The Natural West

The Natural West

*Environmental History
in the Great Plains
and Rocky Mountains*

BY DAN FLORES

University of Oklahoma Press : Norman

ALSO BY DAN FLORES

Jefferson & Southwestern Exploration (Norman, 1984)

Journal of an Indian Trader: Anthony Glass & the Texas Trading Frontier, 1790–1810 (College Station, 1985)

(with Amy Winton) *Canyon Visions: Photographs and Pastels of the Texas Plains* (Lubbock, 1989)

Caprock Canyonlands: Journeys into the Heart of the Southern Plains (Austin, 1990)

(with Eric Bolen) *The Mississippi Kite* (Austin, 1993)

Horizontal Yellow: Nature and History in the Near Southwest (Albuquerque, 1999)

Published with the assistance of the National Endowment for the Humanities, a federal agency which supports the study of such fields as history, philosophy, literature, and language.

LIBRARY OF CONGRESS CATALOGING-IN-PUBLICATION DATA

Flores, Dan L. (Dan Louie), 1948–
    The natural west : environmental history in the Great Plains and Rocky Mountains / by
    Dan Flores
        p. cm.
    Includes bibliographical references (p. 239).
    ISBN 0–8061–3304–X (alk. paper)
    1. Human ecology—Great Plains—History. 2. Human ecology—Rocky Mountains Region—
    History. I. Title.
GF504.G74 F57 2001
333.7'0978—dc21   00–047962

1 2 3 4 5 6 7 8 9 10

To the memory and legacy of Walter Prescott Webb

CONTENTS

ILLUSTRATIONS

Figures

Maps

ACKNOWLEDGMENTS

The genesis of this book, or more accurately my introduction to many of its ideas, hearkens back two decades to a Ph.D. dissertation in history I completed in 1978. It is only proper that I give due thanks to the people on that committee: Keith Bryant, Garland Bayliss, Vaughn Bryant, Harry Shafer, the late Alan Ashcraft, and Lloyd Taylor, who died before I finished my degree but profoundly influenced me. It was my mentor, Herbert Lang, who not only introduced me to environmental history but handed down to those of us who studied the West with him the legacy of Walter Prescott Webb. To all these, plus the late Bob Calvert, I owe a long-overdue debt of thanks—and an apology for a less-than-expeditious move toward publication. Evidently there were some big ideas in parts of that dissertation that needed a couple more decades of study and thought.

Earlier or partial versions of several of the chapters in *The Natural West* have been published previously. Chapter 1 originally appeared in briefer form in Andrew Kirk and John Herron, eds., *Human/Nature: Biology, Culture, and Environmental History* (Albuquerque: University of New Mexico Press, 1999); chapter 2 is rewritten from an article first published in the *Southwestern Historical Quarterly* (1984); the bulk of chapter 3 appeared in the *Journal of American History* in 1991; chapter 5 is reworked from a version originally appearing in *Environmental History* in 1994, and the core of chapter 7 is from a piece in the same journal (then called *Environmental History Review*) in 1983. Chapter 8 is expanded from an article originally published in *Montana, the Magazine of Western History*. Much of chapters 9 and 10 originated as anthology chapters, chapter 9 in Fred Samson and Fritz Knopf, eds., *Prairie Conservation: Preserving North America's Most Endangered Ecosystem* (Washington: Island Press, 1996) and chapter 10 in Bob Keiter, ed., *The Native Home of Hope: Community, Ecology, and the American West* (Salt Lake City: University of Utah Press, 1998). My thanks to all these presses and journals.

Thanks also to the A. B. Hammond Fund for Western History at the University of Montana-Missoula and to the National Endowment for the Humanities for research, travel, and photographic funding. And thanks to Diana DiStefano and Robert Chester for their help with the manuscript, and to Ellen Browning for her careful editing.

Mom and Dad, and Minette, you've made it all possible, and wonderful.

And of course, thanks to all those colleagues and graduate students and reflective pals scattered across the West and the country, whose dinner/late-night/partying/hiking/river-floating conversations have stimulated and refined many of the ideas here. This is your book, too, so if anyone disagrees with any of it, I'm going to blame it all on you.

The Natural West

An Art of People and Place

"Dreams and beasts," Emerson once wrote, "are two keys by which we are to find out the secrets of our nature." In entire deference to Emerson—and to Freud and Darwin, who certainly took him to heart—I wonder if that aphorism is not somewhat myopic. As any advocate of past as prologue might query, where does *history* fit into Emerson's equation as an avenue for exploring human nature? Dreams are indeed something of a pathway, and not just to our aspirations and hopes but back to our animal selves. But what of the historical dream, particularly the one that involves humans and nature and animals all yoked in common to places with great power in our imaginations?

I write this sitting in my hand-built adobe-style home looking out on the Bitterroot Valley, one of the state of Montana's storied Rocky Mountain paradises. It's a place where the "Old" West and the "New" confront one another daily in often bizarre ways. There are ranches in the foothills around me that still make nostalgic use of draft horses in their haying operations, and there are families with logging (and barfighting) traditions going back to Marcus Daly's time at the turn of the last century. Meanwhile, at the turn of this one, among other neighbors are famous writers, intellectuals, and ex-politicians living dotcom lives in what recently was a very remote valley. Even the Dali Lama has looked at Bitterroot property. I'm a sort of a New Westerner myself. Because of relatively recent inventions like solar panels, satellites, cell phones, composting toilets, and four-wheel drive vehicles, I'm able to live where no one has since the Salish had the valley. The New West, maybe. Or perhaps it all just seems new because the prism through which we're accustomed to view the history of the region has only recently been polished sufficiently to gain the deep view.

Ten miles from here, in 1841, the Belgian Jesuit—Father Jean Pierre DeSmet—founded the first Christian mission in the northern Rocky Mountains. By the terms of conventional history in the American West, that's pretty early; in terms of the deep view back through this ancient homeland, DeSmet is barely yesterday. Even in conventional terms the Bitterroot Valley has a rich history, though, similar in outline to that of much of the rest of the Great Plains and Rockies. But the conventional narrative is lumpy, a story that glosses what passes for quiescence to focus on "events": the appearance of Lewis and Clark and DeSmet, the removal of the native Salish people, the arrival of railroads, irrigation and logging and town-building, booms in sheep, busts in apples. Settlement, local politics, participation in the nation's wars, schemes to make money. And now the resources are tourism and real estate based on scenery and an amenity lifestyle in a mountain paradise. These seem to be what we think of as history.

Here under the blue skies of a Rocky Mountain day, when by all rights I should be out climbing mountains, I've spent most of the last few days looking at information to help me reimagine the history of the surrounding valley. It's a history, if you will, that digs into the stratum below the ones that carry wars or political affairs, although ultimately this isn't a history that can ignore politics altogether. Although the basis for such history is old, many of the questions are new. Locally as well as on the grander scale of the inland West, they have to do with our interaction with the ecological landscape, with what we might call the "natural West," as both idea in the mind and as tangible rock, grass, and flesh, which of course it is.

At the dawn of the century, global warming has us all mesmerized by the weather. Yet climate and human history are mostly ignored. What, for instance, have been the major climatic cycles in the West since the Wisconsin glaciations, and what have they meant for the natural West in which our cultures are now deeply embedded? Great ecological revolutions ought to interest us, too, for there are ecological transformations in the Western past whose ripples extend into our own time. How long, after all, have American Indians been setting fires in the West, to what effect? How did thousands of years of plant gathering by Indian women and the hunting of animals by men help fashion essential local Western ecologies? What effects have ecological introductions like horses, sheep, cows, and disease pathogens evolved in Old World conditions in the past, to the present infestations by European weeds, had as agents of historical change?

The litany of questions grows. If aridity has shaped the history of the Great Plains, you have to wonder what influence *slope* has had on the Rockies. What has it meant that the Rocky Mountains, and the Great Plains, too, have been exploited for two hundred years by the global market economy? And surely it's intriguing (or maybe inspiring, or maddening, depending on your politics) that the mountains standing over Rocky Mountain valley floors belong to the American people as a whole rather than to the local communities. Finally, consider the charismatic animals with which we've shared the natural West. How has culture fashioned perception of our animal kin? What does it tell us about our arc across time that wolves and grizzlies, ancient natives once virtually extinguished from the West, are now back, or on their way? Or that having been nearly erased by a complex array of nineteenth-century causes—we're only now coming to understand— buffalo are reappearing in larger numbers every year on the great, expansive plains? These are issues, as the current fashionable phrase goes, that have agency in history.

Restoring the West to its "natural condition" seems likely to be the great environmental crusade of the twenty-first century, and here again it strikes me that a less traditional history can help. When we talk about "restoring" the West, what in fact are we trying to recreate? This acts to pose a *really* good question: whose natural West has this been all along? Is it evolution's superorganism, which we Euroamericans have so long called "wilderness"? Or did the United States inherit a natural stage actually shaped by the very long human inhabitation? In other sections here, I am concerned with more classic history/nature questions. Why do places like Hispanic New Mexico, Mormon Utah, and Montana seem so different when nature would seem so similar in all three? Or are they actually all that different?

This last is a way of circling 'round to where this book begins and where it comes to rest from time to time, which is with a very fundamental question that history rarely considers: Are all our desires and the things we value *purely* cultural, springing entirely from our Mormon or Hispanic or Comanche or capitalist traditions? Or is there something else more universal that our richly layered cultures disguise, perhaps something as essential as an evolutionarily derived "human nature" that influences the way we—*all* of us—see and interact with the flux we call the natural world?

The Human Genome Project has demonstrated that as a species we spring from a foundational population of only about sixty thousand individuals, and that many of our genes came from a single female. Amazingly, across the global human population, 99.9 percent of our genes are identical. So the assumption that we all do share a human nature that is part of our biological inheritance (no less than color vision is) simply can't be dismissed anymore. History ought at least to take notice of this effect, which in the twenty-first century is certain to become more widely acknowledged and understood.

To me, this reality argues, for one thing, that the human past in all its specific variations of culture and place belongs not just to (say) the Blackfeet or the Mormons, but to all of us. So in *The Natural West* I'm interested in several people's particular stories. The whole of the past ought to be ours, as a species, to learn from. And for another, it argues that we humans cannot be considered separate from the earth of our evolution. We, too, are "natural." Which does not mean, however, that our every act is sanctioned. We seem fully capable of maladaptive decisions, of foolish insensitivity and disregard for the rest of the world.

Actually, what might be called "human nature" is probably visible at every level of Big Picture Western history. For instance, it seems that irrespective of our cultures or our ethnicities, we've all found the West a magical place. Think of the

Great Plains and Rocky Mountain West, a kind of "dream landscape" in American history. Could this have something to do with our sensory impression and ancient response to a vast, open country of wind-whipped grasses with outsized blue mountains standing above the horizon, a country saturated in yellow light, domed by dramatic skies? In our art and our collective historical memory we yet tend to see it as it was two centuries ago, full of immense herds of big animals and big predators. Does that description seem reminiscent of anywhere?

The humanities have usually left evolutionary human nature to the biologists. But some of the other questions here are not merely grist for my own mill in these essays about the natural West. They are the kinds of questions—not the only ones, to be sure—posed by the multidisciplinary field known as environmental history. As most students of the American West realize by now, environmental history as a legitimate way of seeing the past has been recognized only since the 1970s, when the American Society for Environmental History and its journal, *Environmental History*, got their starts. Plenty of contemporary environmental historians and writers (I am one) were drawn to this new way of viewing history by our interests in the environmental movement or in nature in general. But many of us came to it, too, through a tradition in Western writing that harkens back to the seminal ideas of Frederick Jackson Turner (with his Darwinian frontier hypothesis that tried to explain the "American character"), Walter Prescott Webb (whose most famous book described the interface between the Great Plains environment and technological culture), and James Malin (who

The High Plains. *Photo by author.*

The Rocky Mountains. *Photo by author.*

pioneered in systematic ecological history). All those pioneers in the field wrote between the 1890s and the 1950s. Brilliant contemporary writers like Donald Worster and Richard White may have made environmental history "the coolest history around" (as someone has characterized it) but they didn't invent it. Nonetheless, Western environmental history is evolving rapidly.

By reason of considerable length of residence in two very different parts of the West, the blue-green Bitterroot Valley of Montana and sere, brick-hued Yellow House Canyon at the head of the Brazos River on the Texas plains, my own interest in environmental history in the West has tended to the regionally specific. The Great Plains and Rocky Mountains do not comprise the whole of the West, of course, and (as will be apparent in the essays here) even their boundaries are blurry. The adjoining tallgrass and oak prairies to the east of the Plains, and the great, varied deserts west and south of the Rockies make up as large a share of the West, and there's also the Pacific Rim and Alaska, all of course with their peculiar ecologies and arcs of history. But for two causes that go beyond anyone's affection for home grounds, the Plains and Rockies of the West make, I think, an especially compelling stage for environmental history.

One cause is that the history of the Plains might be called the origin source for environmental history. Webb, Malin, and more recently, Donald Worster have all made the Great Plains the subjects of big, important books about some of the fundamental issues of Western nature. For many writers in the twentieth century, from Webb to the 1937 Committee on the Future of the Great Plains to Frank and

Deborah Popper, the Great Plains are the ultimate proving ground of environmentalism's doomsday predictions for the Modernist experiment in a massively altered landscape.

Interest in the Rockies derives from another source. These two regions, not merely adjacent but anciently spooled together in a kind of ecological yin/yang interlock, have startlingly different environmental histories. I mean less that trail drives are associated with one and miners with the other than that human history has bequeathed a land-ownership pattern in the two settings that is strikingly different. The Plains is western America's great experiment with privatization, the Rockies our historic communal lands experiment. That we're now entering the second century of these two radically different land-use strategies coexisting side by side makes comparative environmental history here interesting (I almost said "critical") to ponder. What happens in the next century will eventually tell us what we think about these two grand Western laboratories. Naturally, I have some ideas about that.

The ten essays that make up this book were written over a span of more than a decade and portions of a good many have appeared in print before, although in those cases the versions that appear here have been reworked and updated. I would not claim that they constitute a full-blown environmental history of the Plains and Rockies, for by no stretch do they. Scholars in the field will be familiar with earlier versions of a few of them, so that for professionals this collection will represent something less than a foray into darkest terra incognita. But unlike, say, quantum physics or poststructural literary criticism, history—and it may be that this is particularly true with respect to environmental history—has no business (or reason for) cloistering itself from public rumination. The true target of this collection is the student of the West, the interested general aficionado of Western nature and Western life. For those of us intrigued with the West, who have looked about at the surrounding world and wondered how it came to be so, these essays may at least provide a start.

And if not, then perhaps they at least might work as a revision of Emerson's idea about dreams and beasts and human nature.

CHAPTER 1

Nature's Children

Environmental History as Human Natural History

How could we *be* were it not for this planet that provided our very shape? Two conditions—gravity and a livable temperature range between freezing and boiling—have given us fluids and flesh. The trees we climb and the ground we walk on have given us five fingers and toes. The "place"...gave us far-seeing eyes, the streams and breezes gave us versatile tongues and whorly ears. The land gave us a stride, and the lake a dive. The amazement gave us our kind of mind.

Gary Snyder, The Practice of the Wild

You will soon find it theologically and factually true that man by nature is a damn mess.

Norman Maclean, A River Runs through It

Nothing fundamental separates the course of human history from the course of physical history.

Edward O. Wilson, Consilience

O
n an invigorating autumn morning in Montana's Bitterroot Valley, with the first big snow of the season draping the sagebrush, and the sun angle yet low enough that as frost settles out of the intense blue the heavens seem to be raining glitter, I strap on skis, whistle for my wolf-hybrid to join me, and set out across the foothills of the Sapphire Mountains to look for elk. It is one of those incredible daybreaks that in late twentieth-century human description (or so the thoughts form in my mind) would come across, frankly, as so beautiful, it's almost corny. It's sunrise. It's the Rocky Mountains, with all their associations. Just to experience the excitement of being in their presence, we're looking for elk, an animal with a peculiar history in this part of the world, a history I can conjure with just a little concentration. I'm in Montana, with a meaning different from anywhere else, skiing literally out the door of my house, with big, official wilderness areas in view, accompanied by an animal whose ancestry is three quarters wolf, and who acts it. It's the American West at the turn of the twenty-first century, and all those names and thoughts have cultural associations in my head that are coded into the synapses. I couldn't get them out if I wanted to.

We move—I glide, Wily lopes, bounds, and sniffs—across foothills covered with Idaho fescue, sagebrush, rabbitbrush, and ponderosa pines, and as my thoughts continue about this flux we call nature, naming things and experiencing emotions that are equal parts personal and cultural as I do, I happen to glance at Wily, who appears to be devouring the morning as avidly as I am. We are connected, this part-wolf and I, by more than personal history, and skiing along I begin to tick off the ways. We are both native Earthlings, for one, both vertebrate mammals of peculiarly social species, with more in common—more DNA, skeletal, and chemical similarities—than not. We're also both male. We share a hunting past and adaptive plasticity. Our apparatus for apprehending the surrounding world, our sensory organs, are exactly the same, even if our separate evolutionary streams have caused him to rely more on smell, me on sight. But the biological drives bequeathed us by natural selection have meant that as species we both have manipulated the world for reasons we barely comprehend. What does it mean, then, that when I look out at "nature" this bright morning, my cultural associations about it are richer than his? What does it mean to our experiences that I am densely cultured, and he (relative to me) is not? And what

Wily and the Sapphire Mountains, Montana. *Photo by author.*

meaning can be divined from the fact that I, after all, am only his rather more reflective cousin—that I, too, am an animal?

I believe strongly that for humans, our animalness may well be the most important thing about us and that in the twenty-first century, recognition of that importance is going to become widely appreciated. But what meaning will we draw from it? For the almost fifteen decades now that our animal origins have been acknowledged by science, and in turn, philosophy, history, and (although grudgingly, if at all) theology, modern humanity's almost instinctive response is that within the animus must lie a core of evil. That is even implicit (if not frankly acknowledged) in the Judeo-Christian conception of original sin, of humans as "fallen." And in our own time, the notion that pristine nature is a garden of harmony that can only be blighted by our touch is one of the most powerful premises of modern environmentalism.

However ancient the wild nature/human culture dichotomy is—whether it dates to Calvinist disgust with the human body or to the Judeo-Christian notion that humans alone possess souls or reaches back even further to the Greek distinction between the earth/body and the heavens/spirit (with its implication of the superiority of the latter) or yet even more distantly to the dawn of individual self-awareness, as anthropologist Claude Levi-Strauss believed—that we humans are now permanently divorced from nature is a tenet of modern life.[1] That's true no less in the church pews and at the mall than among most humanities scholars, who seem convinced that the seemingly infinite plasticity and genius of human culture has separated us from the rest of our biological kin. Even environmentalists, whose most notable creation in America has been the wilderness system, dedicated to the cultural conceit that the continent was virginal and pure when Europeans arrived and therefore that humans should be only visitors for nature to remain at its best, are guilty.[2]

A deep and unquestioned Puritanism—humans as evil animals—seems to glare out of these notions, yet they persist. Political scientist Robert Paehlke's prognostication, *Environmentalism and the Future of Progressive Politics,* pulls no punches about the matter: humans may have evolved on the African savannas and spent 99 percent of our history as hunter-gatherers, but now we should all live in cities and leave nature alone, period. Even historian Roderick Nash, in one of the first issues of *Wild Earth Journal,* proposed a future America that clusters all humans along the coasts, reserving the interior of the continent as wilderness where our light foraging activities would keep our damage to the natural world to a minimum.[3]

To many interested in ideas about nature and humanity, the emergence of environmental history is one of the more intriguing seismic stirrings in academics in recent years. Although environmental history takes as its operative premise that, at base, history ought to be a study of the ecological relationship between humans and the natural world, environmental history actually has not been particularly effective so far in addressing how our evolutionary history ought to inform historical inquiry. Donald Worster's essay "History as Natural History," which calls for an ecological approach to human history similar to the one biologists use with other species, has come closest. But in two more widely read pieces, "Doing Environmental History" and "Seeing beyond Culture," Worster calls on environmental historians to focus primarily on three levels of analysis: the re-creation of natural ecologies, an examination of human cultural values and ideologies, and an analysis of economics of the type Worster is famous for in books like *Dust Bowl* and *Rivers of Empire*. In *Dust Bowl,* in fact, Worster argues that environmental disasters like the collapse of the Southern Plains in the 1930s cannot be explained by "that vague entity, 'human nature,' but rather by the peculiar culture that shaped [farmers'] values and actions. It is the hand of culture that selects out innate human qualities and thereby gives variety to history. It was culture in the main that created the Dust Bowl."[4]

The three widely applied approaches Worster has outlined are not the only ways that writers interested in environmental history have framed their questions, of course. One of the most useful ways to think about and write environmental history has long been via a kind of local history lens, commencing with a place that seems to hang together ecologically and tracing human adaptations to it. In the American West this is a tradition that dates at least back to Walter Prescott Webb's *The Great Plains: A Study in Institutions and Environment* (1931) and to James Malin's various works on the Kansas prairies in the 1940s and 1950s. Some might argue that even their premises borrowed heavily from Frederick Jackson Turner and in turn from Darwin, since this "bioregional" history is nothing if not Darwinian: humans considered as ecosystem animals making adjustments to particular habitats, in other words.[5] Some of the best modern books written by environmental historians, considering regional human cultures as a kind of "adaptive package" to places, have followed this approach. As indicated by several of the chapters to follow, I've attempted to keep Western history at least nominally pointed toward work like this and have argued that environmental history's intellectual roots in the Western work of Turner, Webb, and Malin are in fact Darwinian and bioregional and interested in "place" above all.[6]

Probably because of the back-to-back success within the humanities of, first, materialist Marxist theory and later cultural relativism—along with the lingering power of the old notion that humans have somehow escaped nature—late twentieth-century environmental history has mostly continued to follow the path Worster and other modern pioneers in the field laid out for it. In other words, what has really pushed Western environmental history so far is the story of how people and places have been integrated into the global capitalist economy, a narrative that has become almost formulaic: start with pristine nature, add noble primitives who coexist blissfully with the world, introduce the white capitalists and watch nature and natives go shit-bang in nothing flat. It's Rudyard Kipling history with a green conscience.

Or, in the big wake of Roderick Nash's classic, *Wilderness and the American Mind,* and more recently William Cronon's controversial edited anthology, *Uncommon Ground,* historians of the environment have done the postmodern dance with culture whereby the natural world as a concrete reality (and presumably our evolution in it) disappears into the shimmer of cultural diversity and all the various words and symbols we humans use to explain the world. It is frankly impossible to locate the human animal, fashioned by evolution and still carrying genetic imperatives within us, in either of these approaches. The only major attempt to revise the Worster/Nash model, by Carolyn Merchant, has merely argued that women and reproduction shouldn't be left out of the analysis. Merchant's *Ecological Revolutions* is an excellent example of how the addition of gender studies, useful and needed as it is, has mostly amounted to a gloss on the same old story.[7]

Watching my wolf-hybrid investigate the Bitterroot Valley this lovely morning and thinking about the two Rocky Mountain valleys in question here—the one that pours through our sensory apparatus and the culturally loaded one that exists in my head—I am reflecting that there may be a more fundamental way at least to *think* about the stories that make up environmental history in the American West, or any other place. It's a way that takes a step beyond even bioregional history and into a realm that precious few of us seem to embrace or much want to hear about, and that postmodernism seems bound to deny.

But what about looking at human history by commencing with a frank and open acknowledgment that at core we *are* biological like every other animal on the planet, deeply motivated by impulses (that we *all* share, regardless of cultural background) that are at least hundreds of thousands of years old, impulses that our cultural overlays have conspired to conceal but that still appear to influence in profound ways how we interact with the world? Ways we ought to be up front about and acknowledge?

In part we've already been doing it. Environmental history as many of its best practitioners—Donald Worster, Richard White, Carolyn Merchant, William Cronon—have written it has long involved an application of ecological principles to human affairs. It seems to me, then, that unless environmental history is still willing to entertain the old Judeo-Christian (and anthropocentric) idea that humans are separate from the rest of the ecological world (either because we alone have souls or because culture has elevated us), it has an obligation to take seriously the long, evolutionary history of humanity. For despite the range of cultural and technological variation in human societies, the essence of what we need from the natural world is much the same from one culture to the next.

There is a much larger rift, ecologically speaking, between us and other species than there is between one human society and another.

But first there stands a premise to be examined and justified. Like human evolution, it presents a somewhat long and convoluted story, but the American West does lie at the end of it.

Environmentalists and other liberals, humanist and often activist about creating a better world, have naturally been drawn to cultural history and to economics as their science because those are aspects of human life that seem reformable, that can be socially engineered toward perfection. Indeed, by insisting that the world exists only in the form of words and ideas arising in the human brain, the contemporary intellectual worldview known as postmodernism implies that *simply by an act of the human imagination,* we can create any kind of world we want. Competitive struggle, violence, technological overreach, and human stresses on nature all can be reformed and probably eliminated by collective acts of human will. Or so the arguments appear to unfold.

For example, reading the anthology, *Ecopsychology: Restoring the Earth, Healing the Mind,* which assembles recent work by those presumably conversant with Carl Jung's collective unconscious and Freud's *Civilization and Its Discontents* (both, of course, positing an evolutionary human nature), I have been struck by the realization that even ecopsychologists place all their hopes for healing humanity into tinkering with the institutions enveloping us. Blow up your TV, they say. Raise male children differently, they say. Stop going to the mall and being a pawn to conspicuous consumption, they say. Just say no. And, in essay after essay, they tell us to look for models of environmentally correct behavior in the preindustrial, precapitalist, "preconsumer," "pretechnological" primary cultures of hunters and gatherers and subsistence agriculturalists. New Mexico psychologist Chellis Glendinning, one of the contributors, has published a book with a title that sums up the ecopsychology gestalt: *My Name Is Chellis and I'm in Recovery from Western Civilization.* Every contributor's assumption—perhaps this is endemic to ecopsychology—is that modern (that is, Western-industrialized) peoples are "sick."[8]

Perhaps we are. But I wonder. Reading fairly broadly in history and studying Native American environmental history more closely have left me more than mildly skeptical of a tenet of faith among cultural interpreters: that there is a Golden Age of environmental balance and harmony in the human past, and that all we have to do to create environmental sustainability is to pirate those ancient lessons. Everyone conversant with the late Paul Shepard's dense and erudite arguments knows that from *The Tender Carnivore and the Sacred Game* (1973) right down to his last book, *Coming Home to the Pleistocene* (1998), Shepard has been one of the major voices arguing that the Neolithic Revolution of six thousand to ten thousand years ago was the true "fall" of humanity from ecological grace into ecological madness. While he did include women and plant gathering in his final versions of deep-time humanity's story, Shepard never varied from his conviction that the Paleolithic was the true Golden Age.[9] As he put it flatly in an essay shortly before his death, "Once, our species did live in stable harmony with the natural environment ..."[10] Thus, what is really fundamental to regaining environmental sanity is a recultivation of what Shepard's follower, philosopher Max Oelschlaeger, calls the "paleolithic consciousness."[11]

Hmmm ... this is interesting. For when I peruse Shepard's wondrous books, nowhere can I find a detailed and believable explanation from him for why that ten-thousand-year-old Neolithic Revolution of agriculture and domestication occurred in the first place. Why, if things were harmonious and stable when we existed in that good, green world of the Paleolithic, did we ever leave it? Too, why did the previous fifteen thousand years of human history before the agricultural revolution feature so rapid a spread of humans out of Africa, Europe, and Asia and into Australia, New Zealand, the Americas, and virtually every island chain in the Pacific? And why, given Paleolithic grace, does the extinction of many hundreds of species in the archeological record—the list is an enormous one—dovetail with the appearance of human hunters in all those places they'd never been before?[12] What Shepard leaves out of his story of ancient sanity and sustainability—and many of us much want to accept his version uncritically—I confess I (uncomfortably) think was actually the record of a species that had reached the limits of population with its sophisticated hunter-gatherer technology. I also confess, looking at this deep-time history, that I am not reassured that environmental "sanity" merely requires ransacking the past for a cultural or economic magic bullet.[13]

While history has yet to pay much attention to the concept of humans as nature's children, philosophers—particularly practitioners of a subfield sometimes called "Deep Ecology"—have. Because I think it an essential step that we accept our biological legacy, I am intuitively drawn to Deep Ecology. But I find several of its premises unexamined and unsupported, and probably unsupportable. Out of romance and cultural relativism, Deep Ecology, too, for instance, has embraced the existence of an earlier environmental Golden Age, the hunter-gatherer period whose insights we must somehow recapture.[14] But Deep Ecology philosophers have made no effort to confirm the very foundation of their philosophy. In fact, the study of past cultures, both hunting and agricultural, does present some examples of societies that sustained themselves over long spans of time, but within a longer term and broader pattern of steadily mounting human population and environmental overreach, along with some world-class collapses and human-caused biodiversity simplifications throughout history.

Nor has Deep Ecology been very systematic about which features of our ancient, "saner" past we should learn from. If it's population control, then the lessons are not reassuring ones: hunter-gatherer population regulation often centered on expedients, like killing up to 40 percent of female infants at birth, that seem overly Draconian by modern standards. In fact, the trajectory of *longue durée* history indicates that humanity has never been successful at keeping an effective lid on our populations, which is what fostered the human colonization of every nook and cranny of the globe by eleven thousand years ago, finally bringing us to the agricultural revolution. By the time the colonization of the planet by hunters-gatherers was complete, human numbers stood at four million. They had risen to five million by the initial stages of the Neolithic Revolution, and then as small-scale subsistence agriculture and the settled lifestyle spread across Eurasia, mushroomed to fifty million by 3000 B.P. The organization of states pushed the global population to 100 million by the time of Christ, and to 200 million by A.D. 200. New technological advances quite often were embraced not so much because they allowed living standards to rise, but because breakthrough technology often meant that more infants were allowed to live.[15]

Is a simpler technology the lesson Deep Ecologists and other environmental Golden Agers want us to draw from longue durée human history? If so, its philosophers are silent on the historical evidence for the rapid technological diffusion and adoption of new tools among most primary cultures, one exemplified by the virtually universal scramble to acquire metal implements and tools with the arrival of traders from industrialized markets. And where, one wonders, along the lengthy trail of connect-the-dots that follows tool making out of the prehuman primate's rocks and sticks to our bulldozers and the World Wide Web, could we have stopped? Judged by the human impact on the nonhuman world, the Clovis toolkit that helped push hundreds of megafaunal species to their extinction in the Americas ten thousand years ago was too much technology. Edward O. Wilson believes that since humans evolved, we have reduced the number of bird species around the planet by approximately 25 percent. Most of those losses came not in the twentieth century but in those first waves of human migrations from fifty thousand to ten thousand years ago.[16]

Finally, those like Deep Ecologists who argue for an ecologically wise human past assume that animistic religions, apparently different from Judeo-Christianity by virtue of their premise that humans are not unique, were a key element to the relative sustainability of primary cultures. But adherents of such views may be too dogmatic about Lynn White Jr.'s 1967 argument that anthropocentrism in Christianity (and Western science) is the "one big insight" that explains modern environmental crises.[17] Those who posit the environmental sanity of the Paleolithic have thus insisted that animistic/shamanistic religions were biocentric rather than anthropocentric. I think most anthropologists and historians—

even those like Adrian Tanner or Richard Nelson who have supported the idea that primary cultures were ecologically sustainable—believe it would be more accurate to say that animistic religions accord admirable respect to entities outside the human sphere, but that like those of New Mexico's Pueblo Indians, the ceremonial lives and cosmologies of most primary cultures are actually extremely human centered. The goal is to keep the world working smoothly so that humans and their descendants can continue to inhabit it and live the good life.[18] In fact, much of the work long used to support the idea that animistic religions and population control were at the heart of primary culture environmental sensitivity—among them Harvey Feit's widely used "The Ethno-Ecology of the Wasanipi Cree; or, How Hunters Can Manage Their Resources"[19]—has been critiqued in recent years by anthropologists testing a more materialist model, borrowed from biology, called Optimal Foraging Strategy. Annette Hamilton explains:

> The romanticized image of the hunter-gatherer as the original conservationist was propagated in the mid-1970s. The fact that these societies all possessed strong sentiments of connection to the natural world, although expressed in different ways, lent support to the view that they had remained in a stable relationship to their resource base. This was achieved not merely because there were few of them but because they took care to regulate their utilization of the products of the land, informed always by their respect for nature. There is much truth in this stereotype. The precise mechanisms, however, by which such regulation could occur is a much more difficult question to answer. . . . It is easy to assert that something approaching conservation was going on, but much harder to demonstrate it convincingly.[20]

Optimal Foraging Strategy models since have asserted that what appears to be "conservation" among hunting peoples was (and is) actually a by-product of attempting to maximize hunting efficiency and use of time. Thus hunter-gatherers ignored depleted habitats and placed taboos on certain species not to achieve conservation but in search of maximum yield for minimum effort. As wildlife populations shrank, this hypothesis argues, hunters actually hunted more, and they ranged farther afield. These are assertions that historical evidence buttresses. Anthropologist Raymond Hames has proposed that *the* test for conservation as an adaptation is whether, if conservation is the result of some practice, it is occurring *by design.* His careful study of hunting among the modern Yanomamo "casts doubt on the existence of conservation in lowland Amazonia." Similarly, anthropologist Robert Brightman has concluded that the precontact Cree "respected" animals, but lacked a general concept of animal population dynamics. As for religion, he makes the startling claim that because it taught the Cree that animals regenerated—the Cree idea was *akwanaham otoskana,* or "animal covers its bones"—and fostered the belief that it was arrogance to assume that animal numbers could be influenced by human manipulation, among the Cree, religion would have encouraged unregulated hunting rather than acting as a brake.[21]

Many of us have come to believe that in the interests of ideology (usually to critique the obvious excesses of global capitalism), such romanticism denies native peoples their history and humanity. Simultaneously it creates a dangerous image, an imagined Disney World that subverts the lessons of the past. The affection of many humanities thinkers for Deep Ecology notions is probably on its soundest footing when it promotes the tie that most primary and early societies had to local ecosystems and bioregional living. Yet in the American West, at least, notions that most Native Americans functioned as "ecosystem societies" utterly fails to take into account the elaborate precontact trading networks that allowed (for example) buffalo hunters on the plains and Pueblo farmers in the southern Rockies to live off the resources of two very different ecologies and economies. Such networks are ancient features of human life.[22]

My suspicion from this exercise is that environmental history (not to mention ecopsychology and followers of Deep Ecology philosophy) may have to investigate humanness at a more profound level to come to a deeper understanding of why we interact with the world around us the way we do. Horrifying perhaps as it may be to think so, just as my wolf-hybrid has a wolf nature that no amount of socialization seems able to erase, we humans appear to have a human nature—the one breathless tie we all share, no matter who we are, where we are, or when in the continuum of human history we emerge from the gene pool— beneath all those rich overlays of culture, space, and time. Like Wilson and a slew of other scholars working in what was once called "sociobiology" but is now usually called "evolutionary behavior" or "evolutionary psychology," I am convinced that there is a biological and universal human nature, and that it appears manifest in the historical record. The question is, how might that insight—so disturbing to many, but likely to offer up a fecund way of seeing the environmental past—be folded into the narratives that give our immediate history meaning and power?

What good will it do us to acknowledge forces within that may be harder to alter than a bad law or flawed institution? It seems to me that understanding the animal within may be fundamental to our grasp of history. And more, embracing the ways in which we truly are nature's children may help us discard the notion that once (in our childhood as a species) we were sane, only to have matured to "alienation" or "madness." In fact, human environmental history right down to the present appears to present us in a continuum, a species doing now exactly what evolution so precisely shaped us to do all along. The causes of twentieth-century environmental decay, the specter of a frightening twenty-first century overreach, aren't human insanity, or our tools, or our economics; those are only the cultural symptoms. The causes of the human assault on the world— and, conversely and ironically, the sources of our hope for ourselves and a biologically diverse planet, too—are evolutionary and mammalian. Despite the astonishing panoply of human cultures, religions, mythologies, ideologies, there are patterns in how we've interacted with the material world. And the foundation of the patterns seems to lie in our hardwiring.

The modern fields of study that have attempted to explain human behavior within an evolutionary framework, sociobiology and evolutionary psychology, are usually said to have had their origins with Edward Wilson's two seminal works, *Sociobiology: The New Synthesis* in 1976 and *On Human Nature* in 1978, and Richard Dawkins's *The Selfish Gene*, which also saw print in 1976.[23] In fact, the foundations of the study of humans as animals actually dates back to Darwin's *The Expression of Emotions in Man and Animals* (1872) and *The Descent of Man and Selection in Relation to Sex* (1874).[24] Nonetheless, it was the prodigious thinker Wilson who most clearly recognized the challenge that human evolution threw down before Boasian cultural determinism and its present incarnation, postmodernism. As Wilson wrote in *On Human Nature* in 1978, "We are biological," yet accepting this simple fact is horribly deflating for a species that had so long thought of itself as unique, outside nature, and possessed of an unquestioned free will. Further, if, as Wilson wrote, "our souls cannot fly free," then we have no place to go but Earth, and that changes everything about history.[25]

Remarkably, in the century that elapsed between the appearance of Darwin's works and Wilson's, outrage at public discussion of the idea that humans were animals had if anything grown more shrill. Interestingly, in both the 1870s and the 1970s it was not so much religious conservatives as liberals who reacted most vigorously. The sputtering in the nineteenth century over Herbert Spencer's Social Darwinism, purporting to explain the emergence of America's "Captains of Industry" as the operation of natural selection in human affairs, was a classically liberal position. And so too it was liberals, Marxists, and feminists who reacted to Wilson's books with outraged hostility and charges of biological determinism. For a few years in the 1980s, sociobiological researchers found themselves in the unique position of being rejected by conservatives who resisted evolution *and* by liberals who emphasized free will and the cultural perfectibility of humanity. Their papers were unwelcome in many academic journals, and some realized, as one sociobiologist put it, "that we were involved in an enterprise worse than studying the occult, we were [assumed to be] fellow-travelling with the American Nazi party."[26] The reaction to sociobiology was paralleled at the same time and for some of the same reasons by a rejection of the post–World War II anthropological position on human origins known as the "Killer Ape" or

"Hunting Hypothesis," and its replacement with the idea of the ecological hunter-gatherer, the carnivore who'd tenderly caressed the sacred game.[27]

Wilson's position over the years has been refined but not reformed. His views in *On Human Nature* were that social scientists were engaging in rampant anthropocentrism by insisting that culture took humans outside nature, and he has not changed his mind. Genetic evolution of human social behavior, he argued in 1978, is the product of 5 million years, culture mostly the product of the past ten thousand. Thus his metaphor of human behavior, borrowed from Conrad Waddington, is a ball tumbling through a landscape from highlands to a shore, with steep, sharply trenched biological topography high up, flattening to meandering, coiling topography low down where culture predominates.

That metaphor led Wilson to disagree with culturalists that human behavior is infinitely plastic, and he pointed out that the basis for much of our social behavior (band-type social groupings of ten to one hundred members, male group bonding for resource and territorial competition, sexual dimorphism, a bias in favor of close kin who share our genes, some degree of self-awareness, nominal tool use, and the Lamarckian ability to pass information along to the next generation) is shared with other primates. And that all human cultures share biologically derived patterns that relate directly to ecology, including ethnobotany, food taboos, population policies, notions of property rights, soul concepts, and a desire to control weather. Evolutionary behavior, he has asserted, should be the most general and least rational in our repertoire—things like gendered mating strategies, the importance of status, incest taboos, parental investment, contract formations that make social relations possible, and territoriality linked to aggression. The human instinct for aggression, indeed, appears to reside much in territoriality and protection of our ecologies with conflict aimed at threatening outsiders.

In 1978 Wilson believed that what sociobiology would enable social scientists to achieve was what physics had achieved: a discipline (human history) that was "predictive."[28] By 1993, in an essay called "Is Humanity Suicidal?" he was ready to venture predictions:

> Darwin's dice have rolled badly for Earth. It was a misfortune for the living world, in particular, many scientists believe, that a carnivorous primate and not some more benign form of animal made the breakthrough [to intelligence]. Our species retains hereditary traits that add greatly to our destructive impact. We are tribal and aggressively territorial ... and oriented by selfish sexual and reproductive drives. Cooperation beyond the family and tribal levels comes hard. Worse, our liking for meat causes us to use the sun's energy at low efficiency.... The human species is, in a word, an environmental hazard.... Perhaps a law of evolution is that intelligence usually extinguishes itself.

Wilson ultimately concluded that we are not suicidal, but that survival—especially in a world where biodiversity is preserved—will entail "a reconsideration of our self-image as a species."[29] By the time he wrote *Consilience: The Unity of Knowledge* (1998), his most passionate and lyrical plea yet that the social sciences and humanities embrace the evolutionary synthesis, he had further refined the idea (first introduced in *On Human Nature*) that culture itself is biological and that much of our behavior exists as a "bio-cultural" loop where certain cultural traits are selected by the genes for their survivability.[30] Culture essentially has converted humanity into one immortal superorganism that gets to learn and compile knowledge endlessly over time. It's this trait that has made us aware, finally, of who we really are.[31]

In *Consilience,* much of Wilson's focus is on the evolutionarily derived "epigenetic rules" of human hardwiring that function as "gravitational centers that pull the development of the mind in certain directions and away from others." Since this prepared learning represents natural selection at work (originally in the natural environment, now mostly in the cultural one), it has spread through human populations, along with the genes that dictate it. Some of the most basic epigenetic rules include a tendency to favor vision over the other senses (very different from most animals), an instinctive inclination to employ binary classification, and a tendency in aesthetics that bias us toward bilateral symmetry and the "supernormal stimulus"—signals that exaggerate favored norms and present cues, sometimes metaphorical, about youth, fitness, and reproduction. Wilson argues that the role of the visual arts may be to signify certain traits of human anatomy, certain animals, certain kinds of landscapes, to which we are already drawn biologically.[32] Of additional interest, particularly in a region with a history like the American West, is his following assertion: "People do not merely select roles suited to their native talents and personalities. They also gravitate to environments that reward their hereditary inclinations."[33]

In its more contemporary form—now known as evolutionary psychology —biological interpretations of human behavior skirt some of the ecological questions Wilson raised in favor of a narrower focus on what's called the "maximization principle." The argument, presented in the form of the so-called Modern Synthesis (which some researchers have touted as a new Copernican Revolution) is that "the universe of biological organization is a system of genetic matter in motion obeying the immanent, natural laws of natural selection and genetic variation."[34] In other words, the most deeply internalized prime directive of all biological species is genetic reproduction and survival, and a great deal of what we gendered species do is propelled (without our realization) by sexuality operating on our selfish genes.

"An important principle in EP," two recent researchers write referring to evolutionary psychology, "is that there is a human nature: the human brain is composed of a large number of psychological adaptations that are virtually identical across people everywhere."[35] Among the "immanent, natural laws" to which the genes bend us are ecological ones, like territoriality. But it is the sexual laws of our gendered species that have come in for closest study. This deep hardwiring includes a "male strategy" for procuring mates, through which human evolution has favored males who are successful in marshaling and controlling natural resources in the interest of status; a "female strategy" that maximizes reproductive potential through the selection of high-status mates; and at least some encouragement of partnership stability for childrearing. Finally there is the kinship principle, the equally well demonstrated genetic bias in favor of those who most closely share your genes.[36]

An aspect of evolutionary psychology that continues to intrigue everyone is exactly what the evolutionary adaptive environment (it even bears its own acronym, EAE) that provides us all these ancient cues might have been. Wilson early asserted that this would be found among forest-dwelling primates and some researchers still look for ancestral clues to our behavior there. But others think our most telling EAE was the Pleistocene savannas of our long hunting-gathering past as Homo sapiens.[37] Emotionally and behaviorally we are Paleolithics, dipped in the sticky batter of cultural and technological elaboration for only a few hundred generations.

One of the most intriguing joining of ideas about the human evolutionary adaptive environment with modern environmentalism comes from Wilson's 1984 book, *Biophilia: The Human Bond with Other Species*, and more recently, the anthology he and Stephen Kellert have edited titled *The Biophilia Hypothesis* (1993). Both books examine the viability of Wilson's assertion that our evolution has bequeathed us an "innate tendency to focus on life and lifelike processes."[38] In other words, biophilia is an aspect of human nature that bequeaths us a very positive heritage with respect to the world around us.

The preliminary studies on biophilia (and its opposite, biophobia) remind us how rooted our social behavior is in the primate world. Studies of inherited biophobic responses (to snakes and spiders, for example) as well as what appear to be genetic preferences among humans for savannas, parklands, certain tree shapes, and terrain scales that mimic our evolutionary home in East Africa, center both our fear of the natural world and our love for it in biocultural adaptations selected by evolution over an immense time span. There also appear to be some clear gender differences. Studies of both landscape art and architectural landscaping in places like Victorian England and the United States show that men worldwide respond most positively to depictions of open, park-like terrain with distant views. These, likewise, are the kinds of scenes male landscape artists are more likely to portray and that park and grounds planners most often try to

Great Plains rock art. Shamanistic rock art from the Southern High Plains conveys something of the antiquity of human nature's impulse to manipulate the world for biological need. *Photo by author.*

reproduce. Women, including female painters, seem more strongly drawn to scenes of closed canopies and protected settings. One of the contributors to *The Biophilia Hypothesis*, Robert Ulrich, is willing to make a ballpark guess: genetic biophilias and biophobias may be 20 percent to 40 percent biologically determined, but appear to require triggering by experience and are established as clear preferences essentially through learning.[39]

Two of the most accessible recent books synthesizing the biological position on human history are Jared Diamond's *The Third Chimpanzee* (1992) and Robert Wright's *The Moral Animal* (1994).[40] Readers of history particularly should appreciate biologist Diamond's longue durée approach and his treatment of human history from a biological perspective. As for Wright's readable, sound synthesis of evolutionary psychology, its major contribution is its clean explanation of one of the most troublesome of sociobiology's problems: if the entire biological world is blueprinted around replication of the selfish gene, how can altruism and human morality be explained?

The answer, worked out by two of the founders of sociobiology, Robert Trivers and Robert Axelrod, is reciprocity, expressed by game theory's demonstration of how cooperation could evolve in nature, with rewards that enhance individual success through cooperation with others, an arrangement that is then buttressed by an ethical code (the social contract) designed to govern it. Canadian game theorist Anatol Rapoport's famous "Tit for Tat" (or, do unto others . . .) is thought to represent most closely how reciprocity, altruism, and morality evolved in a selfish gene world.[41] Freud, Wright argues, accurately saw that human inner conflicts result from the animal brain trying to cope with social life, but erred in thinking that the conflict was between the animal and *civilization*, that "primitive man was better off in knowing no restrictions of instinct." In fact, Wright says, it has been a very, very long time since humans knew no restrictions on instincts. The conflict is between instinct and human *societies* of every kind.[42] Such is the nature of the social contract.

Notwithstanding Wilson, Diamond, and Wright, notwithstanding the steady successes in extending biology to the study of humans—particularly in gene mapping of specific behaviors (like risk taking) and in new research on how the brain functions—there remain many quite vocal critics. Environmental historians like Donald Worster and William Cronon apparently think that the richness of human history—at least the histories of individuals and of recent events of the sort most all of us are accustomed to reading—would be reduced to cartoon status if interpreted through the lens of biology. Feminists have asked if we shouldn't be a bit suspicious of a science that seems to confirm and buttress the gender status quo and the cultural anthropologist Marvin Harris once critiqued the "reductionist principles of sociobiology" as underestimating "by several orders of magnitude" the novelty of culture, since culture substitutes rapid learning for the slow operation of genetic feedback loops. While territoriality and gendered sexuality might exist, our cultures (as history richly demonstrates) are after all capable of socializing us into almost any kind of behavior.[43]

The problem, here, I think, may stem from fundamental methodological differences between biology and history: the one is most comfortable studying broad patterns and populations as a whole, the latter most at home dealing with events and individuals. Can history profitably reduce the strivings of Horace Tabor in helping fashion the mining economy of nineteenth-century Colorado to a masculine compulsion to marshal resources so as to attract the notice of Baby Doe, a genetically superior mate? Should we dismiss Lewis and Clark's educational and cultural preparations and explain their fascination with the high plains and Rocky Mountain foothills by noting the West's similarity to the evolutionary adaptive environment of East Africa? I can't imagine that many historians are going to be willing any time soon to apply evolutionary interpretations to the history of events and the actions of individuals. I would not be comfortable doing so myself. Evolutionary insights are too blunt an instrument for such work.

On the other hand, history *should* sometimes think in terms of bigger patterns—long spans of time, whole populations, cultural groups (say, artists or ecologists) who proffer the broad brush strokes of worldviews.[44] And it is just here, I think, that some attention to evolutionary theory's "epigenetic rules," along with all the usual concentration on cultural patterns, might be very useful. So I suspect that it is in thinking about longue durée and the big patterns of environmental history that a consideration of our evolutionary tendencies will be most worthwhile, however uncomfortable such insights might be. The creation of warrior societies among plains and mountain tribes during the two-century period when horses and new technology brought dozens of groups to the buffalo plains, and the intertribal strife over territory and resources (while simultaneously creating status opportunities for men) that resulted, seems a fairly clear example of evolutionary human nature at work in the West.

But we ought not to fall into the trap of imagining only Indian history through this kind of lens. Nineteenth-century Mormon polygamy has usually been studied by analyzing theology, or the Mormon communal economy, but an evolutionist would be inclined to see it as an expression of the domination of Mormon society by high-status men—or even as an adaptation of the female strategy to a shortage of men and resources in Zion. Similarly, the enduring fascination for the West in world-wide popular culture very likely has its origins in our evolution, since for many of us the region seems to represent humanity's last chance for recapturing the authenticity of life in nature. Twentieth-century Western art's great wave of nostalgia at the passing of the "frontier" seems self-evidently an outpouring of mourning for the end of our last chance at the Pleistocene (Zane Grey himself saw it exactly so). Finally, in explaining the escalating pace of ecological destruction in the past two centuries of the West, no history should omit newly exploitive technologies and the growing human population—or even ideology—as clear causes. But perhaps it would help to understand that the genius and allure—and danger—of frontier economic culture (laissez-faire capitalism and the global market) were all about releasing the selfish gene in human nature to act without restraint and that this is precisely the "untrammeled freedom" we're referring to when we describe what we think was so wonderful about the Old West.

As for history's predictability, that, it seems to me, is another question entirely. Until *Consilience,* Wilson did not seem to grasp an idea basic to human history—that it unfolds as a result of choices that are themselves contingent on other choices, as well as entirely unexpected turns of events. Wilson does recognize now what biology calls "exogamous shocks," in historical terms, the alterations in the time line imposed by unexpected events or individuals.[45] But unlike physics' grasp of the subatomic world, in the specific sense, human history can never be predictive, no matter how well we understand human nature. The implication remains, however, that *knowing* ourselves and our tendencies is always going to be important and significant. For one thing, it lays the responsibility for the kind of world we create directly at our feet. No power, aside from our own history, is directing us. While we may have a biological history stirring like a wind at our backs, knowing what we've done—knowing who we are—puts our destiny in our grasp.

Perhaps another specific place marker where a consideration of human history as natural history can help immediately is in addressing what our own Euroamerican/Western culture actually tells us to *think* about human nature.

Early in *Steppenwolf,* the German writer Herman Hesse's surrealistic novel of the 1920s, Hesse characterizes his protagonist this way: "He calls himself part wolf, part man. . . . With the man he packs in everything spiritual and sublimated or even cultivated to be found in himself, and with the wolf all that is instinctive, savage and chaotic."[46]

Viewed across the great expanse of longue durée history, Steppenwolf's dilemma is the most uniquely human of all of evolution's dilemmas. According to Genesis, in the beginning, nature was benign. Then sin came into the world, and with it evil, and the Fall. To Darwinists, however, the classic "sins"—gluttony, lust, greed, envy, and anger—are all stripped-down expressions of impulses emerging out of evolutionary natural selection and the operation of the selfish gene. This dark view of human nature puts modern environmentalists, in particular, in a real box of a dilemma, since it seems to be a non sequitur to think of humans as destroyers and parasites on the earth (the sources of those destructive tendencies lying in human evolutionary history) while nature itself is seen as divine and harmonious. And of course such a view makes it all the more difficult to imagine past societies, where presumably human nature was even rawer and more exposed than under the present constraints imposed by religion and the state, as existing in a Golden Age of ecological harmony.[47] History seen this way sets up the primary function of socialization all along as the sublimation of the animal appetites, the Seven Deadly Sins, to cultivate a reciprocal altruism that mediates both power relations and the use of nature.[48] Religions and environmental regulations limit the selfish gene's freedom to act, which is why every anarchist militiaman in the West has a bizarre conception of religion and the purest of hatreds for the state.

The conclusion that could be drawn for environmental history is simply this: here at the beginning of the twenty-first century, we are *still* engaging the world around us with exactly the same selfish genes, exactly the same sexually based prime directive, precisely the mental and sensory apparatus that evolution bequeathed *Zinjanthropus, Homo erectus, Homo habilis,* and every one of our more recent hunting and gathering (and ranching, farming, and investment banking) ancestors—and that we are oblivious to our motives because natural selection designed us to be.[49] Evolution prepared us to survive; it did not prepare us to penetrate to real self-awareness of our motives, and now they come as a shock. Seen in this light, then, human environmental history is manifestly not a history of a once-godlike creature gone over the edge of sanity, but the story of a wildly successful species that has been doing the same things, for the same reasons, for 3 million years. It's the history of a species that late in its evolution has assumed that it has stepped outside the external limits nature usually imposes on efflorescence and only now has begun dimly to see the role of the ancient imperatives.

The philosopher Max Oelschlaeger has argued that humans are biologically underdetermined, culturally overdetermined.[50] While I concur that this view is applicable to what we usually view as the proper subjects of human history, environmental history presents a more naked expression of human biology in action than does any other form of history. If I am right that the reason we have not been able to stop the destruction of nature in our time is that we refuse to recognize the animal within, then externally delivered checks—new disease epidemics running rampant through overcrowded populations, massive dieoffs from starvation caused by ecological overreach, wars over resources—are what we can expect. And perhaps ultimately an imposed, top-down environmental fascism to keep us from destroying ourselves. All these kinds of fates (except the last) afflict other animals. We have stories like them in modern human affairs. We call them science fiction.

On the other hand, if Wilson and others are correct and there is, as well, a real biophilia residing there in our animal origins, it may be that biocultural evolution has only now proceeded to the point of allowing it full expression. I think the Golden Age may be in our future rather than in our past. And embracing our animalness, recognizing and confronting the role our long evolution plays in modern human behavior, is a critical step. Once we take it, and perhaps see human nature (like nature itself) not as a mess but as the true and positive core of what it means to be human, then our innate biophilia may be fully triggered. If our cultures *are* able to call up the best from the animal within, then I suspect that our ancient instincts for diversity and for living and interacting in local places where feedback loops are short and the world looms about us in sacred detail will surely be a key.

The crux of biological human nature as cause in environmental history is that, read negatively, it gives us faint hope. But there is a positive reading that gives us, the Mountain and Plains West, and the world a chance for a future with dignity. While there are some who fear that conceding that we are not really a special creation, that we're merely evolved animals, could destroy the social glue that binds society, that view misunderstands evolution. In fact, properly understood, the very web of kinship rules, reciprocation, and ethics that lie at the core of most human cultures is itself a bequest of our biological legacy.

And of course we have our history. And history, like biology, offers us the opportunity to understand the ancient dangers—and the wondrous potential—of being human animals.

CHAPTER 2

The Ecology of the Red River in 1806

Peter Custis and Early Southwestern Natural History

The following objects...will be worthy of notice. The soil and face of the Country, the growth and vegetable productions...the animals of the Country generally.

Thomas Jefferson

I n the course of a lecture to the Philadelphia Linnaean Society early in 1807, the famous early American naturalist, Benjamin Smith Barton, alluded to the important work one of his students had carried out on the little-known Red River of the American Southwest during the preceding year.[1] Barton didn't suppose it necessary to remind this assemblage of Northeastern scientists that the young man whose Western natural history survey he mentioned had been the designated naturalist of President Thomas Jefferson's second major exploring expedition into the Louisiana Purchase. But perhaps he did realize that some promotion wouldn't hurt, even among scientists presumably in the know, for already the dramatic discoveries of Meriwether Lewis and William Clark and Jefferson's embarrassment at the outcome of the Southwest exploration—in combination with some really bad luck—were threatening to obscure the young man's Red River work from the science of natural history in the early West.

Barton had good reason to fret, for Dr. Peter Custis of Virginia remains today an almost unknown figure in the ecological story of the American West. And yet for one of environmental history's more compelling projects—the task of re-creating "baseline" ecologies in order to grasp cause and subsequent environmental change[2]—naturalist Peter Custis's detailed examination of the edge of the Southern Plains during the Jeffersonian era is one of the best time machines in the West.

The story of Peter Custis's pioneering scientific work in the Southwest, performed nearly two decades before the expeditions of Thomas Nuttall, Edwin James and Thomas Say, and Jean Louis Berlandier, is almost as interesting for its obscurity in history as for its value in environmental study. For a variety of reasons, principal among them the Red River expedition's failure to complete its exploration because of Spanish opposition, along with the understandable desire on the part of the Jefferson administration to focus on its success with Lewis and Clark rather than failure amidst the murky diplomatic tangle in the Southwest, the Thomas Freeman and Peter Custis expedition has long remained a lost incident in Western history.[3] Yet Jefferson's Red River probe was the first major American exploration to include an academically trained naturalist, a fact that tells us a great deal about the fusion between government and Enlightenment Age science in America. And while the natural history aspect of the effort has shared in the entire exploration's relative invisibility, the accounts of this 1806 examination of the Red River Valley provide an important and provocative description of the evolving ecology on the borders of the Great Plains. What Custis's long-lost reports address so effectively, in fact, is one of environmental history's great revisions in the American nature story: Just whose West was it that exploring Euro-Americans encountered? Was it "nature's" West, a pristine wilderness in a state of organic harmony? Or something else entirely?

Few who are familiar with Thomas Jefferson's intense curiosity about the American West should be surprised to learn that the Lewis and Clark survey of the Missouri and Columbia Rivers was only one of several expeditions Jefferson envisioned. In fact, he originally planned to send at least four government expeditions into what for European Americans was an uncharted landscape. In order of his own ranking of them, following the Missouri/Columbia probe, Jefferson was keen to have the Red/Arkansas Rivers of the Southwest explored, followed by the Platte/Kansas Rivers and the Des Moines/Minnesota.[4] Once Congress had appropriated money for the first of these and Lewis and Clark were en route on their epic journey, Jefferson quickly turned his energies to what he considered the next most valuable survey, the Red/Arkansas expedition. This examination was to target the Red River primarily, which Jefferson thought "next to the Missouri, the most interesting water of the Mississippi," and his contemporaries believed (from a range of evidence) to have its sources in the Rocky Mountains northeast of Santa Fe. From there Jefferson hoped to have his explorers cross the Southern Rockies to the headwaters of the Arkansas and descend that stream. Judging by what we now know about Southern Rockies and plains topography, there was a significant geographic problem with this plan. Unknown to Jefferson and his contemporaries, the Red River does not in fact head in the Sangre de Cristos but heads instead on the huge plains plateau of the Llano Estacado. That was precisely the kind of unforeseen situation that Jefferson hoped his explorers might bring to light. Unfortunately, Jefferson was not destined to live long enough to see the puzzle of the Red River's sources resolved.[5]

The Red River. *Photo by author.*

As he did with the more northerly probe, the president viewed his Southwest exploration as a multipurpose journey. His letters make it clear that he thought the expedition could serve an important diplomatic function in winning the Indian nations of the Southwest over to the Americans. Privately, judging from the dinner he had at the White House with expedition leader Thomas Freeman in November 1805, Jefferson apparently believed that American commercial interests might be served if the Red River provided a highway to the Spanish city of Santa Fe (afterward Freeman confided to his friend John McKee that the expedition was to take him to "the Neighborhood of St. Afee ... and to the Louisiana mou[ntains]" and then asked McKee, "How would you like to be my Cashier in that country?").[6] Given the strained atmosphere with Spain following Jefferson's promotion of the Rio Grande as the true southern boundary of Louisiana, the president was also convinced that careful celestial readings and map work on the Red and Arkansas Rivers would cement the United States' claim to the southern drainage of the Mississippi. This would provide him an attractive alternative if compromise on the boundary question became necessary.[7]

Finally, of course, scientific and intellectual curiosity would be well served by an examination of the wispily known environs of southern Louisiana. Certainly the stories from the Southwest were tantalizing enough. Relying upon the account of Antoine Simon Le Page du Pratz from the preceding century, the Committee on Commerce in the House of Representatives (chaired by the eminent naturalist, Samuel L. Mitchill) favored an expedition up the Red because of the natural curiosities purported to be found there. William Dunbar, the southern scientist and friend of Jefferson, had relayed to the president reports of medicinal plants in the area, as well as all kinds of minerals, mountains of pure or partial salt, water serpents, and "wonderful stories of wonderful productions" along the Red and its tributaries.[8]

Phillip Nolan, the trader and "Mexican traveler," further aroused Jefferson's enthusiasm with descriptions of immense herds of wild mustangs, descended from Spanish-Arabian stock, running free on the Southern Plains.[9] Still another southwestern traveler, Natchitoches Indian agent John Sibley, sent reports gleaned from French hunters indicating a rich and diverse fauna. "I asked [Mr. Brevel] what animals were found in the Great Prairies," Sibley wrote Henry Dearborn, the secretary of war, continuing: "He told me, that from Blue river, upwards, on both sides of Red river, there were innumerable quantities of wild horses, buffalo, bears, wolves, elk, deer, foxes, sangliers, or wild hogs, antelope, white hares, rabbits, &c., and on the mountains the spotted tiger, panther, and wild cat."[10]

It is not surprising, then, that Jefferson, in his seven-page letter of instructions regarding the Red River expedition, devoted a generous portion to natural history, detailing the entry of meteorological and topographical information, as well as complete observations of all new species, floral and faunal. Add to these a page of directions relative to the recording of data on the ethnology, ethnobotany, and sacred places of the Indians encountered, and it is apparent why popular opinion in the United States supposed the expedition had no purpose other than to inspect natural curiosities.[11] The administration probably fostered such an impression with a view to allaying Spanish concern; obviously, the addition of a naturalist to the expedition could serve a diplomatic function by underscoring the scientific nature of the probe.

For a number of reasons, not the least of which was encouragement by General James Wilkinson, particularly in his "Reflections on Louisiana" missive to the Spanish government in March 1804, Spain was highly suspicious of this expedition aimed at its border, and especially of the explorers' intentions toward the "faithless" Indian tribes of the upper Red River. With the southern boundary of Louisiana unsettled, Spain viewed the expedition as a potential threat to its territorial integrity and not only refused a passport for the party but launched two military parties of more than a thousand troops to confront the perceived threat from the United States.[12]

Yet as is evident from the care exercised and the difficulty experienced in selecting highly trained personnel to direct Jefferson's Southwest reconnaissance, the search for a naturalist was not merely a diplomatic charade for Spain's benefit. The appointment to the Red River tour was actively sought, and the competition, while not fierce, did allow Jefferson to make the selection in a manner that anticipated methods used in later scientific surveys sponsored by the government.

It appears likely that Jefferson, himself an able naturalist as well as a fellow in the American Philosophical Society, may have been criticized by some of his contemporaries (as he has been by historians) for entrusting the scientific work on the Missouri-Columbia Rivers probe to a man with no formal training in science. Talented woodsman though he was, Meriwether Lewis had had only about two months' instruction in natural history and celestial observation—crash courses given to him by Pennsylvania academics.[13] As Wayne Hanley, a natural history writer, observed in *Natural History in America*: "The failure of Thomas Jefferson to assign at least one naturalist to the Lewis and Clark expedition never has been adequately explained." Hanley goes on to suggest that Jefferson at least could have appointed a "promising young student" as naturalist for Lewis and Clark. That's precisely the course of action the president eventually took in manning what the administration came to call the "Grand Excursion," or "Grand Expedition," into the Southwest.[14] Since Jefferson had once actively promoted botanists Moses Marshall (in 1792) and André Michaux (1793) for Western natural history excursions, however, his decision to appoint a naturalist to the Red River party hardly signified a major turn in his thinking. This common criticism of Jeffersonian science loses some of its sting when you realize that for his Red River expedition, Jefferson spent fifteen months and spoke with several of the most famous naturalists in the country before selecting his man.[15]

The plan for the Grand Excursion began to assume form early in 1804 when William Dunbar accepted Jefferson's suggestion that he assume direction of the exploration from his home in the Mississippi Territory. Dunbar, an active and talented Scottish émigré who had an outstanding observatory on his plantation, The Forest, in the hills south of Natchez, played a role that had no parallel in the Lewis and Clark expedition and that considerably enhanced the scientific potential of the tour. He was, in essence, the director of the expedition—assembling stores, setting up experiments, supervising construction of boats, and writing letters of introduction.[16] His trial run up the Ouachita River in the winter of 1804–5, with Dr. George Hunter, a Philadelphia chemist and mineralogist, confirmed his opinion that the absence of a trained naturalist on forays into little-known territory was a serious oversight.[17]

Much of the time that Jefferson devoted to the Red River project in the early part of 1805 was spent in the selection of a field leader. In July the appointment was given to Thomas Freeman, an accomplished Irish-American engineer and astronomer who also had experience as an Indian negotiator. Freeman's capture of this plum began in the spring of 1805, when Jefferson corresponded with Robert Patterson, professor of mathematics at the University of Pennsylvania, about a method of taking longitude readings without a timepiece. Patterson apparently suggested that the president contact Thomas Freeman. Freeman entered this conversation with a background of service to the United States government, including survey work in Washington, D.C., Tennessee, and the Indiana Territory. Although his early career had been clouded by an infamous quarrel with the noted mathematician Andrew Ellicott, which resulted in his dismissal from the survey of the boundary between Spanish Florida and the United States in 1798, he had well-placed friends in such people as Alexander Hamilton and General James Wilkinson. From the standpoint of performing scientific tasks, Freeman was a much better trained exploration leader than either Meriwether Lewis or Zebulon Montgomery Pike, his contemporaries in Western exploration.[18]

The appointment of Freeman, with his geographic expertise, liberated Jefferson to continue the search for a pure naturalist with similarly high credentials to accompany the expedition. At the close of 1804, Jefferson had received a letter that must have encouraged him and, perhaps, firmed his resolve to find such a person. It was an inquiry from the brilliant, but already erratic, Constantine Samuel Rafinesque, then only twenty-one.[19] Rafinesque proposed: "If it ever seems worthwhile to you, to send a Botanist in Company with the parties you propose to make visit the A[r]kansas or other Rivers, I cannot forbear

Mentioning that I would think myself highly honored with the choice of in [*sic*] being selected ..."[20]

Despite his youth, Rafinesque was already well along on a remarkable career, and Jefferson at first tentatively offered the post to him. By the time the letter was mailed, however, Rafinesque had already returned to Italy.[21]

With Rafinesque out of the picture, Jefferson turned to United States academic circles and asked Benjamin Smith Barton to suggest a promising young naturalist. Barton must have believed that Jefferson wanted someone already on the scene of the exploration, for he initially recommended Dr. Fred Seip or Dr. Garret Pendergast, both of Natchez. With Freeman, who spent most of November and December in Philadelphia purchasing scientific instruments, Barton began to interview potential candidates at length in that citadel of natural history study.[22] Scientific training evidently was not the only requisite; ideally, candidates were to be young and unmarried and to possess a woodsman's physique. The considerable danger posed by the dissatisfied Osages, as well as by the suspicious Spanish officials of the Provincias Internas, in fact led Freeman to wonder if it would be possible to find a scientist "willing to hazard [travel] in the Neighborhood of St. Afee."[23]

The approaching deadline—the expedition hoped to depart in the early spring of 1806—led Jefferson to pursue another possibility. Sometime in late November of 1805, following a private dinner with Freeman at the White House, he wrote to William Bartram, the famous Pennsylvania naturalist whose lyrical book *Travels through North and South Carolina, Georgia, East and West Florida* . . . was already a classic (it provided a wealth of material for the emerging Romantic Movement in Europe), inquiring if the great naturalist would be interested in having "the department of Natural History in the voyage up the Red River."[24] Perhaps Jefferson did not really expect the sixty-six-year-old Bartram to accept; more likely the president hoped that he could recommend a protégé. While Bartram declined for himself, he did know someone he could highly recommend, and on 6 February he wrote the president and forwarded a letter from the applicant. The eager candidate was Alexander Wilson, the Scottish-American poet and naturalist whose bird drawings and nine-volume *American Ornithology* (1808–14) have justifiably qualified him as the father of American ornithology.

In his letter of application, Wilson phrased his hopes: " ... hearing that your Excellency had it in contemplation to send travellers this ensuing summer up the Red River, [and] the Arkansaw ... I beg leave to offer myself for any of these expeditions; and can be ready at a short notice to attend your Excellency's orders." Unfortunately for Alexander Wilson, and likely for the fame he'd have brought to the affair, the search for a naturalist had been over for a month by the time he applied.[25]

Documents relating to the successful conclusion to Jefferson's search are few and sketchy. We do not know, for example, how many of the two dozen or so senior students working with Barton at Pennsylvania applied, nor do we know whether the position was offered to such people as William Darlington, a prize pupil of two years before who was still in the Philadelphia area, or Frederick Pursh, who explored the central Appalachians for Barton that same spring. What is known is that in the first week of 1806, Freeman and Barton decided that they could do no better than to offer the post to young Peter Custis, a senior student in the medical program at Pennsylvania. Only twenty-five, Custis was a native of Deep Creek, Virginia, not far from Jefferson's Monticello. His family was related by marriage to the Byrds, Randolphs, Lees, and the late president George Washington. Little is known of Custis's early life, except that he apparently asked his father to sell at least part of the family estate so that he might receive "a Latin education" and "be brought up to one of the learned professions."[26]

Custis had entered the medical program at the University of Pennsylvania in 1804 and soon became a student and protégé in Barton's natural history classes. In 1806 he was still a year away from his doctorate, but under Barton's tutelage he had been educated in a diversified natural history curriculum.[27] Clearly he possessed impressive taxonomical skills, as well as a command of contemporary Latin binomials, but he does not appear to have had previous experience in the field. Since Freeman and Barton had selected him, Jefferson could only "hope we have procured a good botanist."[28] In retrospect what he seems to have found in Custis was an enthusiastic young medical student with a talent for natural history but no experience. And the job was a huge one. The outcome of Jefferson's efforts tells much about the status of nature study in the early United States.[29]

Following an overland journey from Philadelphia in the winter of 1806, Freeman and Custis arrived in March at Dunbar's Natchez plantation where they found Dunbar still assembling goods for the expedition. Two years of congressional appropriations (five thousand dollars in 1805 and three thousand dollars in 1806), plus an additional three thousand dollars' worth of trade goods placed at their disposal in Natchitoches, favored the expedition with more than three times the original funding for Lewis and Clark. This sum easily covered Custis's salary of three dollars a day and traveling and equipment expenses and enabled him to lay in the scientific tools necessary for exploration. In addition to instruments for taking and preserving specimens, these tools included a portable barometer, a microscope, two thermometers, a sextant for the geographic work, and a camera obscura—an optical device used to trace topography on paper.[30]

Custis's texts, no doubt chosen in consultation with Barton, played a critical role in his natural history examination. Not specifically mentioned in his natural history entries, but obviously used (and perhaps carried along), were Jefferson's *Notes on the State of Virginia*, Bartram's *Travels*, and both Barton's

Fragments of the Natural History of Pennsylvania and his new textbook, *Elements of Botany*. Clear references are made in Custis's entries to Humphrey Marshall's *Arbustum Americanum*, to Thomas Walter's *Flora Caroliniana*, and to du Pratz's *History of Louisiana* (evidently the single-volume London edition of 1774). Custis did not include a volume that would have been highly useful, André Michaux's *Flora Boreali-Americana* (1803), perhaps because it was unavailable to him. Instead, as his major references he relied on the most compact Linnaean works he could find. Zoologically he was well served by the four-volume *Systema Naturae* (the 1789 edition compiled by J. F. Gmelin). The botanical text he used, however, was either the 1784 or 1786 version of *Systema Vegetabilium* edited by J. A. Murray. A single-volume condensation, Murray's work would have saved space on the cramped boats, but omitted much descriptive material and all references to geographic distribution. This text led the inexperienced young naturalist into many errors.[31]

Recall that Jefferson's original plan for a southwestern exploration had specified an ascent of the Red River and then a portage across the Southern Rockies to the headwaters of the Arkansas, to be explored descending back to the Louisiana settlements. However, Dunbar's experiences with portages on the Ouachita trip had convinced him that this was impractical. By the spring of 1806 Lewis and Clark had not yet reported their own successful portages in the Northern Rockies. Jefferson delayed the decision to confine the southwestern expedition to only one river until May, although discussion as to whether it ought to be the Red or the Arkansas continued virtually until the departure of the expedition, with Dunbar insisting that Spain would certainly interfere with a probe of the Red. But probably for diplomatic reasons and perhaps the lure of science on the Red, the president (indirectly through Dearborn and Freeman, primarily) would not give up on the Red as the main objective. And as a counter to Spanish opposition, he went so far as to give orders for an additional military escort to be added to the party at Natchitoches. Dunbar's own reluctance to agree to this plan is self-evident in his letter of May 18: "Therefore [there is] not[h]ing to do but acquiesce."[32]

After a series of delays that put the party far behind schedule, the "Exploring Expedition of Red River," as the leaders styled it, at last swung into the muddy current of the Mississippi in late April 1806. Both of the experimental flatboats, which measured twenty-five feet by eight feet, featured "commodious Cabins," one of which Custis made his laboratory, although he had to share it with Captain Richard Sparks, commander of the twenty-man military escort attached to the expedition. Custis's catalogues begin on 2 May, the day the men poled the boats into the mouth of the river the French had called "Rivière Rouge" and the Spaniards, "Rio Rojo" or "Rio Colorado."

Although he was working ultimately under the directions in Jefferson's letter of exploring instructions, Custis's work was also guided by Dunbar's directives and by the scientific method he had learned in Philadelphia. Dunbar, for example, had Custis keep a meteorological chart that was so thorough it recorded not only storm and wind data, but also the temperature—of both air and water—three times daily.[33] All this preparation certainly encouraged a thorough reconnaissance, yet Dunbar's insistence that Custis participate in the geographic work of mapping the river, combined with "Mr. Freeman's great anxiety" to proceed as rapidly as possible, limited his natural history examination to the immediate environs of the river valley, with "no time to make botanical excursions" into the hinterland, he lamented.[34]

During the 185-mile leg of the journey from the mouth of the Red to Natchitoches, a former French outpost and, in 1806, the last bastion of Euro-American settlement below the wild lands upriver, Custis worked to perfect his techniques in a region already inhabited by French and Spanish settlers for almost a century. The water of the river, he wrote Secretary of War Henry Dearborn in his first report, which was posted from Natchitoches on 1 June, "is of a reddish brown colour caused by the suspension of an argillaceous marle." The clay soils composed of this substance "appear to be not worth cultivating, but far from it they are found to be more productive than the best Mississippi lands." Most of the lands not subject to overflow were already inhabited; the settlers—a mixture of French, Spanish, and Anglo-American pioneers, along with some African Americans and migrant southeastern Indians—were engaged in hunting, stock raising, and cotton growing.[35]

Custis's natural history notes on this region are intriguing. Hunting pressure had already reduced quadrupeds to scarcity, but he did describe the three kinds of Louisiana fox squirrels (not differentiated by zoologists until the twentieth century) and is still credited with the description of one of them: *Sciurus niger ludovicianus* Custis, the fox squirrel of the mid-South uplands.[36] Alligators (*Alligator mississippiensis* Cuvier) he noted, were "very abundant, and of a very large size"—a "small one" he measured was twelve feet long. In a lake below Natchitoches, Custis found a strange new amphibian much like the greater siren, but with four legs; he named it *Syren quadrupeda*. Among the sixteen birds he catalogued in this stretch, two among the most common then are now extinct: the Carolina parakeet (*Conuropsis carolinensis ludovicianus* Gmelin) and the ivory-billed woodpecker (*Campephilus principalis* [L.]).[37]

Although he regretted the superficiality of his botanical examination, Custis did catalogue fifty plant species in this stretch and provided invaluable notes on trees indigenous to the area. The native pecan, which he named *Juglans petiolata* (now considered a synonym of *Carya illinoinensis* [Wang.] K. Koch), he found "the most abundant tree of the lower Red." These old growth pecans were enormous; one measured nineteen feet in circumference five feet above the ground.

The party found the whole country from the mouth of the Red to the confluence of the Black with the Red to be subject to overflow, but beyond this confluence Custis encountered the first stands of towering bald cypress (*Taxodium distichum* [L.] Rich.), as well as a few white cedars (now *Chamaecyparis thyoides* [L.] B. S. P.), a tree no longer found anywhere on the Red River. Nearing the Rapide Settlement (present-day Alexandria, Louisiana) the party entered the great longleaf pine barrens, a subclimax parkland preserved by fire, where "almost the only undergrowth . . . found on this river for a pretty considerable extent" was the spicewood (*Lindera benzoin* [L.] Blume). Abundant all along the river was a second shrub he could not identify because it was not flowering. A previously unidentified genus, it is now known as the swamp privet (*Forestiera acuminata* [Michx.] Poir).[38]

In Natchitoches the news was not good. Information that a large Spanish force was on its way to confront the exploring expedition led Jefferson to add a second military contingent to the initial military escort of twenty-one men. Along with guide and translator François Grappe and three Caddo Indians, Talapoon, Cut Finger, and Grand Ozages, the Grand Excursion had now become the largest U.S. exploring expedition of the decade. A total of seven pirogues, plus the two cabin barges, barely carried the forty-eight-man contingent. "The party," Custis wrote Dearborn, "are all in the enjoyment of health and unanimity, pleased with the prospect, & resolved on the prosecution of the expedition let what will oppose."[39]

Leaving Natchitoches on 2 June, the expedition soon passed the beautiful pine-clad bluffs called Grand Ecore and the last scattered French houses. For the next 430 miles they would pole and drag their boats through a lush and seemingly wild country, untapped and fertile ground for a naturalist.

The Red River Valley possessed some ecological features that were typical of the western Mississippi drainage, while others were atypical and singular. Among the latter, the most dramatic was the Great Raft. The raft was an enormous log-jam born sometime around A.D. 1200 when, geologists believe, a Mississippi flood backed up the waters of the Red, producing a reverse flow that caused an accumulation of driftwood the river could not wash out. Over the centuries the raft had climbed upriver like a gigantic snake, adding nearly a mile of timber to its upper end every spring. Its basic skeleton was composed of exceedingly durable red cedar from the great old growth stands of the middle Red River, so that its lower end rotted away at only two-thirds the rate of accumulation. By 1806 the Great Raft was a tangle of drifted timber almost one hundred miles long.[40] Moreover, as Freeman's and Custis's notes make clear, the Great Raft was disrupting the environment and changing the river valley. As it climbed the river, it blocked the mouths of tributary streams, annually creating new lakes and swamplands, killing the climax hardwood forests that had been at least ten centuries evolving, and replacing them with a world of black waters and rotten, standing timber. By damming the river, in effect, and diverting its flow through adjacent lowland tributaries, the raft had also contributed to the development of vast floodplain prairies, as the slowed river dumped its sediment load over extensive stretches of country upriver.[41]

Two weeks after leaving Natchitoches, their way blocked by the Great Raft, the party left the river and detoured eastward into the logjam's most recent creation—a large swamp that must have rivaled the Okefenokee. For fourteen days and one hundred miles, measured by log line, "of incessant fatigue, toil and danger, doubt and uncertainty,"[42] the explorers puzzled their way through bayous, lakes, and interlocking channels, in a maze that baffled even their guides. In the Great Swamp, Custis added more than forty entries to his botanical catalogue, including a rare lobed-leaf southern catalpa (*Catalpa bignonioides* Walt.), which he thought was new and named *Bignonia triloba* (now a synonym).[43] And he was captivated by nature's wild effusion there. Of the "almost impenetrable Swamps and Lakes," he wrote, "one who has not passed through these cannot form an Idea of the great difficulty attending it," and then continued, "but when effected you are more than compensated by the beauty of the country."[44]

Attaining the river once again in late June, the explorers rested and regrouped at a river-bluff village of emigrant Alabama-Coushattas, located just south of the current Arkansas boundary.[45] Here the expedition members met with the legendary Caddo chief Dehahuit, who arrived with forty warriors from their nearby village, Sha'-childni'ni. This meeting gave Custis an opportunity to assemble ethnological data on the customs and mythology of one of the last remnants of the great Mississippian mound-building cultures of American antiquity. Custis described Caddoan hunting and marriage customs and set down their oral tradition of a great flood in their past, a tradition that today sounds a little too suspiciously like the Biblical flood grafted onto a native account featuring local species. As for the Caddos themselves, Jefferson's naturalist wrote that they were "a very small race of men without the least appearance of savage ferocity" and that they were consummate artists with the bow, whose skill reminded him of passages in Homer's *Iliad*.[46]

Custis's report of 1 July, posted by dispatch from the "Coashutta Village, Latt. 32.47 N.," is a far more interesting account than that of 1 June. Large species of wildlife, like black bears (*Ursus americanus luteolus* Griffith) and the native white-tailed deer of the area (*Dama virginiana macroura* [Raf.]), were now "very numerous." "Serpents," surprisingly, were "very rare." The July report added seventy-odd additional plants to his list, including several that were used medicinally by either the Caddos or the Alabama-Coushattas.[47] And the layover afforded time to assemble specimen collections. Included in the mineral collection was a "pumice stone," which he believed served "to strengthen the report of there being

Volcanoes on some of the waters of this River."[48] A botanical collection of twenty-six items from above the Great Raft featured representative prairie, swamp, and hill plants. It was among the first plant collections from the Trans-Mississippi West.[49] Finally, Custis included careful descriptions of two new species. One, "a species of *Mus*," was clearly the plains pocket gopher (*Geomys bursarius dutcheri* Davis), an animal not differentiated by mammalogists until the twentieth century. The other he recorded, in a passage that demonstrates the skill and care of his work, as

> A species of *Falco* which I have not seen described.—Cere, lores and bill black; legs yellow; head and neck blueish white; body and wing coverts lead colour; quill & tail feathers black-brown,—each tail feather with white stripes extending half way across; claws black; belly bluish; wings below with white & ferruginous spots; inside fulvous. 14 inches long.[50]

The bird was a young Mississippi kite (now *Ictinia mississippiensis* Wilson), a worthy species for a Jeffersonian explorer to discover and a bird that would go on to play an intriguing role in Southwest natural history for another century. Unfortunately, in his haste to finish the report in time to post it downriver by 1 July, Custis neglected to append Latin binomials to either of his new discoveries. Alexander Wilson's 1811 description and name thus won Custis's rival for the Red River position credit for this beautiful bird of prey.[51]

By mid-July the party was ready to trace the serpentine river with its

Mississippi kite, a common Southern Plains species first scientifically described by the naturalist Peter Custis. *Photo by author.*

flanking sandbars and cottonwood canopy into the "extensive prairies." Entering present southwestern Arkansas, they were deeply impressed by the beauty and tranquility of the setting they entered. "The Valley of the Red river is one of the richest and most beautiful imaginable," Freeman wrote in his journal, to which Custis added, "Were the Rafts removed . . . this country in a very short time would become the Paradise of America . . . in point of beauty & fertility & Salubrity there is not its equal in America, nay in the world."[52]

From the explorers' notes may be drawn an image of the natural setting. The low bank of the river was lined with willows (*Salix* spp.) for several yards and beyond them by the upper-story successive sere of cottonwoods (*Populus* spp.), which were "so covered with vines and creeping plants, as to present an impermeable mass of vegetation." Stretching out for two to eight miles from the river were vast prairies covered with dense stands of giant cane (*Arundinaria gigantea* [Walt.] Chapm.), tall grasses, and wild strawberries (*Frescaria virginiana* Duch.). Where the prairies abutted the hills there were often clear blackwater lakes fringed with lofty bald cypress. The sandy hills were forested with oaks (*Quercus* spp.) and loblolly pines (*Pinus taeda* L.), "all of large dimensions." Except for the native prairie sennas *(Cassia spp.),* a primary colonizer in burned forests that were "found to overspread the whole country as far as [we] ascended," the upland forests were almost entirely free of undergrowth.[53]

As the party moved rapidly upriver, Custis's daily routine was occasionally interrupted by opportunities to visit the ruins of deserted Indian villages. Extensively populated only decades before, the middle Red River was now wildlands almost without inhabitants. The ravages of Old World diseases alien to the Red River Valley, combined with pressure from the Osages, an expansionist southern Siouan tribe, had by 1806 driven the Caddos from sites they had occupied for hundreds of years. One of the largest of the ancient Kadohadacho towns, and one of the last on the river to be abandoned, had been deserted in 1795 following a surprise attack and massacre by the Osages. At this location, the Caddoan guides showed the explorers their sacred hill, Chacanenah ("place where tears were shed"). A rocky, narrow ridge rising abruptly some 250 feet above the valley floor, the hill was central to Caddoan creation and flood mythologies. Freeman and Custis were permitted to ascend this ridge with Cut Finger and Grand Ozages, who wished to visit the summit and speak with Caddi Ecco, the supreme being, as their religious leaders had done since time immemorial. On the plain below, the wild plants of a vast stretch of riverbank prairie were taking over the deserted Indian fields.[54]

Just beyond this village site, as they neared the location of present Texarkana, the party passed through one of the remarkable phenomena of the nineteenth-century Red River Valley—a forty-mile forest of towering red cedars (*Juniperus virginiana* L.).[55] Here a wildlife trail crossed the river, and they saw the first evidence of bison (*Bison bison bison* [L.]), which no longer ranged onto the prairies farther south because of the disruption caused by the Great Raft. On 24 July, Custis entered the first scientific natural history observation for present-day Texas when he sighted peregrine falcons (*Falco peregrinus* [L.]) along the river. At this point the party was nearing the site of the principal Caddo village, deserted in 1792 following a series of smallpox and cholera outbreaks, and of Bénard de la Harpe's French outpost, Poste des Cadodoquious, which had been occupied by a small French garrison from 1719 until 1778.[56] Now, two-and-a-half weeks upriver from the Alabama-Coushatta village, they were approaching the present eastern border of Oklahoma.

Custis was on the edge of the post-oak savanna ecoregion and only a week's travel from encountering great ecological changes in the blackland prairies. Although fear of Spanish patrols confined him to the river, the naturalist was beginning to sight and record Great Plains animal species, including a "*Lepus Timidus* of a very large size" (evidently the black-tailed jackrabbit, *Lepus californicus melanotis* Mearns) and at least one purely plains plant, a new species of *Orobanche* or broomrape. Custis mistakenly thought it was a new genus and named it *Bartonia* after his mentor.[57]

The guides now told him the party would soon be able to see a "very numerous" new species of wolf. Custis called them "White wolves"; very probably they were *Canis lupus nubilus* Say, the plains lobo wolf. "They are perfectly white, except the feet and half the legs," he wrote from the guides' descriptions, "and are seen in large herds." The Indians also described an animal soon to be encountered upriver that he correctly guessed to be "a species of Antilope." It was, of course, the American pronghorn (*Antilocapra* spp.), a plains animal whose skin and skeleton Meriwether Lewis had already forwarded to Jefferson from the Missouri. Eastern wild turkeys (*Meleagris gallopavo silvestris* Viellot) had become numerous, and Custis wrote that he soon expected to see not only wapiti, or elk (*Cervus merriami* Nelson), but also vast herds of bison. "Some say they have seen Ten Thousand at a sight," he continued, but this was "most probably an exaggeration."[58]

Unfortunately, the consternation the expedition had induced in the Spanish Southwest (a reaction encouraged, it now appears, by the conspiracy of Aaron Burr and James Wilkinson), now reached a climax. On 28 July the exploring party was confronted on the river by an army of Spanish cavalry, commanded by Captain don Francisco Viana, that outnumbered the explorers four to one. Having standing instructions from Jefferson to return with the information they had gathered rather than lose their data and risk their lives in an armed confrontation, Freeman reluctantly decided to abandon the probe. The expedition began descending the river by the first of August, having explored some 615 miles, or about half the total length of the Red River.[59]

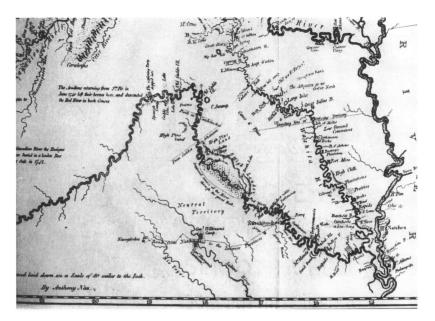

Route of the Freeman and Custis expedition as it appeared on the American maps as early as 1807. Detail from Anthony Nau's 1807 map, *The First Part of Captn. Pike's Chart of the Internal Part of Louisiana.*

Until 1 September, while the Louisiana-Texas border country geared itself for war over the river confrontation and related troop movements, Peter Custis continued to enter natural history data for his last report, posted from Natchez on 1 October 1806. In addition to those species already mentioned, this report included the description of what he believed was a new species of mouse, which Custis named *Mus ludovicianus*,[60] as well as an account obtained from Lieutenant Robert Osburn of "a rabbit in the upper parts of Arkansas about the size of a common Buck . . . having one horn in the middle of the forehead bending downwardly & inwardly."[61] Custis also enumerated an additional twenty-eight herbs and forbs and submitted his completed catalogue of fifty-six species of trees found on the Red River. This list featured a description of the southern endemic, the bois d'arc (*Maclura pomifera* [Raf.] Schneid.), the western reports of which had much excited easterners because of its flexible wood and usefulness as a natural hedge. Custis correctly surmised that it was a new genus, but he was unable to offer a name for it, since he was trained in the sexual system of classification and the tree he examined was not in flower.[62] Finally, the 1 October report included a second mineral collection, his extensive chart of meteorological observations from the tour, and an apology:

> I have to lament that a more complete opportunity had not occurred, that
> I might have been enabled the better to perform the duties allot[t]ed me, but

it is a thing well known that a person subject to the movements of another has little, or I might add, no time to make botanical excursions.... I have to return my most sincere thanks for the appointment with which you honored me, & to regret the failure of the expedition. [63]

In spite of his medical responsibilities and Dunbar's insistence that he participate in the time-consuming geographic work, Custis had catalogued nearly 80 birds and animals and close to 190 plants in four months on the Red River. Of the 267 total species he enumerated and described (and not including his 26 specimens), he had recognized 22 as new and had proposed 7 new scientific names. Most of the latter are synonyms today (see the appendix).

Custis had had an enviable opportunity to fix his name permanently and widely in natural history nomenclature, because dozens of the species he encountered had been previously unknown to science. Inexperience and the inadequacy of his texts in enabling him to make literary identifications (that is, to identify plants from texts rather than specimen comparisons) were major problems, but another difficulty seems to have been his training in the United States, which, unlike that of European naturalists, apparently did not prepare him to recognize that every ecoregion produces its own peculiar speciation.[64] Unfortunately, his botanical collection was damaged, and today only two specimens in the Barton Herbarium survive from it. One of the two, the prairie gentian (*Eustoma grandiflorum* [Raf.] Shinners), was, according to a note attached to the existing specimen, a western prairie species never collected before 1806.[65]

For an environmental historian interested in what the "virgin wilderness" along the edge of the Great Plains actually was like two centuries ago, Peter Custis's natural history reports—with their misidentifications corrected as carefully as possible—make up one of the most detailed examinations that exists of a major western river ecosystem at the time when U.S. explorers began to probe the West. So, despite regrets all around that Jefferson's southwestern counterpart to Lewis and Clark was far less successful, Custis's work is a valuable and intriguing source for re-creating a kind of baseline ecology for the Red River country.

Immediately apparent is that the river valley that Custis describes bears little relation to the Red River of the turn of the twenty-first century. Most of the more dramatic species Custis reported to be common and numerous are now extirpated on the Red River; some of them are lost to us entirely. That list is almost a who's who of once-common Southern Plains species: the Carolina parakeet, the ivory-billed woodpecker, the cougar, the plains buffalo wolf, the Merriam's elk, the peregrine falcon, the whooping crane, the white cedar. Bison still exist in the Red River country today, particularly on the Wichita Mountains National Wildlife Refuge in Oklahoma, but not as a wild species.

One of Custis's surviving botanical specimens, a Great Plains species (the prairie gentian) today housed with Lewis and Clark specimens at the Philadelphia Academy of Natural Sciences.

Custis's data yield other, more startling conclusions. Any further fantasy of a "virgin West" at the time of the Louisiana Purchase should be forever marred by the discovery in Custis's botanical lists of sixteen European exotics, most medicinal herbs growing near the settlements along the lower river but some as weeds deep in the upriver valley. Obviously, the missionary and trading activities of the French and the Spaniards in this part of the world had already introduced alien species as early as 1806. Custis's account is the earliest to document this phenomenon in the West.

Custis's floral and faunal descriptions also make abundantly clear that our long-standing perceptions that the West represented a pristine world, shaped solely by natural processes and untouched by the human hand, is one of the grand fantasies of American history. For one thing, Custis documented for the Red River country a phenomenon that unquestionably was widespread across a continent long inhabited by an ancient and numerous Indian population: a prior human transfer of wild species of plants, especially food and medicinal plants, across the countryside. Near the Indian villages the exploring party visited, Custis found an unusual abundance of species such as the jimson weed, *Datura stramonium* L., and the great blue lobelia, *Lobelia siphilitica* L., used in medicine and ceremony. He describes, as well, a successional pattern of plants taking over abandoned Indian fields that was far different from that in nearby prairies, further evidence that Indian agricultural practices extensively modified the landscape along the Great Plains.[66]

Perhaps most important of all are two other indirect bodies of evidence of the ancient role of the native peoples as shapers and managers of the West's ecology. For one, Custis's careful cataloguing of undergrowth in the upland forests away from the river paints a picture of an open, parkland forest with a light understory confined to fire-adapted species (especially the *Cassias*). This parkland forest, along with the extensive bluestem prairies that appeared along the upper river, suggest widespread alteration of the environment by Indian fire ecology, very probably to the point of extending the grasslands (and prairie species) eastward along the plains ecotone that the party penetrated during the last days of their probe. In fact Freeman himself—in the first published explanation by an American observer on the origins of the prairie—suggested as much, writing in his journal that "neither the nature of the soil, nor any other natural cause, gives rise to these extensive and rich pastures, with which Western America abounds." He asserted that instead they owed their existence "to the custom which these nations of hunters have, of burning the grass at certain seasons."[67]

Equally telling are Custis's (and Freeman's) accounts of the abundance of large animals, including the presence of buffalo—albeit only tracks—in the vicinity of Indian villages abandoned because of disease epidemics or warfare with the Osages. Earlier as well as later accounts by white travelers along the Red River describe a far different situation, with animals like deer and buffalo especially scarce in a region that before the smallpox epidemics of 1777 and 1801 was densely populated by large villages of the Kadohadacho Confederacy. Large animals again grew scarce when groups like the Choctaws and Creeks settled the area and the United States relocated the Quapaws in the country above the Great Raft. Freeman and Custis seem to have been describing a phenomenon now reported elsewhere across the continent, where wildlife populations suppressed by Indian hunting were "released" when disease depopulated a region. The wildlife ecology of the Red River in 1806 very likely was a singular and short-lived phenomenon, a snapshot in time.[68]

Finally, Custis's observations on the Great Raft, which, as it climbed the river, was literally changing the face of the countryside, extending the swamplands and species like Spanish moss (*Tillandsia usneoides* [L.] L.), far to the north of where they are found today, call into serious question ecology's old perceptions of a smoothly functioning "climax" paradise in the natural West. And it was not just the raft that was involved in this natural alteration of the face of the countryside. Perhaps in response to a warming climate as the Little Ice Age cycled toward its end in the nineteenth century, Custis reported tropical invaders, notably the coffee senna (*Cassia occidentalis* L.) and the sicklepod (*C. obtusifolia*) "to overspread" and "infest" the entire river valley as far as the explorers traveled.[69]

With Jefferson's second great exploration into the West ended after only four months, before Freeman and Custis could penetrate along the Red even farther into the real heart of the Southern Plains and perhaps on to the Rockies (although the drainage of the Red would have played out with their powder-blue uplift still nowhere in sight), Peter Custis returned to Philadelphia in the autumn of 1806 to complete his medical degree. While writing a thesis titled "Bilious Fever of Albemarle County [Va.]" during that winter, Custis saw two versions of his Red River work appear in print. His mentor, Benjamin Smith Barton, published Custis's June report (on the river below Natchitoches) as "Observations Relative to the Geography, Natural History, Etc., of the Country along the Red-River, in Louisiana," in an 1806 issue of *The Philadelphia Medical and Physical Journal*. Perhaps to linger over its study, Barton omitted Custis's description of his prize specimen from that region, the *Syren quadrupeda*, from the article, however. Custis never got credit for his creature, which actually represented an entire new family, the Amphibiumidae, not recognized until 1821. The species was the three-toed congo eel, *Amphibiuma tridactylum* Cuvier.[70]

In March 1807, as Custis prepared for graduation, the only official version of the expedition that the government ever printed, combined into a single third-person narrative and redacted by Nicholas King (who also drew the official map of the survey), appeared in a limited print from the offices of the administration newspaper, *The National Intelligencer and Washington Advertiser*. Today only ten copies exist.[71] Worse than limited distribution, though, this official version confused the organization of Custis's four reports, making it impossible (until I found the manuscript versions in 1982) to determine just where on the Red Custis had sighted his species. Far worse for Custis's reputation at the time, however, King was apparently unable to read Custis's carefully penned Latin binomials. The majority came out so badly garbled as either to be unrecognizable or to convince savvy readers that Jefferson's naturalist on the Red River expedition had been totally incompetent. How large a role these events played in Custis's subsequent turn away from natural history or in the almost complete obscurity of his work on the Red River, I cannot say, but Custis never worked up his two remaining (and more interesting) reports for publication. And of all the western explorations of the age, the Red River survey was the only one that Samuel L. Mitchill failed to report in his widely read journal, *The Medical Repository*. So deep was the hole into which Custis's work fell, in fact, that in 1817, when Rafinesque reworked and published C. C. Robin's *Florula Ludoviciana; or, A Flora of the State of Louisiana*, not even a former competitor for the Red River post (and one as widely read as Rafinesque) knew of Custis's work.[72]

In 1807 Dr. Custis returned to Drummondtown, Virginia, near his boyhood home.[73] For a time he collected plants in Virginia for his mentor's herbarium, but after 1808 their correspondence ceased. Within two years of the exploration, he had turned exclusively to medical work, eventually settling down to the life of gentleman physician in New Bern, North Carolina, where he married, successively, the daughters of two of his fellow physicians. An acquaintance of later years described him as a "highly popular" physician in North Carolina, although "somewhat blunt and caustic in his manner, and the life of all social companies in which he appeared." According to his will, drawn up in 1840, he had named his first-born Linnaeus and his second son Peter Barton (after his mentor?), some testimony to a continued interest in natural history. But he does not appear to have published in natural history after 1807, nor did he even become a subscriber to a work like Alexander Wilson's *American Ornithology* when Wilson appeared in New Bern in 1809 and successfully sold subscriptions to several other leading citizens of that city.[74] Dr. Peter Custis, Jeffersonian explorer, died on 1 May 1842, in New Bern, outliving all the other leaders of the Jeffersonian age of American exploration by a considerable margin, and no doubt convinced that the work he had done as naturalist for the Red River exploration had been an exercise in futility. Only with the passage of almost two centuries and the modern blending of historical and ecological interests into environmental history has Custis's work assumed its proper place as a snapshot of a world long gone but endlessly fascinating for what it tells us about our own.

CHAPTER 3

Bison Ecology and Bison Diplomacy Redux

Another Look at the Southern Plains from 1800 to 1850

One day, a Kiowa woman awoke early and went from her camp in the mountains down to a spring ... As the woman knelt down to get water, she saw something mysterious ... Out of the mist came an old buffalo cow leading a herd of wounded and tired buffalo and a few small calves.... As she watched, the old buffalo cow led the last herd through the mist and toward the mountain. Then the mountain opened up before them, and inside of the mountain the earth was fresh and young.... Into this beautiful land walked the last herd of buffalo and the mountain closed.

Old Lady Horse, Kiowa

L ike some tremendous, crashing sound that ceased abruptly just at the moment we turned to listen but whose reverberations ricochet around in the topography yet—that's how more than a thousand centuries of buffalo moving across the landscape of the West strikes many of us at the beginning of the new century. So there is great excitement that this sole holdover of the West's Pleistocene megafauna, the very emblem of the natural West, is back in numbers not seen since the 1880s, and in Yellowstone National Park is now interacting with wolves in the West for the first time in three-quarters of a century. And excitement that there is increasing talk of allowing buffalo, which were the only big Western animals denied the privilege, of being wild animals on public lands once again. As I argue elsewhere in this book, buffalo recovery is almost certain to be one of the biggest stories of restoring the West in the twenty-first century. All of which makes understanding what actually happened to the buffalo in the nineteenth century a more practical concern than most history.

This chapter appeared in its original version in the *Journal of American History* in 1991, and as a new, multicausal interpretation of what befell the great herds on the Southern Plains it has attracted attention since. Naturally I've been gratified to see its conclusions confirmed and extended by other scholars. Historians Jim Sherow and William Dobak have ably demonstrated how problematic horses could be to Plains Indians, and that similar patterns in the way buffalo disappeared from the American Plains also held true in Canada. And in a trio of fine recent books, Elliott West, Shepard Krech, and Andrew Isenberg have extended many of my arguments—along with plenty of points I hadn't thought of—to the eradication of buffalo across the Central Plains and the West in general. As I write this, several other scholars are working on a variety of new angles relating to buffalo in history. It seems that an important revision in the buffalo story, long the great conservation warning in American history, is now well underway.[1]

As part of a new preface to the paperback edition of his *The Fur Trade of the American West, 1803–1840*, published in 1996, geographer David Wisart spoke of this revised buffalo history in a way that makes sense to me. For fur trade historians accustomed to inferring that Indian entanglement in the market had led both to damaged ecologies and to Indian "dependency" on an animal-products-for-industrial-goods exchange, he wrote, what was new about "Bison Ecology" was its reliance on an array of causes for the bison's decline—in other words, the focus on a changing climate, grazing competition from horses, and new bovine diseases.[2] Nevertheless, to many historians and most readers of "Bison Ecology," it was the Indian role in the bison's destruction that was startling. That Plains Indians could or would have participated in the commercial devastation that nearly wiped the North American buffalo off the

Buffalo in rock art. *Photograph courtesy of Minette Johnson.*

continent forever was an image jarring to pop culture (*Dances With Wolves*) notions about ecological Indians.

The new bison story—or so it seems to me—lands close to the heart of the great debate in anthropology and other social science fields over whether there is something universal (and biological) in all of us that strongly influences how we use the world around us, or whether we are so infinitely malleable under the impress of culture that no such thing as a human nature exists.[3] My sense is that efforts to explain how Native Americans became ensnared in the undertow of the global market economy using cultural relativism alone (as in Calvin Martin's famous *Keepers of the Game*) have not been very successful.[4] At any rate, my assumption that historic Indians (like Indians today) were human beings, motivated by the same impulses as people everywhere, is central to this interpretation.

While this chapter focuses on the first half of the nineteenth century, when all the necessary patterns fell into place for the great herds' subsequent crash, I feel an obligation to add that the years from 1800 to 1850 on the Plains shouldn't constitute an apologia for the period that followed. By no means does the Indian robe trade exonerate the white hide hunt that delivered the knock-down flurry, or make the federal government's refusal to implement a conservation policy for buffalo during the 1870s any easier to condone. Far from it.

Just why the government followed a course that allowed the Plains quite literally to be debuffaloed in the 1870s and 1880s has a folk explanation today: that a conspiracy between the Grant administration, the Reconstruction government in Texas, and the American military actively *promoted* hide-hunter slaughter of the buffalo as a form of Indian policy.[5] This story makes a certain amount of sense. Bills introduced in Congress to protect buffalo in the 1870s were allowed to die, one by a presidential pocket veto (which Grant never explained). And to be sure there were people in high places in government, notably Grant's Interior Secretary Columbus Delano, who remarked that they would "rejoice" at seeing buffalo erased from the Plains. But such facts don't constitute a policy. And as the new bison history is discovering, beyond them lies shaky ground, with little or no good evidence (in fact, quite a bit of evidence to the contrary) for either a conspiracy or a policy that truly tied *active* promotion of the buffalo's demise to the government's hopes to turn Plains Indians to agriculture and reservation life.

Many of us, indeed, are growing convinced that in the American West, as was true in Western Canada, no conspiracy was required to annihilate the buffalo, and the only "policy" necessary was not to have one.[6] The economic doctrine of laissez faire—let the market do its work—was a religion to American administrations of the Gilded Age. Besides, no federal environmental legislation protecting any animal existed as precedent then. While it may not be as satisfying an explanation for those who prefer the federal government as proximate cause in most evils, the new bison story is coming very close to an argument that the unregulated market—along with human nature—were sufficient in themselves to almost destroy the American buffalo in the nineteenth century. We ought to hold that foremost in our minds as we attempt to return buffalo under the aegis of market forces in the twenty-first century.[7]

The new buffalo story relies much more on Indian sources than was the case in the past, but we all ought to keep in mind that the intent of history is not to make one group look better, or worse, than another now. The intent is to use as wide an array of evidence as possible to figure out what happened in the past. Native people who remain convinced that bison and Indians have had a special relationship for centuries shouldn't see in the following story an argument that over the long term this was not the case. I in fact would insist that more than eight thousand years of bison hunting on the Great Plains constitutes the longest-sustained human lifeway in North American history.

Yet virtually all Plains Indians have in their tribal lore stories of past times when, as a result of human hubris or miscalculation, bison went away. My argument is that as a result of their capture by the global market economy, Plains people experienced another such time in the nineteenth century. In any case, that all our ancestors—irrespective of their cultures, worldviews, or religions—were as humanly fallible then as we all are now ought not to stun us. That idea is essential to compassionate history.

What I actually advocate here, as will be evident by the end of the story, is not so much an environmental history based purely on the market or even human nature—nothing quite so materialist or universalist—but biocultural history. The following events were unique to their time and place. And as always, it was in the realm of religious and spiritual beliefs that culture unfurled most strikingly into the ecological world.

In the bright spring light on the Great Plains of two centuries ago, Governor Juan Bautista de Anza failed in the last of three crucial tasks his superiors had set for him in reforming New Mexico's Comanche policy. For more than five years, De Anza had followed one success with another. He had brilliantly defeated the formidable Comanche war leader Cuerno Verde in 1779, and as a consequence, in 1786 he had personally fashioned the long-sought peace between New Mexico and the swelling Comanche population of the Southern Plains.

But the New Mexico governor found the third undertaking an impossible one. Observers of Plains Indian life for 250 years and committed to encouraging agriculture over hunting, the Spaniards were certain that the culture of the horse Indians was ephemeral and that the bison on which they depended were an exhaustible resource; de Anza pleaded with the tribes to give up the chase. The Comanches found him unconvincing. Recently liberated by horse culture and by the teeming wildlife of the high plains, their bands found the Arkansas River pueblo the governor built for them unendurable, and they returned to the hunt with the evident expectation that their life as buffalo hunters was an endless cycle.[8] And yet, de Anza proved to be a prophet. Within little more than half a century the Comanches and other tribes of the Southern Plains were routinely suffering from starvation and complaining of shortages of bison. What had happened?

Environmental historians, and ethnohistorians whose interests have been environmental topics, have in the two past decades been responsible for many of our most valuable recent insights into the history of Native Americans since their contact with Euro-Americans.[9] Thus far, however, modern scholarship has not reevaluated the most visible historic interaction, the set piece if you will, of Native American environmental history.[10] On the Great Plains of the American West during the two centuries spanned by 1680 and 1880, almost three dozen Native American groups adopted horse-propelled, bison-hunting cultures that literally defined "Indianness" for Americans and most of the world. It is the end of this process that has most captured the popular imagination: the military campaigns against and the brutal incarceration of the horse Indians, accompanied by the astonishingly rapid elimination of bison, and of an old ecology that dated back ten thousand years, at the hands of commercial hide hunters. This dramatic end, which occurred in less than fifteen years following the end of the Civil War, has by now entered American mythology. Yet our focus on the finale has obscured an examination of earlier phases that might shed new light on the historical and environmental interaction of the horse Indians and bison herds on the plains.

In the nineteenth-century history of the Central and Southern Plains, there have long been some perplexing questions for which environmental history seems well suited to suggest answers. Why, for example, were the Comanches able to replace the Apaches on the bison-rich Southern Plains? Why did the Kiowas, Cheyennes, and Arapahos gradually shift southward into the Southern Plains between 1800 and 1825? And why, after fighting each other for two decades, did these Southern Plains peoples effect a rapprochement and alliance in the 1840s? What factors were operating to bring on such an escalation of Indian raids into Mexico and Texas in the late 1840s that the subject assumed critical importance in the Treaty of Guadelupe-Hidalgo? If the bison herds were so vast in the years before the hide hunters, why are there so many reports of starving Indians on the Plains by 1850? And finally, given our standard estimates of bison numbers, why is it that the hide hunters are credited with only some 10 million market hides, including no more than 3.5 million from the Southern Plains in the 1870s?

Apposite to all of these questions is a central issue: how successful were the horse Indians at creating a dynamic ecological equilibrium between themselves and the vast bison herds that grazed the Plains? That is, had they developed sustainable hunting practices that would maintain the herds and so permit future generations of hunters to follow the same way of life? This is not to pose the "anachronistic question" (the term is Richard White's) of whether Indians were ecologists.[11] But how a society or a group of peoples with a shared culture makes adjustments to live within the carrying capacity of its habitat is not only a valid question to ask of the historical record, it may be one of the salient questions to ask about any culture. Earlier Plains Indian scholars who have addressed this problem have differed. The standard work, Frank Roe's *The Buffalo: A Critical Study of the Species in Its Wild State* (1951), has generally carried the debate with the argument that there is "not a shred of evidence" to indicate that the horse Indians were out of balance with the bison herds.[12] Using the new insights and methods of environmental history to examine events on the Southern Plains in the first half of the nineteenth century, it now appears possible systematically to analyze and revise nineteenth-century environmental history on the Western Plains. Such an approach ought to be capable of resolving some of these questions, including advancing our understanding about when and why bison declined in numbers, and the intertwining roles that Indian policies—migrations, diplomacy, trade, and ecology—and the growing pressures of external stimuli played in that decline. The answers are complex and offer a revision of both Plains history and Western Indian ecological history.

Working our way through to them requires some digression into the large historical forces that shaped the Southern Plains over the last hundred centuries. The perspective of the longue durée is essential to environmental history. What transpired on the Great Plains from 1800 to 1850 is not comprehensible without taking into account the effect of the Pleistocene extinctions of ten thousand years ago, or the cycle of droughts that determined the carrying capacity for animals on the grasslands. Shallower in time than these forces but just as important to the problem are factors that stemmed from the arrival of Europeans in the Americas. Trade was an ancient part of the cultural landscape of the continent, but the Europeans altered the patterns, the goods, and the intensity of the trade. And the introduction of horses and horse culture accomplished a technological revolution for the Great Plains. The horse was the chief catalyst of an ongoing remaking of the tribal map of western America, as new Indian groups moved onto the plains and incessantly shifted their ranges and alliances in response to a world where accelerating change seemed almost the only constant.

At the beginning of the nineteenth century, the dominant groups on the Southern Plains were the two major divisions of the Comanches: the Texas Comanches, primarily Kotsotekas, and the great New Mexico division, spread across the country from the Llano Estacado Escarpment west to the foothills of the Sangre de Cristo Mountains, and comprising Yamparika and Jupe bands that only recently had replaced the Apaches on the high plains.[13] The Comanches' drive to the south from their original homelands in southwestern Wyoming and northwestern Colorado was a part of the original tribal adjustments to the coming of the horse to the Great Plains. There is reason to believe that the eastern Shoshones, from whom the Comanches were derived before achieving a different identity on the Southern Plains, were one of the first intermountain tribes of historic times to push onto the plains. Perhaps as early as 1500 these proto-Comanches were hunting bison and using dog power to haul their mountain-adapted four-pole tipis east of the Laramie Mountains. Evidently this movement was a response to a wetter time on the Central Plains and larger bison concentrations than earlier.[14]

These early Shoshonean hunters may not have spent more than three or four generations among the thronging Plains bison herds, because by the late seventeenth century they had been pushed back into the mountains and sagebrush deserts by various tribes, especially the Assiniboines and Blackfeet, newly armed with European guns, that were filtering westward from the region around the Great Lakes. If so, they were among a complex of tribes southwest of the lakes that over the next two centuries would be displaced by a massive Siouan drive to the west, an imperial expansion for domination of the prize buffalo range of the Northern Plains and a wedge that sent ripples of tribal displacement across the Plains.[15]

The people who became Comanches thus may have shared with the Apaches and, if linguistic arguments are correct, probably the Kiowas, the longest familiarity with a bison-hunting lifestyle of any of the historic tribes.[16] Pressed back toward the mountains as Shoshones, they thus turned in a different direction and emerged from the passes through the Front Range as the same people but bearing a new name given them by the Utes: Komantcia. They still lacked guns, but now began their intimate association with the one animal, aside from the bison, inextricably linked with Plains life. The Comanches began acquiring horses from the Utes within a decade or so after the Pueblo Revolt of 1680 sent horses and horse culture diffusing in all directions from New Mexico. Thus were born the "hyper-Indians," as one scholar has called the Plains people.[17]

The Comanches became, along with the Sioux, the most populous and widespread of all the peoples that now began to ride onto the vast sweep of grassland to participate in the hunter's life. They began to take possession of the Southern Plains by the early 1700s. By 1800 they were in full control of all the country east of the mountains and south of the Arkansas River clear to the Texas Hill Country.[18] Their new culture, long regarded as an ethnographic anomaly on the Plains because of its Western and archaic origins, may not be so different from that of other Plains groups as older scholars have supposed it to be—at least if we believe the new Comanche revisionists such as Thomas Kavanagh and

Melburn Thurman. On the other hand, as Gary Anderson has argued in a new ethnohistorical study of the Southern Plains, Comanche culture quite likely is one of the best representations we have of ethnogenesis—literally, a peoples' re-creation of themselves—under the impress of bison availability plus the pull of the global market.[19] What everyone seems to agree on is that when the Comanches began to move onto the Southern Plains with their new horse herds, their culture was adapting in interesting ways to the wealth of resources now available to them.

For the Comanches, the Southern Plains must have seemed an earthly paradise. The Pleistocene extinctions nine thousand years earlier had left dozens of grazing niches vacant on the American Great Plains. Nature's solution was to evolve a dwarf species of bison that had a higher reproductive capability than any of its ancestors and to flood most of those vacant niches with an enormous biomass of one grazer. In an ecological sense, bison were a weed species that had proliferated as a result of a major disturbance.[20] That disturbance still reverberated, making it easy for Spanish horses, for example, to reoccupy their old niche and rapidly spread across the plains. And it made the horse Indians a group of humans who throve on a unique environmental situation that has few parallels elsewhere in world history.

The dimensions of the wild bison population on the Southern Plains, and the Great Plains in general, have been much overstated in popular literature. For one thing, pollen analysis and the archeological data indicate that for the Southern Plains there were intervals, some spanning centuries, others decades, when bison must have been almost absent. Two major times of absence occurred between 5000 and 2500 B.C. and between A.D. 500 and 1300. These times when bison bones disappear from the archeological sites correspond to pollen data indicating droughts. The severe Southwest drought that ended early in the fourteenth century was replaced by a five-hundred-year cycle of more mesic conditions and a return of bison in large numbers to the Southern Plains from their drought refugia to the east and west.[21] This long-term pattern in the archeological record seems to have prevailed, as well, on a smaller scale within historic times. During the nineteenth century, for example, droughts of more than five years duration struck the Great Plains four times at roughly twenty-year intervals, in a long-term dendrochronological pattern that seems to show a drying cycle (shorter drought-free intervals) beginning in the 1850s.[22]

More important, our popular perception of bison numbers based on the estimates of awed nineteenth-century observers is probably too high. There very likely was never anything like 100 million or 60 million bison on the Plains during the present climate regime because the carrying capacity of the grasslands was not that high. The best technique for determining bison carrying capacity on the Southern Plains is to extrapolate from U.S. census data for livestock, and the best census for the extrapolation is that of 1910, after the industry crashes of the 1880s had reduced animal numbers to something realistic, but before the breakup of ranches and the Enlarged Homestead Act of 1909 resulted in considerable sections of the Southern Plains being broken out by farmers. Additionally, dendrochronological data seems to show the turn of the century as median, between-droughts-years for rainfall on the Southern Plains, rendering the census of 1910 particularly suitable as a baseline for carrying capacity and animal populations.[23]

The 1910 agricultural census indicates that in the 201 counties that then comprised the 240,000 square miles of the Southern Plains, the nineteenth-century carrying capacity during periods of median rainfall would have been about seven million cattle—equivalent grazers, specifically for 1910, about 5,150,000 cattle and 1,890,000 horses and mules.[24] This does not translate directly into a bison population figure, since their migratory grazing patterns and coevolution with the native grasses made bison as a wild species about 18 percent more efficient on the Great Plains than domestic cattle. And varying climate conditions during the nineteenth century, as I will demonstrate, noticeably affected grassland carrying capacity so that the ecological reality was a dynamic cycle that could swing considerably from decade to decade.[25] But if the Great Plains' bovine carrying capacity of 1910 expresses a median reality, then during prehorse times the Southern Plains might have supported an average of about 8.2 million bison, the entire Great Plains perhaps 28–30 million.[26]

Eight million bison on the Southern Plains may not be so many as we've been led to believe, but to the Comanches the herds probably seemed limitless. Whether the Comanches came to the Southern Plains because of horses or because of bison, bison availability through horse culture caused a specialization that resulted in the loss of two thirds of their former plant lore[27] and to a consequent loss of status for Comanche women, an intriguing development that seems to have been true to a greater or lesser extent among all the tribes that moved onto the plains during this period.[28] As full-time bison hunters, the Comanches also appear to have abandoned all the old Shoshonean mechanisms, such as infanticide and polyandry, that had functioned to keep their population in line with resource availability. These were replaced with cultural mechanisms such as widespread adoption of captured children and male polygyny, adaptations to the plains that were designed to keep Comanche numbers high and growing.[29] At least two ecological factors were operating to select for this course of action. That these changes seem to have been conscious and deliberate argues, perhaps, both for Comanche environmental insight and for some form of centralized leadership and planning.

Comanche success at seizing the Southern Plains from the native groups that had held it for several hundred years was also centered in ecological choices.

Unlike the Comanches, many of the Apache bands had heeded the Spaniards' advice and had begun to build streamside gardening villages that became death-traps once the Comanches located them. Apache vulnerability, then, ironically stemmed from their willingness to diversify their economy. Moreover, given the overwhelming dominance of grasslands as opposed to cultivable river lands on the plains, the specialized horse/bison culture of the Comanches exploited a greater volume of the thermodynamic energy streaming from sunlight into plants than the economies of any of their competitors—until they encountered Cheyennes and Arapahos with a similar culture.[30] The horse-mounted Plains Indians, in other words, made very efficient use of the available energy on the Great Plains, something they seem instinctively to have recognized and exulted in. From the frequency with which the Comanches applied some version of the name "wolf" to their leaders, I suspect that they may have been cognizant of their role as human predators and their ecological kinship with the wolf packs that likewise lived off the bison herds.[31]

The Comanches, as is well known, were not the only people on the Southern Plains during the horse period. The New Mexicans, both Pueblo and Hispanic, continued to hunt on the wide-open Llanos, as did the Prairie Caddoans, although the numbers of the latter were dwindling rapidly by 1825. The New Mexican peoples and the Caddoans of the middle Red and Brazos Rivers played major trade roles for the Southern Plains, and the Comanches in particular. Although the Comanches did engage in the classic Plains exchange of bison products for horticultural produce and European trade goods, and did trade horses and mules with a series of little-known Anglo-American traders from Missouri, Arkansas, and Louisiana, they were never a high-volume trading people until relatively late in their history.[32] Early experiences with American traders and disease led them to distrust trade with Euro-Americans, and on only one or two occasions did they allow short-lived posts to be established in their country. Instead, peace with the Prairie Caddoans by the 1730s, and with New Mexico in 1786, sent Comanche trade both east and west, but often through Indian middlemen.[33]

In this classic period between 1800 and 1850, the most interesting Southern Plains development was the cultural interaction between the Comanches and surrounding Plains Indians to the north. The Kiowas were one of those groups.

The Kiowas are and have long been an enigma. Scholars are still interested in their origins because their own oral tradition is at odds with the scientific evidence. The Kiowas, as is well known, believe that they started their journey to Rainy Mountain on the Oklahoma plains from the north. And indeed, in the eighteenth century we do find them on the Northern Plains, near the Black Hills, as one of the groups being displaced southwestwardly by the Siouan drive for the buffalo range. Linguistically, however, the Kiowas are southern Indians. Their language belongs to the Tanoan group of Pueblo languages in New Mexico, and some scholars believe that the Kiowas of later history are the same people as the Plains Jumanos of the New Mexico period, whose rancherias were associated during the 1600s and early 1700s with the headwaters of the Colorado and Concho Rivers of Texas. How the Kiowas got so far north is unclear, but they are known in historical times as consummate traders, especially of horses, and since the Black Hills was a major trade citadel they may have begun to frequent the region as traders and teachers of horse lore.[34]

Displaced by the wars for the buffalo ranges in the north, the Kiowas began to drift southward again—or perhaps, since the supply of horses was the Southwest, simply began to stay longer on the Southern Plains. Their rapprochement with the Comanches came between 1790 and 1806, and thereafter they were so closely associated with the northern Comanches that they were regarded by some as merely a Comanche band, although in many cultural details the two groups were dissimilar.[35] Spanish and American traders and explorers of the 1820s found them most closely associated with the two forks of the Canadian River and on the various headwater streams of the Red.[36]

The other groups that increasingly began to interact with the Comanches during the 1820s and thereafter were also Northern Plains in origin. These were the Arapahos and the Cheyennes, who by 1825 were beginning to establish themselves on the Colorado buffalo plains from the North Platte all the way down to the Arkansas River.

The Algonkian-speaking Arapahos and Cheyennes had once been farmers living in earth lodges on the upper Mississippi. By the early 1700s both groups were in present North Dakota, occupying villages along the Red and Sheyenne Rivers, where they first began to acquire horses, possibly from the Kiowas. Fur wars instigated by the Europeans drove them farther southwest and more and more into a plains, bison-hunting culture, one—as Holder has pointed out—that the women of these farming tribes probably resisted as long as possible.[37] But by the second decade of the nineteenth century, the Teton Sioux wedge had made nomads and hunters of the Arapahos and Cheyennes.

Their search for prime buffalo grounds and for ever larger horse herds, critical since both tribes had emerged as middlemen traders between the villagers of the Missouri and the horse reservoir to the south,[38] first led the Cheyennes and Arapahos west of the Black Hills into Crow lands and then increasingly southward along the mountain front. By 1815 the Arapahos were becoming fixed in the minds of American traders as their own analogue on the Southern Plains: the famous Chouteau-DeMun trading expedition of that decade was designed to exploit the horse and robe trade of the Arapahos on the Arkansas.[39] By the time Stephen Long's expedition and the trading party including Jacob Fowler penetrated the Southern Plains, the Arapahos and Cheyennes were camping with the

Kiowas and Comanches on the Arkansas. The Hairy Rope band of the Cheyennes, renowned for their ability to catch wild horses, was then known to be mustanging along the Cimarron.[40]

Three factors seem to have drawn the Arapahos and Cheyennes so far south. Unquestionably, the vast horse herds of the Comanches and Kiowas was one, an unending supply of horses for the trade, which by 1825 the Colorado tribes were acquiring through daring raids. Another was the milder winters south of the Arkansas, which made horse pastoralism much easier. The third factor was the abnormally rich wildlife bounty of the early nineteenth-century Southern Plains, the direct result of an extraordinary series of years between 1815 and 1846 when, with the exception of a minor drought in the early 1820s, rainfall south of the Arkansas was considerably above average. So lucrative was the hunting and raiding that in 1833 Charles Bent located the first of his adobe trading posts along the Arkansas, expressly to control the winter robe and summer horse trade of the Arapahos and Cheyennes. Bent's marketing contacts were in St. Louis. Horses that Bent's traders drove to St. Louis commonly started as stock in the New Mexican Spanish settlements (and sometimes those were California horses stolen by Indians and traded to the New Mexicans) that got stolen by the Comanches, then stolen again by Cheyenne raiders, and finally traded at Bent's or St. Vrain's posts, from whence they were driven to Westport, Missouri, and sold to outfit American emigrants going to the West Coast![41] Unless you saw it from the wrong end, as the New Mexicans (or the horses) seem to have, it was both profitable and a culturally stimulating economy.

Thus, at the outset of the period from 1825 to 1850, the Comanches and Kiowas found themselves at war with Cheyennes, Arapahos, and other tribes to the north. Meanwhile, the Colorado tribes opened another front in a naked effort to seize the rich buffalo range of the upper Kansas and Republican Rivers from the Pawnees. These wars produced interesting ecological developments, developments that seem to have been typical across most of the continent. Where the boundaries of warring tribes met, buffer zones of various sizes that neither side occupied became established where some hunting was allowed but was usually light. One such buffer zone on the Southern Plains was along its northern perimeter, between the Arkansas and North Canadian Rivers. Another was in present western Kansas, between the Pawnees and the main range of the Colorado tribes, and a third seems to have existed during this time from the forks of the Platte to the mountains. The importance of these buffer zones is that they left game within them relatively undisturbed and allowed the buildup of herds that later might be exploited when tribal boundaries or agreements changed.[42]

The appearance of American traders like Bent and Ceran St. Vrain marked the Southern Plains tribes' growing immersion in a market economy increasingly tied to world-wide trade networks that were dominated by Euro-Americans. Like all humans, Indians had always altered their environments. But as most modern historians of Plains Indians and the Western fur trade have realized, Western tribes during the nineteenth century not only had become technologically capable of pressuring their resources, they were becoming less "ecosystem people" year after year.[43] Despite some speculation that the Plains tribes were experiencing ecological problems, previous scholars have not been able to ascertain what role market hunting may have played in this dilemma, what other combination of factors was involved, or what the tribes attempted to do about it.[44]

The crux of the problem in studying Southern Plains Indian ecology and bison is to determine whether the Plains tribes had established a society in ecological equilibrium, one where population does not exceed the carrying capacity of its habitat and so maintains a healthy, functioning ecology that can be sustained over the long term.[45] Resolving such a question involves an effort to come to grips with the factors affecting bison populations, those affecting Indian populations, and the cultural aspects of Plains Indian utilization of bison. None of these puzzles is easy to resolve.

Studies done on the fertility of modern, protected bison herds on the plains indicate that bison are a prolific species that increase their numbers by an average of 18 percent a year, assuming a normal (51/49) sex ratio with breeding cows amounting to 35 percent of the total.[46] In other words, if the Southern Plains supported 8.2 million bison in years of median rainfall, the herds would have produced about 1.4 million calves a year. To maintain an ecological equilibrium with the grasses, the Plains bison's natural mortality rate would have had to approach 18 percent as well.

Today the several protected bison herds in the West have a natural mortality rate, without predation, ranging between 3 percent and 9 percent.[47] The Wichita Mountains herd, the only large herd left on the Southern Plains, falls midway between with a 6 percent mortality rate. Despite a search for it, no inherent naturally regulating mechanism has yet been found in bison populations, necessitating active culling programs at all the Plains bison refuges. The kind of starvation-induced population crashes that affect ungulates like deer[48] seemingly were mitigated on the wild, unfenced plains by the bison's tendency—barring any major impediments—to shift its range great distances to better pasture.

Determining precisely how the remaining annual mortality in the wild herds was affected is not easy, because the wolf/bison relationship on the Plains was never studied. Judging from dozens of historical documents attesting to wolf predation of bison calves, including accounts of the Indians, wolves do seem to have played a critical role in Plains bison population dynamics and not just as culling agents of diseased and old animals.[49]

Human hunters were the other source of mortality. For nine thousand years

Pecos National Monument, New Mexico, where for centuries Pueblo and Plains Indians carried on a mutualistic trade featuring bison products. *Photo by author.*

Native Americans had hunted bison without exterminating them, perhaps building into their gene pool an adjustment to human predation. But there is archeological evidence that beginning about A.D. 1450, with the advent of "mutualistic" trade between new Puebloan communities recently forced by drought to relocate on the Rio Grande and a new wave of Plains hunters (probably the Athapaskan-speaking Apaches), human pressures on the southern bison herd had accelerated, evidently dramatically if the archeological record in New Mexico is an accurate indication. That pressure would have been a function of both Indian population size and their cultural utilization of bison. The trade of bison-derived goods for the produce of the horticultural villages fringing the Plains meant, of course, that bison would be affected by changes in human populations periphery to as well as on the Great Plains.[50]

One attempt to estimate maximum human population size on the Southern Plains, that of Jerold Levy in 1961, fixed the upper limit at about 10,500 people. Levy argued that the availability of water would have been a more critical resource than bison in fixing a limit for Indian populations. While Levy's population figures are demonstrably too low, and he lacked familiarity with the somewhat drought-resistant sources of water on the Southern Plains, his argument that water was the more critical limiting resource introduces an important element into the Plains equation.[51]

The cultural utilization of bison by horse Indians has been studied by Bill Brown in an article published in 1986.[52] Adapting a sophisticated formula worked out first for caribou hunters in the Yukon,[53] Brown has estimated Indian subsistence (caloric requirements plus the number of robes and hides required for domestic use) at about forty-seven animals per lodge per year. At an average of eight people per lodge, that works out to almost six bison per person in a year's time. Brown's article is not only highly useful in getting us closer to a historic Plains equation than ever before, it is also borne out by at least one historic account. In 1821 trader Jacob Fowler camped for several weeks with seven hundred lodges of Southern Plains tribes on the Arkansas River. Fowler was no ecologist; in fact, he could hardly spell. But he was a careful observer, and he wrote that the big camp was using up a hundred bison a week. In other words, seven hundred lodges were using bison at a rate of about fifty-two per lodge per year, or six and a half animals per person.[54] These are important figures. Not only do they give us some idea of the mortality percentage that can be assigned to human hunters, by extension they help us fix a quadruped predation percentage as well.

Estimates of the number of Indians on the Southern Plains during historic times are not difficult to find, but do tend to vary widely, and for good reason, as will be seen when we look closely at the historical events of 1800 to 1850. Although observer population estimates for the Comanches do go as high as thirty-thousand, six of the seven population figures for the Comanches between 1786 and 1854 fall into a narrow range between 19,200 and 21,600.[55] Taken altogether, the Kiowas, Cheyennes, Arapahos, Plains Apaches, Kiowa-Apaches, and Wichitas do not seem to have exceeded ten thousand to twelve thousand during this same period. The combined Cheyennes and Arapahos, for example, are estimated at forty-four hundred in 1838, five thousand in 1843, and fifty-two hundred in 1846.[56] If the historic Southern Plains hunting population did reach as high as 30,000, then even that level of human pressure would have accounted for only a 195,000 bison per year at an estimate of 6.5 animals per person.

But another factor must have played a significant role. While quadruped predators concentrated on calves and injured or feeble animals, human hunters had different criteria. Historical documents attest to the horse Indians' preference for and success in killing two- to five-year-old bison cows, which were preferred for eating and for their thinner, more easily processed hides and their luxurious robes.[57] Studies done on other large American ungulates indicate that removal of breeding females at a level that exceeds 7 percent of the total herd will initiate the onset of population decline.[58] With 8.2 million bison on the Southern Plains, this critical upper figure for cow selectivity would have been about 574,000 animals. Reduce the total bison number to 6 million and the yearly calf crop to 1.08 million, probably more realistic median figures for the first half of the nineteenth century (see below), and the critical mortality for breeding cows would still have been 420,000 animals. As mentioned, thirty thousand horse-mounted bison hunters, hunting for subsistence, would have harvested bison at a yearly rate of fewer than two hundred thousand. Hence I would argue that, theoretically, on the Southern Plains during favorable climate episodes (like that of 1550 to 1850), the huge biomass of bison left from the Pleistocene extinctions would have supported the subsistence needs of more than sixty thousand Plains hunters.[59]

All of which raises some serious questions when we look at the historical evidence of 1800 to 1850. By the end of that period, despite an effort on the part of many Plains tribes at population growth, the population estimates for most of the Southern Plains tribes were down, and many of the bands seemed to be starving. William Bent's letters were full of accounts of the dire straits of the Cheyennes.[60] The Comanches were reported to be eating their horses in great numbers by 1850, and their raids into Mexico increased all through the 1840s, as if a resource depletion in their home range was driving them to compensate with stolen stock.[61] In Mooney's Kiowa Calendar history, the notation for "few or no bison" appears for four years in a row between 1849 and 1852.[62] Bison were becoming less reliable, and the evolution toward a raiding/true horse pastoralism economy was well underway. Clearly, by 1850 something had altered the situation on the Southern Plains. The "something," in fact, was a whole host of ecological alterations that historians with a wide range of data at their disposal are only now, more than a century later, beginning to understand.

As early as 1850 the bison herds had been weakened in a number of ways. The effect of the horse on Indian culture has been much studied, but for the purpose of working out a Southern Plains ecological model, it is important to note that horses had requirements of their own that directly affected bison numbers. By the second quarter of the nineteenth century the horse herds of the Southern Plains tribes must have ranged as high as a quarter million animals (at an average of five to ten horses per person),[63] with an estimated two million wild mustangs overspreading the country between south Texas and the Arkansas River. That many animals of a species with an 80 percent dietary overlap with bovines and, perhaps more critically, similar water requirements, must have had an adverse impact on bison carrying capacity, especially since Indian horse herds concentrated the tribes in the moist canyons and river valleys that bison also used for watering.[64] Judging from the 1910 Agricultural Census discussed earlier, two million or more horses would have reduced the median grassland carrying capacity for the southern bison herd to fewer than six million animals.

Another factor that may have already started to diminish overall bison numbers was the effect of exotic bovine diseases. Anthrax seems to have been introduced into the bison herds from a sourcepoint in Louisiana around 1800; its effect is most pronounced on animals whose immune systems have been weakened by droughts or harsh winters. Bovine tuberculosis apparently was brought to the Plains by feral and stolen Texas cattle and by stock on the overland trails. It quite likely was one of these diseases that accounted for inexplicable masses of dead buffalo, like those Charles Goodnight saw along the Concho River in 1867. Brucellosis perhaps arrived too late on the continent (the 1880s) to have had an impact on wild bison ecology, although if it were present then Indian women butchering buffalo would have been at risk for contracting the human version of the disease, undulant fever.[65]

Earlier I mentioned modern natural mortality figures for bison of 3 percent to 9 percent of herd totals. On the wilderness plains, events like fires, floods, drowning, droughts, and stress-related die-offs may have increased this percentage considerably. But if we hold to the upper figure, then natural mortality might have taken an average of 50 percent of the annual bison increase of 18 percent. Since thirty thousand subsistence hunters would have accounted for only 18 percent of the bison's yearly increase (based on a herd of six million), then the long wondered-at wolf predation perhaps was the most important of all the factors regulating bison populations, with a predation percentage of around 32 percent of the annual bison increase. (Interestingly, this dovetails closely with the Pawnee estimate that wolves got three to four of every ten calves born.)[66] Canids are known for their ability to adjust their litter sizes to factors like mortality and resource abundance. Thus, while mountain men and traders who poisoned wolves for their pelts may not have significantly reduced wolf populations, their tactics may have inadvertently killed thousands of bison, for poisoned wolves drooled and vomited strychnine over the grass in their convulsions. Many Indians lost horses in this way.[67]

The nineteenth-century climate cycle, strongly linked correlatively with bison populations in the archeological data for earlier periods, must have simultaneously interacted with these other factors to produce a decline in bison numbers between 1840 and 1850. Except for a dry period in the mid-to-late 1820s, the first four decades of the nineteenth century had been a time of above-normal rainfall on the Southern Plains. With the carrying capacity for bison and horses high, the country south of the Arkansas sucked tribes to it as into a vortex. But beginning in 1846, rainfall plunged as much as 30 percent below the median for nine years of the next decade. On the Central Plains, six years of this same time span were dry.[68] These droughts, in fact, marked the end of the three-century-long wet cycle known as the Little Ice Age. But now the growth of human populations and settlements in Texas, New Mexico, and the Indian Territory blocked the bison herds from migrating to their traditional drought refugia on the periphery of their range. Thus, a normal climate swing combined with unprecedented external pressures to produce an effect unusual in bison history—a core population, significantly reduced by competition with horses and by drought, that was quite susceptible to human hunting pressure.

Finally, alterations in the historical circumstances of the Southern Plains tribes between 1825 and 1850 undoubtedly had serious repercussions for Plains ecology. Some of these circumstances were indirect and beyond the tribes' ability to influence. Traders along the Santa Fe Trail shot into, chased, and disturbed the southern herds. New Mexican Ciboleros continued to take fifteen thousand to twenty-five thousand bison a year from the Llano Estacado.[69] The U.S. government's removal of more than eighty thousand Eastern Indians into Oklahoma accelerated the pressure on the bison herds at a level impossible to estimate, although the Southern Plains tribes considered it a threat, and they refused to abide by the Treaty of Fort Holmes (1835) when they discovered it gave the eastern tribes hunting rights on the prairies.[70]

Insofar as the Southern Plains tribes had an environmental policy, then, it was to protect the bison herds from being hunted by outsiders. The Comanches could not afford to emulate their Shoshonean ancestors and limit their own population. Beset by enemies and disease, they had to try to keep their numbers high, even as their resource base diminished. For the historic Plains tribes, warfare and stock raids addressed ecological as well as cultural needs and must have seemed far more logical solutions than consciously reducing their own populations as the bison herds became less reliable.

For those very reasons, after more than a decade of warfare among the buffalo tribes, in 1840 the Comanches and Kiowas adopted a strategy of seeking peace and an alliance with the Cheyennes, Arapahos, and Kiowa-Apaches. From the Comanche point of view, it brought them allies against Texans and Eastern Indians who were trespassing on the plains. The Cheyennes and Arapahos got what they most wanted: the chance to hunt the grass- and bison-rich Southern Plains, horses and mules for trading, and access to the Spanish settlements via Comanche lands.[71] But the peace meant something else in ecological terms. Now all the tribes could freely exploit the Arkansas Valley bison herds. This exploitation of a large, prime bison habitat that had been a boundary zone for Indian hunters may have been critical. In the Kiowa Calendar the notation for "many bison" appears in 1841, the year following the peace. The notation appears only once more over the next thirty-five years.[72]

One other advantage the Comanches and Kiowas derived from the peace of 1840 was freedom to trade at Bent's Fort. Although the data to prove it are fragmentary, this conversion of the largest body of Indians on the Southern Plains from subsistence/ecosystem hunters to a people intertwined in the European market system may have added catalyst stress to a bison herd already being eaten away on a variety of fronts. How serious the market incentive could be is indicated by John Whitfield, agent at Bent's second fort in 1855, who wrote that 3,150

Cheyennes were killing 40,000 bison a year.[73] That is just about twice the number the Cheyennes would be expected to harvest through subsistence hunting alone. (It also means that every Cheyenne warrior was killing forty-four bison a year, and Cheyenne women each were processing robes at the rate of almost one a week.) With the core bison population seriously affected by the drought of the late 1840s, the additional, growing robe trade of the Comanches likely brought the Southern Plains tribes to a critical level in their utilization of bison.[74] Drought, coupled with Indian market hunting and cow selectivity, must stand as the critical element—albeit augmented by more minor factors such as white disturbance, new bovine diseases, and increasing grazing competition from horses—that explains the bison crisis of the midcentury Southern Plains. It is an explanation that may serve as well to illuminate the experience of the Canadian Plains, where bison disappeared without the advent of white hide hunting.[75]

Perhaps it would have happened on the American Plains as it did in Canada if the tribes had held or continued to augment their populations. But the Comanches and other tribes fought a losing battle against their own attrition. While the new Comanche institutions worked to build up their numbers, the disease epidemics of the nineteenth century repeatedly decimated them. In the 1820s the Comanches were rebuilding their population after the smallpox epidemic of 1816 had carried away a fourth of them. But smallpox ran like a brushfire through the Plains villages again in 1837–38, wiping whole peoples off the continent. And the '49ers brought cholera, which devastated the Arkansas Valley Indians to such an extent that Bent burned his fort and temporarily left the trade that year.[76] John C. Ewers, in fact, has estimated that the nineteenth-century Comanches lost 77 percent of their population to disease.[77]

To the question, did the Southern Plains Indians successfully work out a dynamic, ecological equilibrium with the bison herds?, I would argue that the answer remains ultimately elusive because the relationship was never allowed to play itself out. The trends, however, seem to suggest that a satisfactory solution was improbable. One factor that worked against the horse tribes was their short tenure. It may be that two centuries was too brief a time for them to have created a workable system around horses, the swelling demand for bison robes generated by the Euro-American market, and the expansion of their own populations so as to hold their territories. Some of those forces, such as the tribes' need to expand their numbers and the advantages accruing from participation in the robe trade, worked in opposition to their creating an equilibrium with the bison herds. Too, many of the forces that shaped their world were beyond the power of the Plains tribes to influence. Indeed, from the modern vantage, it is clear that the ecology of the Southern Plains by the mid-nineteenth century had become so complicated that neither Indians nor Euro-Americans of those years could have grasped how it all worked.

Catlin portrays the Plains Indian hunt during the height of the robe trade as something approaching a frenzy. *Courtesy National Museum of American Art, Smithsonian Institution.*

Finally, and ironically, it seems that the Indian religions, so effective at calling forth awe and reverence for the natural world, may have actually inhibited the Plains Indians from completely understanding bison ecology and their role in it. True, native leaders such as Yellow Wolf, the Cheyenne whom James Abert interviewed and sketched at Bent's Fort in 1845, surmised the implications of market hunting. As he watched the bison disappearing from the Arkansas Valley, Yellow Wolf asked the whites to teach the Cheyenne hunters how to farm, never realizing that he was reprising a Plains Indian/Euro-American conversation that had taken place sixty years earlier in that same country.[78] But Yellow Wolf was marching to his own drummer, for it remained a widespread tenet of faith among most Plains Indians through the 1880s that bison were supernatural in origin. As a first-hand observer and close student of the nineteenth-century Plains reported, "Every Plains Indian firmly believed that the buffalo were produced in countless numbers in a country under the ground, that every spring the surplus swarmed like bees from a hive, out of great cave-like openings to this country, which were situated somewhere in the great 'Llano Estacado' or Staked Plain of Texas."[79]

This religious conception of the infinity of nature's abundance was poetic and on one level also empirical: bison overwintered in large numbers in the protected canyons scored into the eastern escarpment of the Llano Estacado, and Indians had no doubt many times witnessed the herds emerging to overspread the high plains in springtime.[80] But such a conception did not aid the tribes in their efforts to work out an ecological balance amidst the complexities of the nineteenth-century Plains.

In a real sense, then, the more familiar events of the 1870s only delivered the coup de grace to the free Indian life on the Great Plains. The effects of exotic diseases and wars with the encroaching whites caused Indian numbers to dwindle after 1850 (no more than fourteen hundred Comanches were enrolled at Fort Sill in the 1880s).[81] This combined with bison resiliency to preserve a good core of animals until the arrival of the hide hunters, who nonetheless can be documented with taking only about 3.5 million animals from the Southern Plains.[82]

But the great days of the Plains Indians, the primal poetry of humans and horses, bison and grass, sunlight and blue skies, and the sensuous satisfactions of a hunting life on the sweeping grasslands was a meteoric time indeed. And the meteor was already fading in the sky a quarter century before the Big Fifties began to boom.

CHAPTER 4

Dreams and Beasts

The Grizzly and the West

That which happens to men also happens to animals; and one thing happens to them both: as one dies so dies the other, for they share the same breath; and man has no pre-eminence above an animal: for all is vanity.

Ecclesiastes 3:19

Wednesday 11 Sept. 1805. a beautiful pleasant morning. . . . passed a tree on which was a number of Shapes drawn on it with paint by the natives. a white bear Skin hung on the Same tree. we Supose this to be a place of worship among them [*sic*].

Joseph Whitehouse, *Bitterroot Valley*

As a boy growing up in Louisiana, the world of nature I experienced was the world that we all experience—the one that history has fashioned around those of us who share time and place. With its bayous, its arrowing flights of waterfowl, its fecund and enveloping woodlands with all their smells—the ones I can conjure most easily are the turpentine incense of soaked pine after days of rain, the musky woodsiness of fox squirrels in pungent autumn dusk, the split-cucumber smell of water moccasins on a humid summer day—rural Louisiana in the 1960s was the real thing, a kind of American natural paradise. And I made the most of the place. I roamed the woods, hunted the whitetail deer that were then making an astonishing comeback after their near eradication. I built cabins, set traplines, had a childhood that not many Americans get to have anymore.

Even so, from somewhere, and at a young age, there dawned a recognition that my world was an incomplete one. I think I had already read enough by adolescence to recognize that the part of America I knew as homeland was tragically disadvantaged and not just in the way much of the South in the Civil Rights era was as it confronted its own special historical burden. Louisiana's natural world had been spoiled by decades of overhunting and corporate oil and

Grizzly bear and mouse, George Catlin. *Courtesy National Museum of American Art, Smithsonian Institution.*

timber extraction with their accompanying senseless pollution, a reality I saw dimly and tried to grasp. So an English teacher, perusing my attempts at essay on this theme, pressed Thoreau into my hands in high school. I may have even read back then what to my mind is Thoreau's most moving journal entry, often called "To Know an Entire Heaven and an Entire Earth," although I don't recall as much. But the sentiments in it were certainly my sentiments as an adolescent. In his 23 March entry for 1856, Thoreau wrote that experiencing *his* natural world was like nothing so much as listening to a symphony with all the best instruments gone—without the bass lines of the oboe, the cymbals silenced, the French horns missing, the clarinets extracted. As he reflected on the fact that moose and cougar and wolf were all missing from his Massachusetts, he concluded that he would never know the full manner in which nature signaled the seasons, the richness of its changes. It was a sobering thought, because Thoreau realized that what he wanted more than anything was the chance to know "an entire heaven and an entire earth."[1]

This was a sentiment that came to me, growing up in Louisiana, in much the same way it seems to have come to Thoreau—by reading historical accounts about the diverse world that had existed only decades or centuries before *on my own spot of ground.* And what that reading led me to recognize was that my time and place were a mere shadow of what they should have been, that in my time the bayous that had once echoed with the howls of the red wolves that John James Audubon described in the Louisiana nights now no longer did. And that I did not get to step out onto my Granddad's back porch with the hair on my neck lifting to the screams of the "painters" my grandparents still talked about in hushed tones—"like a woman screaming" those old-timers in Louisiana and East Texas liked to say—while I could only sit with wide eyes and try to stretch my imagination to encompass cougars in my woods.

Then there were the bears. Once, Louisiana was a paradise of bears and the stories of them still wafted around in the humid air, mostly echoes of stories, faint like the snick of the dominos in the pool halls. One of my boyhood rivers, a tributary of the Red River called the Sulphur, had been called rather more romantically *Riviere de L'Ours* (River of Bears) when France owned Louisiana. In 1806 an Indian family living very near where I grew up had attained some small degree of enduring fame for having killed in a single autumn, for their grease and pelts, 118 of the black bears that inhabited my woods. As late as the twentieth century, President Theodore Roosevelt had come to Louisiana specifically to hunt bears.

And there was Ben Lilly, too, a fellow Louisianian whom David Brown, in *The Grizzly in the Southwest: Documentary of an Extinction*, calls "the archetype of the Southwestern grizzly hunter." When Lilly finally pulled up stakes and disgustedly left Louisiana for points west in 1906—the lower Mississippi's entire black bear population was down to fewer than forty animals by then, he believed, and he was probably right—his personal vendetta against bears had left Louisiana 180 bears poorer. A religious fanatic, Lilly went on to a career with the government's Predator and Rodent Control in New Mexico and Arizona, where in the name of Jesus and Civilization (that's exactly the way he thought of it) he waged a kind of John Brown campaign against all bears and lions, a jihad that went far toward bringing grizzlies to the extinction that has become their fate everywhere in the Southwest in the twenty-first century, with the exception, perhaps, of Colorado.[2]

My personal Louisiana experiences, I realize, stand in about the same relationship to my objectives in this chapter on the natural West and the grizzly as Louisiana stands in its relationship to the Southwest—marginal and peripheral at best. But I think not hopelessly peripheral, because just as the black bear virtually vanished from my home state and is only now returning, history documents and predicts a similar vanishing act for the grizzly, whose range and numbers in the past three centuries have shrunk like a prairie lake boiled away to its last couple of puddles under the relentless, empty sky glare of a drought. Bringing the grizzly back so that more of us can know an entire heaven and earth in the West? That's one of the issues that makes the *idea* of the grizzly bear totemic for the natural West (as Claude Levi-Strauss might have put it). Simply, the grizzly is an animal we should incorporate into our understanding of how we've thought about the West, and of how we're coming to think of it.

How it was that the grizzly once thrived and was widespread in the same West where in our own time it exists primarily only in isolated national park pockets, and why history makes its present restoration in the Rocky Mountain states of Montana and Idaho so problematic, might seem questions with entirely obvious answers. I do not think that I can amplify much on how and why Western stockmen hated predators, nor go beyond Tom Dunlap's treatment, in *Saving America's Wildlife*, in explaining why the federal government was for so long willing to subsidize the eradication of many of the continent's most extraordinary big animals.[3]

I have, in other words, no new insights on America's jihad against predators. Certainly there was a powerful cultural psychology at work: American puritanism's disgust with all that was earth and flesh engendered a profound hatred of the animal within ourselves, and that may have led us to a kind of religious quest to eradicate those animals that most symbolized the untamable wild within our own natures. Euro-Americans, to put it another way, were caught up in a Freudian feedback loop with respect to their continent. Its wildness produced enough unease about the thinness of civilization's veneer that we reacted with a numb orgy of destruction aimed at the animals that we subconsciously saw as exposing in raw form our own base instincts as animals. "Nonhuman nature," D. H. Lawrence once wrote, "is the outward and visible expression of the mystery that confronts us when we look into the depths of our own being."[4] For much of American history, that exercise, when we've indulged it, has not pleased us, producing a self-hatred that we've deflected outward. And now, since the grizzly and the wolf were animals our grandfathers so labored to eradicate, many Westerners find it repugnant to confront the possibility that their own ancestors were wrong. As Paul Shepard put it in one of his last books, "By disdaining the beast in us, we grow away from the world instead of into it."[5] That line stands as an evocative summary of much of the history of the American West.

It might be enlightening here to draw on a few representative human/grizzly stories from the history of this Western totem of our imaginations to help us reconstruct the way culture has created the bears in our heads. The bears of our evolving historical imagination have arguably been more important to what has happened to the grizzly, and what *might* happen to the grizzly, than the flesh and blood bears in the mountains. And if that is true—if the Great Bear has indeed been largely configured in the Far Cerebellum of our cultural imaginations— was there perhaps a way out, a path not taken? Perhaps a path that still might be taken so that modern humans and the most formidable and awe-inspiring big animal on the continent can exist side by side, even if uneasily?

I think there was. It is undoubtedly our ancient human nature, an instinct deeply imbedded in our primate origins, that produces such quick fear and considered respect (along with a certain amount of morbid fascination) with big predators that can (and sometimes do) regard us as prey. But fear, respect, even morbid fascination should not stand as synonyms for *eradication*. So an examination of why they have should start with Euro-American stories about bears, since they alone can articulate the foundational reasons why, from a continental population of a hundred thousand five centuries ago, fewer than one thousand grizzlies now roam wild in the Lower 48. I have no intention of ignoring other ways of seeing bears; far from it. But for reasons related to the particular trajectory of this chapter, I'd like to consider those "other," earlier ways of seeing not so much (as we tend consistently to do in Western culture) as a point from which we've traveled, but instead as a potential destination.

Despite a scattering of Euro-American encounters with grizzlies as early as the seventeenth century, for two centuries after Europeans settled the continent, grizzly bears were little known to folk knowledge and existed only as rumors in the Western scientific grasp of North America. The first known description of grizzlies we have by a European was left by Spanish explorer Sebastian Viscaino in the year 1602. Traversing the California coast, near where Monterey would one day stand, two centuries before the Lewis and Clark expedition would bring "white bears" to the attention of Western taxonomy, Viscaino saw grizzlies clambering with astonishing nimbleness over the carcass of a whale washed up on the beach of the Pacific Coast. Three-quarters of a century before Russian traders and naturalists first described large brown bears in Alaska, the Hudson's Bay trader Henry Kelsey became the first European of record to kill a grizzly bear. That event, pregnant with portents for the future, took place in 1690 in present Saskatchewan. Of equal significance, Kelsey's act was one that greatly alarmed his Indian companions, who warned him that he had struck down "a god."[6]

Other unknown Russian, English, and American traders along the Pacific Coast had no doubt encountered grizzlies by 1800, and the Spaniards in California and the Southwest and French traders penetrating inland certainly had experiences with grizzlies by then. But at the beginning of the nineteenth century, journal-keeping Anglo-Americans had not yet begun to push on foot into grizzly country. Archeological evidence along with probable, early sightings has established the entire western half of North America—not just the Rockies but (following the riparian stringers of cottonwoods and water) far out into the high plains and along the island stepping stones of mountain ranges in the southwestern deserts—as falling into the grizzly bear's range two hundred years ago.[7] Even by 1800 no Euro-American settlements save those in the Spanish Southwest and California lay within this immense sweep of country, inhabited by perhaps two million Indians, twenty-five million to thirty million buffalo, and perhaps fifty thousand to sixty thousand grizzlies. So many grizzlies, indeed, that Ernest Thompson Seton says Spanish travelers reported seeing thirty to forty in a single day in Northern California.[8]

Although by no means the first Euro-Americans to encounter grizzlies, Lewis and Clark occupy a prominent place in the grizzly's history, in large part because they stand as such an obvious cultural template for the American reaction to grizzly bears. By the Jeffersonian Age, American attitudes toward wildlife were complex and already deeply internalized. If one does accept the premise of evolutionary psychologists and sociobiologists, in our resident Paleolithic genetic programming we must preserve an ancient core of evolutionary reaction not just toward big predators as a whole but toward giant bears specifically. Bears do not lie extremely far back in time for primates; early human migrants would have begun to confront bears perhaps a hundred thousand years ago, as our species moved from Africa into the northern latitudes. The noted biologist Valerius Geist, in fact, believes that North America's Pleistocene species, the short-faced bear (*Arctodus simus*)—which by every reconstruction seems to have been a long-legged, gracile, and exceedingly active and aggressive predator—likely preyed on humans, and until its extinction twelve thousand years ago may have been singularly responsible for keeping migrating human parties from entering North America.[9]

Atop that ancient anomie, whose sketchy outlines in pagan Europe nonetheless demonstrate that bears once served as both totems and gods there, later Western religion and science layered a complex cultural matrix that richly colored Euro-American experiences with grizzlies in North America.[10] Virtually all the strands are evident in the Lewis and Clark encounters, which were so widely read in early America that they became a kind of nineteenth-century guidebook for how to think about the West and its inhabitants.

Jefferson's explorers had heard before they left Washington about the possible presence of a different kind of bear in the West, a bear rumored to be as large as an ox and as fast in a flat-out run as a race horse. Wintering at the Mandan villages in 1804–1805 the explorers were exposed to more direct evidence from the Indians and had indeed already seen the tracks of a "white bear" in present South Dakota, where some of the hunters claimed to have wounded one. But Lewis and Clark's firsthand experiences with grizzlies really began in April 1805 in present Montrail County, North Dakota.

According to volume 4 of Gary Moulton's *Journals of the Lewis and Clark Expedition*, this is how Euro-Americans and grizzly bears first interacted in the West:

> *April 13, 1805: [Lewis]. we found a number of carcases of the Buffaloe lying*
> *along shore, which had been drowned by falling through the ice in winter an*

*lodged on shore by the high water. . . . we saw also many tracks of the white bear
of enormous size, along the river shore and about the carcases of the Buffaloe, on
which I presume they feed. we have not as yet seen one of these anamals, tho'
their tracks are so abundant and recent. the men as well as ourselves are anxious
to meet with some of these bear. the Indians give a very formidable account of
the strengh and ferocity of this anamal, which they never dare to attack but in
parties of six eight or ten persons; and are even then frequently defeated with the
loss of one or more of their party. the savages attack this anamal with their bows
and arrows and the indifferent guns with which the traders furnish them, with
these they shoot with such uncertainty and at so short a distance, unless shot
thro' head or heart wound not mortal that they frequently mis their aim & fall
sacrefice to the bear. two Minetaries were killed during the last winter in an
attack on a white bear. This anamal is said more frequently to attack a man on
meeting with him, than to flee from him. When the Indians are about to go in
quest of the white bear, previous to their departure, they paint themselves and
perform all those supersticious rights commonly observed when they are about
to make war uppon a neighboring nation.*[11](31)

Over the next few days, as the party traced the Missouri across North
Dakota toward the present Montana border, grizzlies continued to tease their
imaginations. On 14 April, Clark wrote in his journal that they had seen "*two
white bear running from the report of Capt. Lewis Shot, those animals assended
those Steep hills with Supprising ease & verlocity*" (39). On the 17 April Lewis was
moved to write that although they "*continue to see many tracks of the bear we
have seen but very few of them, and those are at a great distance generally runing*

Woodcut of a scene from the Lewis and Clark expedition in Patrick Gass's published
account, 1807. The grizzly's beatific expression is a dubious detail; it had been shot
multiple times and clubbed over the head.

from us; I therefore presume that they are extreemly wary and shy; the Indian account of them dose not corrispond with our experience so far" (48).

The party's first real encounter came on the morning of 29 April in what is now either Roosevelt or Richland County, Montana. Lewis describes it this way:

> *I walked on shore with one man. about 8 A.M. we fell in with two brown or (yellow) bear; both of which we wounded; one of them made his escape, the other after my firing on him pursued me seventy or eight yards, but fortunately had been so badly wounded that he was unable to pursue so closely as to prevent my charging my gun; we again repeated our fir and killed him. it was a male not fully grown, we estimated his weight at 300 lbs... The legs of this bear are somewhat longer than those of the black, as are it's tallons and tusks incomparably larger and longer.... it's colour is yellowish brown, the eyes small, black, and piercing ... the fur is finger thicker and deeper than that of the black bear. these are all the particulars in which this anamal appeared to me to differ from the black bear; it is a much more furious and formidable anamal, and will frequently pursue the hunter when wounded. it is asstonishing to see the wounds they will bear before they can be put to death. the Indians may well fear this anamal equiped as they generally are with their bows and arrows or indifferent fuzees, but in the hands of skilled riflemen they are by no means as formidable or dangerous as they have been represented.* (84–85)

That optimistic arrogance, coupled with a typical American faith in scientific technology's ability to prevail where the tools of lesser cultures left them vulnerable, wasn't destined to last. On 5 May, in present McCone County, Montana, the American explorers were given considerable pause by their first encounter with a full-grown grizzly. Here is how Lewis put it:

> *Capt. Clark and Drewyer killed the largest brown bear this evening which we have yet seen. it was a most tremendious looking anamal, and extremely hard to kill notwithstanding he had five balls through his lungs and five others in various parts he swan more than half the distance acoss the river to a sandbar & it was at least twenty minutes before he died; he did not attempt to attact, but fled and made the most tremendous roaring from the moment he was shot. We had no means of weighing this monster; Capt. Clark thought he would weigh 500 lbs. ... this bear differs from the common black bear in several respects ... the heart particularly was as large as that of a large Ox. his maw was also ten times the size of the black bear, and was filled with flesh and fish.* (113)

In his account, Clark called this bear "*a Brown or Grisley beare*" and "*the largest of the Carnivorous kind I ever Saw*" (115). Lewis noted after campfire discussion that night that:

> *I find that the curiossity of our party is pretty well satisfyed with rispect to this anamal, the formidable appearance of the male bear killed on the 5th added to the difficulty with which they die when even shot through the vital parts, has staggered the resolution several of them, others however seem keen for action*

with the bear; I expect these gentlemen will give us some amusement shortly as they soon begin now to coppolate. (118)

Five days later, on 11 May, having passed the mouth of the Milk River— which some biologists of pre-Columbian America believe was a kind of epicenter of grizzly bear range and numbers on the Great Plains, perhaps because it had long been a buffer zone between warring groups like the Blackfeet and Shoshones—the party had an experience that cemented the evolution in attitudes that was taking place. Once again, let's let Lewis describe it:

> *About 5 P.M. my attention was struck by one of the Party runing at a distance towards us and making signs and hollowing as if in distress ... he arrived so much out of breath that it was several minutes before he could tell what had happened; at length he informed me that in the woody bottom on the Lard side about 1 1/2 [miles] below us he had shot a brown bear which immediately turned on him and pursued him a considerable distance but he had wounded it so badly that it could not overtake him; I immediately turned out with seven of the party in quest of this monster, we at length found his trale and persued him about a mile by the blood through very thick brush of rosebushes and the large leafed willow; we finally found him concealed in some very thick brush and shot him through the skull with two balls ... it was a monstrous beast... we now found that Bratton had shot him through the center of the lungs, notwithstanding which he had pursued him near half a mile and had returned more than double that distance and with his tallons had prepared himself a bed in the earth ... and was perfectly alive when we found him which could not have been less tha:1 2 hours after he received the wound; these bear being so hard to die reather intimedates us all; I must confess that I do not like the gentlemen and had reather fight two Indians than one bear; there is no other chance to conquer them by a single shot but by shooting them through the brains ...* (141)

This initial American confrontation with the largest predator on the continent continued to worsen, primarily because the members of the party seem not to have learned the rather obvious lesson and kept on shooting grizzlies. On 14 May six hunters spotted a grizzly on open ground and went after him, approaching to within forty yards. According to Lewis:

> *Two of them reserved their fires as had been previously conserted, the four others fired nearly at the same time and put each his bullet through him, two of the balls passed through the bulk of both lobes of his lungs, in an instant this monster ran at them with open mouth ... the men unable to reload their guns took flight, the bear pursued and had very nearly overtaken them before they reached the river... [they] concealed themselves among the willows, reloaded their pieces, each discharged his piece at him as they had an opportunity they struck him several times again but the guns served only to direct the bear to them, in this manner he pursued two of them seperately so close that they were obliged to throw aside their guns and pouches and throw themselves into the*

rivr altho' the bank was nearly twenty feet perpindicular; so enraged was this anamal that he plunged into the river only a few feet behind the second man . . . when one of those who still remained on shore shot him through the head and finally killed him . . . they found eight balls had passed through him in different directions . . . (151)

Absorbing the mounting tension of these journal entries almost two centuries later, you're almost prompted to shout aloud at Meriwether Lewis, "Christ Almighty, order them to stop shooting up grizzly bears!"

Of course no one except the Indians and some of the Hispanics thought to stop shooting up grizzlies for a very long time to come. I think a historian has to pose the question—why, once specimens for science had been collected, did Lewis and Clark and other Anglo-Americans feel such a compulsion to react to Western animals by shooting them? What had history lodged in the American psyche that made the left-and-right, wholesale slaughter of animals—more than 500 million of them is Barry Lopez's estimate, although no one can ever know—such a part of the story of Western history? Why, for example, would Colonel Richard Dodge and four companions feel it a worthy expenditure of their time to slaughter, in three weeks of lounging about on the Cimarron River (according to Dodge's obsessively kept scorecard) 127 buffalo, 13 deer and antelope, 154 turkeys, 420 waterfowl, 187 quail, 129 plovers and snipe, assorted herons, cranes, hawks, owls, badgers, raccoons, even 143 *songbirds*—a total of 1,262 animals, most of which functioned only as convenient live targets?[12] Why did an Indian rock art panel portraying a wagon train that I once hiked to in West Texas show virtually every stick figure traveler brandishing a gun and firing in every direction? Apparently because this is the way Euro-American men, particularly, viewed the West—over the sights of a rifle, a powerful signifier of their ability to affect the world.

This initial Lewis and Clark encounter with the grizzly bear may give us some clues as to why that was. Some of the reasons were, and are, so deeply internalized that virtually the only way we are able to recognize that they aren't universal is to contrast Western attitudes toward animals with those of other cultures. At least since the time of the Greeks, and the notion was broadly disseminated through all classes of Western culture by Judeo-Christian traditions, Western Europeans had absorbed the idea that humans were the true measure of the divine on Earth, the only one of God's creations made in His image, the only ones possessing that abstract animation referred to in Christianity as a *soul*. Animals were created solely for the benefit of humans, according to Genesis I:28, for humans to do with as they would. Over that basic idea, the Scientific Revolution of the Age of Reason had layered Descartes's assumptions that, lacking souls or sentience, animals were little more than automatons, living machines with no capacity for self-awareness, not even the capacity to experience injury. These were fictions that anyone who shot a grizzly and heard it roar its rage and pain ought to have questioned. But few did. So by the Jeffersonian Age, for Americans, individual animals were less teachers of universal truths about being a human animal than they were target practice. Or they could be specimens collected for dispassionate scientific study. Or fiends that represented a danger to civilization and its apparently shaky veneer. Or, indeed, worthy opponents against which to pit one's woodscraft, daring, and skills.

And one's technology. Lewis and Clark are exemplars of yet another Western notion that is evident from reading their journals about grizzly encounters, and that is the Western faith in technology, and the peculiar temptation to test technology's outer limits on what were regarded as challenging and dangerous phenomena like grizzly bears. What is striking upon rereading their accounts is their repeated disbelief that America held an animal so powerful and with so tenacious a will to live that Western scientific technology was incapable of easily conquering it. It's the exact theme that Herman Melville explored in *Moby Dick*, wherein an American puritan is driven mad by his inability to control and subdue nature in the form of another great and dangerous beast.

Lewis and Clark's accounts were not the only ones that filtered in from the West about the grizzly bear, of course. One of the ones that most of the compilations of bear stories routinely miss was one from the Southern Rockies, a story that passed by word-of-mouth back to places like my home state, perhaps even inculcating Ben Lilly with the idea that grizzly bears were the very minions of the devil, and that all of them deserved speedy death at his hands. I am talking about the story of the first recorded death at a grizzly's hands on the southern Great Plains.

It was 1821 when this encounter with a grizzly took place on what was christened "White Bear Crick," now known as the Purgatory River southeast of Pike's Peak. A group of Missouri and Louisiana traders had worked their way up the Arkansas to trade with the Comanches, and when the cold snaps of November hit they moved toward the mountains to seek winter quarters. For many of the semi-illiterate Southern traders involved, this was their first inkling that the West held anything like a grizzly bear. I still find this account, flavorfully preserved and creatively spelled in the journal of a trader named Jacob Fowler, one of the most chilling grizzly encounters I've ever read. This is how Fowler told the story in the daily journal he kept.

> *13th novr 1821 tusday: Went to the Highest of the mounds near our Camp and took the bareing of the Soposed mountain Which Stud at north 80 West all So of the River Which is West We then proceded on 2 1/2 miles to a Small Crick Crosed it and ascended a gradual Rise for about three miles to the Highest ground in the nibourhood—Wheare We Head a full vew of the mountains this must be the place Whare Pike first discovered the mountains Heare I took the*

bareing of two that Ware the highest. . . Crossed [the creek] and Camped in a grove of Bushes and timber about two miles up it from the River We maid Eleven miles West this day—We Stoped Hare about one oclock and Sent back for one Hors that Was not able to keep up—We Heare found some grapes among the brush—While Some Ware Hunting and others Cooking Some Picking grapes a gun Was fyered off and the Cry of a White Bare Was Raised We Ware all armed in an Instent and Each man Run his own Cors to look for the desperet anemel— the Brush in Which we Camped Contained from 10 to 20 acors Into Which the Bare Head Run for Shelter find[ing] Him Self Surrounded on all Sides—threw this Conl glann [Colonel Glenn] With four others atemted to Run But the Bare being In their Way and lay Close in the brush undiscovered till the[y] Ware With in a few feet of it—When it Sprung up and Caught Lewis doson [Dawson] and Pulled Him down In an Instent Conl glanns gun mised fyer or He Wold Have Releved the man But a large Slut [dog] Which belongs to the Party atacted the Bare With such fury that it left the man and persued Her a few steps in Which time the man got up and Run a few steps but Was overtaken by the bare When the Conl maid a second atempt to shoot but His [gun] mised fyer again and the Slut as before Releved the man Who Run as before—but Was Son again in the grasp of the Bare Who Semed Intent on His distruction . . . the Conl now be Came alarmed lest the Bare Wold pusue Him and Run up [a] Stooping tree—and after Him the Wounded man and Was followed by the Bare and thus the[y] Ware all three up one tree . . . [but] the Bare Caught [Dawson] by one leg and drew Him back wards down the tree . . . I Was my Self down the Crick below the brush and Heard the dredfull Screems of [the] man in the Clutches of the Bare—the yelp- ing of the Slut and the Hollowing of the men to Run in Run in the man Will be killed . . . but before I got to the place of action the Bare Was killed and [I] met the Wounded man with Robert Fowler and one or two more asisting Him to Camp Where His Wounds Ware Examined—it appeers His Head was In the Bares mouth at least twice—and that When the monster give the Crush that Was to mash the mans Head it being two large for the Span of His mouth the Head Sliped out only the teeth Cutting the Skin to the bone Where Ever the[y] tuched it—so that the Skin of the Head Was Cut from about the Ears to the top in Several derections—all of Which Wounds Ware Sewed up as Well as Cold be don by men In our Situation Haveing no Surgen nor Surgical Instruments—the man Still Retained His under Standing but Said I am killed that I Heard my Skull Brake—but We Ware Willing to beleve He Was mistaken—as He Spoke Chearfully on the Subgect till In the after noon of the second day When He began to be Restless and Some What delereous—and on examining a Hole in the upper part of His Wright temple Which We beleved only Skin deep We found the Brains Working out—We then Soposed that He did Hear His Scull Brake He lived till a little before day on the third day after being Wounded—all Which time We lay at Camp and Buried Him as Well as our meens Wold admit. Emedetely after the fattal axcident and Haveing done all We Cold for the Wounded man We turned our atention [to] the Bare and found Him a large fatt anemel We Skined Him but found the Smell of a polcat so Strong that We Cold not Eat the meat—on examening His mouth We found that three of His teeth Ware broken off near the guns Which We Sopose Was the Caus of His not killing the man at the first Bite—and the one [tooth] not Broke to be the Caus of the Hole in the Right [temple] Which killed the man at last.[13]

Stories such as this one, circulating through the frontier towns and among the ranks of traders and trappers that became the foundation of many of the West's later settlers, were instrumental in casting all grizzlies as fearsome brutes to be hunted down and shot to death at every opportunity—a "wrathful monster" as the writer Frances Fuller Victor wrote of a Yellowstone grizzly in her book, *The River of the West*, published in 1870.[14]

In their *Tales of the Grizzly: Thirty-Nine Stories of Grizzly Bear Encounters in the Wilderness*, compilers Tim Clark and Denise Casey see in their stories, which chronicle grizzly/human encounters in the Northern Rockies from 1804 through 1929, "a complex, changing relationship between man and nature."[15] They chart what they believe are five distinct periods in this evolution of the human relationship with grizzlies: 1) The Native American period, when bears were mythic figures, teachers of medicines, helpers, a species whose physiological similarity to humans offered the possibility for transmigration in both directions. This precontact Indian relationship with nature, they assert, would have been "almost incomprehensible to most modern Americans";[16] 2) the Exploration/Fur Trade period, exemplified by the grizzly encounters of Lewis and Clark and Jacob Fowler, which expose the Western assumption of human dominance and faith in technology, and created the initial impressions of grizzlies as *Ursus arctos horriblis*—the wilderness fiend that offered Americans a reminder of the dangers of uncontrolled, chaotic nature.

The third and fourth periods in this chronology are the periods of conquest and settlement, when it had become a Christian duty to exorcise grizzlies and other formidable wildlife in order to liberate the wilderness for God and the Grand Old Party. During this phase, tens of thousands of grizzly bears were shot on sight; 423 are documented as having been killed in the North Cascades alone in just five years, 1846–51.[17] After 1890 the Great American War on grizzly bears featured an alliance between livestock interests and Animal Damage Control of the U.S. Biological Survey, whose employees made official the war on predators, in the process creating (as environmentalists have loved to point out) a form of early federal subsidy for the Western ranching industry.

Matt Cartmill, in his recent intellectual history of hunting, *A View to Death in the Morning*, has unearthed an unusual Thoreau quotation: "He is blessed who is assured that the animal is dying out in him day by day."[18] One wonders what was being banished, and what embraced, by the rapturous pursuit of bears as their numbers dwindled. At the turn of the century, many sport hunters took to heart President Theodore Roosevelt's advice that "The most thrilling moments of an American's hunter's life are those in which, with every sense on the alert and with nerves strung to the highest point, he is following alone . . . the fresh and bloody footprints of an angered grisly." For hunters, eliminating "bad animals" like predators made sense not just in terms of growing the numbers of huntable elk and deer; going after Western grizzlies also had become the ultimate nostalgic capture of the vanishing frontier, the hunter's version of a Frederic Remington or Charlie Russell painting. As Roosevelt put it, tellingly, "No other triumph of American hunting can compare with the victory to be thus gained."[19]

I find merit in the straightforward chronology of *Tales of the Grizzly*, but I'd like to extend the interpretation in at least two ways that seem to me to be historically significant, by pursuing the evolution of ideas about bears in both directions from the early twentieth century.

First, as grizzly numbers dropped drastically in the late nineteenth and early twentieth centuries, an interesting phenomenon emerged in the way many grizzlies and wolves were perceived. More and more single animals of both species were individualized, indeed, personified with their own personalities and names. Among grizzlies there was the Wyoming bear known as Big Foot Wallace, the notorious California grizzly, Club-Foot, the Colorado grizzly named Old Mose, Idaho's Old Ephraim, and the Greybull River bear Wyoming ranchers named Wab, whose life story, in much fictionalized form, was told in Ernest Thompson Seton's 1927 book, *The Biography of a Grizzly*.

This individualization of grizzlies was an interesting development. It rested on a sentiment, clearly widespread in America at the turn of the century, that had its sources in Darwinian thought as popularized by the natural history writers of the day. According to Lisa Mighetto's *Wild Animals and American Environmental Ethics*, writers like Seton, Jack London, William Burroughs, Enos Mills, and John Muir were struggling to erase the Tennyson imagery of a Darwinian world as "nature, red in tooth and claw."[20] They used literary devices such as the personification of animals, an emphasis on animal individuality, cooperation, intelligence and reasoning, and the strategy of telling their stories from the point of view of the animals (as in London's *Call of the Wild* or James Oliver Curwood's *The Grizzly King*) to effect a more favorable treatment of animals. Humanitarian animal reformers at the turn of the century even discussed the hitherto unimagined possibility that animals had souls; one eccentric Eastern faction went so far as to found a church to save the souls of the beasts around them. As H. W. Boynton, a book reviewer following these trends summarized, the message for a world distressed by the implications of Darwinism seemed to be: "If we are only a little higher than the dog, we may as well make the dog out to be as fine a fellow as possible."[21]

Despite the sympathetic view of grizzlies presented in Seton's *The Biography of a Grizzly* (which climaxes with Wahb's[22] suicide as his West fills with settlers and tourists) and Curwood's *The Grizzly King* (wherein the wounded but peace-loving grizzly lets his hunter/antagonist walk away unharmed in the end), at least three more decades of rehabilitation by biologists would be required to rescue predators from a general hatred in America. The real Wab, for example, met a rather different end than Seton prepared for him. He was shot by a rancher, the fourth grizzly the hunter had killed that day.

Indeed, in the minds of most scientists and wildlife managers, the individualizing of animals has been forever tarnished by the "nature-faker" controversies of the period. While individual grizzlies were steadily extirpated across the West—the last grizzly in Texas was killed in 1890, the last one in California in 1922, Utah's last one in 1923, Oregon and New Mexico's last grizzlies in 1931, Arizona's last one in 1935—professional wildlife management moved under the influence of the Murie brothers, Aldo Leopold, and Eugene Odum in the direction of ever more macro perspectives. Following their leads, the exclusively anthropomorphic ideas inherent in the Western worldview gave way in biology to more holism, a stance far more biocentric and ecosystem oriented than before. This new biological holism, however, has halted at rights for *individual* animals; its realm has been the health of species as a whole, and more recently the health of ecosystems. The idea of the Greater Yellowstone Ecosystem emerged as a concept first applied by the famous biologist brothers, John and Frank Craighead, to manage Yellowstone grizzlies as a species and as components of a larger habitat.[23]

According to Lisa Mighetto, the last great American environmental thinker who was willing to try for a blend that respected both species *and* individual animals was John Muir. Since Muir, the idea of animal individuality—although it is genetically logical, readily observable in animals in virtually any context, and in fact enjoys practical application today in the treatment of "problem" bears and wolves—has been a target of special ire by ecologists and biologists. This seems to be so for two reasons. First, individuality still carries with it the unsavory historical association of nature-faking (as in the sarcastic reference to one of Seton's books as "Wild Animals I *Alone* Have Known"). These stories are an essential part of Biology 101; by graduate school all biologists of worth are required to swear eternal enmity to such sentimentality. Second, and if anything, even more disturbing to biologists, animal individuality plays into the arguments of the modern descendants of the nineteenth-century humanitarians. Contemporary animal advocates assert an apparently radical doctrine: that individual animals have rights, and that the circle of ethical treatment, which in the Western tradition has expanded through history to confer rights to individuals of groups once denied legal standing, such as women, blacks, and Native Americans, ought to and must be extended to animals on an individual basis.[24]

Earlier in this chapter I mentioned a path not taken, and in closing I'd like to return to that theme. If advocates of the natural West are serious about preserving not just the one thousand grizzlies now left to us, but biodiversity of all kinds, then there may be some merit in reconsidering the concept of animal individuality and even analyzing how individual animal rights might be conferred. I cannot say that traditional history stands behind this assertion, because traditional Western American history, in particular, has consistently been written as if animals were nothing more than lumpen species, resources, or convenient live targets that inevitably had to give way to progress. A history that judges as individuals those "monster bears" that Meriwether Lewis and Jacob Fowler described, bears whose home territories and berry patches had been invaded, who deserved better than being shot on sight, might go farther toward awakening a biophilic conscience than the big abstractions that remove us farther from the immediacy of life and death. By big abstractions I mean conservation biology and ecosystems management.

I don't want to give the wrong impression. I fully recognize the logical and practical problems inherent in going from *writing* history this way to conferring actual legal standing and *managing* this way. In fact, in practical application both the wolf and grizzly restoration projects of the Endangered Species Act do treat some wolves and grizzlies—specifically the "problem" ones—as individuals. But in reality these animals are controlled (usually shot) for the political good of the restoration projects, which is interpreted as the best course for the species.[25] That is not quite what animal rights activists have in mind when *they* speak of individual animal rights.

Nor is it how animal individuality worked in Indian cultures.[26] Reading about Native American mythologies, imagery, and rituals associated with bears in a book like David Rockwell's 1991 *Giving Voice to Bear*, you have to be struck by the possibilities that such thinking offers. It could be that the reason there were still a hundred thousand grizzlies even after eleven thousand years of Indian inhabitation of America was because, as Meriwether Lewis asserted, Indian technology was not up to the task of getting rid of them—although you have to note in this regard that mammoths were pretty formidable critters, too, yet Clovis technology managed to wipe them out.

All the same, without trying to appropriate anyone's culture or romanticize anyone's past, it is difficult not to conclude that a way of thinking that recognized bears as essentially humans in another form, thus conferred individuality to bears, and thus a corpus of rights to bears—among them the simple right to exist—must have played some role in the historical fact that millions of people and hundreds of thousands of bears were able to live together in America for so long.[27] Was it a wilder and more dangerous continent then? Yes. Absolutely it was. It was a heaven with all the stars intact.

I am intrigued that Indian grizzly stories do not whitewash bears. The bear

George Catlin captured the likeness of this Blackfeet grizzly-bear shaman in 1832.
Courtesy National Museum of American Art, Smithsonian Institution.

personalities in stories from the Blackfeet to the Nez Perce to the Kiowas are complex ones, which is exactly what grizzly bears are in nature. Almost always the bears possess traits valuable to humans; in culture after culture, grizzlies are almost universally regarded as teachers of medicines and herb knowledge, as in the Blackfeet's "Friendly Medicine Grizzly." At other times, though, as in the Gros Ventres story of how the Big Dipper came to be, grizzlies are "monsters" that lay rapacious waste to human communities and chase people into the sky.[28] But consistently, as in the lusty Athabaskan story of "The Girl Who Married the Bear," for instance, or the male anxiety tale from the Nez Perce called "The Bear Woman with a Snapping Vagina," these are stories premised on a real-life biophilia in practice. The bears are both good *and* evil, are valued and respected in either case on an individual basis, but their inherent right to exist is never an issue. In the stories of Western Indians about bears, both bears and humans are, in essence, mirrors of each other. Indeed, one constant theme is that humans and bears play interchangeable roles.[29]

The historical arc of the great bear's story over the five centuries since we Euro-Americans have been here, on the other hand, is far less nuanced and has a crystal-clear direction. The way Euro-Americans thought about bears was catastrophic to the grizzly's survival: the great bear has undergone a hundredfold reduction in numbers and range. Yet in truth there is little that is inevitable about history, environmental or otherwise. Because that is a truism, we ought not to be content that a perspective on bears like the one in thousands of years of Indian stories is either "incomprehensible" or too alien to embrace. Biologists may well argue that the bears in these Indian stories are anthropomorphs. Anthropologists may insist that we Others cannot meaningfully grasp another culture's worldview, any more than Indians could really fathom what was important to a grizzly. Modern nature writers like Bill McKibben will no doubt continue to insist that we humans have so separated ourselves out of the natural world, and then "humanized" the wild, that nature itself is dead and there is no longer a path home. And historians may continue writing history involving animals without questioning the assumptions of human dominance.

All that may happen, and perhaps will. But having grown up near a River of Bears in Louisiana where bears no longer roam, I have personally experienced the consequences of a culture and a place that were insufficiently flexible in protecting nature.[30] That way is not the way. It is precisely the reason I now live in Montana, where a couple of months before writing this, in the early fall of 1998, a huge, half-ton boar grizzly killed a cow on the Blackfeet Reservation and halted travel on a major highway for half a day by charging cars as they passed by his kill. That is an "entire heaven and an entire earth," and it makes me think the stakes are high. So if the sociobiologists and evolutionary psychologists—and the Indians—are right about us and our animal natures, then hanging on to the great bear may be nothing less than an act of self-preservation.[31]

Humans and bears, each with rights. Western science and the Indian view that animals are individuals, just like us, joined together. That ought to up the ante of philosophy, as well as the unfolding history of the natural West, considerably.

CHAPTER 5

Place

Thinking about Bioregional History

Every continent has its own great spirit of place. Every people is polarized in some particular locality, which is home, the homeland. Different places on the earth have different
vital effluence, different vibration, different chemical exhalation, different polarity with
different stars: call it what you like. But the spirit of place is a great reality.

D. H. Lawrence, "Spirit of Place"

As he told the story, Walter Prescott Webb—widely accepted among American environmental historians as one of the founding fathers of this new
discipline—began to conceptualize his most famous work, *The Great
Plains: A Study in Institutions and Environment,* at the age of five. Raised as a
young child in Panola County, Texas, deep in the heart of Southern culture,
where thickly timbered rolling hills screened the horizon and even the over-
head sky was only partially visible through the soaring loblolly pines, Webb had
not yet started school when his family moved to Central Texas. In the Western
Cross Timbers province at the edge of the Great Plains, the future thinker of big
ideas found himself stimulated by another world. Here no loblolly pines
blocked the skies, and across the grasslands the horizon was miles distant, visible like the encircling rim of a bowl in every direction. Here King Cotton and
backwoods truck-garden farms gave way to fenced spreads enclosing the
Sacred Cow. Young Walter Webb was fascinated at the differences in those two
worlds, remained fascinated as an adult, and with his books and articles went
on to stimulate reading Americans into pondering the peculiar dialogue
between the Western environmental setting and human technological adaptations to it.[1]

Like Frederick Jackson Turner (whom he claimed not to have read prior to
writing *The Great Plains*) and his frontier thesis, Webb and his approach to

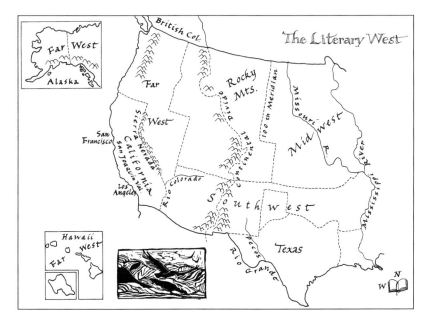

Place and region as expressed in art: the most recent conception of the Literary West. Map by Barbara Whitehead, 1997, from Western Literature Association, *Updating the Literary West. Courtesy Texas Christian University Press.*

history have taken their hits over the years. Fred Shannon's two-hundred-page savaging of Webb's book in 1940 was the first of those critiques, made all the more famous by Webb's laconic refusal to acknowledge Shannon's points; his response to Shannon's critique was that he had conceived and written *The Great Plains* not as history, but as art.[2] In our own time, even his sympathizers acknowledge that Webb's basic ideas were a rank exercise in environmental determinism, an approach that geographers and anthropologists had long since abandoned. Somewhat in the manner of an intellectual Ulysses S. Grant, it has been asserted, Webb was moved to write big idea books like *The Great Plains* and later *The Great Frontier* (1950) essentially because he lacked the education to know better.[3]

I disagree. I think Webb was so moved because as a child he paid attention to what his senses told him about the difference between the piney woods and the Western Cross Timbers in Texas. Just as Frederick Jackson Turner's essentially Darwinian idea that new environmental settings ("frontiers") transformed those peoples who experienced them into new peoples (Americans in Turner's thinking), Webb's intellectual vision also continues to influence environmental historians, especially environmental historians of the American West.[4] Donald Worster, for example, has pointed out that Webb's insistence that aridity is a defining characteristic of the American West has taught us correctly that "the

West" was not a process, but was and is a *region* whose perimeter can be sensed on the ground and marked out on a map.[5] Beyond that, Webb's approach remains valuable in environmental history because of the attention he forces us to pay to the confluence between specific ecological realities and specific human adaptations (in the relatively simple terms of *The Great Plains*, such as the use of windmills and barbed wire in semiarid, open grasslands) that are a part of the evolution of cultures in place.

Having struggled with terms like "region" and "place" in writing a pair of books about West Texas/New Mexico and the larger American Southwest, I think I would argue that the intuitive foundation that Webb built—albeit in a refined form—ought to remain central to the way we think about ourselves in the context of history.[6] In fact, it seems to me that the particularism of distinctive *places* fashioned by our peculiar interpenetration with all the vagaries of topography, climate, and evolving ecology that make up landscapes—and the continuing existence of such *places* despite the homogenizing forces of the modern world— ought to cause us to realize that one of the insightful ways for us to think about the human past is in the form of what might be called *bioregional* histories.[7] Although at first glance looking at cities that way might seem counterintuitive, even urban areas sprang into existence, and most often continue to depend, on environmental circumstances that lie just below the level of our awareness. From the time humans located regularly visited hunting camps and early river-valley farming settlements, human places have been superimposed on environmental settings. They still are.

"Place" is a term that attracted much attention as the twentieth century closed, particularly in literature and postmodern geography, in a way not seen in America since the 1930s, when artistic regionalism with its active encouragement of regionalist literature and art, actively promoted place-based thinking.[8] But during the half century after the New Deal's WPA programs helped fuel this kind of thinking, "place" and regionalism in America were supposed to have been washed away by capitalist integration and by the cloudburst of television/modern communication. The literary scholar Bill Bevis, for example, has argued that "Capitalist modernity seeks to create a kind of no-place center to which all 'places' . . . are marginal." Similarly, in his "Sense of Place" chapter (the title borrowed from a famous essay by Wallace Stegner) in the provocative book *Dust Bowl: The Southern Plains in the 1930s*, historian Donald Worster has described in graphic terms how Haskell, Kansas's, sense of place was subverted by American capitalism and more national sentiments.[9]

In the 1970s, however, America began a process of rediscovering that we are all place based. One researcher concluded that we inhabitants of this single nation of fifty states in fact regard ourselves as going about our day-to-day lives in 295 different local regions.[10] But while American places in fact seemed to have survived the onslaught of modern life, writing about—or even thinking systematically about—place in America is not as easy as it once was. In part this is because as a people (the New Deal period excepted), we have not usually been encouraged to set place high in our hierarchy of values. Too, late twentieth-century postmodernism, including geography among its other converts, has clouded place study with its argument that place actually exists only in the human imagination, that landscapes should be seen less as "real" ecological and historical entities than as "texts" that human cultures have fashioned out of the flux of the world.[11]

And there is this peculiarly American difficulty about place: according to census data from the 1990s, we are still one of the most transient peoples in the world. With the U.S. population now cresting 280 million, a whopping 40 million of us still relocate every year. Between 1993 and 1994 nearly 43 million Americans, median age 26.8, changed residence. The average residence in place for all Americans is only ten years. Demographers have also charted an ethnicity of relocation: Hispanics are the most mobile, with 22.6 percent of their population moving in 1993, while 19.6 percent of the black population and 16.0 percent of whites without Spanish surnames moved. America's long-standing transience does seem to be slowing in recent years. By 1995, when 16.3 percent of the population relocated, Americans were moving at the lowest rate since 1948. Indeed, the rate has dropped steadily since the 1980s. Among regions, residents of the Northeast are least likely to move (12 percent). Westerners, however, remain the most transient citizens in the United States—21 percent of Westerners were still relocating annually by 1996.[12]

The American West is by no means the only region where the insights of bioregionalism seem to be valuable to environmental history, but because it is my region of study (and because its transience seems closely linked to its history), the West of the Great Plains and Rocky Mountains is my focus here. While according postmodernism its due for showing us very well the roles that culture, imagination, and words have played in creating the world, I am convinced that there are tangible ecologies of place out there, and that one of environmental history's tasks is to fold the stories of those ecologies into human history.[13] The word "plains" may carry cultural freight, but it still denotes a different ecology, and a tangible and real one, from "mountains." And we remain biological even with all our bewildering array of cultural dressings.

Despite a too-easy perception by many that the interior American West is a generic land of a few creased-faced horse whisperers squinting at far horizons, one initial insight is that here at the beginning of the twenty-first century, the Great Plains and Rockies are not one thing (or even two) but a great diversity of place republics. I'm reminded of a conversation historian Patricia Limerick recounts in one of her essays in *Trails: Toward a New Western History*, when after one of her public lectures she was approached by a man who said something like, "I enjoyed your speech, but since I'm not a Western historian, everything you said was obvious to me."[14]

He's not alone. At the University of Montana where I teach, the graduate students in history and environmental studies tend to be young, bright nonresidents seeking exposure to the mountain West. Many of them take advantage of their location to travel widely, from Montana south to Texas, and sometimes northward through Canada to Alaska. I suspect this is why they are as puzzled as Patricia Limerick's acquaintance when they read historical essays positing various reasons why the American West as a whole comprises a distinctive, singular region much as the American South appears to do. Their questions often follow these lines:

"So, if aridity is the defining characteristic of the West, then Alaska doesn't belong, and the Pacific Northwest doesn't either? And you mean that those high, wet lifezones disqualify the Rocky Mountains?"

"Kind of ironic, isn't it, that Texas has produced some of the most potent Western symbols, but isn't really a part of the West because it lacks the defining system of federal land ownership?"

"To me, Colorado seems so different from Utah. But you're telling us that they were shaped into a consistent form by the same forces of global economic integration that forged the rest of the West?"

Uncorrupted by an impulse toward the broadly inclusive and generalized definitions of regionalism that professionals have been trained to apply, these students see the obvious. I have noticed with interest the testimonies of Westerners recorded in the anthology *A Society to Match the Scenery* assembled at the Center of the American West at the University of Colorado in 1991 as an exercise in envisioning the future of the West. Among the voices appearing in that anthology were Dan Kemmis and Camille Guerin-Gonzalez, both residents of the Rocky Mountains (Missoula, Montana, and Santa Fe, New Mexico), both inhabitants of similar topographies where federal land ownership and management are everyday facts of life, where resource extraction and tourism prevail economically, where water problems and an influx of wealthy newcomers dominate local discussion. Yet after listening to Kemmis's remarks about life in the Northern Rockies, Guerin-Gonzalez claimed that the northern New Mexico she knows bears no relationship whatsoever to what Kemmis described.[15]

The answer to the puzzlement and to the denial of uniformity expressed above is that no set of generalized definitions, regardless of how inclusive, accurately explains the loose cluster of subregions comprising the huge swath of continental topography and ecology that is the western United States. Neither aridity and its effects, nor federal land ownership, nor economic integration into the

Missoula, Montana, in the Northern Rockies, 2000. *Photo by author.*

global market at a time of mature industrial development, nor the presence of Indian reservations, nor proximity to Mexico or to the Pacific Ocean, nor a legacy of conquest, captures the particularism that is the historical reality of *place* in the western United States.[16] I doubt that broadly generalized interpretations work very well to capture historical sense of place elsewhere, either. But as it has done for a century now, the country west of the Mississippi River continues to work well as a kind of national laboratory for testing ideas in culture and ecology.

Let me here define and explain my promotion of bioregional thinking by positing three lines of investigation. First, if we grant that specific human cultures and specific landscapes can and do intertwine to create distinctive places, then to understand place, why not just turn to local county histories of the type that amateur history has generated in Wal-Mart quantities and that already fills so much space in local libraries? If thousands of such local histories already exist—admittedly, often done uncritically as a kind of pioneer family-ancestor worship—what, in fact, would constitute the rationale and the basis for "bioregional history"? Second, if the theories promulgated half a century ago by Walter Prescott Webb and others of his generation are passé or too obscure and eccentric (in James Malin's case) to serve as models to think about history and place, what kinds of approaches and ideas ought we to use to look for environmental histories of human places? And finally, how much work is already out there that demonstrates the value of bioregional histories of place in the western United States?

On one semantic score, a defense of sorts may be necessary. There are traditionalists for whom use of the terms "bioregion," "bioregional," and "bio-regionalism" may perhaps appear as either an unnecessary resort to jargon or as a surrender to fad. On the contrary, for all its association in the United States with countercultural environmentalism, "bioregion" should in fact be recognized as a precise and highly useful term of art in environmental history. The word appears to have had its genesis in the early 1970s with the writings of the Canadian Allen Van Newkirk and since then has been most closely associated with the California counterculture and back-to-the-land prophets like Peter Berg, Raymond Dasmann, Gary Snyder, and Stephanie Mills.[17] In the publications and the journals of these visionaries—*CoEvolution Quarterly* and *Raise the Stakes*—bioregions act as the essential natural human settings for bioregionalism, which has come to stand for what Berg calls "a kind of spiritual identification with a particular kind of country and its wild nature [that is] the basis for the kind of land care the world so definitely needs."[18] Geographer James Parsons, calling the bioregional movement to the attention of the world in 1985, noted that it "has attracted a remarkably sensitive, literate group of adherents" who, while they might seem like "misty-eyed visionaries caught up in a New Age semantics, . . . may be the unwitting architects of a new popular geography, a grass roots geography with 'heart.'"[19]

Bioregionalism as a modern social movement is an interesting phenomenon in its own right. But it is not merely bioregionalism's focus on ecology and geography, but its emphasis on the close linkage between ecological locale and human culture, its implication that in a variety of ways humans not only alter environments but also adapt to them, that ties it to some central issues of Western

Santa Fe, New Mexico, in the Southern Rockies, 1998. *Photo by author.*

history. While the history of politics and diplomacy and (sometimes) ideas may be extracted from the environmental setting and studied profitably, the kinds of subjects that make up modern history—legal, social, gender, ethnic, science, technology, and environmental issues—cannot be taken on without sophisticated reference to places or what people think about places. But there is an irony here. Professional history, especially in the United States, has long regarded an interest in place as limiting, provincial, even antiquarian. Unless the topic is New England or California, local, state, and regional history is often thought of as provincial.

There are some very good environmental histories of place out there that have already made strides in eroding this sniffing condescension, for in truth, to an extent, all history is the history of *some* place. But environmental history has gone beyond traditional history and justified its reputation for new insight by following the lead of ecologists, geographers, ecological anthropologists—and bioregionalists—in drawing the boundaries of some of the places we have studied in ways that make real sense ecologically and topographically. That is something new in the way we've thought about our history.

It ought to be agreed that with rare exceptions, the politically derived boundaries of county, state, and national borders are mostly useless in understanding nature. Naturally, history continues to rely heavily on the documentary trail generated by political life, but there are significant limitations inherent in that dependency. The founders of environmental history like Webb and Malin realized this and pointed the way toward a more ecologically oriented kind of study more than half a century ago.[20] Clearly, the first step in recognizing the value of environmental histories of place is a recognition that natural geographic systems—ecoregions, biotic provinces, physiographic provinces, biomes, ecosystems, in short, larger and smaller representations of what we probably ought to call "bioregions"—are the appropriate settings for insightful local history.

Without county/province/state/national borders to provide clues for delimiting place history, to what sources should we turn for ideas if we want to understand the natural ecologies we inhabit? For the American West, one of the best is the earliest. In 1890, John Wesley Powell laid before a Congressional committee a remarkable and beautifully colored map of the arid West mapping out 24 major natural provinces, and further subdividing the region into some 140 candidates for "commonwealth" status based on drainage and topographical cohesion.[21] Powell's ideas for the West of 1890 conform startlingly with many twentieth-century delineations, such as those in Wallace Atwood's *The Physiographic Provinces of North America*. The modern movement among federal resource bureaus in the West for ecosystems management could be said to stand on Powell's shoulders.[22]

More ecologically precise and recent than Powell, however, is Robert Bailey's *Ecoregions of the United States* (first published in 1976 and newly revised in 1994–95) and its accompanying map. Assembled by the U.S. Department of

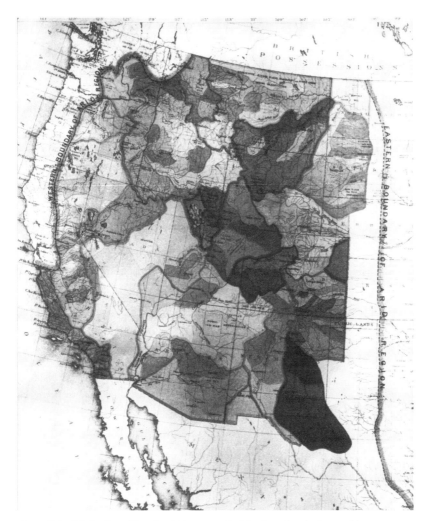

One of John Wesley Powell's early 1890s maps of a West based on hydrographic common-wealths. John Wesley Powell, "Arid Region of the United States, Showing Drainage Districts." U.S. Geological Survey, Eleventh Annual Report, 1889–90. Irrigation Survey, pt. 2.

Agriculture from a broad range of soil, climate, floral, faunal, and topographic sources, but based primarily on plant study, this work creates a taxonomy of North American nature ranging from the macro (four "domains" further differentiated into twenty-five "divisions") to the micro (the divisions are further refined into fifty-two "provinces"). Bailey's provinces range considerably in size. His Southeastern Mixed Forest Province, for example, extends across parts of ten states; his Great Plains-Palouse Dry Steppe Province covers all of the northern and central Great Plains. On the other hand, the superficially similar Rocky Mountain region is conceptualized in Bailey's mapping as comprising seven ecologically unique provinces. His system does not specifically locate and bound ecosystem corridors such as major rivers and their drainages, which have demonstrably played key roles in human history. But in his taxonomy, an area that modern Westerners might be tempted view in the round, like the Intermountain Great Basin, is subdivided into no fewer than five distinct provinces.[23]

Typically, experts closer to the local ground tend to subdivide to the even more specific. Today, in my adopted states of Montana and New Mexico, for example, bioregional particularism is rife. In Rocky Mountain Montana, Bailey's three provinces are carved by state ecologists into four categories: the Columbian Rockies, the Broad Valley Rockies, the Yellowstone Rockies, and the Rocky Mountain Foreland. More recently, ecosystems ecologists in Montana and Wyoming have recognized the dynamism of bioregions, as well as the role played by cultural developments, with their designation of two modern natural systems they call the Greater Yellowstone Ecosystem and the Northern Continental Divide Ecosystem. As for New Mexico, the majority of ecologists see the state as an extraordinarily artificial creation that cobbles together no fewer than *six* individual bioregions, from creosote desert to alpine tundra, across its wild run of elevation and topography.[24] Beyond providing us with a new axle upon which to spin our ideas about where we live, bioregional study at least partially explains why a place like Texas, say (with ten to eighteen bioregions) cannot decide whether it is properly Southern, Western, Southwestern, or just Texan.

The particularism of human places that is often so observable to travelers is explained by the geographer Yi-Fu Tuan's equation: space plus culture equals place.[25] So beyond ecological concerns, the second basis for thinking about bioregional history, of course, is the existence of a diversity of human cultures across both time and space. Since I began this essay by invoking Webb, it is worth mentioning as a foundation for understanding the dialogue between nature and culture that Webb was properly criticized in his day for his resort to environmental determinism in writing *The Great Plains*. As he saw it and wrote it, certain characteristics of nature on the Great Plains presented so many challenges to American settlement culture as it had evolved in the Eastern woodlands that the Great Plains served up an "institutional fault line" that significantly modified the settlement strategies (by which Webb meant primarily technological and economic culture) of the peoples who settled there. In something of a major misreading of history, Webb believed that Hispanic New Mexicans and Tejanos had failed to adapt to the plains to the same extent that horse Indians and Anglo-Texans did and that this adaptive failure explained why more technologically innovative Anglo-Americans seized the region.[26]

James Malin, among other historians, corrected Webb's naive assumptions about environmental determinism with his application of an interpretive framework known as "possibilism."[27] Although Malin still accepted a dichotomy between the world of nature and the world of humans and had an inordinate faith in technological fixes, with possibilism he gave human cultures a sturdier freight and responsibility in creating places. The possibilist idea is now well understood to imply that a given bioregion and its resources offer a range of possibilities, from which a given human culture makes economic and lifeway choices based upon the culture's technological ability plus its ideological vision (what postmodernists would call the "discourse") of how the landscape is seen and ought to be shaped and used to meet that society's definition of a good life. While the possibilism idea is scarcely new, and in the social sciences has long been retired from the cutting edge of interpretation, I suspect that the idea has a continuing relevance for thinking about environmental history, where we're much interested in the wake of events that follows from ideology and from the choices we make through time.[28]

As a theory for how we live in and use nature, possibilism was a reaction to environmental determinism. It continued the nature/culture dichotomy and carried with it the danger of playing to our modern conceit that ever since the scientific and industrial revolutions, human culture had triumphed over nature and the natural world hardly mattered anymore except as potential commodities. Too, possibilism can give the impression—and this is a frequent failing of the bioregional movement's own philosophy—that historical decisions about place are formed exclusively by local populations. Most of us know by now that this isn't how our world works.

Since the early 1970s we've had a set of mechanisms—that sprang particularly from ecologist Eugene Odum's influential studies of ecosystems—known collectively as "systems theory" to explain the diverse web of connections that tie local places to larger economic and ideological systems.[29] Since Odum's insights, one sort of footbridge has been constructed to span the apparent chasm between nature and culture, for not only biological processes but cultural ones appear to operate as functional, and evolving, systems.[30] Some of the best recent place-based environmental histories—Donald Worster's *Dust Bowl* (1979), Richard White's *Roots of Dependency* (1983), William Cronon's *Nature's Metropolis* (1991)—have made the concept of systems central to their work, primarily (following the lead of anthropologists like Marvin Harris) by tracing the role of the global market in a materialist age. So Worster blames the Dust Bowl not on farmers but on the "system" of capitalism in a fragile place, White shows how the global market system ensnared Indians so that eventually their ecologies broke down, and Cronon shows how an urban area like Chicago created a system that exploited everything from soil to buffalo hundreds of miles distant.

One remaining kind of cultural study that is relevant to bioregional thinking is a recent refinement of cultural adaptation theory that Walter Webb brought to his work more than half a century ago. Inspired by the Odum-derived thought that human systems might, after all, be living organisms, in the late 1970s social scientists Karl Butzer and Roy Rappaport applied the precepts of organic evolution to cultural adaptation and tried to sort out its mechanisms in various simulations of real life, as in the feedback loops of a land management bureaucracy dealing with an environmental crisis, for example. While Butzer wondered whether entire human societies might not *be* organisms,[31] Rappaport went on to assert that, ultimately, adaptation's function is the same whether it occurs in organisms or societies. That function is to aid survival. "Since survival is nothing if not biological," he wrote, "evolutionary changes perpetuating economic or political institutions at the expense of the biological well-being of man, societies and ecosystems may be considered maladaptive."[32] In Rappaport's view, then, adaptation is critical to understanding the long-term successes (or the short-term failures) of human cultures in specific places. In other words, a "positive adaptation" for the town or region where you live would aid its long-term survivability. And good adaptive choices likely vary widely from one bioregion to another.

For residents of particular places, thinking about how local bioregional history has unfolded should commence with the recognition that our historical places exist on a base of nature. Given the natural human preference for ecotone edges, interesting settings for human history won't always be bounded in the way Bailey maps out his ecoregions. Pre-Columbian Indian cultures in North America hewed fairly closely to the larger bioregional divisions we now recognize, and individual bands often conformed in their home ranges roughly to slices of topography that Bailey has identified in his provinces. On the other hand, Western cultural groups like the New Mexican Hispanics and the Mormons occupied and adapted to several kinds of bioregions in the American West. Any number of intriguing histories have resulted in the West from the experiences of distinctive groups—I think of Hutterites or Mennonites on the Great Plains—existing side by side with peoples of different traditions in a bioregion with its own historical arc.[33]

In a recent essay, Western historian Hal Rothman expressed concern that histories of place, even environmental histories, might succumb to provincial bias if they are written about places to which the authors have an emotional tie. That *could* be a danger for someone whose connections are to local culture, who might take offense at environmental history's tendency to set biodiversity, say, on an equal basis with human economic success. In the books that exist so far, though, I think that you'd have to look very hard, say, to find much native Kansan sympathy (although his family springs from a Kansas background) in Worster's *Dust Bowl*; Worster's bias in *Dust Bowl* is an environmentalist one, an identification with what he presents as a healthier Great Plains during Native American tenure. My own experience in writing bioregional books is similar: an emotional tie to the natural world has made me critical of some of modern society's choices in the Southwest even when my own ancestors were involved. On the other hand, the best writing and most informed research spring from passion. Places can summon that.[34]

Anyone looking for a sophisticated modern environmental history of place is probably going to have to make peace with a current view of a natural world that is dynamic. Far from serving as some pristine baseline of climax harmony, our bioregions as presented by the new ecology have to be accepted as endlessly evolving through time. Ecologists now speak of "internal change," "blurred secessional patchworks," and "moving mosaics." Disturbance is the natural state, and adjustment to it is ongoing and fundamental. There has been some resistance to this among historians who have hoped, in the environmentalist tradition, that there *is* a harmonious, stable nature out there against which we might view human activity as arrayed in a destructive assault.[35] But while ecologist Daniel Botkin's view, that "Nature undisturbed [by human activity] is not constant in form, structure, or proportion, but changes at every scale of time and space," might be problematic for environment romantics, I don't see it so for history.[36] In fact, recognizing that the ground of the natural world is shifting and always has can be another bridge tying the activity of human culture back into nature.

If they make any claim to apprehending reality, our bioregional stories should capture that changeability. Indeed, in modern techniques like repeat photography, fine-resolution remotely sensed data, and the manipulation of spatial information with computers (historic maps I have seen recently showing vegetation and fire patterns in the Northern Rockies come to mind), we now have the ability to track these kinds of changes at a denser grain than ever before. Personally, I do not see how acknowledging the fact of ongoing, natural disturbance in nature prevents us from critiquing human disturbances or choices that foolishly endanger us or are reprehensible with respect to the diversity of life.

Perhaps one thing that distinguishes bioregional history from traditional histories, even of places, is a precise spatial application of famed historian Fernand Braudel's longue durée. For proper perspective, the bioregional story ought to aim for the "big view," not through wide geographic generalizations in shallow time, but through analyzing deep time in a single place. As I attempted to show in chapter 3, an accurate understanding of shallow time often isn't possible without the context of the longue durée.[37] To think about the story of human history in the Southern or Middle Rocky Mountain Steppe Province or the Great Plains Steppe Province, you should properly commence with geology and landform, then take up climate history using an array of modern approaches from ice cores and pollen analysis to packrat middens and dendrochronology. Climate has always been and remains one of the most visible forces interacting with human history. The climate record of place can then position us to understand the ebb and flow of floral and faunal species across space and time the way our eyes enable us to track cumulus clouds drifting across an open basin by the shadows they cast on the ground.

Although there are past cultures, no question, that saw and utilized nature differently than we do, history is coming to the view that human stress on nature is very ancient. Superficially, bioregional history might seem to confirm our suspicions that the ancient ways were morally superior; closer examinations, however, usually turn out to be more sobering. Too, at every level of time (including our own), we need finally to become comfortable with the idea that there is no distinction between "nature" and "civilization," no bright line separating "us" and "them."[38] The preliminary studies in biophilia and biophobia research, for example, indicate in rather striking ways that genetically, it is ludicrous to think that humans ever stepped outside nature. Evolutionary psychology and sociobiology remind us how rooted our social behavior is in the primate world. As I explained in chapter 1, studies of inherited biophobic responses (to snakes and spiders, for example) as well as genetically transmitted biophilic preferences (to savannas, parklands, certain tree shapes, and terrain scales) seem to center human fear of the natural world, as well as our settlement strategies and even our aesthetics, in adaptations selected by evolution over deep time.[39] The extraordinary range that human cultures have taken around the world and throughout time may make such a statement seem counter-intuitive, but we remain children of nature. Unless we are so strongly socialized to ignore our natural surroundings that we take no cognizance of them at all, our cultures endlessly react to the "natural" world around us, even if only to fear or dread it.

When human cultures in specific places address adaptation directly, those ideas can be seen as adaptive packages of "captured knowledge" about living in particular places.[40] As an example of how this might work in a historical case in the American West, geographer William Riebsame has recently melded some of the ideas of systems analysis and adaptation theory to distinguish between positive adaptation (a culture's willingness to change in the face of new circumstances) and cultural resiliency (a system's resistance to change, and if disturbed, to return rapidly to its former condition). In Riebsame's view, the Southern Plains' response to the Dust Bowl of the 1930s is a classic instance of resiliency rather than adaptation. Rather than a wholesale rethinking of the premise of plowing the grasslands up to create wheat and cotton farms, the regional and national response to the Dust Bowl represented a tinkering with the existing system. And while that tinkering (in the form of new agronomy techniques and a small-scale return of marginal farmland to grass) was seen by residents as a successful adaptation, Riebsame thinks that over the long term, with continuing droughts and collapses, those actions will be reinterpreted as having been a resilient rebound to the status quo and hence ultimately maladaptive.[41]

The narrative line of bioregional history is essentially imagining the stories of different but sequential cultures occupying the same space and creating their own succession of "places" on the same piece of ground. It is important to realize in this kind of narrative that successive cultures inhabiting a space interact with a "nature" more or less altered by the previous inhabitants.[42] And we ought to understand that the structure of the dialogue—and that is the proper way to describe it—between local ecologies and human culture is the same kind of dialogue that exists between habitat and species in natural selection. We alter our places in accordance with our ideological visions, and in turn we are shaped by the power of our places.[43] Just as we now understand organic evolution to work, significant change in human history can be expected to occur as punctuations in equilibria, a rapid ratcheting (or "ecological revolution," to borrow historian Carolyn Merchant's term) to some new condition that recreates place.[44] Some of these "punctuations" are materialist, or economic, naturally enough. But some of the most important ones spring from ideologies, values, literature, art—the endless and changing ways we humans have *imagined* ourselves and our places.[45]

Such stories about the past are our guides to an essential insight: we live in an anciently inhabited continent. What makes history so useful to the reading public (as opposed, say, to anthropology) is that it can communicate generalities with stories of individuals, whose experiences carry the scent of life for readers.[46] It is just this "fuzzy" propensity for anecdote, history's inherent wish to tell stories with beginnings, endings, and lessons, that makes it so useful. As geographer Yi-Fu Tuan wrote two decades ago in *Topophilia*, affection for history, as with place, tends to focus on smaller and more personal scales than the large political boundaries of the modern world, and human sense of place has everything to do with a shared sense of history.[47] I take this as confirmation that there is a very eager audience for lovingly crafted bioregional history.

Bioregional histories of the kind I've described here do not yet exist in great quantity, but the list is growing. Despite its county focus and overly academic title, Richard White's first book, *Land Use, Environment, and Social Change: The Shaping of Island County, Washington* (1979), was a promising start to modern bioregional history. It's a book that shows well how a small place can encapsulate and exemplify many broader historical themes, and in the Pacific Northwest it is now regarded as basic to bioregional literature.[48] Worster's *Dust Bowl* of the same year *is* bioregionally centered and certainly explores adaptation, but since its topic is a specific event, it only superficially examines sequential cultures or deep time. The literature and art it explores are those of event rather than place. Nonetheless, it's a superb place book. To the extent that it examines the Imperial Valley of California especially, the same can be said of Worster's *Rivers of Empire: Water, Aridity, and the Growth of the American West* (1985). These two books are almost indispensable to environmental history, although neither is quite a bioregional history.

The country east of the Mississippi River has been better served than the West. William Cronon's *Changes in the Land: Indians, Colonists, and the Ecology of New England* (1983), Carolyn Merchant's *Ecological Revolutions: Nature, Gender, and Science in New England* (1989), Richard Judd's, *Common Lands, Common People: Society, Landscape, and Conservation in Northern New England* (1996), Albert Cowdrey's *This Land, This South: An Environmental History* (1983), Timothy Silver's *A New Face on the Countryside* (1989), Mart Stewart's *"What Nature Suffers to Grow": Life, Labor, and Landscape on the Georgia Coast, 1620–1920* (1996), and Jan Albers, *Hands on the Land: A History of the Vermont Landscape* (1999) have made the bioregions of the Eastern United States perhaps the best studied on the continent. Cowdrey's book, although it mentions deep time, essentially is a broad geography/shallow-time work, far different from Stewart's, which covers a broad stretch of history and is an exceptionally multicultural and sophisticated book. Cronon's, Merchant's, and Silver's are all more temporally focused and do explore processes and changes that create places across cultural lines, although without much reference to adaptation. Of the New England books, Merchant's is the broadest, but theory and jargon poke through the fabric of the writing; Cronon's and Judd's books are the most readable. Finally, Philip Scarpino established a different and useful bioregional category with his *Great River: An Environmental History of the Upper Mississippi, 1890–1950* (1985), a book that is somewhat narrow temporally but stands alongside Philip Fradkin's 1995 *A River No More: The Colorado River and the West* to give rivers a special role in bioregional history.[49]

Among the growing number of books concentrating on Western bioregions, geographer Robin Doughty's pair of 1980s works, *Wildlife and Man in Texas: Environmental Change and Conservation* (1983) and *At Home in Texas: Early Views of the Land* (1987) can be taken together as a shallow-time place history, of the bioregions of Central Texas. Hal Rothman's *On Rims and Ridges: The Los Alamos Area since 1880* (1992), a book on mounting competition for resources among ethnic groups on the Parajito Plateau of New Mexico, Peter Boag's *Environment and Experience: Settlement Culture in Oregon* (1993), which richly and imaginatively tells the story of the Calapooia Valley in Oregon, Elliott West's *The Way West: Essays on the Central Plains* (1990), and Robert Bunting's *The Pacific Raincoast: Environment and Culture in an American Eden, 1778–1900* (1997) are the kind of wonderfully place-specific books that are retelling Western history in an exciting new way. My own pair of bioregional books—*Caprock Canyonlands: Journeys into the Heart of the Southern Plains* (1990), about canyons of the Llano Estacado plateau of Texas/New Mexico, and *Horizontal Yellow: Nature and History in the Near Southwest* (1999), which uses rivers flowing eastward off the Southern Rockies to define the boundaries of its stories—

experiment with ways to tell history, but I did try to incorporate into them the kinds of ideas I've discussed here.

That the simple fact of aridity has bent Western bioregional writing toward rivers and canyons shouldn't be any surprise. Richard White's brilliant little 1995 book, *The Organic Machine,* was followed by another environmental history of the Columbia, Blaine Hardin's *A River Lost: The Life and Death of the Columbia,* the following year. The Missouri River of the northern Great Plains finally attracted its biographer with Robert Schneider's *Unruly River: Two Centuries of Change along the Missouri* in 1999. That was the same year that Stephen Pyne masterfully wrote the Grand Canyon's cultural history, *How the Canyon Became Grand*, and Jared Farmer's marvelous *Glen Canyon Dammed: Inventing Lake Powell and the Canyon Country*, lyrically told us how geology's Colorado River canyon was transformed from a geological human place to a technological one.

Probably the most successful Western bioregional history, Bill deBuys's *Enchantment and Exploitation: The Life and Hard Times of a New Mexico Mountain Range* (1985), a lovely *longue durée*, multiethnic book about the Sangre de Cristo Mountains, almost single-handedly joined mountain ranges to rivers and canyons as the landscape settings writers have favored most for this new kind of history. While deBuys himself focused on the Colorado River with *Salt Dreams* (1999), Tom Wolf's *Colorado's Sangre de Cristo Mountains* gave us still another environmental history of a Western mountain range in 1995. And Devon Peña's edited anthology, *Chicano Culture, Ecology, and Politics: Subversive Kin* (1998), is a kind of native's rejoinder history of the Southern Rockies, which Peña and his coauthors call the Río Arriba bioregion.

In its brief three decades, modern environmental history has made a name for itself primarily as a field that has offered stimulating studies of environmentalism as a socio-political movement, of intellectual ideas about nature, and specific environmental events of historical importance. For its theory it has mostly borrowed, yet in the work of Turner, and particularly Webb and Malin, there existed from the beginning a focus on places and their history, and at least the rudimentary foundations of how to approach that kind of study. As Malin put it in the 1960s, the "proper subjects of study" for a specific bioregion are "its geological history, its ecological history, and the history of human culture since the beginning of occupance by primitive men."[50]

Perhaps it has been a serious mistake in our ability to go native to the natural West that we've so long devalued local and regional stories in favor of endless histories that present the nation-state, its wars, politics, and empire, as the true measure of what history ought to be. Or, alternatively, we've favored histories that have attempted to impose upon a diverse continent some interpretive framework and then set about forcing the world around us into a facsimile of that model.

More enlightened and useful kinds of history for contemporary life, it would seem, are those that go after the reality of the specific, that present sophisticated, deep-time, cross-cultural, environmental histories of places. Histories that bring us to think about ourselves as inhabitants of places, of watersheds and topographies, of an evolving piece of space (with an evolving set of fellow inhabitants) different from every other one.

A new kind of history called "bioregional history," in other words.

CHAPTER 6

Islands in the Desert

The Rocky Mountains in Environmental History

I live not in myself, but I become
Portion of that around me; and to me
High mountains are a feeling, but the hum
Of human cities torture ...

Lord Byron

Mountain landscapes and mountain peoples are best characterized by their infinite variety and great complexity. Despite a rapidly increasing research effort, they remain virtually unknown.

Jack Ives, "The Future of the Earth's Mountains"

So far as civilization is concerned, the mountains are negligible. Unless they contain minerals they are of relatively little importance in the development of human society.

Walter Prescott Webb, 1931

Anyone living in the Rocky Mountain West—the fastest growing section of the United States at the beginning of the twenty-first century, and one now famous as "The Last Best Place" on the continent—would undoubtedly be startled by the last quotation on mountains above, one penned by the famous historian Walter Prescott Webb in his environmental classic, *The Great Plains: A Study in Institutions and Environment*. I am a great admirer of Webb's body of work, which stands as one of the foundations of environmental history, and the clarity of his writing has led me to imagine more than once that on those early mornings when he sat down to write, his mind switched on like a blowtorch in the dark. But "so far as civilization is concerned, the mountains are negligible"? I've read those dismissive lines more than once and wondered what on earth a historian so attuned to environmental influences could have possibly meant by them—or whether they were merely the equivalent of a literary migraine, the result of some sweltering daybreak on his Friday Mountain Ranch in the Texas Hill Country that momentarily addled a sensible man's judgment.

But the truth is, I have come to think that Webb meant what he said, and that he not only believed it but that he has subtly shaped the history of the American West with it ever since. Certainly modern environmental historians have internalized Webb's assertion that regional distinctiveness in the American West is less the result of a historical *process* (as in Frederick Jackson Turner's frontier hypothesis) but more accurately the end product of environmental uniqueness that made the West different from everywhere else in North America. The most important of these Western ecological truths, according to Webb, was the overwhelming influence of aridity across the region.

Western aridity was already a full-blown idea when Webb articulated and popularized it, thanks largely to the legacy of the nineteenth-century West's most important federal bureaucrat, John Wesley Powell.[1] The first map tens of thousands of readers have seen upon opening Webb's *Great Plains* in the almost seventy-five years the book has been in print was a Powell-adapted map of western America, with a series of concentric circles drawn around it to demonstrate the tightening grip dryness had on the region. From Powell to Webb, and through them, that imagery and its ideas colored yet another highly influential twentieth-century book about the West, Wallace Stegner's *Beyond the Hundredth Meridian*, a biography of Powell that even used the aridlands concept in its title. Right up until his death in 1992, Stegner continued to articulate the aridlands theme, as in this passage from *The American West as Living Space*:

> Aridity, and aridity alone, makes the various Wests one. The distinctive Western plants and animals, the hard clarity … of the Western air, the look and location of Western towns, the empty spaces that separate them … the pervasive presence of the federal government as land owner and land manager, the even more noticeable federal presence as dam builder and water broker, the snarling states'-rights and antifederal feelings, whose burden Bernard DeVoto once characterized in a sentence—"Get out and give us more money"—those are all consequences, and by no means all the consequences, of aridity.[2]

Potent mind pictures conveyed in potent words. Reading them or hearing them, you can smell the sagebrush, feel the lips crack, taste dry dust in the mouth. Yet, as with much truly powerful writing, there's reductionism going on here. Stegner and Webb, both champions of discarding myth and seeing reality, were themselves engaging in a bit of myth making.

Because the truth is, the American West is not a uniformly arid province at all. It does possess deserts, and slickrock canyons, and much vast and open shrubland of greasewood and sagebrush. And the Great Plains, at least west of about the ninety-eighth meridian, still present badlands and in places great

Grand Tetons and Snake River, Northern Rockies. Strangely, relative to the Great Plains, the Rockies have been an overlooked setting in Western environmental history. *Photo by author.*

grassy sweeps rivaled only by trans-Ural Asia as the premier dry grasslands of the world. But not all of the West is desert influenced. It consists, as well, of a Pacific Northwest that in some respects replicates the environmental conditions of Western Europe; the southern Cascades, for example, produce more annual runoff than most of New England.[3] More directly relevant here, the interior West also includes myriad sets of mountain chains rising skyward, emerald islands in the lowland sea of encircling plain, sagebrush steppe, and cactus desert. As a consequence of Mountain West complexity, because the mountains do not present an unbroken face throughout, and because of peculiar difficulties they have presented to human settlement, this Mountain West has been more difficult to characterize—oddly enough in view of their imposing visual presence, more difficult to *see*, if you will—than simpler landscapes like the deserts or plains.

But neither in world history nor in American history have mountains been "negligible" in human civilization. And in the Rocky Mountains, the fact of mountain ecology—mountains as snow fountains of moisture, mountains as the head sources of the West's surging rivers, mountains as homes to alpine-adapted life forms very different from those of the dry lowlands, mountains belted by dense evergreen forests that grade into scrubby forms both low down and high up—gives the lie to aridity as the sole and preeminent shaping influence of the natural West. Indeed, a good many of the Western characteristics that Stegner attributed to aridity in *The American West as Living Space* are actually a consequence of the mountain presence, and of course the author of *Big Rock Candy Mountain* and *The Sound of Mountain Water* knew that. My intent with this chapter, then, is to revisit the basis of Western environmental uniqueness and to assert a kind of dual natural primacy—both aridity's effect *and* the stamp of the complex mountain environment—in giving western American environmental history its look and arc.

Where I reside, in the Bitterroot Valley of western Montana and just south of the Sangre de Cristo Mountains in New Mexico, what I'm most aware of is that mountains are standing visible against the sky. I don't know what the peaks of the Bitterroot Valley or the Sangres mean to others, but to me they seem to encircle my spots on the planet like a tribunal of earthly gods, their heads in the rarified heavens. Godlike, wild as creation itself, they forge the very weather; they're beyond time as I experience it. How does the Taoist phrase put it? "The state is shattered; mountains and rivers remain."

Like most everyone else in the Rocky Mountain West, I live where I do in large part because of the mountains, and I watch them ceaselessly. I also wonder why I feel about them the way I do (when someone like Webb obviously felt so differently), why the low, rolling Sapphire Range with its parkland meadows strikes me as human scale and inviting, why it's the high-drama rocky places—the granite canyons and peaks—of the Bitterroots or the faces of the Truchas Peaks that stun the endless dialogue in my head to silence. In short, why do mountains seize us the way they do?

Start with this set of premises, all of which according to current reflection on human nature seem to be true. (More or less.) That humans are a primate animal. That our genesis as forest foragers gave us stereoscopic color vision to measure forest distances and to pick out ripe fruit against the dim background of green. That perhaps pushed out of the ancestral forests by competition with other apes, our ancestors emerged into the bright, expansive world of the grasslands, and straightened up and blinked into consciousness. That the openness and the essential forms of the *place* where this experience unfolded—horizontal yellow earth and domed sky in a yin/yang balance, cone-shaped green mountains standing above the intersect plane, even the tree forms of a fire-swept savanna—became genetically internalized as consciousness budded. That this place imprinting in the deep genes has been dancing a slow waltz with radiating culture ever since, flickering into existence an array of human aesthetics amounting—essentially—to variations on a set of themes. That the long tail of the *visual* in our evolution is apparent in the preponderance of words in our languages dealing with vision as opposed to the other senses. That words define the world. That because biocultural evolution is an endless conversation between genetic human nature and culture, the world around us has shifted and shimmied like a swaying cobra the more we've looked at it and talked about it.

If you've followed all this, and have silently nodded more than a couple of times, then you're already on the downhill of this deductive trail: we avuncular chimps must have come up with some really obsessive, imaginative, and colorfully entertaining notions about all those ancient visual archetypes of our deep experience. Like, for example, *mountains*, whose resonance in our lives is manifest throughout history. Given our past as a species, it's no wonder that people the world over are obsessed by the power of the simple pyramidal form whose geometry points toward the sky.[4]

We Americans have had an intense love affair with our own mountains, especially with some of the ranges of the American West, which, via great national preservation schemes, we've made into a peculiarly American form of sacred places. That's no particular insight, of course, but on the other hand, the savvy mountain observer of five hundred years ago probably would never have predicted that Americans would invent national parks and the wilderness idea in order to preserve our mountains. What makes our journey such a long strange trip were the gymnastics in thinking about mountains that got us from mountains as the lair of Satan in the Middle Ages to artist Albert Bierstadt's and Thomas Moran's nineteenth-century Sacred Mountains as the Face of God, and on in our own time to the mountain-based wilderness preservation system.

Worldwide, mountains have always been formidable landscapes for human societies, with a set of complex environmental problems that amount in some ways to a base-reversal of those encountered in arid flatlands.[5] The fundamental, organizing principle for biological life in most mountain ranges is not aridity, but *slope*. Just as dry has far-reaching consequences for biological life, that deviation from the horizontal we call "slope" presents interesting problems and opportunities for life. In mountains big enough, slope means complex topography, stratified life zones, and a complicated mosaic of ecological opportunities, hence biological diversity. In big ranges, slope produces elevations that stress life to its limits; some mountains, including Asian ranges like the Himalayas and American ones like the Andes and even parts of the Rockies, present difficulties of inhabitation that humans have not evolved to handle. While we evolved as exploiters of diverse edge habitats, our ecological history is that of a lowland species. Humans are naturally savanna, not mountain, apes. We may have spent much of our life as a species looking at, admiring, or dreading the looming, triangular shapes of big mountains, but they are not our natural home.

Slope and elevation are not the only significant physiological characteristics of mountain country. Latitude combines with them to give mountain ranges like those in the American West a variety of different looks. In the Northern

Hemisphere, mountain ranges near the equator and north of about thirty-five degrees are considerably cloudier and receive heavier precipitation than ranges that lie between about twenty and thirty-five degrees—accounting for visible differences in aspect between a range like the Bitterroots in Montana and the Sangre de Cristo in New Mexico. And like vast plains, where radiating heat can generate anvil-head thunderstorms and even tornadoes, mountains that are big and bulky enough are able to create their own weather systems, including effects like chinooks and inversions that are significant in human affairs, and not merely in the complications they create for Westerners deciding what to wear on a particular day.[6]

And big mountains are able to go beyond making their own weather. They are also able to fashion their own individual ecologies. As Edwin James, the first scientifically trained botanist to collect alpine plants in the Rockies in 1820, discovered, the Southern Rockies are high enough to act as settings for relict ecologies from latitudes a thousand miles to the north.[7] We still use C. Hart Merriam's turn-of-the-century names for the ascending bands of progressively more northern life zones—Upper Sonoran, Transition, Canadian, Hudsonian, Alpine—that are found on big mountains.[8] Additionally, ranges like those in the Great Basin, where the moist peaks of high ranges are separated, one from the other, by thirty to fifty miles of searing desert, in the twentieth century have become laboratories for the study of island biogeography and specially evolved endemics.[9] Consider mountain biogeography anywhere around the world, and you can't help coming away convinced, as Stephen Trimble has said, that "the patterns of life repeatedly show how fragile and fleeting is any one incarnation of reality."[10] As one example in the American West, during the late Wisconsin glacials, when the Pleistocene lakes, Missoula and Bonneville, were etching the shorelines we still see on the slopes of the mountains above Missoula and Salt Lake, there were no piñons or junipers in the Southern Rockies, and no ponderosa pines in the Northern. During these glacial episodes of only 140 centuries ago, alpine tundra and boreal forest spread two thirds of the distance to the equator along the spine of the Rockies; relicts of those life communities remain there still. Now the trend of floristic migrations is reversed, with desert-evolved species like piñon pines steadily advancing northward into present Wyoming and Idaho.[11]

These might seem like random and irrelevant facts until you face their consequences in human economy. More so than the biological life of the arid grasslands or the deserts, that of the mountains is remarkably diverse from foothills to mountaintops, tends to endemism, and also changes dramatically under both climatic and human influences. As one example, unlike the vegetation of the Great Plains, neither the boreal meadows nor the Southwestern shrublands that are chasing one another up and down the length of the Rockies evolved in conjunction with large herds of grazing species. With the introduction of Eurasian grazers into Western mountains over the past four hundred years, the Western mountains have been more susceptible to exotic plant invasions under grazing than any other Western ecoregions.[12] In other words, at its most fundamental what I want to say here is that the Mountain West has not presented a changeless face to human inhabitation through time, but has been a moving target, changing independently from the human presence, but also as a result of it.

Accepting that the elevated mountains—with their verticality, their life-forms, and their moisture—by all logic ought to stand alongside aridlands as the yin and yang of defining influences in Western ecology and history really ought not to stretch our imaginations. Yet historical tradition hasn't seen the West that way. John Wesley Powell set us to thinking about the influence of aridity in the West as early as 1878 with his *Report on the Lands of the Arid Region*; Webb made "semiaridity" and the Great Plains virtually synonymous for us since the 1930s. Aridity (and the Great Plains) have stood at the crossroads of historical interpretation of the West every since. Yet outside of geography and such contemporary books as Bill Wyckoff and Larry Dilsaver's recent geographical compilation, *The Mountainous West: Explorations in Historical Geography* (1995), Terry Jordan, Jon Kilpinen, and Charles Gritzner's, *The Mountain West: Interpreting the Folk Landscape* (1997), and Wyckoff's *Creating Colorado: The Making of a Western American Landscape, 1860–1940* (1999), thinking about the West has almost uniformly tended to follow Powell's, Webb's, and (most popularly) Stegner's leads in emphasizing aridity as the key to the West. Beyond the historical geographers, social sciences and humanities writers have never strongly conceptualized the Rockies, Cascades, and Sierra Nevada as asserting a primary environmental influence in Western history.

In part, I think, because the mountains of Western America have been settled by diverse ethnic groups that have created their own mountain places, scholars surveying the mountain Wests of Pueblo and Salish Indians, New Mexican Hispanics and Utah Mormons, Californians and Coloradoans, Montanans and Canadians, have experienced difficulty recognizing the Mountain West as a unified subregion of the West. Two examples make this point. Despite mounting evidence in archeological study for some long-term inhabitations by Indian cultures with specially adapted mountain cultures based on nomadic transhumance and (significantly) on sheep hunting, cultural anthropologists examining historic Western tribes still have not recognized a "mountain culture area" in the American West.[13] Evidently this has been because many mountain-based groups (the Mountain Crows, Utes, and "Flatheads," or Salish, for example) adopted a veneer of plains bison hunting traits when horses became available to them.[14] Nor, in fact, does cultural geography recognize a unified Rocky Mountain region up and down the Rockies today, divvying the American Rockies up between Southwestern, Mormon, and "Rocky Mountain" (Colorado, Wyoming, Montana, and Idaho) cultural regions.[15] It was not until the late 1990s that contemporary scholars of the arts studying regional literature recognized a literature of the Rockies, preferring (until the weight of notable Mountain West writers became too crushing) to lump Rocky Mountain writers into "Plains" or "Southwest" categories.[16]

Since the Powell/Webb/Stegner view yet appears to influence us, perhaps we need a refurbished mountain-based perspective and appreciation in the American West. To achieve that may require some general grasp of mountains in world history. Just as understanding the proper and primary role of the Mountain West in American environmental history seems to me to call for an acknowledgement of the function and role of mountain landscapes in deep-time human history, maybe we need some geographical diversification of perspective. Some knowledge of the separate perceptions of mountains in the East vs. the West; a familiarity with the evolving image of mountains during the past seven hundred years in Western culture; and the use of mostly European and Asian ranges as apotheoses of human-caused environmental disasters during the critical late nineteenth-century period of American conservation—these, you'd assume, should enrich our view about the significant and shaping environmental influences mountains have had in Western American history.

The number of world civilizations that have regarded mountain homelands as their cradles is probably impossible to calculate accurately. But despite the difficulties that great elevation and steep slope have presented to humans, few mountain ranges anywhere in the temperate latitudes have gone unoccupied. The anthology *Mountain People* lists well over two dozen contemporary groups of mountain dwellers worldwide in the late twentieth century, and it does not cover Europe.[17] According to the geographer Yi-Fu Tuan, while steep mountain ranges may have been the last of the major habitat types that Paleolithic hunters exploited, nonetheless, ten thousand years ago it was mountain valleys that became the setting of the great agricultural, or Neolithic, revolution. Perhaps that is why a mountain valley with a river coiling through it seems to function as a kind of ideal habitat, an Eden narrative, in the human imagination. The earliest landscape representations in human art are mountain valleys coursed by rivers. These scenes are a mirror of gender dualism. The watered valley symbolizes an enveloping and fertile femininity. The surrounding mountains represent the masculine, and particularly in the Eastern tradition they act as ladders of transcendence to the spiritual.[18]

In the East for a very long time, the reaction to the great mountains of interior Asia seems to have been one of awe and spiritual sublimation. A mountain, as Lao Tzu describes one in the *Tao te Ching*, is "A thing confusedly formed, born before heaven and earth, silent and void."[19] Yin and yang originally referred to the shady and sunny sides of a mountain—the opposites that replace one

Rock art, Bighorn sheep. *Photo by author.*

another in a natural Möbius loop.[20] In his recent book, *Landscape and Memory*, Simon Schama characterizes the Taoist tradition with respect to mountains this way: the universe was anchored by four mountains with a fifth at its center, whose peaks were the "above" of immortals who had successfully sought the way of the Tao. So the Taoist tradition invested mountains with a sacredness. Great mountains, while their iconic pyramidal forms might be symbolized in incense burners or other replications, were not profane landscapes of work and inhabitation the way valleys and plains were. Their heights were not absolutely off-limits, but they could only be ascended, and lived in, by shaman monks, for their peaks were guarded by dragons that feasted on the unworthy.[21] Indeed, even with modern developments like the Maoist and Cultural revolutions, this kind of special regard for high mountains has not entirely been erased. It was not until 1986, for instance—and then primarily because Westerners threatened to do it first—that Chinese explorers finally traversed the upper stretch of China's longest river, the Yangtze, from its sources on the Tibetan Plateau.[22] Japan's Fujiyama anciently and still today functions as a major sacred site for the Japanese people; *Sanjo-ga-take,* the Golden Mountain of the Omine Range, is so holy that women are still not allowed to approach it.[23]

By contrast, mountains in the Western tradition more than any other type of landform have gone through a striking evolution in the way culture has seen them. Of all the earthly configurations of soil and design thrown up by geology, mountains have been problematic in the West for at least the last two thousand years. This has much to do with history. In the Europe of two thousand years ago, the ancient and widespread Bronze Age ideas that mountains were symbolic, earthly ladders (or as the Greeks had it with Mount Olympus, the actual abode) for the gods, began to change dramatically.[24] This changed status for mountains in Western civilization led in some strange and unexpected directions.

The direct cause was the spreading triumph of Christianity over the pagan nature religions. In discrediting both pagan ideas and their high-country shrines, Christian theologians made a useful discovery: mountains are nowhere mentioned in the Judeo-Christian account of the Creation. This very odd absence appeared to offer proof that mountains, suspiciously, were not a part of the divine plan. The mountain's principal role in the Biblical tradition, in fact, is as the setting for the Satanic temptation of Christ in Matthew 4:8. Think about it: a landform that doesn't appear in Genesis, and is Satan's favorite haunt in the New Testament, surely must have had a spin problem among European Christians. Indeed, in a famous seventeenth-century book, *Telluris Theoria Sacra (Sacred Theory of the Earth),* theologian Thomas Burnet explained mountains as the chaotic residue of the Great Flood, tangible flotsam of Yahweh's punishment that ought to be regarded as warts, pustules, or carbuncles on the face of the planet. Mountain air and the instinctive euphoria of great panoramas? The devil again, tempting the unwary back to paganism with the sensuous pleasures of the flesh.[25]

But to borrow from the title of Marjorie Nicolson's famous book, *Mountain Gloom and Mountain Glory,* which traces the intellectual history of mountains in the traditions of Western civilization, somehow, like the ancients, we twenty-first–century Americans see "glory" where our near ancestors saw gloom. That requires explanation. The solution to less revulsion toward mountains in Western culture was, in part, experiential immersion. Inevitably this happened as population grew in Europe, and it took the form of the Benedictine monasteries in ranges like the Pyrenees where—in the tradition of Saint Jerome—acolytes could renounce participation in the worldly, as Jesus had done when tempted on the mountaintop.

It also took the form of mountain ascents and mountain observations by Europeans who lived in the proximity of great mountains, ascents that were first intellectual and religious and then became gradually more aesthetic and spiritual as dragons, fairies, and elves retreated farther around the corners of the European imagination.[26] Consider one of the great mountain-climbing stories of Western civilization. While Petrarch's famous ascent of Mont Ventoux in Provence in 1336 could still plunge the scholar, primarily interested in resolving an academic debate, into a soliloquy on the sensuous temptations of earthly scenery, Petrarch's debate with himself about scenery viewed from great heights set a new progression in motion.[27]

By the dawn of Romanticism in Europe, the Western mind had effected a transformation with regard to mountains. The European landscape painters Salvator Rosa, Claude Lorrain, F. M. W. Turner, and eventually the critic John Ruskin were converting European ranges like the Alps into, as Ruskin put it, "the beginning and the end of all natural scenery."[28] Edmund Burke's 1757 *Philosophical Inquiry into the Origin of Our Ideas of the Sublime and Beautiful,* with its classically Romantic fascination with chaos, mystery, and wildness as the template of the Sublime—and of great mountains as the form of that template—completed the evolution. It was an intellectual odyssey that prepared nineteenth-century American Romantics to regard their mountains, complexly, but potently, as the freshest representatives of God's handiwork, even the seat of America's moral superiority over Europe. As Thoreau put it—shrieked it, really, with the wind in his hair atop Maine's Mount Katahdin in August 1846—there was an American mountain refrain in the nineteenth century, and it sounded like this: "What is this Titan that has possession of me? Talk of mysteries! Think of our life in nature,—daily to be shown matter, to come into contact with it,—rocks, trees, wind on our cheeks! the solid earth! the *actual* world! the *common sense! Contact! Contact!*"[29]

Altitude equals beatitude. That was the message in nineteenth-century American high culture's take on mountains, and it has made mountains, especially Western ranges like the Rockies, Sierra Nevada, and Cascades, the apotheosis of the American landscape aesthetic. Yet this is an operative aesthetic that has been with us as a people for only a couple hundred years. It became an operative force in Euro-American life only from the moment Asher Durand's 1820s discovery of Thomas Cole's Catskill Mountain paintings initiated the Hudson River School's canonization of mountain scenery, and reached its ecstatic frenzy only when American Romantic culture encountered the far West. The maturing science of geology, explaining all that chaos of topography, helped.[30] So did experiential immersion with mountains—mountain climbing, in other words—which had the effect of chasing the hobgoblins beneath the scree forever.

But it was people like Albert Bierstadt, a German-American landscapist who first portrayed the Wind River Range by accompanying the Frederick Lander expedition westward in 1859, and Thomas Moran, who initially painted the Northern Rockies for the Ferdinand Hayden survey of the Yellowstone Plateau in 1871, who for Americans effected a final transformation of mountain gloom into ranges of light. Culturally, many of us put the spectacles of Romanticism on then and there, and we've only wiped them a time or two, never removed them, since. It's the view that tilled the American mind for the national parks and federally legislated wilderness areas that are a principal American cultural contribution to modern world history.[31]

Bierstadt, Moran, even the photographers who often were alongside them in this portrayal of the Mountain West, were shamans of the first rank, as visual translators obsessed by the mystery of the once-forbidden mountain landscape. Their art turned the former warts into *scenery*, the reflexive human awe (our deep-time hardwired reaction) at vastness and topographical complexity into the positive emotion called the Sublime. And since Romanticism by no means had escaped religion's influence, mountains that once had been Satan's lair now became *wilderness*, places unpolluted by the presence of "fallen" humans. In short, the Romantics had performed the hat trick of entirely inverting the previous idea: mountains were now holy, the freshest example of God's handiwork. And now it was civilized, fallen humanity that was suspect. In the play of holy Western light in a work like Bierstadt's *The Rocky Mountains, Lander's Peak* (1863), the mountain becomes the face of God—powerful but benign, looking down with compassion on the Shoshone encampment below. Or the Rockies are imagined as a majestic, timeless, unspoiled Eden, and that in good part because of our absence, which is the kernel of the wilderness idea.[32]

Through the eyes of Romantic mountain artists of the last century, the very existence among us of monumental ranges like the Tetons, the Beaverheads, and the Winds became testimony to American destiny and moral superiority. So who cares now that Bierstadt mostly made up his canvases of the Wind Rivers from scenes in the Alps and Yosemite, or that Thomas Moran fudged a bit (combining several locations) when he painted that ultimate confirmation of God in America, the Mountain of the Holy Cross in Colorado? Or that American mountain "wilderness" was mostly myth anyway, since the continent had seen more than 350 generations of people come and go by the time the painters got there? For most of us, verticality has meant sublimity ever since, and we've fashioned our world in the American West around the idea. For several decades, actually until the 1930s in the case of the national parks, American parks were synonymous with the Western mountains or great canyons fashioned by flowing water. Wilderness, for the most part, still is.[33]

The mountain ranges of western America have not been interpreted solely through the lens of Romanticism. As a historical experience like that of Montana exemplifies, the resources of the Western mountains were targeted by the global market as early as the fur trade of the 1820s. The historical tension between the two ways of seeing the West—that of the Romantic aesthete, who in the person of someone like John ("of the mountains") Muir became a champion of mountain preservation, and an agent of economics like Marcus Daly, whose interests were in resource extraction where mountains just happened to be, have clashed spectacularly for a century now. The story of that confrontation, so loudly a part of modern Western history, offers another reason why the Powell/Webb/Stegner aridity hypothesis alone can't explain Western history very well. In the modern history of the American West, the land-use debate has centered around the public lands. And the largest slice of the truly semiarid West, the largely privatized Great Plains, has experienced relatively little of that debate.

The public lands are today the most visible institution that differentiates the Mountain West from the rest of the United States. It might be helpful in recognizing the important role of the mountains in Western history to remember that in the 1890s, when the U.S. government began to withdraw large parts of the public domain from privatization to remain under public ownership and federal management, that program was aimed specifically at the mountains of the West, not at the arid deserts or plains. It had been George Perkins Marsh, in his remarkably modern *Man and Nature, or The Earth As Modified By Human Action* (1864), who had set America's Western mountains in a historical continuum of mountain land abuse in Europe and Asia, and who had first offered a rationale for public retention and management of America's Western mountains as federal commons.

As Marsh told Americans, "There are parts of Asia Minor, of Northern Africa, of Greece, and even of Alpine Europe, where the operation of causes set in action by man has brought the face of the earth to a desolation almost as complete as that of the moon."[34] Fashioning the first compelling linkages between forest cover and streamflow, Marsh was able to demonstrate that in the kind of mountainous country that Americans were then encountering in the West, there were dangers in market forces and privatization. Although his book mentions examples of land collapse in the Orient, Marsh's primary examples of mountainscapes that had suffered ecological collapse through logging and grazing were the French Alps. Marsh quoted a French observer to make his readers understand that,

> The Alps of Provence present a terrible aspect. . . . one can form no conception of those parched mountain gorges where not even a bush can be found to shelter a bird . . . where all the springs are dried up, and where a dead silence, hardly broken by even the hum of an insect, prevails. . . . Man at last retires from the fearful desert, and I have, in the present season, found not a living soul in districts where I remember to have enjoyed hospitality thirty years ago.[35]

These examples extended to both the southern and northern flanks of the Alps, as well as the entire Pyrenees chain, Marsh wrote. America's mountains would experience the same disasters if the country did not act. And how to act? In passages that scientists of the time did not miss, but that historians like Walter Webb apparently did, Marsh asserted flatly that "It is, perhaps, a misfortune to the American Union that the State Governments so generally disposed of their original domain to private citizens." If not privatization? Marsh continued, "It is desirable that some large and easily accessible region of American soil should remain, as far as possible, in its primitive condition . . ."[36]

Mountain water for the lowland deserts: Rio Grande Gorge near Taos. *Photo by author.*

This, I have to observe, was the inception of what history must consider the most significant event in the fashioning of the Mountain West as a distinctive region, one with far more long-term resonance than Lewis and Clark, or extractive industry, or the respective impacts of Buffalo Bill Cody, Frederic Remington, the Homestead Act, or even dam building. The original creation of a permanent Western public domain in the form of forest reserves came in 1891, at a time when eight European nations had already set aside their own mountains as public commons. In the United States the move was intended to satisfy Marsh's call to recognize the ecological—and economic—reality of sloped and elevated country. As the water fountains for their surrounding aridlands, the mountains made the dry West wet; they made inhabitation possible for hundreds of miles downstream by protecting the headwater forests of Western America's mountain lands.[37] Other uses—logging, grazing, human recreation, protection of habitat for the Western wildlife that was consolidating in the mountain fastness—came later. But far more than their mining history, their logging history, or their status as sublime landforms or recreational destinations, the Mountain West's salient contributions to Western history are the core national forest public lands that today define the region as unique in the United States. That fact alone is what makes the aridlands thesis as a stand-alone environmental explanation for the West come up so short.

As environmental history and historical geography conceptualize the American Mountain West today, that critical step—the communal ownership and regulated use of the high mountain zones by an American culture whose nineteenth-century arc, after all, was pretty brassily an Adam Smith blend of entrepreneurship and laissez-faire—stands as something of a startler. I think it is the most important in a list of characteristics that describes a central and highly significant role for mountains in Western history. These characteristics[38] include mountains' function as barriers to movement; their sporadic spacing of resources useful to human enterprise; the ecological complexity created by elevation, exposure, and latitude; and their precious snowpacks, which through a problematic but classic irrigation and diversion technology have made the rest of the West inhabitable. In this last, the streams flowing down the mountains of the American West have been manipulated by a hydraulic apparatus that functions much as do the Grand Canals, the Southern Waters North project, and the Three Gorges dams in spreading the mountain waters of the Yangtze across arid China.[39] Sublime modern marvels of engineering technology or tragic environmental catastrophes, these dammed, artificial extensions of mountain canyons are a fact of modern life almost everywhere mountains stand as islands in some desert. And perhaps the thing they make obvious is that overcoming aridity *requires* mountains. The aridity hypothesis itself cannot function without mountains on the horizon.

In his 1898 essay for *Century* magazine, John Muir—like Enos Mills of the Colorado Rockies—found in the Rocky Mountains of what is now Glacier National Park the nexus of reasons that mountains have played so important a role in the modern history of the American West. With the Great Plains falling under private ownership and the great herds of abundant grasslands wildlife only a memory there, Muir (and many others) observed that all the great, charismatic animals of the West had by the end of the nineteenth century fled to the hills. The Rockies now served as the last refuge for elk, grizzlies, wolves, even buffalo—and have continued to do so since. Yellowstone, Glacier, Rocky Mountain, and Grand Teton national parks were established in the Rockies in large part because, as almost uninhabitable highlands ("rocks and ice" in the contemporary phrasing), their only tangible function seemed to be that they preserved the last great wildlife habitat left for the big animals of the West. Western environmental historians refer to this idea, crucial in both national park and wilderness system history, as the "wastelands hypothesis." (That's a valuable insight, although to the *railroads* in search of tourist dollars, the parks turned out to be more akin to the Mother Lode. The Great Northern's ad campaign on behalf of Glacier ranks up there with Moran's art in defining the Rockies in our imaginations).[40]

What Muir was onto was the thread that led not just to the big Rocky Mountain parks but, eventually, to the twentieth-century development that had virtually all the first nine million acres of wilderness of the 1964 Wilderness Preservation Act (and a very high percentage of Wilderness Preservation System lands even now) in the high mountains of the West. Until environmentalists recently protested the omission of other land types, alpine country and the wilderness experience came very near to synonymity in the late twentieth century.[41] How much of this Muir anticipated I cannot say, but apparently he had at least some portent of things to come. As he put it:

> Go to the Flathead Reserve; for it is easily and quickly reached by the Great Northern Railroad. . . . in a few minutes you will find yourself in the midst of what you are sure to say is the best care-killing scenery on the continent,— beautiful lakes derived straight from glaciers, lofty mountains steeped in lovely nemophila-blue skies and clad with forests and glaciers, mossy, ferny waterfalls in their hollows, nameless and numberless, and meadowy gardens abounding in the best of everything. . . . give a month at least to this precious reserve. The time will not be taken from the sum of your life. Instead of shortening, it will indefinitely lengthen it and make you truly immortal.[42]

As the undisputed champion of the importance of access to nature for his fellow Americans, Muir is the logical spokesperson for this end result of the slow-cooked Western appreciation for mountains as aesthetically and spiritually inspiring places. Until our newly acquired taste for deserts and canyons emerged midway through the twentieth century, mountains were where we've gone in the American West when we've wanted natural experiences. Even with the new desert aesthetic, Yellowstone, Glacier, the Bob Marshall Wilderness, the Pecos Wilderness are where the bulk of us still go—a democracy of recreators that would send Petrarch hurtling downslope in confusion and terror, convinced that there be goblins for sure.

But human access and recreation in the mountain public lands isn't the ultimate end of an appreciation of mountains in environmental history. Because of their marginality as inhabitable places for us, mountains worldwide have tended to be set up as commons.[43] Thus they have served as a kind of "training topography" for human cooperation, management strategies, and settlement patterns. In any true appreciation of the American West, this kind of mountain history ought to be front and center, particularly as the pattern is so obvious and so old. By allowing private lands almost exclusively only in the valleys, public ownership in the Mountain West has served to create what historian Thomas Alexander has called an "Oasis Civilization."[44] So most interestingly, our modern highlands commons of national forests, parks, and wildernesses now preserve most of the wild country and the aesthetic views to the distance that have been central in converting the Mountain West, in our time of satellite communication and air travel, from rural backwater to Last Best Place.[45]

Overcoming the antimountain religious forces of Western civilization, the mountain ranges of the modern American West have in our time become a kind of sacred space for a secular society. Not an exact emulation of Asian traditions, but close. Because of the arc of settlement history and the fact of the mountains as public lands, we inhabitants of the Rockies are not, for the most part, truly mountain people. Unlike the Tibetan monks or the Benedictine hermits of the High Middle Ages, or the Gurungs and Sherpas of the Himalayas, we rarely live in the true alpine mists. We are actually valley people, which has meant that we have, indeed, lived mostly where the ground is more bare, the air dryer and more translucent, close in with the smell of sagebrush. But we do live with the sound of mountain water in our ears, mountains close by and accessible—mountains on our horizons and reflecting from our eyes.

And the mountains, right there alongside aridity, are very much in our history.

CHAPTER 7

Zion in Eden

Phases of the Environmental History of Utah

This earth was once a garden place.
William Phelps, hymn of the Church of Jesus Christ of Latter-Day Saints, ca. 1835

We were the first to plant out orchards and to improve this desert country, making it like the Garden of Eden.

Brigham Young

On 21 May 1996, 6:45 A.M., I am on the west bank of the Escalante River, Utah, just below the confluence of the green, rippling Escalante and Harris Wash. I descended to this spot between 10 A.M. and 4 P.M. yesterday, wading the beaver ponds as Martian-red Kayenta cliffs soared above me, falcons worked the thermals, and wrens trilled their clear, curved song of the canyon country. Now I'm sipping my first cup and idly watching dawn sunlight saturate the coloring around me, whacking the odd cedar fly, listening to this emerald river murmur ten feet away.

Big doings, this Escalante country in the late 1990s. It's the old river named for the Spanish fathers (who crossed the Colorado below its mouth in 1776), of course, but also the river of that ultimate vagabond for beauty, the young poet/painter Everett Ruess, who disappeared off the face of the earth here in 1934. And it was also Wallace Stegner's river, the thread around which he hoped to fashion a great Southern Utah national park in the early 1960s. Now, judging by the cars parked at the trailhead and the folks I've seen along the trails, it's become the ultimate Western hippie environmentalist backpacker's river, too. And as I sit in this brick dirt in May 1996, I know from murmurings out of the Green rumor mill that President Clinton is considering declaring a large swath of the surrounding country a national monument—the Grand Staircase/Escalante—to add to Utah's quintet of great parks.

This Grand Staircase/Escalante issue and an even more vitriolic debate over Utah's Redrock Wilderness Bill (proposing 9.1 million acres of wilderness across the roadless public lands of southern Utah) are only the most recent confrontations in a part of the West that has ably entertained itself and the rest of the world with its environmental history for a good 150 years. My experience yesterday—before putting on my backpack and dropping off into Harris Wash—in the nearby little community of Escalante stands in my mind this morning as a kind of emblematic summary of this story, which puts modern, secular environmentalism in basal opposition with an older, Christian view of how the world works.

What had happened was this. After a fourteen-hour drive down from Missoula, I'd gotten to Escalante around dark and at random picked a thirty-dollar motel run by a talkative elderly Mormon couple, both of fourth-generation, pioneer LDS (Latter-Day Saints) roots. As I stood in their office listening to them cluck (they did not rant) their dismay over environmentalists, to make conversation I confessed not only to being a writer about the Western environment but (in a miscalculated effort to sidestep a *Book of Mormon* pitch for bedside reading) to having grown up in a Mormon family myself.

The next morning I'd gotten up early and had breakfast at the Blue Dog Café, where locals glared at me and my out-of-state license plates as if I were a fellow-traveler of the anti-Christ and my Mazda an invading half-track lander. Then after buying a sheaf of maps at Escalante's combination hiking/liquor store

Southern Utah landscape, a focus of major environmental disputes at the turn of the twenty-first century. *Photo by author.*

I returned to the hotel to discover that the owners had been giving my situation some thought.

"Were you really raised LDS?"

I explained, briefly. They listened intently, then scribbled down a scripture for me to read (Moses 6:63). And then *reminded* me (it was my turn to listen with real intent) how at Satan's expulsion from Heaven his destination had been our own Earth, that he was *still* here, that certainly I must know that environmentalism was not only misguided but bespoke Satan's presence, that God's plan of redeeming the earth was secondary (since it is not "our real home") but was in any case a different sort of redemption than these environmentalists envisioned. All this was delivered as a reminder of what I surely knew, having had the proper upbringing.

I writhed loose from this conversation as politely as I could, not willing to tell them that since I'd been inside a Mormon church only once since I was eighteen, I didn't in fact recall all these details. But to convey the nuances of the scene entire, I ought to include that as I drove off, the male half of the pair suddenly came loping into the street, flagging me down, all earnestness and concern. I stopped, dropped the window, but I admit not all the way.

"Would you happen to be married?"

"No. No, I'm not."

"Well, when you finish your hike, you drive over to Boulder. Two of my wife's nieces work at the museum, neither one married. Smart girls. Cute girls. You stop by."

"Thanks for the tip," I say, and drive away thinking how much this man reminds me of my father. Also that in Escalante and Boulder, Utah, sparking the local LDS women is a certain and foregone recipe for trouble. Isn't that one of the possibilities for what happened to Everett Ruess?

In seeking to discover the causes of modern ecological dilemmas, American environmentalism in the last half of the twentieth century developed a penetrating critique of a number of mainstream American institutions. In the 1960s, historians Lynn White Jr. and Roderick Nash, for example, credited Judeo-Christian religious culture—with its anthropocentric convictions that only humans were created in the image of God and only humans have everlasting souls and that the planet is subservient to our destiny—as central to environmental callousness and mismanagement.[1] Philosopher Eugene Hargrove, among many others, has argued that our European tradition of Lockean, private-property concepts may be too exclusive, too unconcerned with impacts on larger society, to permit the emergence of an ecologically sound society based around property rights.[2]

With the collapse of Communism across much of the world in the 1980s, a common observation was that environmentalism had emerged as the major new critique of capitalism. And indeed, in its first decades of influence, environmental history, most accessibly through the widely read works of Donald Worster, skewered capitalism as a deeply rooted cause of America's environmental problems.[3] While disposed to trace many current problems to technology and scientific specialization, ecologist and political figure Barry Commoner, in a number of books that were widely read in the 1970s and 1980s, also argued that capitalism and ecological values were disharmonious.[4] Thus mainstream environmentalism in the United States finds itself largely in sympathy with public ownership of resources, along with strong legal restraints on private development. The result since about 1990 has been an increasingly vocal property-rights and "Wise-Use" movement emerging from the rural, conservative, and often religiously based opposition side of the environmental debate.[5]

Those looking to history in this clash of values have often pointed to the example of the American West, a region opened up to capitalism and the market between about 1820 and 1900, where a wide-open nineteenth-century laissez-faire development appears to proffer a portentous example of individualistic, competitive, unplanned, disruptive, wasteful, and undemocratic natural resource exploitation.[6] This lesson drawn from Western history is often presented as if it were a monolithic one, a history where the places that became, say, Texas, Colorado, Nebraska, and Idaho all experienced the world in much the same way.

No one need observe, of course, that we still don't know as much about the environmental history of the American West as we need to in order to draw many meaningful conclusions. But the monolithic idea certainly doesn't work. As a starting point we now recognize that diversity—of ethnicity, values, and experiences—was much the norm in the nineteenth-century West. So aside from a sprinkling of Indian cultural groups, perhaps the Pueblos of New Mexico, for example, were there any other nineteenth-century societies in the American West that experimented with group planning and noncapitalist approaches in their interaction with the natural world of that time? That attempted an egalitarian distribution of resources? If there were a nineteenth-century Western society that came closer to emulating some of the ideals of a modern, socially conscious model, how successful might that society have been in terms of its environmental record? Finally, if such a society had existed in the West, how might it have reacted when modern environmental concepts—based around public lands and mounting ecological knowledge about the realities of life in the arid West—were introduced with the force of government and a dominant culture?

Of course I've loaded the deck with the previous paragraph, because such a society did exist in the history of the American West and for nearly half a century it brought to bear upon some of the most ecologically sensitive of Western bioregions a unique set of values about people and nature. This is a story, I think, that allows a certain degree of testing of some of our ideas about individualism and Western exploitation, about planning as the correct way to create sustainable communities, and about the issues that environmentalists and social justice advocates still argue. The society, of course, was created by the Mormons in Utah, a group centered around the Church of Jesus Christ of Latter-Day Saints, which in 1847 initiated a series of settlements along the western edge of the Rocky Mountains, centered along the Wasatch Front of present Utah. Their experiences there afford history a surprising kind of model from which to speak to a variety of interesting questions about the West, religion and society, and environmental history.

Founded by Joseph Smith of upstate New York in the 1820s, the Mormon Church emerged in America at a time when utopian, communal, and socialistic experimentation was widespread, and centralized planning in economic matters was not considered threatening. These influences on Smith's pronouncements have been well documented: one of his close collaborators in the early years of the church, Sidney Rigdon, was an intellectual reformer who had been involved in several communal experiments in the Midwest.[7] The societal plan that emerged from Smith's one hundred or more "revelations" (some of which were institutionalized in *The Doctrine and Covenants*) featured the essence of the liberal thought of the time. (Smith even believed that animals, even the earth, had souls.) The Law of Consecration and Stewardship, later a basis for the Mormon communal societies of the United Order, attempted to establish a socialism for the Saints (as they sometimes prefer to be called) by conferring all individual wealth to the church, which would then redistribute it according to need.[8] After an initial experiment with this doctrine in the Midwestern Mormon communities, it was abandoned, although some of its principles were tried sparingly in the West on a trial basis. But its existence in the early doctrines did pave the way for a number of radical doctrines that were widely utilized in Utah.

The two most important early Mormon doctrines with respect to environmental history were the church's retention of ownership of natural resources, and the ideology of communalism as practiced by Utah's pioneers, who endeavored to prepare for Jesus' return by creating a society, Zion, that under divine church guidance would woo a garden from the Rocky Mountain wilds. As Young said, the Mormons would cleanse and beautify a "cursed earth" through a "pragmatic mastery of the forces of nature." With these lines and others like "We had to leave our homes and possessions of the fertile plains of Illinois to make our dwelling places in these desert wilds, on barren, sterile plains amid lofty mountains," Brigham Young set in motion what could be called the mythology of the Mormon transformation. It consciously devalued the Wasatch Front environment—which actually had favorably impressed church leaders in 1847—and set up a narrative of environmental transformation in which the Mormons took a Fallen desert wilderness and restored it to the Garden from which humanity had once been expelled. Both the name "Zion" and Young's promise that the Lord would help the Saints in this transformation came from Isaiah (51:3): "For the Lord shall comfort Zion; he will comfort all her waste places, and he will make her wilderness like Eden, and her desert like the Garden of the Lord."[9]

The opportunity to try these ideas in a Western setting did not come before Joseph Smith's death, but Brigham Young was an able successor, a pragmatist who nonetheless shared Smith's utopian concerns. Hounded and persecuted in the Midwest, by 1846 the Mormons were considering an emigration to Texas, Oregon, California, even Vancouver Island. But in May of 1844, explorer John C. Frémont had returned from an expedition to California by way of the Great Basin, and at the foot of the Wasatch Front had found (as his published account put it) "a region of great pastoral promise abounding with fine streams . . . [and] soil that would produce wheat," although "this fertility of soil and vegetation does not extend far into the Great Basin."[10] Before his death, Smith wrote in his diary that he had dreamed that "the Saints . . . would be driven to . . . [and] become a mighty people in the midst of the Rocky Mountains."[11] Given that prophecy and the desired isolation of the Wasatch Front, when Frémont's report was read to the assembled Mormon Quorum, the issue was settled. The American "Great Trek" was about to begin.

In order to track the nuances of the environmental history that follows, I think it's useful to re-create with some precision the ecological outlines of the setting the Mormon pioneers entered when they emerged from Emigration Canyon in the late summer of 1847. Fortunately a number of useful first-hand accounts, as well as subsequent studies by ecologists, exist to make this possible.

The environment of the region pioneered by the Mormons was the result of both nonhuman and human forces that had been at work for many thousands of years. The setting was dominated, of course, by the massive Wasatch Range, itself a product of nearly 300 million years of uplift, faulting, erosion, and sedimentation.[12] Stretching like an irregular massif more than two hundred miles north and south, and rising to elevations exceeding twelve thousand feet, the Wasatch was rent by a series of structural troughs that had been carved into westward-trending canyons by water and glacial action. Through these tumbled sparkling mountain streams that the Mormons, ignoring their existing Indian names, would give the names Bear, Ogden, Weber, Provo, Jordan, and Sevier, as well as dozens of smaller creeks.

Rivaling the mountains in importance was the contoured basin floor that abutted them on the west. Nearly perfectly flat out away from the mountains, this basin was the legacy of ancient Lake Bonneville, a gigantic freshwater lake produced from the melt of the Wisconsin Age glaciers. Dozens of times over thousands of years, Lake Bonneville had alternately risen and fallen to create a series of lakeshore terraces on the face of the Wasatch and on the smaller Oquirrh

Range twenty-five miles west. Bonneville's many guises had also left numerous delta fans and elevated benches where the mountain rivers had spilled their sediments into the varying levels of the lake. Lake Bonneville reached its highest shoreline on the Wasatch about sixteen thousand years ago, but within a thousand years the enormous pressure caused the natural dam at Red Rock Pass to give way. The lake almost drained itself overnight, carving the Snake River Canyon with an enormous rush of waters. As the glacial climate warmed, the lake continued to fall until at eleven thousand years ago it was at roughly its present level and had become a salty remnant without drainage—the Great Salt Lake. But it had left deposited along the transitional Upper Sonoran Zone of the Wasatch a narrow, rich alluvial piedmont of fans, deltas, and terraces, through which meandered the sweet, clear water of the mountains.[13]

As the Rocky Mountain ranges go, the Wasatch has a unique hydrography in that it lies within the reach of the rainshadow of another, higher range, the Sierra Nevada. It is this rainshadow, in conjunction with the Great Basin's lack of an external drainage, that produces desert conditions in the Basin itself, with precipitation averaging less that five inches annually. But thrust up at right angles to the prevailing winds, the peaks of the Wasatch form an orographic barrier that induces precipitation, so that the high mountains get up to fifty inches most years, while the narrow Transition Zone at their western base gets thirteen to eighteen inches. The great bulk of the precipitation in the highlands falls as snow, and its melting annually sends from eight to ten million acre-feet of water surging through the drainages in late spring and early summer.[14] In response to precipitation cycles whose causes still aren't well understood, during certain climate regimes, local convectional cells sometimes formed over the mountains in summer to produce violent rainstorms (at intensities up to eight inches an hour for short periods). Observing these storms and their effects in the early twentieth century, hydrologists convinced themselves that prior to Mormon arrival, the mountain watersheds handled such violent weather with no problems.[15]

These east/west altitude and precipitation zones effected a corresponding zonation of soils, and hence biological life, in the Wasatch. In the high mountains lie chernozem soils that are dark and humus-rich but often rocky, while on the flats below, where drainage brings down mineral residues, alkaline sierozem soils prevail. Between these, though, the deltas and benches of the transitional Upper Sonoran featured sandy, porous chestnut soils that by the mid-nineteenth century lay fertile and rich with lime.[16]

In combination with the diversity of altitudes, precipitation, and exposures, two centuries ago these soils grew a remarkable array of vegetation that ecologists, using the reports of early observers, have been able to reconstruct to provide a pre-Mormon baseline ecology for the Wasatch Front. On the highest peaks of the Wasatch, Mount Timpanogos, for example, a relict alpine tundra features fellfields of cushiony forbs, short sedges, dwarf bluegrasses and wheatgrasses, even Arctic willows. Below these isolated patches of tundra, in the narrow Hudsonian Zone, elfinwood timber like Engelmann spruce and limber and white pine are typical. The high ranges of the Wasatch feature some true montane Canadian Zone forests, with ponderosa and lodgepole pines and Douglas and white firs interspersed with meadows of Letterman needlegrass and beardless wheatgrass and cloned groves of quaking aspen. But the largest expanse of midrange (five thousand to eight thousand feet) slopes in the Wasatch Mountains has for a few thousand years been slightly too dry for ponderosas and instead is covered in a deciduous dwarf maple and oak forest, the Wasatch chaparral, largely ancient, cloned groves of Gambel's oak. Below this zone, especially along the rocky canyons, is an evergreen zone dominated by Utah junipers and a diversified understory of shrubs. These junipers, mountain mahoganies, and other shrubs gave way to stringers of riparian cottonwoods where the mountain streams coiled westward out of the mountains.

In the all-important zone where the Wasatch fronts the Great Basin, two centuries ago the benches and valley were carpeted with tall, waving wheatgrasses and bluegrasses and a variety of forbs. At the time the Mormons arrived, less than 20 percent of the floristic component of this zone seems to have consisted of shrubs like junipers or half-shrubs such as big sagebrush or rabbitbrush, although rabbitbrush and more salt-tolerant species became dominant parts of the flora farther out in the desert basin.[17]

As for its native fauna of two centuries ago, the Wasatch was typical of the rest of the Rocky Mountain West. Most of the principal native species, including Rocky Mountain bighorns, elk, mule deer, pronghorns, and predators like wolves and coyotes, along with white-tailed jackrabbits, were cosmopolitan across the entire region, the larger ungulates often migrating from one life zone to another with the changing seasons. Black-tailed jackrabbits were confined to the desert floor, while grizzlies, cougars, black bears, and moose ranged only in the mountains, canyons, and high valley meadows. Bison, too, had once been a feature of this ecology, but apparently under hunting pressure from trappers and Indians had disappeared from the Wasatch shortly before the Mormon migration.[18]

Environmental history can no longer afford to indulge the assumption, common in traditional histories of the West, that Indians somehow floated above a landscape like this without producing significant impacts on it. In fact, like most of North America, the Wasatch Front had been occupied by men and women who had long sought to alter the country to their needs for at least ten thousand years before the coming of the Mormons. At first they were the Paleolithic hunters who stalked and killed and may have precipitated the extinctions of the megafauna of the Pleistocene. When the mammoths and camel were gone, this lifeway was replaced along the Wasatch by gatherer/hunters of the Desert

Archaic, who painted ancient rock art like the Great Gallery on Utah's canyon walls. They were followed a thousand years ago by horticultural groups like the Anasazi and Fremont cultures, more than likely Uto-Aztecan speakers who were the direct ancestors of the Utes and Paiutes encountered by the Mormons in the 1840s.[19]

Among what must have been a wide and significant range of alterations these peoples made to the west slope landscape, they all certainly used fire as a basic technology of hunting, a means to drive animals as well as produce more succulent pasturage that could manipulate animal migrations. This long tradition of anthropogenic fire, without question, produced direct and far-reaching consequences along the Wasatch Front. Walter Cottam, the respected Utah ecologist, has argued in fact that it was previous generations of native peoples who created the essential ecology of exactly the landscape the Mormons found most compelling. Through centuries of firing the Wasatch they had been able to maintain—against a bench/foothill regime of junipers, shrubs, and half-shrubs well suited to the modern climate—a relict community of grasslands more typical of wetter and cooler climates.[20]

Into this centuries-old environment, with its delicate balance of water, slope, vegetation, and fire, stepped more than sixteen hundred Anglo-American farmers with thirty thousand head of cattle and "an immense number of sheep" and armed with the unusual cultural baggage of Mormonism.[21] Interestingly for Mountain West history, as Richard Jackson has shown, the impression the early Mormon pioneers had of the Wasatch was not of a "desert," but of "the most fertile valley . . . clothed with a heavy garment of vegetation."[22] To people used to the prairies and woods of Illinois and Missouri, this mountain country must have seemed strange and incomprehensible. But under Young's leadership the Mormons threw themselves zealously into the task of colonizing Utah, thus proving that in communal action there existed an alternative to the capitalistic order that worked, as Brigham Young put it, "to make a few rich, and to sink the masses of the people in poverty and degradation."[23]

With their centralized leadership and their belief that the earth and all its products were the property of a divine entity,[24] the Mormon's possessed a brand of stewardship that was less theoretical than Christian stewardship as it is generally understood: individual Mormons, for example, held ceremonies dedicating land and projects to the divinity. Additionally, the doctrine of continuing revelation was not only a boon for coping with a new environment, but endowed church decrees on natural resources with the power of supernatural sanction. The Mormons thus provide the closest American example of the Judeo-Christian stewardship ethic, what some have called the "Abrahamic Land Concept," in action in the West.

Mormon stewardship modified the Lockean view of private property use.

The earth could not be "owned," but it could be occupied temporarily provided the occupant "improved" it, or used it "beneficially." To Mormon thinking this meant changing nature to make it more productive of the things most useful to themselves. Land, it was decreed, must be distributed democratically, and members were even expected to give over part of theirs if a project or a new arrival needed it. Between 1847 and 1869 the church assigned titles, of usually no more than twenty acres, by drawing and petition.[25] These small plots were a clear recognition that arable lands were limited in Zion and that in a dry climate against the mountains it was irrigation that made their benchland farming possible.

The mountain topography of the country they now inhabited had left the areas receiving the most adequate rainfall too high and rocky to farm. To combine the water of the highlands with the fertile land below, the Mormons followed the lead of both Indians and Spaniards in North America. In this way the Wasatch environment reinforced their yen for communal action, for irrigation was an intimidating undertaking for the most rugged individualist who ever lived. The church leaders also borrowed certain features of Hispanic water law, specifically community ownership of water combined with a priority right ("first in time, first in right") of diversion for users. It planned and controlled the collective construction of canals and laterals, and the allotment of water. An early historian of institutions called these projects "one of the greatest and most successful community or cooperative undertakings in the history of America."[26]

Centralized control over land and water on behalf of the community was also extended to other major resources, notably timber and grass, even minerals. As Young told a band of new arrivals in 1847: "There shall be no private ownership of the streams that come out of the canyons, nor the timber that grows on the hills. These belong to the people: all the people."[27] Timber was obviously sparse relative to the Eastern conditions the Mormons had known, and it was much more difficult to get at. Using it sensibly necessitated restraint. After a brief experiment with unfettered use, the church decided to grant monopolies, or concessions, to responsible LDS men who through their own labor would open roads to resources in the mountains. Even today many of the canyons into the Wasatch—like Parley's Canyon, which once accessed Wasatch timber managed by Parley P. Pratt—bear the names of their nineteenth-century concessionaires. The extent of the regulation in these mountain concessions went beyond the mere charge of a toll for road use, for in 1851 a territorial ordinance established the rather stupendous fine of a thousand dollars for anyone convicted of wasting timber or firing the forest. Yet full use was implied, and since there were no attempts to reseed, the stands of ponderosas, lodgepoles, and Douglas firs were drawn down quickly by the steady increase in population. Within less than a decade of settlement, most of the timber in the vicinity of Salt Lake City was gone.[28]

With grass, the approach was similar and oriented more toward democratic distribution than conservation.[29] The communal herding of stock did eliminate competitive use of the range so long as the Mormons had only themselves to compete against. Yet Mormon stockmen, possibly somewhat bewildered by the strangeness of the Mountain West with its complicated life and water zones, appear to have overgrazed these relict, Indian-preserved grasslands very quickly. The Indians first voiced concern about the decline of grass for wildlife herds in the 1850s. By the 1860s, the Mormons themselves were uneasy over its scarcity.[30]

Mormon communities, unlike those that sprang up elsewhere in the Mountain West, were not organized around exploitation of only one resource, but instead made use of a variety of natural products. Parley P. Pratt's scouting parties thus ranged up and down the Wasatch Front in search of suitable benchland sites where later farms and villages (or "stakes") could be planted. Although the idea predated the move west, coming from Joseph Smith's "Plat of the City of Zion," which evolved from utopianist experimentation with the New England village, this kind of farm/village community was one particularly suited to an environment like that of the Western Rockies, where suitable settlement locations existed as oases. Church policies respecting natural resources were handled within a particular valley by stake presidents and councils and at the level of the individual irrigation ditch by the ward bishop. This was a necessary delegation of powers given distances and transportation and communication in the Mormon empire. Far from being independent and self-sufficient, however, these scattered villages were actually cogs in a societal economic system. Mormon villages "called" to locations in "Dixie"—the red rock canyonlands extending across Utah into Arizona—were launched to produce semitropical crops that couldn't be grown farther north. By 1900, nearly five hundred of these little Mormon villages had been established along the western slope of the Rockies from Arizona to Idaho.[31]

While Mormon economic stability across this far-flung empire rested almost from the beginning on a good deal of trade with "outsiders" plying the trails to the West Coast, Mormons consciously attempted to remain outside the spirit of laissez-faire capitalism that characterized American society during the post–Civil War years. For many it was a struggle to remain uncontaminated, but Brigham Young remained mostly unyielding. During the 1870s he went so far as to resurrect the communism of Smith's early theories by starting several United Order colonies—small, self-sufficient, entirely communal villages—and as late as 1868 held before the Saints as a whole this vision of collectivism: "I have looked upon the community of Saints in vision and beheld them organized as one great family of heaven ... working for the good of the whole more than for individual aggrandizement; and in this I have beheld the most beautiful order that the mind of man can contemplate ..."[32]

For a variety of reasons, though, the communal, egalitarian society advocated by the early church leaders began to crumble economically, if not religiously, during the 1870s. "Gentiles" who found Mormon ways authoritarian and un-American, began passing through Utah regularly as early as 1849, and with the completion of the transcontinental railroad in 1869 arrived in numbers that soon rivaled the Mormon presence. Forced increasingly to compete for resources with them, many Mormons (such as the Godbeite organization of Mormon businessmen) lost their affection for egalitarianism. When Young's death in 1877 removed the major advocate of the old order, under federal pressure Mormons in Utah began a process of "Americanization" (one author has compared it to Southern Reconstruction) that ended in 1896 with Utah's statehood and an almost complete incorporation into the laissez-faire American mainstream. Although separation of church and state and abandonment of plural marriage were the most symbolic reforms required to "bring the territory into conformity with national standards," Americanization in process had meant a tacit recognition that use of nature should be more a matter of competition, less of planning.[33]

Leonard J. Arrington, the dean of Utah historians, once asserted that Mormon resource policy "seems to have protected Utah from the abuses and wastes which characterized many frontier communities in the West." Yet from the perspective of environmental health, Utah's very landscape, read as an historical document, indicated otherwise. Even before the rush of Gentiles into the territory, the sensitive aridlands ecology along the western slope of the Rockies was showing signs of deterioration. In its efforts to provide for the growing numbers of converts by making "the desert bloom as the rose," the Mormons seem to have pushed the Wasatch environment into a sudden, ecological shift toward new conditions. From 1,637 Saints in 1847, Zion's population had shot up to 97,229 by 1870, with 55 percent of them residing along the Wasatch Front.[34] Raised and nurtured on landscapes in the wetter and less sharply sloped Northeast and Midwest, unfamiliar with Western plant succession or the fragile relationship between precipitation and mountain vegetation and forced to provide for ever larger numbers of Saints while competing with non-Mormons for resources, the Mormon leaders and their church were not able to develop a conservation ethic capable of preserving Zion in the ecological state they'd found it. Their doctrines provided well for the democratic distribution of resources. But given the goal of reclaiming a Fallen nature, the church was facing an array of environmental problems, for Zion was yearly becoming less productive and more instable. Rather than taking a Fallen desert and restoring it to the Garden of Eden, the Mormons had settled lushly grassed mountain benchlands that were now in danger of becoming overgrown with weeds and shrubs and inundated in flood debris.

The consequences of altering and disrupting the Wasatch ecology they had originally found so compelling in 1847 particularly disturbed the LDS bishop Orson Hyde. Addressing the General Conference of Saints in 1865, Hyde invoked both continued material success and the Saints' responsibilities as God's stewards as reasons that Mormons ought to pay close attention to what was happening to the environment around them: "I find the longer we live in these valleys that the range is becoming more and more destitute of grass; the grass is ... eaten up by the great amount of stock ... and where grass once grew luxuriantly there is now nothing but the desert weed.... There is not profit in this, neither is it pleasing in the sight of God ... that we should continue a course of life like unto this."[35]

Although Hyde did not mention it, timber was likewise beginning to come under heavy assault by the 1860s. At the beginning of that decade there were twenty-eight sawmills operating in the Wasatch. Twenty years later they had increased to a hundred, and by 1900 the entire west slope of the mountains had been denuded to such an extent that, according to Forest Reserve employee Albert Potter, "It would be difficult to find a seedling big enough to make a club to kill a snake."[36]

Because of traffic over the Mormon Cutoff, Gentiles were obviously in Utah with their herds during much of the 1850s and 1860s. According to the Works Progress Administration grazing researchers, the "chief injustice" done to Utah grasslands was done by these transient operators rather than the Mormon herders. Utah's cattle population peaked before 1880, and soon cattle were giving way to sheep, many of them herded around the West wherever forage could be found. By 1889 a million sheep and 350,000 cattle were in Utah; by 1899 the cattle population had stabilized, but now 4 million sheep were in the state. Like the wild grazers that they considerably replaced, these stock animals grazed the valleys in winter and followed the melting snows into the high mountains during spring and summer. Supplemental winter feeding of this stock broke the old natural balance by keeping alive thousands of animals that as wild grazers would have died. These enormous stock herds tramped and gouged the waterlogged spring soils and ate the meadows down until individual sheep bands could be spotted from the valleys below by the dust clouds they raised.[37]

Another barometer for gauging the ecological change set in motion by the Mormons and accelerated by the arrival of non-Mormons in Zion was a striking change in the face of the landscape as seen in the vegetation patterns of the western slope. By comparing the records kept by early observers (such as Peter Skene Ogden) with those of later scientific expeditions and survey parties, ecologists in Utah have been able to map a landscape response in the region that modern residents of Utah would be hard-pressed to imagine. For about fifteen years the grasslands of the valleys and benches managed to recover from the grazing pressure of introduced Mormon stock. But these were not grasses that had evolved with heavy grazing pressure. And with the removal of the Utes from the Mormon corridor, the ancient practice of firing the grasslands to replenish them ended. By 1870 a new regime had emerged that began to erase much of the flora the Mormons had found in 1847. The grasslands began to give way to shrub and half-shrub communities of big sagebrush, rabbitbrush, and shadscale, followed by a remarkable invasion of Utah juniper, which in a century would expand its density six-fold. And after 1900, exotic invading annuals like Russian thistle (tumbleweed) appeared, along with that bane of twentieth-century Utah ecology, cheatgrass, to overspread a country once carpeted with waving native grasses.[38]

In 1878, emerging from the scientific study of the Mountain West begun by Lewis and Clark and continuing through Ferdinand Hayden's Geological and Geographical Survey of the Territories, John Wesley Powell published his landmark *Report on the Lands of the Arid Region of the United States, with Special Reference to Utah*. A part of Powell's argument in 1878 was that communally based Mormon society ought to be used as the model in a new general plan of settlement in the West.[39] Of course, like most of his visionary ideas for Western inhabitation, Powell's plan was not adopted in Congress—and given his endorsement of the privatization of the high mountains in that 1878 blueprint, modern environmentalists probably ought to be applauding its defeat. But by holding up Mormons as its model, the Powell monograph pointed up a growing belief among American scientists that a new Western land-use plan to replace unchecked individualistic grabbing had become critical. Yet many within American scientific circles—among then Chief Forester Bernard Fernow and Franklin Hough of the American Association for Science—looked not to Powell for inspiration but to George Perkins Marsh, author of *Man and Nature* (1864), who argued that the high mountains of the West should not be privatized but instead retained in national ownership and their use regulated to protect the watersheds on which the West depended.[40]

So on the most elemental question of Western land use, including privatization of the commons, where Powell stood rejected, Marsh found his own ideas embraced. The new Western land-use plan was not Mormonism writ large across the face of the West, either, although the basic concepts of Mormon (and Pueblo and Hispanic) communalism and planning did become central to this "New West" of the 1890s. And the Mormon idea of "making the desert bloom as the rose" via water manipulation did find expression through the work of the Bureau of Reclamation (1902). But the late nineteenth-century plan that was adopted was actually a *federal* rather than a bioregional one, and instead of emulating the Mormons' regional and concessionaire systems, it replaced their program (and those of other long-standing local groups like Indians and Hispanics) with one featuring national retention and management of the high mountain country—

as I've mentioned, arguably the most important idea anyone has ever translated into policy about the West as a whole.

For something so important, this idea for a New West was written into law with astonishingly little fanfare. In 1891 Congress attached to the end of a twenty-four-part revision of a General Land Office bill a rider that empowered the president of the United States to set aside from private entry "forest reserves" to protect Western watersheds. Unimaginably, the bill passed both House and Senate virtually without comment.[41] Refined by Gifford Pinchot and significantly elaborated by Theodore Roosevelt's administration, the national forest system with all its principles of federal ownership, bureaucratic management, and multiple uses (with fees and permits for most uses) was in place within fifteen years. And with passage of the Taylor Grazing Act in 1934, the same principles were extended to low-elevation desert and valley lands still in the public domain West, first regulated by the Grazing Service and later the Bureau of Land Management.

In Utah, these fundamental institutions went into effect the year following statehood, when Utah got its first Forest Reserve (Uinta); by 1910 there were ten more, now called National Forests and covering nearly all of the mountainous areas, or about 14 percent of Utah land. Perhaps because early church regulation of resources had established a precedent of control, the people of early twentieth-century Utah were more solidly in favor of the National Forest plan that was generally the case in the West. The concept was supported by the Mormon church, and Senator Reed Smoot of Utah was one of the only Western legislators who championed its cause.[42] Yet for national forest users, even in Utah immediate economics still outweighed theories like conservation of watersheds. Their constant pressure on the Forest Service for more freedom of use was indirectly aided by a number of scientists and scientific bureaus (notably the Army Corps of Engineers and the U.S. Weather Service) that openly began to doubt the postulated relationship between vegetation and runoff that had provided the rationale for the creation of the system.[43] A century later the debate between locals and federal managers, now as hot in Mormon country as anywhere in the West, drones on.

Just how extensively a half-century of Mormon occupation along the Western Rockies altered and damaged regional ecology in the nineteenth century is difficult to say. But as with Hispanics in New Mexico and Navajos in the Southwest, the new managers in Washington were convinced there was solid evidence that the damage had been considerable. Indeed, the very landscape of the Mormon experiment seemed to provide proof of the connection between vegetation and watershed health. Beginning in 1881 and continuing for the next six decades with mounting frequency and fury, the Utah high country began periodically to send tons of debris, soil, and boulders rolling into the streets and irrigation works of the Mormon towns below. The Moab region in the canyonlands of southeastern Utah, for example, settled by Mormons since 1862, began flooding in 1888. Although local petitions closed the Manti/LaSal National Forest to grazing in 1904, nine devastating floods struck the area between 1888 and 1909. By 1930 thirteen Mormon communities in the red rock country of southern Utah had been abandoned because of flooding.[44]

What federal and state hydrologists considered a genuine land collapse, on a scale they were convinced had not occurred in Utah since Lake Bonneville's great flood fifteen thousand years before, began in earnest by the 1920s. Between 1928 and 1930, sixteen Utah counties suffered such devastating floods that Governor George Dern appointed a Flood Commission to study the causes of a phenomenon that had been unknown to the early settlers. After two years of study, the commission concluded that the mountain topography of Utah was incapable of absorbing the kinds of heavy summer rains the region had been experiencing with the watersheds so depleted from grazing, logging, and a rash of fires associated with the highly flammable exotic, cheatgrass. The commission in fact warned of continuing catastrophe if large-scale mitigation was not undertaken.[45]

In response to this report, a handful of critical watersheds were cross-terraced to break up gullying and then replanted and closed to grazing. The Forest Service also began an investigation of grazing that led to a first round of national forest permit reductions in the 1930s. But floods continued. In 1945, two years shy of the centennial celebration of the Mormon migration, Salt Lake suffered a flood that caused nearly half a million dollars in damage when a single patch of cheatgrass less than eight hundred acres in extent burned and left a vulnerable watershed bare and exposed. By the time of the Mormon centennial, twenty watersheds in Utah stretching from the canyon country to the northern Wasatch were considered flood prone.[46]

By the that time it had become apparent in Utah that floods and altered plant succession were only two manifestations of the widespread environmental deterioration. During the 1930s, the "West Desert" at the north end of the Oquirrh Range, specifically Tooele, Skull, Cedar, and Rush Valleys—only sixty years before praised as an excellent grassland of waving native species—became the only dust bowl in Rocky Mountain history. Eventually forty-six thousand acres lay bare to the winds, and in 1935 the Department of Agriculture anticipated that the town of Grantsville would have to be abandoned. The Soil Conservation Service closed the area to use and made it a demonstration plot in revegetation, but Utah's battle with surface wind erosion and dust bowls did not abate. After particularly severe problems struck again in 1955 and 1960–61, Utah ecologist Walter Cottam predicted that Utah was, as he put it, "Sahara-Bound."[47]

Contributing to the general ecological degradation was the twentieth-century transformation of Utah's agriculture. Hastened by government reservoir development and an increase in average farm size from 30 acres in 1870 to 212 in 1900 (and 1,032 in 1977), commercial agriculture and its techniques now held sway. When the Office of Foreign Seed and Plant Introduction imported strains of strong, red winter wheat from Siberia, a flurry of dry farming began, pushing the fields up mountain slopes as steep as 20 percent. Yet even the booms in wheat, sugar beets, and horticulture could not submerge the serious problems in soil erosion, malaccumulations of water and salt from irrigation, and canal seepage losses (more than 50 percent in some systems). By 1950 half the arable lands in Utah were being artificially fertilized. And although one of the legendary events of early Mormon history had established a precedent for biological pest control, commercial monoculture in Utah had so built up harmful insect populations that in the last half of the twentieth century, Utah joined the rest of the country in dousing its crops with malathion, endrin, and a host of other pesticides to keep its version of the Green Revolution going.[48]

Out here in the world of the twenty-first–century West, of course, the question is what to make of Mormon environmental history, what lessons to draw from it. In our New West, fascinated with a communitarian and bioregional vision of the future, Mormon history in Utah would seem to provide a veritable treasure trove of ideas. The problem is that while environmental history serves as a kind of key to unlock it, the contents of the box seem to be a fairly messy grab bag. They mirror reality's complexity.

As I look inside, here's the way I see the contents. First, the general patterns of Mormon society vis-à-vis a sustainable West are admirably worthy of study. Early Mormon socialism, at least within the parameters of its own group members (nineteenth-century Mormon policies toward Indians and Gentiles were another matter), does seem to have created for a time the kind of social justice and democratic access to natural resources that Americans value highly. Mormon communalism was also a positive virtue in another way, the way in which it so enticed Powell: it was the most effective way to create successful, *long*-term communities out of Western space. The careful study Mormon leaders did of every valley and bench setting along the western slope is one of the admirable features of the Mormon approach to the West. History would seem to count Mormon leadership as similarly wise in leaving the high mountain zones a form of commons, too, and for being one of the few groups to recognize the importance of this part of the Forest Service plan at the turn of the twentieth century. Finally, the self-sufficient regional economic model developed in Zion, which actually attempted to function for a time outside the global market, bears a close relationship to the sort of small-scale economies of place that bioregionalists talk about today.

The problem is that the treasure chest of Mormon history contains some jarring images, as well. The environmental history of Mormon Utah as I've told it here, for example, does not sound like the success story Mormon mythology portrays. Why not?

As with all human environmental history—and this is true of the ecological world in general—the answer unfortunately is not a simple one. The conclusion I draw from Mormon environmental history is that, first, like other nineteenth-century Christians, Mormons did not accord the natural world around them any particular rights. Natural Zion, in the LDS mind, was a world of utility that God gave to them to make them strong enough to stand against their enemies. Their brand of Christian stewardship, then, was little more than a humble-before-God anthropocentrism. For that reason, along with their lack of familiarity as New Englanders and Midwesterners with how arid countries function, the Mormons paid too little attention to the tenuous nature of the natural forces that held Zion together.

With a few exceptions (like Orson Hyde) their antennae as the nineteenth century marched on were tuned less to the unraveling mountains around them than to missionary efforts, growth, and a consolidation of their political power in the territory. With our better grasp of ecology today as opposed to a century ago, of course, we have to wonder a bit at the cause-effect relationship federal and state hydrologists saw between Mormon practices and landscape degradation in Utah. The native grasslands that vanished under Mormon settlement were, very certainly, relics preserved by Indian management. Plenty of wandering, itinerant herders piled their flocks and herds atop Mormon stock to help degrade Zion's mountain watersheds. And many scholars (see chapter 8) now see a climate cycle as perhaps the chief culprit in the gullying and flooding phenomenon of the period from 1880 to 1940.

Competing with environmental-degradation-portrayed-as-mythic-success for historical irony, though, is the LDS church's wholesale commitment to economic Americanization as requisite for acceptance into mainstream society. That perhaps helped make Mormons the most malleable of all the preexisting Western societies when the federal land-use plan was implemented, and for most of the last century it has made Mormon Utah a bastion of commonsensical conservatism and Republicanism. But lest anyone forget that Mormonism is as much religion as culture, Americanization has not brought Mormonism into secular embrace of environmentalism. In fact, outside relatively cosmopolitan (and far from exclusively Mormon) Salt Lake City, contemporary Utah seems less open to environmental sympathies than virtually any other part of the modern Rocky Mountain West.

Part of this has to do with environmentalism's embrace of ecological science as its explanation for the world and of biocentric respect for the diversity of life as a driving force in contemporary policy making. Meanwhile, traditional Mormons (along with a large share of other Americans) cling to a scriptural and fundamentally religious worldview that unquestioningly accepts humanity's role as the central story of creation. Utah ecologists J. H. Paul, Ray Becraft, C. L. Forsling, Reed Bailey, Walter Cottam, and Stephen Trimble—ably assisted by native environmental literary figures from Bernard Devoto and Wallace Stegner to Terry Tempest Williams—appear to have been far less convincing in their observations about Utah nature than the early Mormon leadership was with its religious pronouncements. When the first of several environmentalist-sponsored conferences on the future of Utah's environment was held in Salt Lake in 1968 it found itself confronting a Mormon population that had not only embraced individualistic capitalism but even the Western version of state's rights.[49] It was Utah's perpetual senator, Orin Hatch, who in 1980 introduced Bill S. 1680 calling for the "return" to the Western states of all national forest and BLM lands within their boundaries! With scant appreciation of Zion's once warm embrace of the federal plan, Hatch went on to become a leader of the Reagan-era sagebrush rebellion and publicly referred to environmentalists as "toadstool and dandelion worshippers." More recently he's questioned President Clinton's "moral authority" in setting aside Grand Staircase/Escalante.[50]

As I found out in the village of Escalante in May of 1996, the classic Mormon conception of the Divinely ordained transformation of the West endures today. But like other early Mormon ideologies, the twentieth-century version of the idea seems to have undergone something of a metamorphosis, too. "In the [modern] Mormon mind," *Northern Lights* editor and environmental journalist Don Snow has written, "the earth as we know it is a temporary state of affairs, soon to be cleansed 'in the twinkling of an eye' by the redeemer. If industry makes a mess of air or watersheds, that's of little consequence."[51] While that view does not seem to be official LDS policy, traditional Mormonism today does seem generally unsympathetic to environmental crusades, especially on behalf of issues like wilderness preservation. Perhaps only those who know something of Utah's early history can appreciate the gleeful irony with which Edward Abbey cast a Mormon bishop as the anti-environmental antagonist in *The Monkey Wrench Gang* in 1975.

Since replacing Mormon Zion with federalist Utah a century ago—augmented by its periodic creation of high-drama national parks and monuments like Dinosaur (1915), Zion (1919), Bryce (1928), Cedar Breaks (1933), Canyonlands (1964), Arches and Capitol Reef (1971), and now the Grand Staircase/Escalante—the federal government rather that the LDS church has been the principal force of environmental policy in Utah.[52] With rather stronger support from the church, the fed has simultaneously been a force of environmental disruption, from above-ground nuclear testing to the infamous damming of

Ranges isolated by surrounding desert, such as Utah's Henry Mountains drained by the Fremont River, are cradles for specially involved endemic species and unending environmental debates. *Photo by author.*

remarkable Glen Canyon (while preserving Echo Canyon in Dinosaur National Monument from a similar fate) as the culminating act of the Colorado River Storage Project.[53] Both were configuring events of Utah environmental history at mid-twentieth century. That schizophrenia continues today, as the fed simultaneously promotes Utah's growth with the $325-million Central Utah Water Project and at the same time endeavors through environmental impact studies and Forest Study Plans to reverse the long-term "declining condition of millions of acres of rangelands caused by overgrazing."[54]

I emerged from the sandstone embrace of Escalante Canyon three days later convinced that for the past hundred hours I had been enveloped in a energy hologram ricocheting from red stone, jade water, and that fathomless blue that will be here after all of us are gone. There had scarcely been a waking hour when the sights and sounds and smells of Escalante Canyon hadn't pressed a serotonin cascade of euphoria into me, and as I walked out through the undulating badlands called the Red Breaks, the hike (and, no doubt, a summer off from university duties) had me in a state of near religious conviction. Anyone, I was thinking, anyone at all who actually experiences this Utah world firsthand has to be moved to want it to remain capable of inducing such feeling for all time.

Then I drove that astonishing tightrope highway north to the little Mormon village of Boulder. Didn't stop at the museum—it was Sunday and the museum was closed, anyway—but I did pull in at a café for coffee and something to eat. And immediately upon opening the door was confronted with a rack of gimmee caps and bumper stickers expressing the gestalt of traditional, rural, Mormon Utah: "No More Wilderness."

CHAPTER 8

The Rocky Mountain West

Fragile Space, Diverse Place

Man makes the mountains.
                Colin Turnbull

T he world," Ralph Waldo Emerson wrote in his famous essay, "On Nature," "is mind precipitated." By which the sage of American Romanticism might be taken to mean that the way we *see* the world, including Nature, is almost a by-product of the evolution of the human imagination.[1] As generations of American readers can attest, Emerson was at his best as an essayist when he distilled his thoughts into pithy one-liners like this, and here he clearly was onto something important. And since it was in what Emerson called the "nervous, rocky West" that he believed the ultimate American destiny would be shaped, perhaps we twenty-first–century Westerners ought to take Emerson at face value and suspend judgment on what would seem at first glance a hopelessly anthropocentric statement so that we can reflect again on this old philosophical question that postmodernism has adopted as its own.[2]

Consider, for instance: in 1991 the Center of the American West at the University of Colorado-Boulder published an anthology about the future of the West called *A Society to Match the Scenery*, the title borrowed from a poetic line in Wallace Stegner's book, *The Sound of Mountain Water*. Among the voices whose Western hopes were preserved in that anthology was that of Missoula mayor Dan Kemmis, a native Montanan who introduced his own singular vision of Western community, a kind of bioregional market strategy combined with some hope for the revival of the Sagebrush Rebellion, with his conviction that "the world spirit is alive in Western valleys."[3] Nature, in other words, is the key to history of the Mountain West.

But, as I mentioned in chapter 5, Camille Guerin-Gonzales, in an essay called "Freedom Comes from People, Not Place," took issue with that remark. The northern New Mexican West that she knows, she objected, was nothing like western Montana as she had experienced it. Why? Because while *nature* might not be so different in the Northern and Southern Rockies, the *people* certainly are.[4] To round out this argument over nature vs. culture, Sally Fairfax, famous for her laborious and detailed (and, one suspects, not altogether joyous) updating of *The Handbook of Range and Forest Management*, asserted that the whole central notion of the conference was a sham. The West is not a place, she said, and it is not a region, and it is not unique. Western scenery by no stretch of the human imagination translates into a common societal agenda, unless it lies in the commodity value of selling cowboy hats—and that ain't no culture, according to Sally Fairfax.[5] Facing Western history as a layer-cake continuum of decisions and events that stretches away in both temporal directions from the point we now occupy, what are we to make of all this?

In the subtitle of this chapter I've used the terms "space" and "place" for what seem to me to be sound reasons of definition. So before stepping boldly and hip deep into the sticky intellectual bog of Western nature and Western culture, let me clarify my terms. Leapfrogging the two terms for the moment, I should point out in deference to the primary title that irrespective of all the ways that the American West has been bounded—whether by terms of human process, like frontiering or economic integration; or by environmental parameters, like aridity or altitude—the Rocky Mountains are consistently and universally considered to comprise the viscera of the West. In fact, if a recent poll of Western historians and writers has any value, the Rocky Mountain West might be said to constitute the most "Western" part of the West.[6] The spine of the Rockies, extending in the United States from Camille Guerin-Gonzalez country across six states and fifteen hundred miles to Dan Kemmis country, is regarded by people who make their living thinking about such things as the *ne plus ultra* West, the essence and apotheosis of whatever characteristics the West is made of.

"Space" and "place" I can deal with more perfunctorily. Although they might seem synonyms, they are not. I am using "space" here in the traditional way that earth science scholars and at least some environmentalists do, as a synonym of nature (or environment). In truth, this is an uneasy use, because it bifurcates reality, into the natural world on the one hand and human beings on the other, in a way that more and more of us are convinced is a distortion. But since the human cultures I want to talk about have in fact been added as a new element to Rocky Mountain nature over the past several hundred years, this sort of deconstruction is not altogether a deceit. As for "place," you need to understand it in the sense that geographers reserve for the term—as the evolving product of interactive nature and human culture. Place, in other words, adds humans and their cultures to nature and rejoins the bifurcation into the reality of the inhabited West that we all recognize.[7]

As the sample remarks quoted above ought to show, the question of whether it has been environment or human culture that has played the critical role in Western history is one that generates disagreement among environmental historians and geographers that is not too different from the "nature vs. nurture" controversy among psychologists. The resolution of this question might seem clear to many: while environments undoubtedly shaped the cultures of primary human cultures, since the Industrial Revolution science and technology appear to have given human culture the dominant role. Nature—dominated, conquered, manipulated, exploited—clearly seems to be on the run in our own time. Anyone conversant with late twentieth-century environmental problems in the Mountain West can offer a litany of the subjugation of Rocky Mountain nature to the human will.

Human minds have done rather a good deal of precipitating around this issue, and in modern times one of the regions where those intellectual rain-showers have fallen abundantly is on the West. That American environmental history had its genesis in the history of the West is no accident of fate, of course; the field is imbedded about as deeply in Western history interpretation as it is possible to go. Beyond that concession, and because his general ideas are so familiar to everyone who reads Western history, there is no point in rehashing Frederick Jackson Turner's conclusions about "the frontier's" role in shaping the American character. However, I might emphasize William Cronon's point in the *Western Historical Quarterly* (1987) that Turner's argument—that European interaction with the North American environment produced a new "type" (the American)—is a classic Darwinian concept, pure and simple.[8] In Turner, this understanding of nature as selective force and human societies as evolving organisms is more metaphor and literary device than outright scientific phenomenon, but it is a point that bears some additional investigation later in this chapter.

The writer-historian who carried Turner's idea to its logical extension in Western history was Walter Prescott Webb, who wrote his *The Great Plains: A Study in Institutions and Environment* in 1931.[9] Although he gave it the veneer of an analysis, Webb's approach was as old as Herodotus and Hippocrates, both of whom had noticed a certain confluence between geographies and cultures. The rhetoric of *The Great Plains*, that the aridity of the Western grasslands had created an "institutional fault line" to which American pioneers responded with mostly technological innovations (barbed wire, windmills, Colt revolvers, sod houses), was presented so forcefully that it seemed to be a flash of real insight. But despite its lyricism and continuing popularity with readers and historians, the thesis of *The Great Plains* rests in a mono-causal environmental determinism that, as I explained in chapter 5, anthropology and geography have long since moved beyond.[10]

In contrast to history, the social sciences by midcentury had rejected environmental determinism—the argument that environmental settings literally force human societies into specific forms—in favor of the theoretical approach that became known as possibilism. Environmental determinism cast human societies as too passive and too reactive. Obviously, human cultures—especially their perceptions of nature and their technological abilities—needed to be given due credit. An environment like the Great Plains, say, offers *possibilities*, but even its apparent limitations do not predetermine the outlines of human societies, as Webb had argued. Kansas University historian and more-or-less professional curmudgeon James Malin, who is now often considered along with Turner and Webb to round out a founding holy trinity of American environmental historians, pressed possibilism to its logical end in his series of eccentric books and articles about the Great Plains in the 1950s. Human cultural ingenuity as expressed through technological fixes to living in place, Malin argued, made nature's apparent limits chimerical. Possibilism, to Malin, implied that the possibilities were unlimited.[11]

But how do the viscera of the West, the Rocky Mountains, fit into these scenarios? The Rockies, for all the individuality of their separate ranges—the volcanic Jemez, the towering San Juans and Sawatch, the chiseled Tetons and Bitterroots, the abrupt verticality of the Rocky Mountain Front—seem at first glance to present a fair ecological consistency from northern New Mexico to and beyond the Alberta border. To a good degree that is chimerical, too, yet the American Rockies do stand generalization in one sense: they are a blue-green island archipelago, water fountains set in a sea of surrounding dry that laps against their uplift like waves against a shore. I've already mentioned the Rockies as metaphorical viscera of the West, but as many of the native peoples conceptualized them, the architecture of the Rockies' topography actually seems skeletal— like the backbone of some great continental beast. Extending the metaphor, the mountain snowpack can be thought of in terms of a slow heartbeat, pumping the West's water through a dendritic circulatory system that reaches three oceans.

But more important to Rocky Mountain space—at least as we perceive homeland possibilities—this circulatory system has fashioned within and along the Rocky Mountains many dozens of grassy valleys, holes, and parks. Mountain valleys were the setting of the Neolithic Revolution, and perhaps (as I argued in chapter 6), that is why mountain valleys still function as habitats of the ideal in the human imagination. But the reality for ten thousand years has been that a significant preponderance of the topography of the Rocky Mountains is just too rocky, and too cold and snowbound, for humans to live there year 'round, or to do very much of anything else there year 'round until professional recreation and contemplation gained some adherents. The *valleys* shaped by flowing mountain water were another situation altogether.

Sangre de Cristo Range, Southern Rockies. *Photo by author.*

I have already outlined some of the more important of the crucial foundations of the Rocky Mountain environment in chapter 6. They are reasonably consistent from the Sangre de Cristos to the Selkirks. The Southern and Central
Rockies tend to be dryer and higher, the Northern Rockies a bit wetter and lower.
Maximum elevation gain from valleys to peaks is about the same, though—
about nine thousand feet—up and down the Rockies. The inhabitable valleys
average much higher in the Southern Rockies (more than seven thousand feet)
than in the Central Rockies (five thousand to six thousand feet) or the Northern
Rockies (thirty-two hundred to forty-five hundred feet), but latitude and sunlight again compensate toward a broad consistency. What, then, did Camille
Guerin-Gonzalez mean when she professed lack of recognition at a description
of society in western Montana?

I've long suspected that the reason Walter Webb dismissed the mountains as
an unimportant part of the West was because the most superficial look at the
region would have been sufficient to blow environmental determinism out of the
water. It's not that Webb wouldn't have found ample evidence of technological and
cultural adjustment in the Euro-American settlement of the Rockies. Consider
this list, and it is only a partial one: vertical transhumance, or the seasonal
movement of people and animals across mountain life zones; water manipulation
via stream irrigation and, eventually, transmountain diversions; narrow-gauge
railroads to climb mountain grades and penetrate tight mountain canyons; new
snow-plow designs for high mountain railroads; ranching technology like the
"Beaverslide" hay stacker to enable livestock to cope with high-elevation winters;
extractive industry innovations like aerial tramways to move mining ore and aerial logging to haul trees off steep slopes that roads can't penetrate.[12]

In a recent work on folk and material culture in the West, a geographical team led by Terry Jordan in fact found four mountainous hearths of human invention and innovation in the American West. And three of those hearths—Hispanic highland New Mexico, Mormon Deseret, and the high mountain valleys of southwestern Montana—are in the Rocky Mountains.[13]

A sharp look at the mountains, in fact, might have shaken Webb's belief that *technological* adaptation to the environment really is the most important story of Western regionalism. Any fair-minded thinker who looks at the Rockies closely encounters a mosaic of cultural patterns that makes them appear something quite different from a singular landform shaping human societies toward convergence. Assembling evidence for a deterministic aura emanating from environment, someone like Webb could react only with hasty dismissal when confronted with Hispanic New Mexican villagers, Wasatch Front Mormons, and Montanans in the Northern Rockies.

My intention here, then, is to take a survey look at the environmental histories of the above trio of Rocky Mountain "hearth" places (and true enough, my examples do not exhaust the list in the Rockies), but within the context of a refined interpretive framework that may get us closer to the scent of reality in the Mountain West. Since the time of Webb and Malin, one of the breakthrough ideas of historical study has been the rise of systems theories that explain how local regions and cultures become integrated (or ensnared) into larger systems. Fernand Braudel's *Civilization and Capitalism* and Immanuel Wallerstein's *The Modern World System* demonstrated how the net of this new level of human social organization has come to affect most of the planet over the past five hundred years. David Emmons, in a very thought-provoking piece of recent writing, believes that this process of economic integration lies close to the soul of the West as a region.[14]

Also recently, however, as I briefly explored in chapter 5, an older interpretive concept has undergone some interesting refinements. The idea that human societies might actually be living organisms predated Turner's Frontier Thesis and was explored by thinkers as diverse as Arnold Toynbee and Julian Steward in the 1940s and 1950s. But in the late 1970s geographers and anthropologists like Karl Butzer and Roy Rappaport resurrected this line of investigation by applying the rules of organic evolution to cultural adaptation, and they tried to work out some of its societal mechanisms—principally the learned behavior and actions of bureaucracies, special interest groups, and individuals. Rappaport went on to argue that the ultimate purpose of adaptation on the part of both organisms and societies is the same: to survive. Some activities, these scholars conceded, might be both adaptive in the short run yet maladaptive (if they encouraged flawed behavior) in the long run. Finally, societies differ dramatically not only in how they "cognize" their environment, but in how adaptively flexible and responsible their mental maps of the world allow them to be.[15]

There is fairly good historical evidence for an assumption that peoples and places that have been outside the project of global integration have been freer to adapt on their own terms and possess better records of environmental sustainability. We still don't know enough about early Indian adaptations in the Central and Northern Rockies to answer the sustainability question for certain. The implication so far is that the very early Paleo cultures used the Rockies merely as seasonal tool-refit stations, with only occasional travel or hunting in the high country, but that a set of isolated and provincial sheep-hunting cultures occupied the Northern Rockies during Archaic times.[16]

In the deserts and canyons west of the Southern Rockies, however, a different drama unfolded, one of widespread Indian overextension and ecological collapse, and a retrenchment centering on the high valleys of the Southern Rockies about seven hundred years ago. Alvin Josephy and others have argued that the memory of this Anasazi experience, in fact, produced an adaptive response on the part of Pueblo culture. The resettlement locations they chose, and the careful, worshipful, admittedly anthropocentric but also much-admired ceremonies and restrictions they followed right down to the twenty-first century, were the results.[17]

Among the three Euro-American cultures—New Mexican, Mormon, Montanan—there are in fact some interesting adaptive convergences. For instance, all of them followed a similar pattern as valley peoples. The New Mexicans have been in place longest and had the added benefit of the Pueblo presence, a working model to emulate, which seems to have added useful information to what they knew from their Iberian experience about settlement locations, irrigation strategies, and seasonal use of mountain life zones. The initial Hispanic settlements in the Southern Rockies, at Santa Fe and present Española and Taos, were begun in the early seventeenth century. But it was not until the latter half of the eighteenth century that the New Mexicans established most of their high mountain villages—Truchas, Las Trampas, Chimayo, Mora, Vadito, Abiquiu, Chama (at elevations approaching nine thousand feet)—that have been used ever since to define Hispanic adaptation to the Southern Rockies.[18]

Several historians, among them William deBuys, Hal Rothman, and Robert MacCameron, along with sociologist Devon Peña, have explored the continuity and fascinating environmental history of this mountain culture.[19] Although they were part of an integrated global system from the first (albeit in the beginning a not-very-potent mercantilist one), the true mountain villages of northern New Mexico were not founded so much for economic motives but to act as buffers and early-warning outposts against Indian raids. They seem to have functioned more

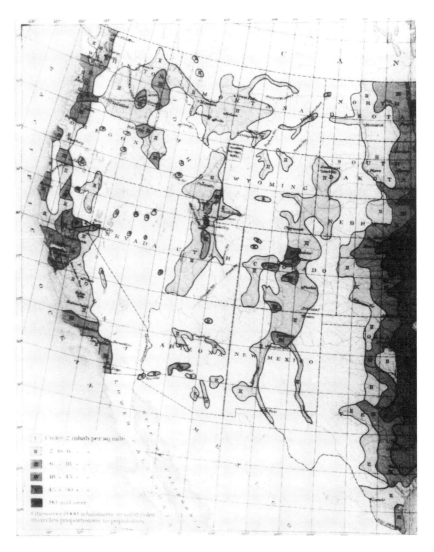

The oasis-like human inhabitation in the Rocky Mountain West a century ago. From the *U.S. Census Report for 1900*, volume on population.

than anything else like medieval villages, socialistic communities based on home industry in production of adobes and furniture, local barter, and communal sharing of critical resources like irrigation water. The surrounding higher elevation life zones of the mountains were granted to these communities, by crown and state, and in the Old World tradition left in commons called *ejidos* that were used to pasture the Eurasian goats, sheep, cattle, and horses that Hispanic settlers introduced into northern New Mexico as early as 1602. The Old World institution of partible land inheritance almost guaranteed mounting population density and resource stress in the inhabited valleys, so as population grew in nineteenth-century New Mexico, *Norteño* grants and villages spread eastward to the Sangre Front and the plains and northward into Colorado valleys like the San Luis.[20]

John Wesley Powell was impressed enough by the model of bioregional watershed living these mountain villages presented that in 1890 he specifically mentioned them as a model of the kind of West he envisioned.[21] And when American artists and literati began to seek authenticity in New Mexico in the early nineteenth century, some of them—Mary Austin, in particular—saw this New Mexican "mountain socialism" as the native model for a new American society grounded in community and environmental values.[22] Few of us looking critically at New Mexican village life today would question, as historian Frances Quintana has written, that the New Mexicans' long tenure in their microbasin (or bioregional) grants gave them a profound attachment to place. Place attachment, or *querencia*, was perhaps influenced by the attitudes and ceremonies of the surrounding Pueblo and *genizaro* (Hispanicized Plains Indians living, usually, as

Regionally and ethnically adapted cultural practice in the Rockies includes the Penitente Cult of the Hispanic Southern Rockies, portrayed here by Ernest Blumenschein, *Sangre de Cristo Mountains* (1925). *Courtesy of the Anschutz Collection.*

indentured servants in the New Mexico settlements) populations, for the New Mexicans referred to land as "madre," and on San Isidro Day in places like Abiquiu and Cañones, the priest blessed the fields, ditches, and gates. Sociologist Devon Peña has also discovered a body of folk songs and traditions in Hispanic mountain communities in New Mexico and Colorado that relate directly to the surrounding landscape and their use of it.[23]

However, in terms of environmental sustainability, the Norteño lessons are murkier than Mary Austin implied and many Hispanic activists have so eagerly accepted. If early twentieth-century Forest Service accounts of a general Southern Rockies degradation can be trusted—and if the troubled environmental history of the ejidos in Mexico has any bearing on the issue—over a couple of centuries of occupation these same New Mexican villages may have witnessed a profound alteration in the ecology of the Southern Rockies.[24] Indeed, the evidence does seem clear that about the time the U.S. Supreme Court upheld the government's assertions that virtually all the ejidos had always remained crown lands and thus were now part of the American public domain, apparently unusual environmental events were unfolding in the Sangres and Jemez ranges.[25]

When the government took over the old ejidos and transformed them into the Carson and Santa Fe National Forests, they found large animals like elk, sheep, and deer virtually extinguished. Period photos show barren and trampled mountains and a rash of spreading exotic weeds. And now, two centuries after the first New Mexican highland villages had established their ejidos in the Sierra, an episode of flooding and severe gullying commenced on the flanks of the Southern Rockies about 1905 and continued almost unabated into the 1930s. The Department of Agriculture in 1937 reported that 75 percent of the upper Rio Grande drainage in New Mexico had experienced accelerated erosion and that every small valley in the watershed had been gullied.[26] As just one of many stories, a regular accompaniment to an environmental backlash that seemed to spring directly from the land itself, it was said that in 1849 an emigrant had boasted of drunkenly crossing Galisteo Creek south of Santa Fe, on a plank; by 1930 that plank would have had to be 250 feet long to span the gouge the creek had cut.[27]

Answering what would seem to be a simple question—what were the causes of what happened to the Southern Rockies from 1900 to 1930?—has become a politically charged exercise. Virtually all of the government scientists on the scene at the time were convinced that overgrazing by introduced domestic stock was the cause, although they did disagree as to *whose* stock was responsible. Aldo Leopold, building on what was an unfortunate choice of historic materials (James Ohio Pattie in particular, whose account of the Southwest is no longer trusted) blamed Anglo-American pioneers and dated the beginning of the general degradation to 1849, the year of the overland migration to California.[28] Forest Service officials, on the other hand, were convinced that the cause was older and lay with the pressures brought on the mountains by the goats and sheep and other stock pastured on the old Spanish ejidos. Since it was the Forest Service that was in direct charge of the high country, it was their view that prevailed.

The end result of this Southern Rockies debate has been sixty years of permit reductions, spread among the small Hispanic villages as well as Anglo operators with (usually) bigger herds, to bring grazing in line with what the Forest Service believes is an acceptable carrying capacity for the Southern Rockies. As one ranger told sociologist Paul Kutsch in the 1960s, running the ten to twenty head of livestock that the average Hispanic owned was ridiculous hobby ranching; he flat-out ridiculed the Hispanic concept of land and the way they used it.[29] Those who have accepted Hispanic stockraising as the cause for the Southern Rockies' unraveling have pointed to a widespread cultural value, *fatalismo*—the image of the Hispanic shrugging stoically at that he cannot influence—as an explanation for why the short environmental feedback loops of microbasin living were ignored.[30]

Well, maybe. The modern historians who have most directly confronted this issue, William deBuys and Robert MacCameron, have tended in the round to agree with the Forest Service take on the question. MacCameron has pointed out that the livestock and plants (both crop and medicinal) introduced into the New Mexican mountains by Hispanic colonization were after all exotics whose impact in a new environment must have been profound. DeBuys, in a book that it seems to me has been unfairly castigated, argued carefully and sensitively that Forest Service science with respect to carrying capacity for livestock seems irrefutable, but that implementing that policy among villagers still resentful of the loss of their land grants has produced an almost impossible situation. The other principal environmental historian to address this question, Hal Rothman in *On Rims and Ridges* (1992), sees only minor ecological alteration by colonial New Mexicans, and explains the Southern Rockies' environmental degradation through steady population increase and competition for resources among the many different groups.[31]

In contrast to these Anglo historians, Hispanic scholars like Eric del Balso, Reuben Martinez, and Devon Peña have boldly asserted that John Wesley Powell and Mary Austin were precisely on target when they pointed up Hispanic mountain communities in the Southern Rockies as models of environmental management. Peña has written that while "the land grant commons has all but disappeared from the discourse on the environmental history of the intermountain West," nonetheless, "our communities created ecologically balanced lifeways well before 'conservation' entered vernacular speech. Our land-based origin cultures did not need Leopold, Muir, or Thoreau to develop environmental ethics." While he doesn't deny that the Southern Rockies seemed to be unraveling in the early twentieth century, Peña is convinced that this land collapse was a consequence of New Mexico's full incorporation into the global market after 1850, and resulted from the institutions and processes of imperialistic intrusion by Anglo-Americans. And that the arrival of the railroads and Texas herders fleeing overgrazed ranges on the plains were the critical on-the-spot causes of it. Even further, he believes that the usufruct rights under which the ejidos of the old microbasin mountain villages were managed actually produced strong sanctions against environmental damage. Environmental historians, Peña, Martinez, and others charge, have been remiss (or worse) in not recognizing this.[32]

While the very Anglo invasions—from trappers in the 1820s to elk and sheep hunters, itinerant herders, logging railroads, and all the rest later in the nineteenth century—that Hispanic scholars invoke as cause for environmental degradation would seem to argue against the villages' ability to impose anything like strong sanctions against ecological damage in their mountain ejidos, there are those who now argue that the question of *human* cause may have been moot all along. At least with respect to gullying and erosion, a pair of very careful geographers, Yi-Fu Tuan and William Denevan, have made a cogent argument for climate change as the essential cause for the widespread arroyo-cutting and flooding that plagued the Southwest and both the Southern and Central Rockies in the period from 1905 to 1940.

Tuan set this reevaluation in motion with his observation that gully-cutting in this part of the world is nothing new, that geology preserves evidence of a previous gullying episode extending to the pre-Spanish period and that it seems to have been triggered by a climatic anomaly featuring winter droughts (drying the soil and weakening vegetation) with torrential summer storms. Denevan then followed with a study that paired livestock estimates through nineteenth-century New Mexico with a chronology for the onset of gullying and concluded that stock numbers were nearly as heavy (3 million) in the 1820s, with animals much concentrated because of Indian raids, as in the 1880s (5 million). Yet while the period after 1880 produced the red scars of erosion gullies across the region, there is no evidence for arroyo-cutting in the earlier period. Perhaps the small-scale Spanish check dams and irrigation works offset overgrazing then.

But Denevan thinks the real difference lay in climate.[33] In current terms we would say that, in effect, the wetter and cooler climate of the Little Ice Age (roughly 1550 to 1850) was capable of supporting heavy stock numbers in the Southern Rockies, while the warmer and dryer climate characteristic of the period since hasn't supported a vigorous-enough vegetation to do so without the mountains getting sluiced away to bedrock.

Since another chapter in this book explores Mormon environmental history in the Rocky Mountain West in detail, here I'll offer only a few points for the sake of comparison with the pair of other mountain cultures. The Mormons had commenced their settlements farther north along the Wasatch Front half a century after Truchas, New Mexico, was settled, in the same decade that saw Euro-American inhabitation initiated in the mountain valleys of Montana. When John Wesley Powell observed it a quarter century later, the Mormon pattern seemed so adapted to mountain life that he recommended some parts of it as the model for Western settlement in general.[34]

In modern terms the early Mormon approach was a centrally directed, bioregional irrigation economy that until the coming of the transcontinental railroad in 1869 actually managed to keep itself largely outside the pressures of the global market. The New England-style Mormon villages were established in the Transition Zone meadows of mountain benches and valleys up and down the Wasatch, and like that of the New Mexicans, the Mormons' approach featured communal resource sharing, with use of the upper life zones carried out through church grants of monopolies to individuals who then managed the public use of resources like timber and grass.

What the Mormons were up to was a religiously motivated cleansing and beautifying of a "cursed earth," as they put it. It is difficult to escape the impression that this implied a wholesale remaking of the Wasatch Front with exotic plants and animals from Europe. It also seems to have meant a war on "wasters and destroyers" (read, "predators"). And despite the communal sharing of resources it entailed, the peculiar concessionaire LDS management of the upper zones was predicated on intensive use designed to make the Mormons wealthy and powerful against their enemies and to provide for a territorial population that had exploded to almost a hundred thousand by 1870. The fact of Mormon devastation of the Wasatch Mountains was abundantly clear by the 1870s, as grasslands began to give way rapidly to an efflorescence of pigweed, sagebrush, and juniper, and the steeply sloped mountain ecology began to unravel. By the early twentieth century, twenty major watersheds in Utah were flooding and gullying on a regular basis, leading to the temporary closing of two national forests, and ultimately the abandonment of more than a dozen Mormon communities.[35] Occurring within three short decades of John Wesley Powell's pronouncements on the Mormons, this Utah environmental history didn't make Powell much of a prophet.

Finally we come to the third hearth of cultural innovation in the Rockies—western Montana. In contrast to the Sangres and the Wasatch, where American capitalism and federal resource management were forced on existing cultures possessing their own adaptations, Montana's Northern Rockies were settled by Euro-Americans whose folk traditions were derived from what geographers have called the "Pennsylvania Extended" and the "Anglo-Canadian-Yankee-New England" cultural seedbeds.[36]

Visible built-environment reminder of the diverse historical legacies in the Rockies: Jackknife rail fence (of Pennsylvania origins) near the Sawtooth Mountains, Idaho. *Photo by author.*

Montana pioneers also happened to be direct emissaries of and workers in the global market economy from the very beginning. As Joseph Kinsey Howard and K. Ross Toole have taught us, directly and simply it was resource exploitation—first of furs, then of minerals and timber—carried out on behalf of the East and Europe that created Montana.[37] Montana had no great religious ideology fueling its birth, and when farms and towns appeared in its mountain valleys, their settlers harbored no illusions about experiments with utopian socialism. If a state like Texas, say, can be seen as the South's West, then Montana was New England, New York, and Chicago's West.

Although the oasis pattern of settlement characterized Montana as elsewhere in the Mountain West, far from embracing isolation and local barter economies, early Montanans rejected Powell's 1889 suggestion that Montana emulate the New Mexicans and Mormons and organize their local government around watersheds. The Northeastern and Midwestern farmers who settled Montana's mountain valleys were so keyed to cash-crop agriculture that before transportation links to the outside were in place, they almost destroyed themselves through overproduction.[38] From Bannack and Silver City onward, Montana was dollar oriented, secular, and interested in the possibilities of science and technology in manipulating the world. No wonder the Mormon missionaries mostly avoided the state in favor of Idaho and Alberta, that the state slogan ("Oro y Plata") and nickname ("Treasure State") still convey in overt terms its origins as a plunder colony for capitalism—or that Montanans are today precariously perched on top of frighteningly polluted rivers, sediment-laden streams, and mountain slopes branded with clearcuts.[39] While Euro-American stress on the Hispanic and Mormon Rockies was primarily agro-pastoral and small scale until a late subsumation by industrial capitalism, in the Montana Rockies ecological stress and pollution were industrial from the start. If Montana was to some extent New England and Chicago's creature, it was in a larger sense capitalism's creation—capitalism's Frankenstein, some would argue.

Since one of the goals of the global economy has been to integrate and hence homogenize the world, and since those who fashioned Montana were so willingly seduced, the Northern Rockies would not appear to be a fertile seedbed for the kinds of positive societal adaptations to living (and surviving) in place that Roy Rappaport and others have sought. That makes it especially interesting to compare these three Rocky Mountain societies 150–200 years after their founding and to note that of the three, at the start of the twenty-first century, it is Montana that *seems* to have gone farthest in evolving a set of promising adaptations to place. Of course from the long perspective it is not yet clear that embracing ideas like big wildernesses, biological diversity, ecosystems management (for example, Greater Yellowstone and Crown of the Continent ecosystems), and land trusts are necessarily effective adaptations. But commencing with the

Montana's experience of early incorporation into the global market has had an effect on the modern state's relatively progressive environmentalism. *Photo by F. Jay Haynes, courtesy Montana Historical Society.*

Bitterroot Controversy over Forest Service management in the 1960s and continuing today with issues like wolf and grizzly reintroduction, wildlife corridors and conservation biology in general, both issue positions and polls indicate that such thinking is considerably more progressive in western Montana than in northern New Mexico or along the Wasatch. Indeed, Montana's state constitution even has an amendment guaranteeing its citizens the right to a clean and healthful environment.[40]

Part of the explanation for that may have to do with the fact that divisions based on ethnicity and religion were less a part of the Montana experience than was true in Utah or New Mexico. And that no existing *Euro-American* (this obviously ignores the Blackfeet, Salish, and Kutenai) land-use strategies were forcibly replaced in western Montana as in the other two mountain regions.[41] Here at the turn of the twenty-first century an intense homelands attachment (querencia) continues among many of the mountain villagers in New Mexico, but it centers more on ethnicity and the continuing, festering sore of land-grant issues than on the issues of environmentalism, now suspect and identified with the Anglo community. So it is ethnicity and history that color debate in the mountain villages in their confrontations with "Floresta" scientists and environmentalists over restoring the health of the Sangres and Jemez ranges.[42]

Meanwhile, grazing reductions and the general integration of New Mexicans into the cash economy have destroyed many of the bioregional aspects of the Hispanic mountain villages. Traditional New Mexicans like Adrian Bustamante insist that the continuing commodification of Southwest art and folk culture and an endless cycle of domination by new arrivals has meant that cities like Santa Fe and Taos are no longer "real places"—and that if there is anything "real" left, it's to be found in the isolated mountain villages like Truchas and Abiquiu.[43] As for the Mormons of the Wasatch Front and beyond, their great issue of contention with the dominant culture was not ethnicity but religion. And while "Americanization" was forced on the Mormons (as the price of statehood) in the late nineteenth century, the Mormon mainstream seemingly has embraced, even internalized, most aspects of that assimilation. The church itself has fallen even more under the lure of growth and wealth. The doctrine of continuing revelation still gives the church's pronouncements supernatural sanction, but outside an urban core in Salt Lake City, Mormondom yet derides environmental protection. Meanwhile, the Wasatch Front has become a population bomb, with 1.3 million people currently packed into five counties (necessitating extensive transmountain water diversions) and a projected population beyond 5 million by 2050.[44]

So why *is* western Montana different, a more "ecologically aware" mountain place than Mormon Utah or (at least partly) Hispanic northern New Mexico? Environmental history has embraced the idea that the human/nature interaction works like a dialectic. Like all species, we change our environments as a result of our presence, and thus our subsequent adaptations are responses to the changed places that we've created.[45] I rather think something like this explains Montana's situation among the three mountain cultures. Inhabitants of a magnificent setting where charismatic big animals remained more intact than elsewhere in the Lower 48 because of cold, snow, and altitude, and whose essence was then maintained by historical developments that designated national forests and parks and eventually big wilderness areas (the Bob Marshall/Great Bear and Selway/Bitterroot wilderness areas, along with the Frank Church/River of No Return Wilderness in Idaho, are the largest south of Alaska), Montanans have undoubtedly put a spin on their place as a result of their cultural traditions of settlement.

On the other hand, they have been significantly shaped by their place and the peculiarities of their history. Modern environmentalism springs from literary Romanticism's marriage to the science of ecology, both secular developments, and Montana's roots are more secular than is true elsewhere in the Rocky Mountain West. That secularism has combined with Montana's (comparatively) well-preserved wildlands and with the state's singular history to produce some interesting results. As a colony of extractive industry, with (infamously so) decades of outright domination by two great companies, Anaconda Copper and Montana Power, western Montana entered the late twentieth century with the strongest anticorporate zeitgeist—the most profound suspicions about capitalism's effect on nature—anywhere in the interior West. Additionally, while most of the other Western states, New Mexico and Utah included, were transformed by the New Deal and Second World War from pure extraction colonies to more diverse and modern economies, Montana never experienced such a transition. It has gone directly from extraction to ecotourism with no intervening step.[46]

These unique developments have not only made the political debate about the future just as vitriolic in Montana (although for different reasons), they've tended to make it a more fertile seedbed for secular environmentalist sentiments than Hispanic northern New Mexico or Mormon Utah—or neighboring Idaho and Wyoming. In his *Montana Ghost Dance*, geographer John Wright describes a confrontation at a St. Patrick's Day parade in depressed Butte, once the "Richest Hill on Earth" that propelled Montana's per-capita income to first rank in the nation, now symbolic of the extractive crash that has spiraled Montana income to dead last. Assuming that he was a tourist (or a recently arrived Californian, foil for Montana's woes), a drunk kept bellowing at Wright, "Git out! Let Montana be Montana!"[47]

That confrontation distills into a single scene a dimension of modern Montana impossible to miss: a "native" who longs for the glory days of the extractive West confronting a newcomer who appears to represent the New West of environmentalism and ecotourism in the Last Best Place for both. (It only smears the scene with the complexity of the real to know that the geographer had spent most of his life in Montana while the "native" turned out to have grown up in Chicago!) In Rocky Mountain Montana at the turn of the twenty-first century, the major issue of contention is not religion or ethnicity, but economics, a clash between the old West and the new one. And because of what "natural" Montana was and is, set in opposition to the extractive holy hell that capitalism made of the place, this is a clash of place visions one could have predicted for the Northern Rockies. In its embrace of environmentalism, whose origins in Montana are partly indigenous and partly the result of the rapt attention the state gets from national environmental organizations, Montana as a place more resembles Colorado (and for some of the same reasons) than it does any of the other Rocky Mountain states.

Thus are places fashioned.

Given the arc this chapter has taken, it might seem that I have now come 'round to concur with Emerson's statement that "the world is mind precipitated," that human culture, not nature, has been the determinative engine in creating place in the Rocky Mountain West. If that's what you think, you'd be at least partly wrong, and I will leave you with a single but highly significant reason.

Back in the 1970s, a journal called *Human Ecology* published a special issue on mountain cultures. One of the consistencies it found among mountain societies worldwide was a disinclination to place, or leave, high mountain life zones in private ownership.[48] As we have seen, this has been the pattern in the Rockies, as well. For all their cultural divergences, the Indians kept the high Rockies as commons, and so did the New Mexicans, and so did the Mormons. When nineteenth-century American science pushed for recognition that ownership and management of the Rockies ought to be done in the public interest through the creation of the National Forest system, it was, I submit, bowing to the one virtually irresistible force on human environmental adaptation to Rocky Mountain living. Humans have almost never privatized high mountains.

What this sort of macroview of Rocky Mountain environmental history demonstrates, then, is that in broad outlines, the Rockies do appear to have shaped diverse cultures toward general societal responses featuring valley occupation and privatization and public ownership commons in the high country. The specific environmental histories I have outlined here have all been rather troubled, too, which indicates to me an additional theme—the essential ecological fragility of mountains enveloped by surrounding arid lands.

How our various Rocky Mountain cultures have perceived their mountain world and the values they have vested in nature—especially nature in their commons—is still not consistent even with a century of federal National Forest management in all three regions. To me, those differences remain today at the core of evolving Rocky Mountain environmental history. Nevertheless, the very existence of these highland public lands commons continues to define Rocky Mountain life. And they serve to separate mountain history from that of most of the rest of America, including the Great Plains.

So, I suppose, we should continue to pay homage to Emerson and the emphasis on how cultures cause us to see the world differently. But we ought to remember Rocky Mountain Westerner A. B. Guthrie Jr.'s, perspective, too:

"Here in the Mountain West," he once wrote, "space and nature shapes us."[49]

CHAPTER 9

A Long Love Affair with an Uncommon Country

Environmental History and the Future of the Great Plains

The sea, the woods, the mountains, all suffer in comparison with the prairie. . . . The prairie has a stronger hold upon the senses. Its sublimity arises from its unbounded extent, its barren monotony and desolation, its still, unmoved, calm, stern, almost self-confident grandeur, its strange power of deception, its want of echo, and, in fine, its power of throwing a man back upon himself.

Albert Pike, *Journeys in the Prairie*

In the larger context of conserving biological diversity in . . . natural ecosystems in North America, prairies are a priority, perhaps the highest priority.

Fred Samson and Fritz Knopf, *Bioscience*

BEFORE SUNRISE, SUMMER SOLSTICE, 1995

Atop a sandstone ridge that juts like a ship's prow from Texas's Llano Estacado plateau, my companion and I sit a few feet from a snapping juniper fire in the twilight of a Great Plains dawn, sipping hot coffee and waiting. Off across the blue planes into the opalescent distance to the northeast, the direction of the solstice sunrise, homestead lights that looked last night like tiny fireflies on a gigantic lake have now winked out. Once since the coffee was made, car lights flashed momentarily in the middle of those horizontal planes, then were swallowed up.

Since that moment and for minutes since, the panorama of country laid out before us has given every appearance of a *tabula rasa*, an empty and runeless slate across which human history is yet to be written. it's an illusion we're having to allow, of course. But as we sit here waiting out the sunrise, looking off at a landscape so vast and flat it seems we can see to the curve of the earth, we indulge the illusion, pretend that the country below us is not yet Texas and that all the immensity looming beyond is not yet Kansas, South Dakota, Saskatch-ewan. Nature emptied of the modern human presence and its technological clut-ter seems for us late twentieth-century folks an instinctive longing that, in my view at least, very likely is a sensibility lingering from our hunter-gatherer ances-try. If so, we're going to have difficulty letting it go.

So this morning, for a very few moments before the jets begin to drone and the faint grinding of truck gears becomes audible, Catherine and I permit the fantasy. Indeed, we've deliberately enhanced its effect—first by choosing to cele-brate Solstice at all, second, by doing it in remote Caprock Canyons State Park, one of the new nature preserves of a type beginning to appear on the Great Plains in our time. Too, there's the small gathering of rocks Catherine circled together soon after crawling out of her sleeping bag this morning. With a center cairn, it's a miniature medicine wheel, a kind of rock calendar marking the seasons that past cultures of the Great Plains built on hundreds of overlooks up in the northern prairies. As we see it, the wheel and the flint scattered in the dirt all around us represent tangible ties between us and them in this most anciently occupied of all North American landscapes. It's not that we want to ignore the last five hun-dred years of history here, but we recognize that the human drama has been going on the Plains for far longer. The truth is that this is at least the (roughly) 11,200th summer-solstice sunrise people have watched across this ground.

Striped badlands like these form the plains of Montana and the Dakotas. *Photo by author.*

We anticipate a fireball sunrise—the moon rose late in the night as a flaming scimitar crescent—and we're not disappointed. From first glint until it has cleared the earthline by a distance of two diameters, this Solstice sun drifts skyward as a flattened disk, Martian red through the slate blue. It's a skyscape effect I recognize because Georgia O'Keeffe captured it in her art here three-quarters of a century ago. The fireball makes this an easy sunrise to mark, and using the center cairn of our wheel as a sight, we embrace the timeless human ritual of setting down a line of rocks to mark the sun's point of emergence and ascent.

Later, after we've packed back down to the canyon floor, we drive out past a hundred-centuries-old Folsom site that archeologists have interpreted as a shrine to the long-horned bison. The country that we pretended was such an unmarked slate at daybreak is in fact historically rich and diverse. Tule Canyon, where Colonel Ranald Mackenzie had fourteen hundred Indian ponies shot to death after his attack on the last big Southern Plains village in Palo Duro Canyon in 1874, is the next major canyon to the north. Beyond that is JA Ranch country, where Charles Goodnight and John Adair began the Anglo-American ranching empire on the Southern Plains. Atop the Llano Estacado that looms like a flat-topped mountain range to the west lies the quintessential twentieth-century Plains adaptation: an agribusiness empire based on mined aquifer water. And when we drive through the tiny burg of Quitaque, Texas, whose economic fortunes are now closely tied to the nearby park and canyon country trails, I remember that Frank and Deborah Popper walked these streets a few years ago, ruminating on the future of depressed Plains counties like Briscoe, and on the possible twenty-first-century outlines of Great Plains society.

In the history of American places, the story of human efforts at adaptation to landscape and the history of ideas about the past as that history has put eye to microscope on particular continental regions, the American Great Plains stand in the first rank. Other parts of America—New England, the South, the Rocky Mountain West—true enough, possess their own recognizable historical identities. But the grassy heart of the country, those great rolling sweeps of prairie that commence around the Mississippi River, where the rainshadow of the Rockies are first manifest, and stretch away in a steadily rising sea of undulations to the foot of the mountains five hundred miles west, has been home to a human history that is both older and apparently more fragile than that of other American regions. What struck American explorers and homesteaders out of the Eastern woods as a place that was alien and marginal for Anglo-Americans was in truth—as the poet Walt Whitman would recognize—the most anciently American of all living places. But by virtue of its minimalism, the Great Plains are the part of North America, certainly the part of the American West, that captures more transparently than elsewhere the precarious fingerholds by which human cultures cling to the earth. As the last two centuries of Plains history illustrate so well, the wholesale assault on nature that modern, industrial, global-market living implies simply is not sustainable in every environment. And there are consequences of that assault, both to the natural world and to regional human societies, that seem to being playing out on the Western Plains more quickly and transformatively than anywhere else on the continent.

Modern industrial capitalism's assault on nature has fashioned a legacy that often seems to be fraying out around us as we embark on the new century, and to many of us it appears to be serving the Great Plains up as an example. If the Rocky Mountain West, from New Mexico to Montana, is today running scared of growth and Californication—the Rockies were widely recognized as the fastest-growing region of the country in the 1990s—the adjoining Great Plains are an equally large slice of the West that does not share that particular fear. Despite the occasional story of the random Dust Bowl refugee family returning to calmer soils three quarters of a century after parts of the Plains lost nearly 20 percent of their population in the 1930s, the Great Plains are facing different worries. Rather than being overrun by the "lifestyle-amenities" migration that has targeted the Rockies, the Great Plains are hemorrhaging people.

This abandonment migration is a long-term process that actually began as long ago as the 1920s, the decade of the high tide of population for much of the rural Plains, but that accelerated sharply in the 1980s, when large areas of West Texas, Kansas, Montana (and, if you want to get specific about it, thirty-eight of forty-one of arid North Dakota's counties, fifty of fifty-two of Nebraska's, and twenty-two of twenty-three of Oklahoma's western counties), lost as much as 10 percent of their populations in a single decade. In Montana during the 1990s, for example, the three fastest-growing counties in the state were all mountain valley counties in the Rockies. The Bitterroot, Flathead, and Gallatin valleys all registered population gains between 15 percent and 25 percent during the 1990s. The Plains counties? All except Yellowstone, encompassing Billings, were losers: seventeen of Montana's Plains counties suffered population losses in the 1990s, most experiencing 5 percent to 10 percent drops. In Colorado the story has been the same, with the Front Range threatening to become a new Los Angeles at the same time the Plains counties are emptying out.[1]

These losses amount to a hemorrhage because the people who are exiting are the young and the creative, leaving the Great Plains with the oldest population of any part of the country except Florida. Why it's happening, and what the future holds, are questions that point backward as well as forward in time.

For many, the modern Great Plains are a conundrum. A century ago the Plains were the heart of the West, the terrain of Sitting Bull and Crazy Horse and Bill Cody, the setting for Old Shatterhand's adventures in the Karl May novels that have turned a large number of Europeans into aficionados of the West. For a more reliable account of the nineteenth-century Plains, read Lewis and Clark.

When they traversed the grasslands almost two centuries ago, the Great Plains was the Serengeti of North America. Now the region is widely and popularly regarded as ugly, monotonous, uninteresting, unromantic. If the Montana Rockies strike Americans as the Last Best Place, to use writer William Kittredge's phrase, then the Great Plains—home to one fifth of the American land mass and 6.5 million people—has become the West's last place. And its least appreciated one.[2]

Great Plains space serves as preface to talking about how humans and the natural world of this remarkable country have interacted and what the possibilities are of the continuation. In late December 1993, in a single day, I replicated the movement of nineteenth-century Anglo-Americans across the continent from East to the West. I started where I started originally, where my ancestors' bones lie buried in the damp woods along Bayou Pierre in some of Louisiana's most remote eighteenth-century cemeteries, where the only names on the crumbling tombstones are Floreses and Lafittes. And then retraced in twelve hours the journey it took American pioneers eight weeks to accomplish.

Driving up out of the shrouded bayous and misty pineywoods, where the rainfall approaches forty-five inches annually, by sixty miles west of the Louisiana border I had imperceptibly gained higher oak country with the first scatterings of little bluestem meadows, which seemed to become larger and more savanna-like with every mile. By the time I was two-thirds of the way from Shreveport to Dallas, I was out of the woods and into the Blackland Prairie, the country broadening into a true grassland aspect, the gently undulating prairie crests from a mile to three miles distant, one from the other, with riparian tree growth in every declivity. Human sprawl around Dallas/Fort Worth had all but obliterated the north-south finger of oak woods once known as the Eastern Cross Timbers. But through the signs and edge city suburbs, like a mirage from the old Plains, all of a sudden there was the Grand Prairie, a windswept, mid-height grassland built on Cretaceous ocean terraces that a century ago was home to the first big herds of bison and wild horses as one moved west. Beyond that the Western Cross Timbers, a wider finger of oak and junipers that straddles the Red River for two hundred miles in both directions, still strikes the modern traveler as a phenomenon of the continental transformation, although this woodland belt, too, is rapidly being cleared away in our time.

And so on into nightfall, the country climbing higher and spreading out and drying out—annual precipitation down to thirty inches and dropping past Dallas—the trees steadily dwarfing, until with my headlamps lighting Highway 114, I realized that the trees were all but gone when the lights of small towns began to appear miles away in the spreading pancake of flatness. A memory came at me from twenty-five years before, of some of my first trips west onto the

Plains and of the excitement of spacious—Western!—topography, seeing those distant town lights twenty and thirty miles away and having no idea how the country was going to look in the light of day. At this point you know something elemental—that you've come *out*, are no longer *in* country but *on* it. Approaching the shortgrass High Plains, where rainfall drops to under twenty inches a year and emigrants used to watch the wagon wheels shrink loose on their axles, you float up out of choppy swells onto a smoother sea and come to the surface for far seeing. It's a feeling I've lost with more than two decades of living on the Plains, but the emotion is an old one—*euphoria at spaciousness*—a kind of landscape epiphany for us humans, with our evolutionary roots on the savannas of Africa.

This country of grass, space, and sky has been regarded as an environmental anomaly, at least in the United States view of the continent, since the time of Lewis and Clark, Zebulon Pike, and the Long Expedition of 1820. Of course, environmental anomalies, or normalities, result significantly from experiential and cultural biases. Spaniards out of the Meseta or Hispanics up from Mexico returned from their early *entradas* onto the Llanos del Cibolos (Plains of the Buffalo) with impressions of a country that was *cold* (rather than flat or arid), that was densely inhabited by nomadic Indians, and that possessed much potential as pasture for *rancherias*. What they did not think about it was that it was a desert wasteland.[3] As for the Indians, Comanches on the Southern Plains and Salish peoples on the northern sweeps—both groups from farther west—found the Plains superior to the country they had known, a hunter's paradise. But Anglo-Americans out of the woods of northern Europe and the Atlantic Seaboard have the reputation for having long found the Plains alien, deficient, and peculiarly hard to love in their natural state.

One wouldn't have imagined so at reading some of the first American accounts of the region. In 1806, for example, William Dunbar, the Natchez, Mississippi, scientist who was involved in President Jefferson's early exploration of the Southwest, wrote of the Great Plains that:

> By the expression Plains, or prairies ... it is not to be understood a dead flat without any eminences. ... The western prairies are very different; the expression signifies only a country without timber. These prairies are neither flat nor hilly, but undulating in gently swelling lawns, and expanding into spacious valleys, in the center of which is always found a little timber, growing on the banks of brooks and rivulets of the clearest water. ... Those who have viewed only a skirt of these prairies speak of them with a degree of enthusiasm, as if it were only there that nature was to be found truly perfect; they declare that the fertility and beauty of the vegetation, the extreme richness of the valleys, the coolness and excellent quality of the water found everywhere, the salubrity of the atmosphere, and above all, the grandeur of the enchanting landscape which this country presents inspires the soul with sensations not to be felt in any other region of the globe.[4]

In truth, Dunbar was not alone with this kind of glowing reaction to the Plains. Mountain man, poet, and later Arkansas judge Albert Pike, who traversed the Llano Estacado in 1832, was moved to similar rapture by the prairies, as were later poets, writers, and artists like Walt Whitman, Mari Sandoz, Willa Cather, and Georgia O'Keeffe.[5] But almost from the beginning of Anglo-American encounters with the Plains, explorers and observers who felt obliged to respond to the grasslands' potential for transformation into the *agricultural* landscapes that buttressed the expanding American frontier tended to regard the Plains as a place of deficiencies. Zebulon Pike, who traversed the Plains in 1806–1807 and spoke of the country as "sandy desarts," and Stephen Long, whose party crossed the Southern Plains during August of a drought year in 1820, gave the Plains an identity that they have never entirely relinquished as the "Great American Desert." Long put it this way: "The Plains are almost wholly unfit for cultivation, and, of course, uninhabitable by a people depending upon agriculture for their subsistence."[6] Even the national necessity of replacing Great American Desert imagery with imagery of the same region as a Garden of the World in the mid-nineteenth century never quite erased the stigma of these popular initial impressions.[7]

The historians Walter Prescott Webb and James Malin summarized those so-called deficiencies in major works of Great Plains history half a century ago. Interestingly, desert imagery for the American West was associated initially not with the true deserts—the Sonoran, Chihuahuan, Mojave, Great Basin, or Colorado Plateau—but with the semiarid Great Plains. As a result of the rain-shadow cast eastward by the Rockies, the Great Plains were regarded as seriously deficient in moisture; because this semiarid quality made it a grassland, it was seen as deficient in trees. Its rivers were shallow, seasonal, and deficient for navigation.[8] To Webb, these environmental deficiencies spurred pioneers to technological adaptations: Colt revolvers, barbed wire, windmills, sod houses, new land and water law, etc.

But there was yet another way the Plains came to be seen as deficient, and that one is apparently yet another story of the triumph of cultural preparation over the deep hardwiring of genetic memory. Or, at least it speaks to the complex interweaving of biology and culture in how we react to landscape forms. At issue is this: despite our evolution on the African savanna, which has given most of us a preference for open settings and distant views, most Americans now regard the Great Plains as a region that is deficient aesthetically, as well. Elsewhere I've explained this phenomenon as the result of an American nature aesthetic powerfully shaped both by ecological preparation in Northern Europe and on the Eastern Seaboard and by popular Romantic Age painters of mountain landscapes. For most Americans of the past 150 years, though, whose evolving nineteenth-century sense of America's cultural worth actually came to depend on the discovery of monumental and vertical scenery across the continent, the sere, sunlit savannas of the Plains seemed the antipode of what was grand and sublime.[9]

Significantly, it seems to me, this became especially true after the great wildlife herds, the wolves and grizzlies, even the prairie dogs, were shot, poisoned, and otherwise extirpated, and the Indians were shunted off to reservations. Quite suddenly at that critical point—which arrived between 1875 and 1915 for various parts of the grasslands—the Great Plains lost their romance and their beauty. Much, indeed, of what is often referred to as the Nostalgic Era of Western art and literature exemplified by painters of the Plains like Frederic Remington and Charles Russell was literally a mourning for that loss. And without their wild diversity of life, the Great Plains have seemed ever since incapable of triggering our Paleolithic affections.

Environmental and conservation history on the Great Plains has been much shaped by these historical impressions of deficiency ever since. By the early twentieth century, the Plains that William Dunbar and Meriwether Lewis, George Catlin and John James Audubon and many others had rhapsodized over had not only been stripped of most of their wildlife, but much of its ancient expanse was being homesteaded and fenced, and—in a word—privatized. Increasingly, even the grass complexes were being lost, plowed under to plant wheat, cotton, and sorghum. And with that ultimate transformation, the Great Plains lost almost all appeal to our deep-seated biophilic impulses and came to be seen in our own time as a precariously dry and boringly flat version of the Midwestern farm belt.[10]

No matter that the Plains actually continued to harbor scores of grassland ecological complexes or that the widespread perception of "boring flatness" is actually belied by the surprising number of island-like mountain ranges (the Wichitas, the Black Hills, the Sweetgrass Hills, the Bearspaw Mountains, the Crazy Mountains, the Big Belts and Little Belts, the Highwood Mountains, the Turtle Mountains, for example) peppering the grassy sea. Or that there were still wildlife-rich rivers, potholes, and playa lakes. Or that the Badlands of the Northern Plains and the Caprock Canyonlands along the Llano Estacado of the Southern Plains have turned out to be catalysts for artistic creativity and inspiration in our own time.[11] As geographer Bret Wallach pointed out in the journal *Landscape* a few years ago, twentieth-century Americans have not so much had our aesthetic sense filled by the Great Plains as we have come to deny that the Great Plains are aesthetic or much worthy of preservation.[12]

If history is the measure by which regional inhabitants understand their adaptation to place, then it is clear why most citizens of the Great Plains appear not much concerned about their future. Until fairly recently, the history they've been served up—including Webb's 1931 classic *The Great Plains*, supposedly still the most frequently read book about the Plains—has essentially been pioneer celebration of the conquest of nature and the subjugation of the native inhabitants. But the new Western history, a significantly more critical approach, and especially the new field of environmental history, make for rather more useful literature if the purpose of history is not just celebration, but to ground us in place and give us some perspective and context and some powers of discernment.

History used critically can be a very useful tool, but its limitations are obvious. It shares with the sciences some ability to analyze cause and effect, to explain why things have come to be the way they are—but unlike the hard sciences, history is not predictive. Its insights are a one-way street, and the signs point backward. The path of history, as Stephen Jay Gould demonstrated so nicely with his study of the Burgess Shale in *Wonderful Life*, is a layer cake of contingencies, each choice resting on hundreds and thousands of earlier choices. While it is possible to read direction from the tapestry of those choices, the ability to infer the future diminishes the farther ahead we try to look.[13] Who can say now what new matrix of circumstances, knowledge, values, or technology will affect the decisions extending our future? About the best we can say is that we have a reasonable idea where we've come from, and we're pointed somewhere, but we don't have much of an idea what is out there or where we're going.

The historical tapestry indicates that there are elements of the Great Plains environment that have been critical to the human experience on the Plains, and because we are biological, with particular needs from any ecological setting we inhabit, they are most likely are going to remain so. These are best expressed by looking at the long story of human adaptations to the Great Plains, a story that stretches back at least 11,200 years, and one that without question carries lessons for present and future inhabitants.

The story of sequential human cultures interacting with the unique set of microhabitats that make up the American Great Plains environment demonstrates some patterns that are, to say the least, interesting in terms of how we've lived in such vast and open landscapes. One pattern that lends weight to the arguments of those who believe that late twentieth-century Plains culture may have overshot environmentally is simply this: because the Plains environment is made fragile by cyclical drought, the hold human societies have had here has often been disruptive and tenuous. No part of the continent, it seems, invites such easy human environmental alteration, yet can collapse so quickly and completely under that wooing.[14]

Held against the Eastern woodlands or the Rockies, the Great Plains are ecologically a simple system, with fewer of the safeguards built into more diverse systems. It is this that makes the region deceptively fragile. Thus with few exceptions—a several-thousand-year bison hunting continuum on the Northern

Plains appears to be the major one—the big picture of human interaction with the Plains centers around a series of ecological transformations that further simplify the system and lead to ecological crashes, several carrying profound consequences for the natural/human world. In fact, human interaction with the Plains has been so transformative for so long that rather than a howling wilderness untouched by the human hand, for at least 350 human generations the Great Plains have been the environment those early Spanish accounts so honestly portrayed—an occupied landscape much shaped by human activity, especially human-set fires, as Cabeza de Vaca recounted on the very first European encounter with the Plains.[15]

The most far-reaching Great Plains ecological alteration since men and women arrived to take up residence on the grassy sweeps very likely was the first one. Except for the Antarctic and a few isolated islands in the Pacific, the Americas were one of the last human-free places in the world twenty-five thousand years ago. And all over the world, the principal result of our arrival into ecologies that had evolved without the human presence was ecological extinction and diaspora.[16] In the Americas, the Pleistocene extinctions saw thirty-two genera (and many dozens of species) of mammals disappear, evidently largely as a result of the intrusion of highly skilled human hunters from Siberia into an ecological setting that had never before experienced human hunting pressures. This extinction crash, which peaked around ten thousand years ago, not only eliminated almost all of the American-evolved megafauna, leaving only half a dozen grazers/browsers of mostly Eurasian derivation on the Plains, it also eliminated the so-called Clovis and Folsom cultures themselves. In sum, a set of human cultures (the Paleolithic peoples) who occupied the Plains for three thousand years—two hundred times longer than we have—failed when the giant animals they had hunted were gone.[17] The crux is that the bison, elk, and other specific animals we have learned to associate with the historic Plains were in fact the products of extinctions in which early humans were involved.

This ancient phase of Plains history was finished off a millennium later by another major disruption, this one primarily climatic: the great two-thousand-year drought of the Altithermal, when the climate warmed and dried subtly, yet enough in a country so delicately balanced between precipitation and evaporation as to cut plant diversity by as much as 50 percent, particularly on the Southern Plains. There, animal populations and human adaptation evidently could not keep pace with climatic change. While the Northern Plains saw a succession of bison-hunting specialists whose main lifeway existed relatively unchanged for thousands of years after the Pleistocene crash, the Southern Plains were all but abandoned during the Altithermal.[18] A sensible strategy of both animals and people to drought cycles on the Great Plains, abandonment was also the response of the Plains Villager and Plains Woodland cultures of a thousand years ago, which had pushed their riverside farm villages far out onto the Plains, then fell back to the tallgrass prairie perimeter when another significant drought struck around 1300.[19]

A more recent lesson of the fragility and even marginality of human life on the Great Plains is the ranching collapse of the 1880s. What this one seems to demonstrate is that even in a country that evolved with large herds of native grazers, which the Plains did, a policy of land privatization with commercial grazing based on exotic animals was capable of bringing on short-term cultural ruin and long-term ecological alteration. Although traditional ranching historians argue that a variety of human adaptive responses (fencing, irrigated hay pastures, winter feeding, better stock) emerged from the infamous Big Die-off of the late nineteenth century, more recent environmental historians have questioned the grazing adaptation in light of a much transformed grassland ecology on the Plains over the last century.[20] Plains ecology has been more grazing resilient than elsewhere in the West simply because for millennia the Plains have been essentially an immense pasture, home to large wandering herds. But the spread of juniper, sagebrush, and mesquite (mostly due to rancher intolerance for the natural fire ecology), the invasion of exotics (Russian thistles, or tumbleweeds, are the most glamorous, but leafy spurge is almost as dangerous), and riparian destruction and significant alteration of grass species composition all spring from the rancher adaptation.[21]

Another large pattern in the long-term environmental history of the Great Plains has been the tendency for Plains cultures to respond to the apparently limitless resources of the great grasslands with narrow economic specializations. The Paleolithic big-game hunters inhabited the richest, most diverse Great Plains environment men and women have been privileged to see, a North American version of today's Masai-Mara of East Africa. Yet so far the archeological record indicates that their response to the wetter, lusher, more diverse Plains of a hundred centuries ago was a narrow hunting specialization on the lumbering giants of the late Ice Ages. Similarly, when the Pleistocene extinction crash and a stressed climate regime produced that huge biomass of a single species, the modern bison, Plains cultures increasingly specialized in hunting bison. While this adaptation seemed to work rather well on the Northern Plains for several thousand years (and a thousand-year-plus adaptation, one would have to think, merits being called a successful one), the alteration in technology and economic outlook that accompanied the arrival of Europeans on the continent undermined it. Indeed, after the year 1700, many Indian cultures along the periphery of the Plains abandoned horticulture or gathering altogether and became bison specialists hunting increasingly for the market economy. The result of this pressure and other, external ones, was yet another great environmental crash, and the demise of still another way of life, as I detailed in chapter 3.

There are some contrasting examples provided by history on the Plains, but their lessons may be hard to accept for modern inhabitants. That long buffalo lifestyle of the Archaic cultures on the Northern Plains—peoples we know only by their archeological names: Oxbow, McKean, Pelican Lake, Besant, Avonlea, Old Woman's—offers a positive historical legacy of what must have been a carefully honed sense of place, if you will, predicated around local knowledge of the world. Another is the example of the Archaic groups of the Southern Plains, whose record for widespread inhabitation doesn't extend back so far, but who appear to have moved in after the Altithermal ended and in various cultural dress resided in the region for almost forty-five hundred years thereafter.[22]

Although their story remains one of the least understood in the archeological record, the evidence so far is that these various Archaic groups occupied the grasslands longer and more successfully than any other humans before or since. Their secret is instructive, but there was nothing magical about it. Consciously, probably as acts of policy, they kept their numbers small. They were mostly generalist hunter-gatherers whose economies were diverse, so that their effect was spread across a wide range of resources. Although they certainly did alter their environment, using broadcast fire that suppressed shrubs and brush and enlarging the areal extent of the midcontinent grass, their real genius seems to have been not so much alteration of local bioregions as adaptation to the general outlines of the changed world they had inherited from the Paleo peoples.[23] If cultural longevity and integration with intact natural ecosystems make up the essential environmental criteria for human success, then the Archaic lifeway is probably our species' most successful model on the American Plains. We ought to find out as much as we can about it, and study it well.

That all these patterns appear to continue into our own time folds us like layers into the fabric of history. Narrow economic specializations, such as the monocrop dry farming of wheat or the dripping of irrigation water onto skinned prairies revegetated with exotic sorghum and cotton, possess none of the safeguards of diversity—a bigger net beneath potential collapse—inherent in the Archaic lifestyle. And according to most gauges of Great Plains health, mounting internal pressures on the key resources of soil and water, coupled with external pressures from the market and from global climate change, keep our modern economic specializations for this part of the West on the familiar, slippery slope of Plains human history, with periodic ruin grinning up at us with bright teeth.

That the Plains remain a fragile and uneasy place to live even with modern technology has been seared into the American consciousness by the Dust Bowl of the 1930s. Triggered as so many times in the past by drought, the Dust Bowl appears in history as the logical consequence of five decades of the most massive human transformation of the Plains since the Pleistocene. During the preceding half century the Plains had been debuffaloed and dewolved. Now much of it was degrassed. With a series of dry years, first the Northern Plains, then the Southern Plains, basically collapsed in a nightmare of erosion and dust storms—seventy major ones on the Southern Plains in 1935. The ecological collapse and epic human abandonment of the Dust Bowl have become the great historical experience, equivalent to the Civil War, of the modern Great Plains.[24] Yet they are also experiences that many traditionalists have used to argue against doomsday projections for the region, as an example of how hard times acted as a natural selection process to fix more appropriate institutions in place.[25]

There are observers of the Great Plains today—not many, most of them on the periphery, it is true, and, sad to report, very few of them serving the taxpayers well from university positions on the Plains—who believe that the Great Plains are facing yet another watershed. There are worrisome doubts about the success of modern adaptations to the Plains, fears that in fact we haven't done much adapting at all, but have simply imposed patterns from other places, other visions. On the Southern and Central Plains, from Texas to Kansas and Colorado, half a century of irrigated agribusiness has increased the human carrying capacity twenty times beyond what it was when the previous inhabitants—the Comanches/Apaches/Kiowas/Cheyennes/Arapahos—owned the region. Yet the irrigation farming economy has drained the great water resource, the vast Ogallala Aquifer on which it is perched, so much that in Texas alone the wells have stopped pumping on 20 percent of the acreage irrigated in the middle 1980s. On the Southern Plains, which at the beginning of the twenty-first century are home to the most extensive population and two of the largest cities on the entire Great Plains (Lubbock and Amarillo), the aquifer's estimated remaining lifespan is twenty to fifty years, no more.[26] After that, no more water. Compared to the forty-five-hundred-year life of the Archaics, the lifespan of irrigated agriculture—approximately a century—will be a thin stratum indeed in the archeological record.

The litany of problems in the Great Plains part of the American West isn't a short one. The most obvious to the senses is that ecologically the Plains are a mere shadow of the vast grassland that throbbed with diverse and extensive wildlife right down to 125 years ago. Oklahoma Indian friends of mine say that sometimes in their Saturday-night peyote ceremonies, the reverberations of all those migrations, all those animals, all that life drama, can still be sensed vibrating in the spaces across the Plains, so recent was it all.

The eastern third of the Plains, the tallgrass prairie whose areal extent has declined 82–99 percent since 1830 as a result of agriculture, has suffered the greatest loss of natural diversity of any ecosystem on the continent. But the mixed grass beyond the 98th meridian and the shortgrass system within sight of the mountains have also been devastated by agriculture, particularly on the

Northern Plains and in the Canadian provinces, where the percentage of native grasslands remaining ranges from 28 percent (North Dakota) down to 19 percent (Saskatchewan). In Texas a mere 20 percent of the shortgrass Plains country still has native vegetation.[27] The effects of ecological dismantling are graphic and discouraging in the part of Texas I know best; in Lubbock County, where I lived for sixteen years on a ranchette in Yellow House Canyon, only 3 percent of the native grassland remains, and virtually all of that is in the canyon or along its rims.[28] The widely touted Conservation Reserve Program (CRP) that has been in place since 1985 and was hoped to restore, through federal rents, half the croplands on the Great Plains to grass, unfortunately has a mixed record. It has returned grasses to hold the sod year around and create wildlife habitat, which is a great accomplishment. But especially on the Northern Plains, much of the restoration was done with exotic grasses, particularly Asiatic crested wheatgrass, which many private owners prefer for grazing because of its early greenup. And CRP regulations have even encouraged a certain degree of breakout of remaining native prairie.[29]

The results of such stunning, wholesale ecological alteration have been predictable. It's not just the highly visible and charismatic species—the bison that have been reduced to a shadow of themselves and Plains grizzlies and lobo wolves and Eskimo curlews and Merriam's elk and Audubon bighorn sheep that have been entirely erased from the scene—but today fifty-five grassland species are threatened or endangered in the United States, with a whopping 728 Great Plains candidates considered likely or possible for those listings. Great Plains bird species, in fact, suffered a sharper population decline (25–65 percent in the 1980s) than any other single group of continental species. Maybe the most symbolic losses are the unanticipated ones. Prairie-dog colonies almost define the Great Plains in our imaginations, yet by 2000, many animals associated with dog towns, like swift foxes and black-footed ferrets, were either already on the endangered list or, like the mountain plover and the black-tailed prairie dog, were proposed for listing. Prairie dogs now occupy only 1 percent of the range they had a century ago.[30]

Those perceived aesthetic deficiencies that have colored the last century of Plains history—and, during the twentieth century, the fact of privatization—have also figured prominently in the disgraceful lack of Great Plains parks and preserves in the National Park System (NPS). In 1834, when the artist George Catlin issued the first call for "a great nation's park" in the West, it was the Great Plains he had in mind.[31] Yet in point of fact, the Great Plains remain now, at the start of the third century of national park history, the most underrepresented region in the entire NPS system.[32] Through the end of homesteading in the 1930s, the NPS found proposed Plains parks like Badlands and Theodore Roosevelt (in the Badlands of North Dakota's Little Missouri River) and Palo

Duro Canyon in Texas not sufficiently "monumental" compared to the parks of the far West.[33] Its three existing Great Plains parks at the time—Sullys Hill in Nebraska, Platt in Oklahoma, and Wind Cave in South Dakota—totaled fewer than thirty thousand acres, and the NPS did all it could to lose them. One NPS investigator reported Sullys Hill to lack even "comic" value.[34]

It was a struggle to get any significant Great Plains parks at all. In the 1920s the ecologist Victor Shelford and the Committee of Ecology of the Grasslands began to press for large Great Plains preserves based on ecology rather than monumentalism, studied eleven sites, and found four that were more than acceptable; one (spanning three quarters of a million acres in Nebraska and South Dakota) was even proposed to Congress.[35] But the NPS fumbled the ball, and it kept turning down other proposals. A million-acre park enclosing the Palo Duro system at the head of the Red River in Texas was turned down in 1931.[36] Badlands in South Dakota was first proposed as a park in 1909, and did finally become a 150,000-acre national monument in 1939. Initially the NPS thought North Dakota's Little Missouri Badlands "too barren" for a park, and local ranchers opposed the idea vociferously. But rancher opposition swirled away with the Dust Bowl out-migration, and the NPS finally got Theodore Roosevelt Memorial Park in 1947. Both of these Badlands preserves became full-fledged national parks with the Omnibus Parks Bill of 1978, and Badlands got enlarged to nearly a quarter million acres.[37] In the 1980s, Great Plains grassland preserves were augmented with Saskatchewan's creation of its Prairie National Park.[38] And here at the turn of the century, Interior Secretary Bruce Babbit has earmarked $50 million for Great Plains restoration, including a possible consolidation of the new Missouri Breaks National Monument and Charles Russell National Wildlife Refuge in Montana into a Great Plains park in honor of Lewis and Clark.

If the Great Plains as a whole remain pathetically underprotected ecologically, the Central and Southern Plains are almost entirely so. Citizens of places like Texas and Kansas are today among the most divorced of all Americans from any kind of connection with regional nature. With midheight grassland ecology represented by the existing parks on the Northern Plains, however, the pressing need in the future is for large preserves in the shortgrass high plains and the tallgrass prairies. Efforts to create a tallgrass prairie national park have stumbled along for two decades, but the Nature Conservancy's 1990s thirty-thousand-acre acquisition in northeastern Oklahoma may at last serve as a core for tallgrass protection.[39] The Sierra Club, too, has an agenda for the Great North American Prairie Ecoregion, including park or monument designation in the Kansas Flint Hills as well as in some part of the Sand Hills–Niobrara Valley region of Nebraska.[40]

In the 1950s and 1960s it was taken for granted by Plains people and those outside the region that the Great Plains' Dust Bowl had been "fixed" with tech-

Canyonlands of the High Plains of west Texas. *Photo by author.*

nology, and that like the rest of the West and the rest of the country, the arc of history for the region was onward and upward toward unlimited growth and population. Then, in the 1970s, the dust returned. And in the 1980s, as the census reports came in showing steady out-migration and falling revenues, something like a new consciousness emerged about the Great Plains. Serious reappraisal of the burden of modern Plains history really commenced in the 1980s, and surprisingly enough it was academics—like Donald Worster, Bret Wallach, and Frank and Deborah Popper—who began to call the modern agricultural experiment on the Great Plains a mistake, in the much-quoted phrase of the Poppers, "the largest, longest-running agricultural and environmental miscalculation in American history."[41]

Of course, nobody wants to hear that what their granddaddies did was a mistake, and the Poppers' statistics, maps, and prognostications have had, to say the least, something of a spin problem almost everywhere between Oklahoma and Saskatchewan. No great-granddaughter of a pioneer finds cause for rejoicing that maybe the Indian Ghost Dancers were right that the whites would disappear and the buffalo would return. The Poppers needed six deputies as bodyguards when they talked about their Buffalo Commons in McCook, Nebraska. And when Frank Popper was invited by the citizens of the liberal, Rocky Mountain city of Missoula to discuss the idea of a "Big Open" in Montana, his appearance had to be called off because of alleged threats on his life by

Montanans from the Plains. The Poppers did speak in Montana eventually—in Billings—but the situation was contentious.[42]

In 1991, in an article in *Great Plains Research*, Colorado geographer William Riebsame explored the use of evolutionary adaptation models to explain how American society might respond to environmental change on the Great Plains of the future. Riebsame contrasted adaptation (the development of characteristics better fitted to specific circumstances) to what systems theorists call "resiliency" —a system's tendency to rebound to its previous characteristics following a disturbance. Along with Donald Worster, Riebsame thinks that many of the institutional and technological changes that have resulted from modern society's response to the various Plains crises of the twentieth century have actually been resilient rather than adaptive. Contour farming, listing, center-pivot irrigation— all these have been merely technological refinements of the status quo, Riebsame argues, that have enabled Plains society actually to avoid making adaptations to the natural parameters on the Plains.[43] The technological fixes that seemed to "fix" the Dust Bowl, in other words, in reality were oriented toward adjusting to the market rather than to regional nature. What ended the Dust Bowl, truly, was the return of a rainy cycle in the 1940s.

I am one of those who expect the success of modernism's technological fixes to be fully tested on the Plains of the twenty-first century. What makes the environmental future of the Great Plains especially worrisome is, of course, the predicted global climate change, expected by most meteorological assessments and computer simulations to proceed at a rate ten times faster than humans have ever experienced (about one half to one degree Celsius per decade) during the twenty-first century. The Southern and Central Plains repeatedly have been singled out as among the continent's regions that will be hardest hit by global warming, perhaps featuring some significant and rapid advance of Chihuahuan Desert conditions northward.[44] Viewing the future of the Great Plains in the context of aquifer drawdown, rapid climate change, and some emerging awareness by Plains people that troublesome changes really are taking place, it seems fairly obvious (to some of us, at least) that the Great Plains are on the edge threshold of what could be a major paradigm shift. Whether this shift is brought on by an eventual disillusionment with the continuing pattern of cyclical ruin, or by more planned, truly adaptive strategies built around the natural systems and cycles of a restored grasslands, future society here is almost certainly going to look very different.

What form might a new adaptation to the Plains take? There are some models out there. Phil Burgess, of Denver's Center for the New West, in 1994 published a study titled *A New Vision of the Heartland: The Great Plains in Transition*, which posits what the postmodern Great Plains might look like. Burgess calls his version an "urban-archipelago" society, basically the rescue of a few Plains urban centers via high-tech economic development. In other words, "oasis" inhabitation, with the population islands supported by a service economy. Burgess has said little about the fate of the rural lands in between.[45] (For a time Wes Jackson's Kansas Land Institute looked for an answer in Jackson's search for a native grass, maybe a genetically manipulated grama grass, that could replace wheat as a commercial crop.)[46] The Poppers' Buffalo Commons and the Montana version called the Big Open, both of which envision reintroducing the native Plains fauna (including predators) on enormous public refuges, may be more romantic visions and will certainly be difficult to create, but they hold out a promise of sustainability based around the Plains' ancient ecological base. Depending on one's politics, these ideas sound like either Eden or disaster. But they're steadily winning converts.

My own suspicion is that the Great Plains, which after all were the country's Western experiment with privatization, might learn something useful from the model presented by the Mountain West. As in the Rockies, the future of the Plains West may likely hold a consolidation of the human population in a few choice locations near interstates or in favored service hub areas. While there almost certainly will be some agricultural cropping in select locations, perhaps even some small-scale rural water importation, and while private ranching (increasingly with buffalo, the grazers evolved to the country, rather than cattle, the grazers evolved to the market) would continue on a reduced scale, the great experiment that privatized virtually all of the Great Plains will, I think, be substantially reversed over the coming century. The process initiated by the Dust Bowl, with the public reacquisition of 11 million acres of ex-homesteader land, is likely to be reimplemented in some form, or perhaps many forms, before many decades pass.

The future Great Plains almost surely will feature far more publicly owned and managed commons, perhaps regionally or community-managed rather than federal lands. Some no doubt will be used principally for grazing, but even those areas—along with the river corridors and much of the rest—will feature a restoration of the natural ecological diversity that has proved capable of weathering natural change on the Plains so well. A significant part of the structure of the Plains economy will likely end up resting on the human interaction with this restored nature. There's a name for this kind of model, of course. It's called eco-tourism, the kind of economy that defines the emerging twenty-first–century Rocky Mountain West already.

The key to a nature-based sense of place on the American Great Plains thus lies in a democratizing and ecologically restorative approach to a Great Plains landscape that for a hundred years now has been ripped to pieces. As a result of their familiarity and long tenure (in the case of some tribes, extraordinarily so) on the Plains, the Indians should lead the way for us. There's evidence they already are. The founding of the Intertribal Bison Cooperative (ITBC) and its success in getting sizeable buffalo herds on more than a dozen reservations on the Plains during the 1980s and 1990s represents an extraordinary start. The Crows in Montana, who introduced buffalo as early as 1971 and now have fifteen hundred head, and the Cheyenne River Sioux of South Dakota, with a current herd of eight hundred and plans for five thousand animals on one hundred thousand acres, have the largest herds in Indian country.

Regrettably, though, the ITBC has so far failed at achieving buffalo recovery on the Southern Plains because of privatization. Unlike the tribes farther north, through allotment and land rushes the Comanches, Kiowas, Ft. Sill Apaches, and Southern Cheyennes ended up without tribal lands.[47] For the same reason, it's the Northern Plains reservations like Fort Belknap (Gros Ventre/Assiniboine) and the Blackfeet Reservation, with their willing sponsorship of the return of endangered Plains species like black-footed ferrets and swift foxes, for example, that presently offer the best evidence for a major Indian role in the restoration of the Great Plains in the twenty-first century.[48]

For the rest of the inhabitants of the modern Plains, it's perhaps going to be more difficult to accept this kind of future. It's possible that it will require another great collapse on the order of the Dust Bowl to ratchet Plains society to its next stage. With fewer national parks, preserved ecosystems, and far less public land than the Rocky Mountain West, the average turn-of-the-twenty-first-century resident of the Great Plains West now must really struggle to create a sense of place based on a world older and more diverse than Herefords, furrows, and big farm machinery. Even with the Kathleen Norrises, the William Least Heat Moon, the Ian Fraziers, and a growing host of other writers, artists, and photographers who have been trying heroically in recent years to fashion a place-centered Plains society predicated on the natural world of grasslands and prairie dogs, buffalo and badlands, the transformations of the last century make this a process that has, shall we say, a ways to go yet.

On the other hand, as Catherine and I intuited that morning watching Summer Solstice from the escarpment rim of the Llano Estacado, this time we occupy seems, for the Great Plains West especially, to possess all the characteristics of a transition. The longue durée lesson of Plains history certainly seems to show that, no matter, we'll occupy the grassland West creatively, and indefinitely. In contrast to the rest of the continent, however, history may well dictate that there be fewer of us living here a century from now—maybe three million of us instead of six million. But the hopeful possibility is that whatever our numbers, we'll occupy a more complete Great Plains than today, one sufficiently restored that all across the great sweeps of the great horizontal yellow grasslands we can once again intertwine with the natural world in some facsimile of the way its evolution—and ours—points us toward with such compelling force.

CHAPTER 10

The West That Was, and the West That Can Be

Western Restoration and the Twenty-First Century

Sunday May 5th At 9 o'Clock A.M. we set out again and proceeded on: and saw Buffalo, Elk, & deer in gangs in the Prairies, & Goats in large flocks on the Hills on both sides of the River. . . . At 12 o'Clock A.M. we saw 4 Bear on a Sand beach . . . . At one o'Clock P.M. the party halted to dine . . . at this place we saw flocks of Goats & Gangs of Buffalo in abundance on both sides of the River.

Joseph Whitehouse, Upper Missouri, 1805

For any landscape, the model natural ecosystem complex is the presettlement vegetation and associated biotic and abiotic elements.

Reed Noss, 1983

It was in his thirty-eighth year, less than a decade before death came calling in 1862, that hard there by the Atlantic shore, Thoreau fell into his habit of studying the accounts of the early settlers who'd left descriptions of New England two hundred years earlier. As I've previously mentioned, reading William Woods and others, Thoreau realized that his own experience in the Eastern woods, where so many species had already been erased by the previous colonists, meant that the New England he knew was only a partial world, a shadow of what it was supposed to be. As he further considered his situation in time, Thoreau finally decided that his forebears—the "pioneers"—were demigods who had impoverished his universe by, in effect, plucking from the heavens many of the best and brightest stars.[1]

Only a span of years later and a continent farther west, the Crow leader Plenty Coups, speaking of his great vision atop the Crazy Mountains wherein he witnessed in his mind's eye the replacement of buffalo with speckled cattle, summarized the Indian perspective on the changed universe with this cryptic

Eastern Montana's Evelyn Cameron and her husband Ewen may stand as teachers of Great Plains nature appreciation. Here Evelyn photographed her husband with pet wolves around 1900. *Photo by Evelyn Cameron, courtesy the Montana Historical Society.*

remark: "After this, nothing happened."[2] Even Western pioneers who experienced the before/after process in the American West were shocked by it all. As L. A. Huffman, the famous Montana photographer remembered it, when he first went west in the 1870s, "This Yellowstone-Big Horn country was then unpenned of wire, and unspoiled ... One looked about and said, 'This is the last West.' ... There *was* no more West after that. It was a dream and a forgetting, a chapter forever closed."[3]

From any perspective, that great world of sunlight and grass, endless forests and clear streams anyone could drink out of any time, Eden-like abundance amidst a fresh, prismatic natural shine, now seems comet-like in our experience as a people, building across a three-century brilliance to its provocative and compelling Western phase, then winking out suddenly, and apparently forever. Being born literary, Native American, or a sensitive pioneer was and is no requisite to mourning the loss of a world like that, a wilder life on a wilder continent. Most of us interested in the natural world of the American West here as the new century dawns experience the feeling that, as Thoreau put it, "I am that citizen whom I pity."[4]

Walking out my door and stepping into the quintessential West—a Rocky Mountain valley in Montana—I can identity with both Thoreau's pathos and Huffman's lament, and, even if less clearly, I can see what Plenty Coups meant when he said that after the historic period began for the whites, history ended for the Crows. In every direction as I look around at the place where I live, I'm enveloped by a classic Western landscape that, at first glance, seems very little different from what the Salish and Kutenai saw here. The mountain valley and its sagebrush foothills haven't gone anywhere, and neither—in places—have the fescues and bluebunch wheatgrasses, the cottonwood and aspen groves along the river. But like all of us alive in this time, in fact I inhabit an impoverished nature, an impoverishment made emblematic by the erasure of many of the great animals that once lived here. Both the bison herds that the early British traders describe frequenting this valley two centuries ago and the grizzly bears that loom large in the folk stories of the local Indians are entirely gone now from the Bitterroot Valley.

More than once in my mind's eye I've tried to picture this process of erasure. The buffalo here were mostly spillover, animals that drifted into the Bitterroot from the Big Hole or the sagey Idaho valleys farther south, and the herds probably were never large. But whereas they had always appeared before, two centuries ago those appearances became more and more sporadic, until the last time or two (for which we have no record) it must have seemed almost a magical thing, and the animals themselves rather like echoes of a past world than tangible beasts of the present. Too soon the foothills no longer smelled like them, and their tracks no longer appeared along the creeks. Two winters' worth of snows would have melted their droppings into the soil, and the ubiquitous magpies eventually would have hauled off all the lingering tufts of hair left snagged on the sagebrush.[5]

And the grizzlies, the lords of the Bitterroot? They went from *dramatis personae* in the Salish accounts of Bitterroot life to universal target of stockmen, hunters, and settlers. While there are more than a dozen reliable records of grizzly occurrences in the valley around me into the 1930s, no viable population of grizzlies exists here now.[6] Today the only physical evidences that either of these great animals was ever here are the oral memories of the native peoples and accounts like those of the Snake River brigades and nineteenth-century hunters. These—now—are about all that remain to testify that two centuries ago the Bitterroot Valley lay at the Rocky Mountain heart of a great, biologically diverse and rich continent many thousands of years in the making.

For most of the past two centuries the West has been growing smaller before our eyes, and not just because in our time it is possible to traverse in three days what once took three months. For the past two hundred years—and the process actually garnered its foothold four hundred years ago, when the first Spanish colonies were planted along the Rio Grande in northern New Mexico—the human inhabitants of the American West have been dismantling and simplifying the place piece by piece. Beginning 125 years ago, with the preservation of

Yellowstone and Yosemite parks, and at an accelerated pace since the creation of the Wilderness Preservation System in 1964, the visionaries of our culture have checked the dismantling process by attempting to preserve some select pieces as vignettes of what we think the West once was. The parks and wilderness systems in two ways resemble great literature, art, and music: while striving for high expression they rarely obtain it, but nonetheless they serve as cultural landmarks, tangible expressions of something good and noble in the human spirit. Wallace Stegner thought of them as a kind of "geography of hope."[7]

In his late years, Stegner despaired that the West would continue to serve, in the round, as any kind of hopeful geography for America or the world.[8] It was being assailed too rapidly, on too many fronts. His one hope, in fact, was that the West's great deficiencies, its relative aridity and finite water sources, would ultimately serve to slow the assault and place limits on Western growth. Restoring the West was not, indeed, a topic to which Stegner devoted much attention. But in fact many of our conservation visionaries, who originally thought in terms of making Western resources a commons to be shared and managed by the federal planners, and who in another phase thought of preserving parts of the West as parks and wilderness systems, have turned their attention more recently to the theme of restoring the West. In point of fact, the idea of restoration is as old as the first great book of American conservation history, George Perkins Marsh's 1864 *Man and Nature*, wherein Marsh urged that humankind become a coworker with nature in the reconstruction of the damaged fabric of the natural world.[9] If public retention and management of Western resources was the great conservation theme of the late nineteenth century, and preservation of select pieces of the West that of the twentieth, then restoration may well be that of the twenty-first.

As noble a cause as restoration is, however, the plans and processes of it easily raise as many questions as preservation ought to have, but actually has only in reflection—and rather too often after preservation's shortcomings have become apparent enough to tarnish its image. While I personally believe that restoration will be the major theme in the environmental future of the West, acknowledging some of those problems seems commonsensical. If we aim to restore the West, we ought as a first step to have clearly in our minds exactly what it is we're about. In hopes of avoiding some of the mistakes and grand controversies that have come to surround preservation, looking at the problems of restoration dead-on might not be a bad idea.

The place to begin is with the premise, because it's a doozy. What on earth was the West's "original condition," that "virgin" baseline which we so long to recreate? For a long time in American environmental history, certainly for most of the twentieth century, we've felt pretty certain that we've known the answer to that last question. Certainly John Muir, gazing awestruck at the soaring gray granite in Yosemite, was convinced he knew. Since Thoreau, and right down to the time of Aldo Leopold and Stegner, we've been sure we knew what the West was originally. The tradition, as spelled out in the enabling acts of both the National Park Service and the Wilderness Preservation System, has been to seek that baseline condition in the earliest journals of European explorers and travelers. The famous *Leopold Report* (1963) by Starker Leopold, Aldo's son, spelled it all out: American policy ought to be to return the national parks *to the condition they were in at the moment of first European contact.*[10]

So, what was the situation of the Great West at that pregnant moment? This is an image that has fascinated many of us ever since Thoreau, and three-quarters of a century ago Ernest Thompson Seton's famous *Lives of Game Animals* made the first systematic attempt to sketch it out. The Canadian cofounder of the Boy Scouts produced not merely anecdotes but actual extrapolated statistics. Some of Seton's wildlife figures for the "original" West (the bison estimate, especially) have made the journey into popular culture. All of them are truly astonishing, though. What was the West like at that "moment" of the European touch? How about 60 million to 75 million bison, 30 million to 40 million pronghorns, 10 million elk, 10 million mule deer, and 1.5–2 million sheep across the West at the time the first European explorers traversed it. Furbearers? Seton figured 60 million beavers continent wide. Big predators as a sign of a healthy continental ecology? Seton assembled accounts indicating that grizzlies had been so numerous that the rate of encounters in early America ranged from thirty to forty sightings in a single day in Northern California, to nine sightings in a month in the Big Horns in 1877, to bears every fifty yards during salmon runs in Idaho.[11]

Relying less on journal descriptions and more on ecological carrying capacities, more recent scholars (commencing with Victor Shelford) have revised many of Seton's figures, yet the imagery of a great natural garden remains. Great Plains biodiversity? Shelford speaks of an average of four hundred whitetail deer, fifty to two hundred wild turkeys, five black bears, three cougars, and one to three wolves per ten square miles along the edges of the Great Plains in 1500. And while Seton's 60 million buffalo continent wide was no doubt a considerable overstatement, I've done carrying capacity calculations for bison herds on the Great Plains indicating that in times of good grass there must have been as many as 24 million to 28 million—still an enormous number (see chap. 3).

For the Rockies and the country westward in 1492, Frederic Wagner has estimated 20–30 million large mammals aggregate, including 5–10 million bison, 10–15 million pronghorns, 1–2 million bighorn sheep, 5 million mule deer, 2 million elk.[12] And I note in my Hall and Kelson, *Mammals of North America*, that the eastern perimeter of the grizzly's range is originally believed to have stretched from Mexico's Sierra Madre Mountains across West Texas to eastern *Kansas* (!), then due north along the Mississippi to Hudson's Bay.[13] We now think grizzly populations across that vast stretch totaled more than one hundred thousand animals.[14] As for fish diversity, in addition to (now-scarce) natives like cutthroat trout in Rocky Mountain streams or paddlefish on the Missouri, from the Alaskan coast down to the Pacific Northwest and as far inland as present Idaho, salmon runs featured so many different species that it would take a full page just to list them, a living mass that surged up the rivers during spawning runs with such need and power that even those who had witnessed bison herds on the Plains were stunned to speechlessness.

This brief litany of diversity and abundance only scratches the surface, of course. Think of the hundreds of cactus and dozens of reptile species in the deserts of the Southwest. Or, as Stephen Trimble has taught us, an endemic, or two or three, left as populations migrated northward and southward in response to changing climates, on almost every mountain range in the Great Basin.[15] There were so many passenger pigeons in the annual migration flights up from Texas that some scholars believe the Cross Timbers, a four-hundred-mile-long strip of oak woods reaching almost to Kansas, was planted by their droppings and exists today as mute testimony of their presence.[16] So many black-tailed prairie dogs that a single dog town covering virtually the entire Texas Panhandle is believed to have harbored more than 400 million of them.[17] And old-growth giant trees, firs and redwoods and sequoias in the Pacific Northwest and the Sierra, parklands of fat, yellow-bellied ponderosas from the Mogollon Rim of Arizona to the Flathead Valley in Montana. And prairie, of course, the only apt metaphor for which is still today, *oceans*. Great seas of prairie lay across most of the basins and benches and foothills everywhere in the West—tallgrasses, from switchgrass to bluebunch, midheight gramas and bluestems and fescues, and High Plains carpeted with buffalo grass so velvety that Meriwether Lewis described it, as it appeared in North Dakota in the spring of 1805, as resembling nothing else quite so much as a huge "bowling green in fine order."[18]

Such was the West two hundred to four hundred years ago, now eaten away to the point that, to illustrate merely (among too many examples), today there are not 30 million bison but fewer than a quarter million, not one hundred thousand grizzlies, but in the Lower 48 fewer than one thousand, not billions of passenger pigeons, but now only stuffed ones in dioramas in Philadelphia and Reading, Pennsylvania.[19]

The West-That-Was has long gone by a worship word, holiest of the holies, for all parishioners of the environment. Aldo Leopold enshrined it throughout essays like his 1933 piece, "The Virgin Southwest," and since then we've not only made it sacred, we've deeply internalized an ideology of its meaning. Leopold, of course, called the America the earliest European explorers saw "wilderness," and we all know the rest. The Romantic Age and America's cultural need had already made the primeval continent into a metaphor for the Divine, if not actually God, then the best and freshest example of His handiwork. In seminal essays like

"Pioneers and Gullies," our teacher Leopold coupled that idea with a conviction that the presence of humans, or at least Northern European humans, could only detract from or despoil the perfection of that wilderness.[20] The emphasis on that despoliation has become the defining stream in how we think about American environmental history, in the West or anywhere on the continent.

Most of us are aware now that the word "wilderness" (along with "nature") has recently come under assault from academic deconstructionists.[21] And while I am one of those who demur to the conclusions that my fellow historian William Cronon has drawn—that, in effect, since the idea of wilderness is a cultural construction we ought to dispense with it entirely—I do feel obligated to point out (because the evidence is too overpowering to do otherwise) that wilderness is certainly the wrong word for what early America was. It's the wrong word because it's Eurocentric and it obscures more than it reveals. What it obscures, I think, is that the garden didn't have to be free of the human touch to still strike us *as* a garden.

The case here is simple and incontrovertible. At the time of contact between Europe and the Americas, at least 350 generations (probably more) of men and women had been living in and transforming North America across a time span of well over a hundred centuries. Multiply that based on the recent estimates of pre-Columbian population—either William Denevan's cautious estimate 3.8 million in today's United States and Canada, or the estimate of Henry Dobyns that the precontact Indian population north of Mexico was between 9.8 million and 12.25 million—and it means that just in the immediate five centuries prior to that magic moment of contact, the supposed "virgin" American landscape had been home to from 50 million to 200 million people. As geographer Denevan argued in an article he called "The Pristine Myth," the ecological changes that many people could produce over that full span of occupation could only mean that North America when Europeans first saw it *was in fact a managed landscape*, much of its look and ecology the product of the human presence.[22]

Managed? Exactly. Indians had cleared forests, drained swamps, engineered significant water diversions and highway systems. They had built public works in the form of earthen mounds that for two centuries were larger construction projects than anything the Europeans attempted in America. Subject to the undertow of biological human nature just like all the rest of us, they had also engaged in environmental modifications that in our Eurocentric guilt we tend to associate only with industrial societies. Their ancestors had played at least some role in the extinctions of the megafauna of the Pleistocene—and I'll say it again—ecologically the most significant transformation to occur in the West since humans have been here.[23] Indian farmers had introduced dozens of domesticated exotic plants to the West, moved several native species (as Peter Custis found on the Red River in 1806, Chickasaw plums and bois d'arc trees among them) from one location to another. And again as is clear from the early work of naturalists like Custis, the fire ecology they practiced had altered successional patterns and even floral and faunal ranges significantly.[24] There are scholars studying fire now who are beginning to argue that after humans had colonized around the world twelve thousand years ago, the total biomass of annual burning produced a greenhouse effect that helped end the Ice Ages as well as bringing the next cold cycle (the Little Ice Age of 1550–1850) to a speedy, early end.[25]

Thus the great diversity of North America that inspires us to such flights of sentiment was the creation, certainly, of eons of evolution and geology and climate, but equally of thousands of years of the Indian hand. Those thronging herds of animals and grasses were in fact a legacy of simplification—the Americas lost 73 percent of its large fauna ten thousand years ago, including most of the animals like horses and camels that actually evolved here—and the animals that did survive were mostly Eurasian adventives.[26] That the West looked and functioned ecologically the way it did five hundred years ago had everything to do with the fact that Indians managed it with fire as a great gathering and hunting continent, that tribal wars and hunting based on maximum take for least effort kept buffer zones full of animals across the West, that taboos kept some aspects of nature (beaver among the Blackfeet, for example)[27] sacrosanct, that no clear distinctions were drawn between humans and certain, human-like animals such as grizzlies, so that big predators like bears or wolves were not pursued or eradicated.[28]

Buffer zones between warring Indian tribes, for example, have been much underappreciated by ecologists and historians, who have assumed that accounts like those of Lewis and Clark's—which convey a sense of the Upper Missouri as a paradise of big animals—were describing the natural conditions of an untouched continent. Ever since Harold Hickerson's seminal paper, "The Virginia Deer and Intertribal Buffer Zones in the Upper Mississippi Valley," on the subject, however, a few biologists and historians have explored the role of buffer zones in other regions of the continent.[29] Richard White did so among the Choctaws and their neighbors in the Southeast and concluded that the Choctaws recognized full well how buffer zones worked to build up populations of deer—and how quickly they could be depleted of animals when peace came.[30] Warfare had to exist actively to keep the zones functioning.

The question is: did buffer zones work on the Plains, among animals that were less territorial than those in the woodlands? In fact, a number of Western travelers in the nineteenth century described what appeared to be buffer zones of animals thriving where the boundaries of warring Plains tribes overlapped. After two and a half years in the West, William Clark, for example, asserted as the Lewis and Clark party neared St. Louis in August 1806, "I have observed that in

The return of fire to the West, a restoration basic that replicates the Indian-managed continent, is now endorsed by most state and all the federal land-management agencies in the West, and it is increasingly used on private lands as well. *Photo by author.*

the country between the nations which are at war with each other the greatest numbers of wild animals are to be found."[31] An article in the journal *Conservation Biology* by biologists Paul Martin and Christine Szuter in fact is an in-depth exploration of the reason behind Lewis and Clark's reported difference in wildlife east and west of the Divide, and their conclusion is that it was a Blackfeet-imposed "war zone" on the upper Missouri that accounted for the huge number of animals Lewis and Clark reported from the region. And that the large and peaceful Indian population along the waters of the Columbia was responsible for the game sink the explorers found there.[32]

Buffer zones came and went with tribal movements and diplomacy, of course, but I find it striking that many of our accounts of wildlife abundance in the early West seem drawn from descriptions of what were probably functioning buffer zones. The Sweetgrass Hills of northern Montana, the Black Hills region, and the country along the Arkansas River on the Southern Plains are three areas frequently cited to illustrate America's original paradise of large animals. Yet according to W. J. Twining, the astronomer running the "medicine line" between the United States and Canada in 1878, the reason the Sweetgrass Hills had so many buffalo that "the number of animals is beyond all estimation" was that it was a "debateable ground" among several tribes.[33]

As for the Black Hills, according to Richard Dodge:

> A long-continued war between [the Sioux, Pawnees, and Crows] taught at least mutual respect; and an immense area, embracing the Black Hills and the vast plains watered by the Niobrara and White Rivers became a debateable ground into which none but war parties ever penetrated. Hunted more or less by the surrounding tribes, immense numbers of buffalo took refuge in this debateable ground, where they were comparatively unmolested, remaining there summer and winter in security. When the Pawnees were finally over-thrown and forced onto a reservation, the Sioux poured into this country, just suited to their tastes, and finding buffalo very plentiful, and a ready sale for their robes, made such a furious onslaught on the poor beasts, that in a few years, scarcely a buffalo could be found in all the wide area south of the Cheyenne and north and east of the North Platte.[34]

Farther south, as I have shown in chapter 3, it was warfare among the Osages and the Wichitas and Comanches—along with Comanche/Kiowa attempts to keep the Cheyennes and Arapahos out of the upper Red River coun-try—that produced huge numbers of bison and elk along the middle Arkansas and on the upper Llano Estacado. After the Comanches, Kiowas, Cheyennes, and Arapahos made peace in 1840, however, buffalo numbers in those regions declined rapidly. Randolph Marcy noted that in 1852, a dozen years after the peace, the Kiowas and Comanches were doing most of their hunting northward into the former buffer zone by then. And Heinrich Mollhausen in 1853 reported buffalo to be scarce in country that Edwin James of the 1820 Long Expedition had described as a kind of sanctum sanctorum of animals.[35]

Finally with respect to the long Indian impact on the ecology of the conti-nent and its implications for restoration, I think we have to face squarely that the America we rhapsodize about was populated by no more than about 10–12 mil-lion people north of Mexico at the time of contact. And that happens to be just about 3 percent of the present population of the United States and Canada.[36] Even at that relatively modest population level, however, remember that this was an ancient human presence with accumulated effects. The geographer Denevan figures it probably took the European settlers more than 250 years to produce as much ecological alteration in America as existed on the continent at the time of contact.[37]

To make the premises of restoration even more complicated, Denevan, along with geographer Martyn Bowden, who calls the pristine wilderness idea, "The grand invented tradition of American nature as a whole . . . a succession of imag-ined environments," believes that a good deal of the natural diversity and rich-ness conveyed in our literary accounts of "virgin" America actually reflects a continent that was in ecological rebound as a result of Indian depopulation from European disease.[38] In what may be only one in many such examples, bison, which were never seen in the Southeast by a DeSoto expedition that infected the numerous tribes of the region with disease, were widely reported there over the next century or more, until Indian populations rebounded, whereupon bison once again vanished from the region.[39] Several recent paleobiologists, most notably Charles Kay of Utah State University, in fact believe that populations of many ungulate species in the West remained suppressed for more than seven thousand years before being briefly released, by human disease epidemics, from the sixteenth through the early nineteenth centuries.[40] What Euro-American travelers saw, then, was not only an Indian-managed continent, but one across which the managers and primary harvesters were themselves being taken out by diseases, so that populations of hunted animals were mushrooming.

While these arguments may never persuade us to drop the term "wilderness" and substitute "Indian-Managed America" or something like "Continent Undergoing Ecological Rebound," these insights are obviously problematic for restoration ecology. Even if I ever do succeed in eradicating the Conservation Reserve Program's alien Asiatic wheatgrass and the exotic spotted knapweed that have mostly supplanted the native fescues and bluebunch on my twenty-five acres of Bitterroot Valley prairie, and even if I turned a buffalo loose on it, it may be that what I'd have restored is nothing but a snapshot of time and place—not the face of nature as pristine superorganism at all, but merely another of the kinds of landscapes that humans, and history, have produced. For example, should modern conservation biology assume that bison are native to the American South, or no? The answer seems to depend entirely on the time period it selects as "pristine baseline." Even if Lewis and Clark's description of different megafaunal populations on either side of the Divide was a consequence of Indian demographics and warfare, is that sufficient reason to conclude that in the twenty-first century a restored Buffalo Commons ought to be a feature of the Lower Yellowstone in Montana but not, say, the open, grassy Lemhi Valley just over the Divide in Idaho? Now that ecology has discovered history, environmentalists for the first time in this country are being asked to reassess exactly what it is we mean when we say we seek "to restore wilderness."[41]

As one who is drawn to the bucolic life of the country (or, as a friend puts it a bit less romantically, "to my own little gullywhack out in the sticks") and thus has confronted restoring my own little parts of the Plains and the Rockies, I've been forced to do some practical ruminating on this question. And I've decided that, personally, I simply don't care if the image of early America I hold in my head doesn't really deserve to be called wilderness, whose sanctity (I believe) comes from a Romantic conflation that "Virgin Nature" equals God. But I realize I don't speak for everyone. There is a very real philosophical debate over whether (for example) human-assisted wolf recovery in the West under the Endangered Species Act will restore an ecological situation that people value highly, or at least as highly as they would a West where wolves recolonized from Canada and Mexico all on their own. At stake here, obviously, is a crucial question: are we willing to let *ourselves* be natural, too? Or will we continue to insist on separating "cultural" cause from "natural" cause? It's just one more example, to me, why accepting ourselves as evolved animals would help us think through some critical issues of the twenty-first–century West.

Restoration has yet another human nature/biological imperative of sorts. One of the fundamentals of evolution is that all species prefer and gravitate toward the kinds of habitats they evolved in and are adapted to—and this may be why, almost unconsciously, we idealize and seek to restore a biologically rich world with large animals in it.[42] To give credit where it's due, I personally prefer the term "Indian America" when imagining that baseline West of five centuries ago. But acknowledging that what I value springs not so much from God as from evolutionary history, with humanity's hand firmly on the tiller for several thousand years, ought not diminish the luster. In ought, indeed, to make the place even more marvelous and mysterious. And to give us the chance to feel home in it.

On the other hand, all this represents a revision in thinking that we'd best be up front about, because we have to be clear about which West we're trying to restore. Is it the precontact West? The postcontact West, after the disease epidemics? A pieced-together Pleistocene West? Or (accepting that you can never go home again) the best *New* West we can imagine? I have a real soft spot, myself, for a restored West with wild mustangs in it. But that's a *very* specific snapshot in time unless you argue, taking the long view, that horses really are a native taxon. And human finger smudges are all over that snapshot: not only may we have had a hand in horse extinctions in North America, we certainly reintroduced them here.

When we do decide what West we ought to restore, we'll likely as not face (in fact we already have) plenty of questions. How can we expect to restore Indian fire ecology to an America speckled with houses and latticed with roads that act as firebreaks? How do we replicate a continent managed for hunting and gathering with a population thirty times larger? Restoring to a West that entirely lacked industrial development doesn't look likely for an industrialized society as interested as ours continues to be in metals, coal, wood, and hydroelectric power. And there are nuances like this one: returning wolves and building in livestock losses is one thing, but in the age of mass media, we're going to need to be frankly honest that a restored West with expanding populations of mountain lions—or grizzlies returned to the Bitterroot Mountains under the Endangered Species Act—is going to feature lions and grizzlies doing what they've always done, which is mostly to stay out of the way, but to nab an occasional pet and maul the odd hiker now and again. That's a natural West that is a *wilder* West than we've been used to.

True Western restoration implies not only a different mindset about American progress, but a confrontation—quite likely—with so many specific problems it's impossible even to list them. A few examples might give an inkling of the range, though. For one, what we've often destroyed so unthinkingly are not just species but entire ecosytems. Think of the black-tailed prairie dog communities on the Great Plains, which recent research indicates supported more than 150 different species.[43] We certainly don't know enough yet to be able to reassemble whole ecosystems; restoring salmon runs on the tributaries of the Columbia may be simple compared to restoring, in proper chronological sequence, a viable prairie dog/bison/pronghorn community. And as those of us who've supported bison restoration found out when the Poppers called for a Buffalo Commons, not everyone's going to be happy with our visions.[44] I still believe a Buffalo Commons may be the best use to be made of certain parts of the Great Plains, but Reed Noss of the journals *Conservation Biology* and *Wild Earth* thinks that to be viable as wild animals, large ungulates like bison, along with their carnivores, would need an area on the order of 10 million acres to support a population of a hundred thousand animals.[45] None of the great parks we created during the heyday of the preservation movement is nearly that large.

In bison restoration on the Great Plains lies the twenty-first–century restoration's equivalent of Yellowstone or the Wilderness Act. And if practical on-the-ground democracy has been one of the defining triumphs of conservation

The twenty-first century's great environmental restoration project. *Photo by author.*

and preservation, then we have to ask the question: who gets to be in charge of restoration in the twenty-first century? No question, some restorations—of wolves, of fire to the public lands, of bison to the plains, the restoration of the Western grasslands after a century of plowing and grazing abuse and brush spread, the return of salmon to the Columbia—are obviously of national interest and scope. But many restoration projects are not only local but often occur at the level of the shortest feedback loop of all, on private land.

Arresting weed spread in the West is an example of a restoration that has an enormous private-land dimension.[46] Across the West the spread of exotic weeds, one of the largely unintended aspects of European ecological imperialism, is creating biological wastelands at a dizzying rate. The spread is bad enough on the public lands, where 100 million acres in the Mountain West is already dominated by the exotic (and highly flammable) cheatgrass, and where roughly forty-six hundred acres of wildlife habitat are being lost to weeds every day.[47] But the rate of spread (and corresponding loss of natives species) on private land is if anything even more horrifying. In my home state of Montana, a 1988 study found that in three years of invasion, the European exotic spotted knapweed is capable of knocking six of twenty-one native plants in mountain meadows into the "rare" category. A knapweed-infested foothill prairie eventually will lose 95 percent of its native grasses and along with them 95 percent of its deer and elk. Knapweed spread from 4.5 million acres in Montana in 1989 to cover nearly 12 million acres in the state by the middle 1990s.[48]

Like a lot of other people living in the valleys of the Rockies, I've had to confront this mind-boggling weed spread across the Mountain West on the front lines. When the Lewis and Clark party first saw the Bitterroot Valley in the fall of 1805, one aspect of its setting they all seemed to delight in were its "pleasant plains." They remarked of these undulating prairies, extending from the east bank of the Bitterroot River up to the foothills of the rolling Sapphire Mountains, that they had little timber but were thickly covered in grasses and "wild hysop"—the Biblical term the American explorers used for sagebrush—along with some prickly pear cactus. Evidently lacking a thesaurus, Joseph Whitehouse used the term "pleasant" to describe these prairies on four different occasions.[49]

Half a century later, when the Isaac Stevens Pacific Railroad Survey confronted the Bitterroot Valley, one of its members—John Mullan—wrote thus of its upland prairies: "Bitter Root or St. Mary's valley is about eighty miles long from north to south and from four to seven miles wide ... [it] is naturally covered with luxuriant grass, supplying inexhaustible pasture, over which several thousand cattle or horses were roaming scarcely noticed in the vast area."[50]

A good deal of the ecology these nineteenth-century accounts were describing was actually the result of the firing practices of the local Salish peoples, who regularly torched the lower elevations of the Bitterroot Valley to create as much savanna—for their horse herds and for the buffalo that spilled across the Divide—as possible.[51] John Mullan also noticed one other aspect of the natural ecology of the Bitterroot that made it the absolute prize horse-raising locale of a country where Plains groups like the Assiniboines and even the Blackfeet had notorious difficulty getting their horses through the frigid, snowy winters. As Mullan put it: "It has been noted, that when the other valleys of the mountains are covered with snow, in this valley perpetual spring is found to reign during the whole of every year."[52]

These grasses that horses, Indians, and explorers all loved so well were not the buffalo grasses and blue gramas of the High Plains, but bunchgrasses of the Western mountains—Idaho fescues, rough fescue, oatgrass, and Sandburg bluegrass, needle-and-thread, and a waving, eighteen-inch-high miracle called bluebunch wheatgrass—so thickly bunched and softly waving in the mountain breezes that one early observer of the Bitterroot spoke of "rolling seas of Bunch Grass."[53] The grasses and the mild climate of the valley captivated early settlers like John Owens, who famously bought up depleted Oregon Trail stock, fattened them in the Bitterroot, and then sold them back to next year's overlanders. And these bunchgrass prairies were why there were fifty-thousand cattle and sheep in the Bitterroot Valley by the 1930s.[54]

There was just one problem. Mountain fescues and wheatgrasses had certainly been grazed by elk, even buffalo, over the centuries, but evidently they had never evolved with the kind of heavy grazing and trampling that High Plains gramas and buchloe grasses had. Many of them, especially those lovely bluebunch wheatgrasses, wilted alarmingly under commercial grazing. So all that previous history, it turns out, was prelude to what has now befallen these lovely valley prairies. For the ground-zero point of spotted knapweed colonization in the Northern Rockies (late in the nineteenth or early in the twentieth century) was here in the Bitterroot, when knapweed seeds either were accidentally introduced in alfalfa bales or (so the story goes in the valley) deliberately brought in by beekeepers to provide late-summer flowers for bees.

However it happened, by the early 1990s when I bought my little piece of the valley, twenty-five acres draped across a high draw just below the Sapphire Mountains, the knapweed takeover had become a story straight out of science fiction. For the native fescue/bluebunch prairies of the valleys of the Northern Rockies, it's now the Day of the Triffids. Here and there in small spots remote from the roads you can still find patches of ten or fifteen acres of delicate bunchgrasses—tiny little remnants of what the Salish fired and Lewis and Clark saw. But virtually everywhere else—and my little rancheria was as badly infested as any—the grasses and forbs of the native prairie are entirely overcome by a knapweed jungle secreting so much toxin that the native plants exist only in a depauperate state of strangulation and near invisibility.[55] Firing the prairies as the

Salish did? Within a couple years of homesteading my place, I did controlled burns across much of it. As fires always have in this setting, they worked beautifully to thin out the thickets of young ponderosa pines that have emerged in more recent decades of fire suppression. My Paleolithic biases against brushy thickets are strong. Like most everyone else, I much prefer more natural (that is, fire-swept) parkland settings and attempted to recreate them almost without conscious thought. For restoring the original ponderosa parkland on my place, the controlled burns worked beautifully. Unfortunately, the knapweed loved the fires, too. Or at least it emerged unfazed.

The moral of this story isn't clear to me yet, but it has something to do with how far we're willing to go in terms of restoring the natural West. I've tried a plethora of other ways to return the native prairie to my part of the Rockies, from mowing knapweed (or whacking it down with a slingblade) before it sets seed, to laboriously hand pulling it, to waiting hopefully while the state agriculture department continues its two-decades' long search for biological controls. To the spotted knapweed's credit as a competitor, its response to all of these has been a march of unrelenting takeover, what ecologists tell us is an elaborate setting of the stage for a prairie wholly replaced by a postholocaust landscape of weeds— not just knapweed but dalmation toadflax, leafy spurge, and cheatgrass. And as it all unfurls, wildlife and the ancient, evolved biodiversity of the bunchgrass prairies flee in panic or succumb to strangulation.[56]

How far will we go? For fifteen years and prairie restoration in two different settings I have refused to use chemicals. But in the spring of 1998, after first burning and mowing to stimulate the grasses, I donned rubber gloves and boots and a face-mask, strapped on a backpack sprayer, and applied an herbicide to selected parts of property. I felt horrible doing it. I felt like a character out of some futuristic film of environmental collapse. But knapweed will make you think the wasteland future has already arrived, and I don't feel horrible about watching the fescues and bluebunch emerge into the sunlight for the first time in decades.

There's one final, big-picture aspect of restoration I've not yet mentioned, but in a chapter on restoration in a book with a title like *The Natural West*, there's no avoiding it. It's simply this: you can't help but wonder whether in our efforts to restore the West we may not confront an issue that will bewilder all our inspiration and striving. I seem to have shaken hands with it already. Fifteen years ago down in the Texas Panhandle, with literary descriptions and nineteenth-century photographs in hand, I set about using fire to restore to native prairie my little twelve-acre Southern High Plains ranchette, a canyon floor then enveloped in a mesquite thicket almost impossible to walk through. Two or three good burns and the grasses were back—the little blue gramas waving about for all the world like thousands of little quarter-notes stabbed into the ground, the side-oats gramas growing heavy with seed heads that resembled rows of feathers on a lance. It was beautiful.

Then the weather started changing. The period that we associate with classic American wilderness description, 1550 to 1850, in fact was a time of climate anomaly, the Little Ice Age. It was great for grass and for big animals. But present global warming—with its tendency on the Southern Plains, at least, to produce droughts broken by almost unprecedented gullywashers, so that annual rainfall is up while soil moisture is dropping—is in fact favoring Chihuahuan Desert species.[57] So fifteen years after those first burns, I've watched the cactus and the kangaroo rats march onto ground those Indian era photos show was a waving empire of grass.

It's one small "for instance" of what we're likely to face at every level of restoration of the natural West in the twenty-first century, and a further demonstration of the one prediction that history is able to make: what happens next is likely to be awfully interesting. And as always, it will surprise us.

Discoveries of Peter Custis

Apart from his botanical collection, Peter Custis reported twenty-two discoveries and proposed seven new scientific names from his exploration of the Red River in 1806. These discoveries and names appear below with page numbers from Custis's accounts and catalogues in Flores, ed., *Jefferson & Southwestern Exploration*.

Discoveries Custis carefully described and for which he proferred scientific names: (1) *Sciurus [niger] ludovicianus* Custis (228–29), the Louisiana fox squirrel; (2) *Mus ludovicianus* Custis (273), the white-footed mouse(?), the present *Peromyscus leucopus* Raf.; (3) *Syren quadrupeda* Custis (227), the three-toed amphiuma, the present *Amphiuma tridactylum* Cuvier; (4) *Bartonia* Custis (265–66), the genus of the broomrapes, *Orobanche* L.; (5) *Bartonia bracteata* Custis (265–66), the Louisiana broomrape, *O. ludoviciana* Nutt.; (6) *Juglans petiolata* Custis (104–6, 118, 252), the pecan, *Carya illinoinensis* (Wang.) K. Koch.; and (7) *Bignonia triloba* Custis (259), the southern catalpa, *Catalpa bignoniodes* Walt.

Species Custis recognized as new and described carefully but did not offer names for: (8) "A species of *Falco*" (234), the Mississippi kite, *Ictinia mississippiensis* Wilson; (9) "A species of *Mus*" (231), the plains pocket gopher, *Geomys busarius dutcheri* Davis; (10) "Bois d'arc . . . is probably a new Genus" (260), *Maclura pomifera* (Raf.) Schneid.; (11) "A species of *Hibiscus*" (262), *Hibiscus laevis* Allioni; (12) "Cotton tree species of *Populus*" (106, 252), cottonwoods, *Populus* spp. (three types are found on the Red River); (13) "A shrub growing in great abundance every where along this River" (109), the swamp privet, *Forestiera acuminata* (Michx.).

Species he noticed or described as new or different but that were not scientifically rendered: (14) "*Corvus Corax* . . . a variety perfectly white" (268), probably the white-necked raven, *Corvus cryptoleucus* Couch; (15) "*Strix aluco* . . . rather larger than the European species" (234), probably the Florida barred owl, *Strix varia georgica* Latham; (16) "*Lepus Timidus* of a very large size" (272), probably the black-tailed jackrabbit, *Lepus californicus melanotis* Mearns.; (17) "A flying squirrel perfectly black" (274), probably *Glaucomys volans saturatus* A. H. Howell; (18) "White wolves" (274), the plains lobo wolf, *Canis lupus nubilus* Say; (19) "A species of Antilope" (275), the American pronghorn (*Antilocapra* spp.);

(20) and (21) "Two kinds of Plum" (154), in the area of their sighting, probably the Chickasaw plum (*Prunus angustifolia* Marsh.) and either the wildgoose plum (*P. munsonia* Wight and Hedr.) or the Mexican plum (*P. mexicana* Wats.); (22) "A small blue [grape] that ripens about the first of June" (154, 157), probably a muscadine, perhaps *Muscadinia rotundifolia* (Michx.). Small, but possibly a mustang or another species of *Vitis*.

Custis's unicorn was, of course, a chimera.

NOTES

Chapter 1. Nature's Children

1. See Ingerson, "Nature-Culture Dichotomy," 43–66.

2. See especially Cronon, ed., *Uncommon Ground* and "Trouble with Wilderness," 42–45.

3. Paehlke, *Environmentalism,* 249–51. Roderick Nash first developed his antibioregionalist stance in his *Wilderness and the American Mind,* 380–84. Donald Worster argues for a foundation for American environmentalism in Puritanism in "John Muir," 184–202.

4. Worster, "History as Natural History," 30–44; "Doing Environmental History," 289–307; "Seeing beyond Culture," 1132–36; and *Dust Bowl,* 94.

5. Webb, *Great Plains;* Malin, *History and Ecology.*

6. Flores, "Place," 1–18. On human adaptation and humans as part of ecosystems, see Rappaport, "Maladaptation," and in the same volume, Rappaport, "Adaptive Processes," 79–88; Whyte, "Systems as Perceived," 73–78. Also, Hardesty, "Rethinking," 11–18, and McDonnell and Pickett, eds., *Humans as Components.*

7. Merchant, *Ecological Revolutions* and "Gender," 1117–21.

8. Roszak, Gomes, and Kanner, eds., *Ecopsychology.*

9. P. Shepard, *The Others* (see chaps. 1–2 for his last account of the formative Paleolithic) and *Coming Home.*

10. Shepard's original expression of these ideas was in *Tender Carnivore.* For a more recent treatment of his on the topic, see "Post-Historic Primitivism," 40–89.

11. Oelschlaeger, *Idea of Wilderness,* 1–30.

12. In his last book published before his death, *The Others,* P. Shepard finally did grapple with causes for the end of his good, green Paleolithic; he blames the transformation of human attitudes about nature on the taming of the horse, a "nightmare of domestication" and "the instrument and symbol of the human pursuit of a yielding earth" (243–67). A very brief explanation is in Shepard, "On the Shift." Here he blames climate for the demise of big prey, forcing agriculture to develop.

  The range of other literature on Paleolithic ecological overreach is vast, but see particularly Ponting, *Green History,* 18–67. P. Martin and Wright, eds., *Pleistocene Extinctions;* and P. Martin and Klein, eds., *Quaternary Extinctions;* Diamond, "Man the Exterminator," 787–89.

13. See Flores, "Bison Ecology," 465–85.

14. See especially George Sessions, preface and introduction, "What Is Deep Ecology," ix–xxviii, 3–7. Also, Lee and Devore, eds., *Man the Hunter;* Harris and Ross, eds., *Food and Evolution;* D. McDonald, "Food Taboos," 734–48.

15. Ponting, *Green History,* asserts that hunting and gathering was "without doubt the most successful and flexible way of life adopted by humans and the one that caused the least damage to natural ecosystems" (20). Figures on female infanticide and global populations are also from this work, 18–67.

16. E. Wilson, "Conservation Ethic," 21–41. In support of my general arguments about the impact history of prestate human societies on the environment, see P. Martin, "Extinctions," 187–201. Also, Diamond, *Guns, Germs, and Steel.*

17. See L. White, "Historical Roots," 15–31, and Sessions, "Introduction," 97–103.

18. R. Nelson, *Make Prayers;* Tanner, *Bringing Home the Animals.* On the Pueblos, see Tuan, *Topophilia,* 79–83, and *Space and Place,* 91–93. Also Adams, *Origin and Development;* Clews, *Pueblo Indian Religion.* In *Now That the Buffalo's Gone,* Alvin Josephy puts it this way:

> The lessons of history permeated and guided every aspect of Pueblo lives. Their princi-
> pal teaching was the necessity of maintaining a harmonious relationship with everything
> in the world in which they lived.... The people's welfare demanded harmony between
> themselves and the entire spirit world.... Only man could upset the balance by doing
> something wrong. To avoid this, Pueblo society was tightly knit and rigidly conformist,
> ever watchful against any activity that might violate the Creator's directions.... The slight-
> est failure to conduct oneself correctly could upset the balance with nature and harm the
> whole community.(97)

19. Feit, "Ethno-Ecology," 115–25.

20. Hamilton, "Reflections," 240. See also Hames, "Game Conservation," 92–120.

21. Brightman, "Resource Depletion," 121–41. See also the seminal review article on Optimal Foraging Strategy by E. Smith, "Anthropological Applications," 628–32.

22. See chap. 3 for details. Another problem with Deep Ecology is that its attack on the Neolithic Revolution has led to a counterattack by feminists, who hold that domestication of plants and animals was primarily undertaken by women. See Sessions, "Introduction," 265–68; and Fox, "Ecology-Ecofeminism Debate," 269–89; Zimmerman, "Feminism, Deep Ecology," 21–44.

23. E. Wilson, *Sociobiology* and *On Human Nature;* Dawkins, *The Selfish Gene.*

24. Darwin, *Expression of Emotions* and *Descent of Man.*

25. E. Wilson, *On Human Nature.*

26. Kendrik, "Bridging Social Psychology," 6.

27. Cartmill, *A View to Death,* chap. 1. See also, Leakey and Lewin, *Origins Reconsidered.* The hunting hypothesis is regarded as the first truly Darwinian explanation of the origins of humanity.

28. E. Wilson, *On Human Nature,* 60–61, 20–26, 208.

29. E. Wilson, "Is Humanity Suicidal," 183–99, 184–86.

30. E. Wilson, "Culture," 107–26. The essay begins: "This is the essence of the matter as I understand it: culture is ultimately a biological product."

31. E. Wilson, *Consilience,* 127–28.

32. Ibid., 223, 129, 152, 230–32.

33. Ibid., 140–41.

34. Lopreato, "Maximization Principle," 119.

35. Thornhill and Gangestad, "Human Sexuality," 98–102; Blum, *Sex on the Brain.*

36. Dawkins, *The Selfish Gene;* Low, *Why Sex Matters;* Browne, *Divided Labors;* Kendrik, "Sexual Attraction," 5–23; Margo Wilson, "Marital Conflict," 45–62; Thornhill and Thornhill, "Psychological Pain," 73–103; Essock and McGuire, "Social and Reproductive Histories," 105–18.

Thornhill and Gangestad, in "Human Sexuality," argue that a "vast body of empirical evidence" supports ideas about women's strategies and men's, and that new work in fantasies (which show evolved preferences outside the restrictions placed on actual behavior) supports them. Another approach yielding insights into evolution and human nature has been research with very young children. See, for example, Pinker's *How the Mind Works,* chaps. 2, 3.

37. See Small, *Female Choices,* and Mace, "Why Do We," 4–5.

38. E. Wilson, *Biophilia,* and "Conservation Ethic," 31–41.

39. For my points in the text, see, especially, Kellert, "Biological Basis," 42–69, and Ulrich, "Biophilia," 73–137. Heerwagen and Orians, in "Humans, Habitats," 150–53, argue that because they are done to elicit emotional responses, landscape paintings are effective formats to test preferences. Women tend to "show a greater affinity for enclosure and protected places than do males." Sexual division of labor had much to do with selection for these preferences in early human history, with males preferring openness because of game, females preferring more vege-

tated areas likely to yield vegetables and refuge. In a study of paintings by men and women, 52 percent of females' paintings had high "refuge symbolism" compared to only 25 percent of males' paintings. No horizon was visible in 75 percent of the women's paintings. All of these essays are in Kellert and Wilson, eds., *Biophilia Hypothesis.* See also, Conniff, "Natural History."

40. Diamond, *Third Chimpanzee*, and R. Wright, *Moral Animal.* Diamond's treatment of "The Golden Age That Never Was" is particularly good; see 317–48. Also, de Waal, *Good Natured.*

41. Every first move a player makes in "Tit for Tat" is for cooperation, and after that the player makes exactly the move the opponent made the previous encounter, thus avoiding the costs of too much cooperation and getting exploited. In computer simulations, this strategy defeats every other one.

42. R. Wright, *Moral Animal*, 321–25.

43. M. Harris, *Cultural Materialism,* 119–40.

44. See Sahlins, "Return of the Event," wherein he describes event/individual history as "merely surface disturbances, foam on the great tides of history" (38–35).

45. On historical contingency see Gould, *Wonderful Life.* E. Wilson's recent appreciation of the idea is in *Consilience,* 201, 267.

46. Hesse, *Steppenwolf,* 3.

47. R. Wright, "Science."

48. See Butzer, "Environment," 572–84.

49. See Ehrlich and Ornstein, *New World.*

50. Conversation with Max Oelschlaeger, Albuquerque, N.Mex., 6 Apr. 1996.

Chapter 2. Ecology of the Red River

1. Barton, "A Discourse," 23.

2. See Malin, "Grassland, Southern" and "Grassland, Central," 82–119; Worster, "Doing Environmental History," 289–308; and Cronon, "Uses of Environmental History."

3. In the nineteenth century, botanist Edwin James, compiling the 1819–20 Long Expedition accounts (including his own) for publication, was loaned Thomas Freeman's original journal from War Department files. James's *An Account of an Expedition* preserved for us the only existing excerpts in Freeman's own hand, for James never returned the manuscript, and it apparently was lost when he had all of his papers burned at his death. (See Pammel, "Note.") Freeman's version of the journey is preserved in an abbreviated and apparently quite altered form in the official government-sponsored publication, Nicholas King's *An Account of the Red River, in Louisiana.* Fortunately, Custis's account—in the form of four narrative reports to the War Department and to his mentor, plus his natural history lists and descriptions of specimens— was not handed over to James and survived in the papers of the Jefferson administration in the National Archives, where I found them in 1982.

Until the 1980s the only work done on Jefferson's "Grand Excursion" (as the principals titled it) consisted of a pair of works by the great Borderlands and Latin American historian, Isaac Joslin Cox, done shortly after the turn of the century. Cox's *The Early Exploration of Louisiana* was a proto-Goetzmann survey of Jeffersonian Age exploration. He drew an article from it—"The Explorations of the Louisiana Frontier, 1803–1806"—where he matched some research into the pertinent letters on both Spanish and American sides with a summary of the Freeman and Custis exploration drawn from the slim King volume.

By the mid-twentieth century, Custis, particularly, had disappeared as a Western figure. He is absent from Susan Delano McKelvey's massive *Botanical Exploration of the Trans-Mississippi West, 1790–1850* and both Samuel Wood Geiser, *The Naturalists of the Frontier,* and

Harry Oberholser, *The Bird Life of Texas*, believed that scientific work in the Near Southwest began with Thomas Nuttall (1819), Edwin James (1820), and Jean Louis Berlandier even later. Then in 1967, at the urging of John Swanton (director of the Bureau of Ethnology and author of American Indian works), Conrad Morton of the U.S. National Herbarium at the Smithsonian worked up Custis's botany in "Freeman and Custis' Account of the Red River Expedition of 1806: An Overlooked Publication of Botanical Interest." Morton was poorly served by having to rely on the King volume, which unfortunately butchered Custis's natural history work.

In the early eighties, Donald Jackson's *Thomas Jefferson and the Stony Mountains* appeared with a Jeffersonian Age focus much like Cox's. The book did more with the context of the Freeman and Custis exploration than anyone had before; in the chapter devoted to the probe, Jackson made the interesting comment that Custis's science shouldn't be dismissed until it could be analyzed. My work, *Jefferson & Southwestern Exploration*, reproduces all the principal, extant documents of the expedition, including Custis's originals and Jefferson's unpublished letter of exploration instructions to Thomas Freeman, and gives the exploration its first book-length treatment.

The Red River explorers have also been fictionalized. In his *Valley Men*, Donald Jackson sends them up the Arkansas River in 1807—a trip the Jefferson administration actually planned and Freeman was taking until Congress withheld funds. In a novella titled "The River That Flowed from Nowhere," in *Horizontal Yellow*, I let the Grand Excursion into the Southwest proceed upriver for a season of exploring.

4. Jefferson to Meriwether Lewis, 16 Nov. 1803, quoted in Flores, ed., *Jefferson*, 8. Jefferson confessed to William Dunbar that he was compelled by an interest in the Red River that was both scientific and diplomatic. Jefferson to Dunbar, 25 May 1805, Thomas Jefferson Papers. Hereafter cited at TJP.

5. Numerous European explorers had operated on the Red River, but in 1806 its geography was still hazy. See Webb, Carroll, and Branda, eds., *Handbook of Texas,* 2:449–51. Its North Fork was merged with the Canadian on Pedro Vial's untitled 1787 map and with the Pecos in von Humboldt's *Carte générale.* See the copy in the University of Illinois, Urbana-Champaign, Library, reproduced in Flores, *Jefferson,* 20–21. Jefferson received a prepublication copy of Humboldt's map when the cartographer visited Washington in 1804. See Abernethy, *Burr Conspiracy,* 20. Too, a number of French traders told the administration they had ascended the river to the mountains. See esp. Jean Brevel's account in John Sibley's letter to Henry Dearborn, 10 Apr. 1805, in [Thomas Jefferson], *Message from the President.*

6. Jefferson to Dunbar, 25 May 1805, Rowland, *Life, Letters*, TJP, 175. See Freeman to Jefferson, 10 Nov. 1805, TJP.

7. The president's conviction that scientific map work on the Red River would give the United States an undisputed claim to the river is intimated in several letters, most notably one to the territorial governor in New Orleans, William C. C. Claiborne, on 26 May 1805, TJP. See also, Jefferson, "Limits and Bounds," 7–45.

8. See *Annals of Congress*, 8th Cong., 1st sess., 1, 124–26, for the Mitchill committee report. See also du Pratz, *History of Louisiana*, introduction. For Dunbar's promotion of the Red River, see Dunbar to Jefferson, 9 June 1804, Rowland, *Life, Letters*, 133–35 (quotation); John Sibley to Dunbar, 2 Apr. 1805, Rowland, *Life, Letters*, 162–74; Dunbar to Jefferson, 22 Aug. 1801, TJP, first series.

9. "Concerning Philip Nolan," 314, 308–17; *Annals of Congress*, 8th Cong., 1st sess., 1088–1103, 1104 (second quotation). Although he expressed considerable excitement over the fact that Philip Nolan had captured horses in the Southwest at "the only moment in the age of the world" when the horse could be studied scientifically in its wild state, Jefferson never met Nolan, who was killed by the Spaniards in 1801. See "Concerning Philip Nolan," 308 (footnote quotation); Loomis, "Philip Nolan's Entry," 120–32; Flores, *Jefferson*, 32–33 n. 44.

10. Sibley to Dearborn, 10 Apr. 1805, *Annals of Congress*, 9th Cong., 2d sess., 1088–1103, 1104 (quotation). For Brevel's report see *Annals of Congress*, 9th Cong., 2d sess., following Sibley's "Historical Sketches."

11. Jefferson to Freeman, 14 Apr. 1804. An unaddressed version of this predated and heretofore unpublished letter is in TJP; Freeman's addressed, personal copy is now in the Peter Force Collection (Manuscripts Division, Library of Congress); it has been published as Appendix I of Flores, *Jefferson*. The passages concerning natural history and ethnology are identical to passages on those topics in Jefferson's letter of instructions to Meriwether Lewis. Not all of the ideas came from Jefferson's mind alone; we know that a rough draft was circulated among members of the American Philosophical Society for suggestions. See Malone, *Jefferson*, 5:174–78; *The Louisiana Gazette* (New Orleans), 16 May 1811.

12. See Flores, *Jefferson,* 75–84, for details. The quotation is found in Francisco Viana to Antonio Cordero y Bustamante, 3 June 1806, Bexar Archives (Eugene C. Barker Texas History Center, The University of Texas, Austin). Wilkinson's "Reflections" is reprinted in Robertson, ed., *Louisiana, 1785–1807,* 2:325–47. Robertson mistakenly attributed the missive to Vicente Folch, the governor of West Florida. In 1914 Isaac Joslin Cox proved that the work was by Wilkinson; see Cox, "General James Wilkinson." The original of the Wilkinson work is in the Archivo de Indias, Havana, Cuba.

13. For discussions of Lewis's training, see Malone, *Jefferson*, 174–76; Cutright, *Lewis and Clark*, 19–29.

14. Hanley, *Natural History*, 39; McDermott, ed., "Western Journals," 12; Dunbar to Jefferson, 15 Oct. 1804, TJP.

15. Caspar Wistar Jr. to Moses Marshall, 20 June 1792, in D. Jackson, ed., *Letters*, 2:675; Jefferson to André Michaux, 30 Apr. 1793, D. Jackson, *Letters*, 2:669–72; Cutright, *Lewis and Clark*, 10–13; John W. Harshberger, *Botanists*, 106.

16. See Dunbar to Jefferson, 9 June 1804, quoted in Rowland, *Life, Letters,* 133–34. See also in Rowland, *Life, Letters*, Dunbar to Dearborn, 13 May 1804, 128–29; Dunbar to Jefferson, 13 May 1804, 131; Dearborn to Dunbar, 25 Mar. 1805, 150–51; and Dearborn to Dunbar, 24 May 1805, 153. On his functions for the expedition, see Dunbar to [Fre]eman Esqr. And his associates, 28 Apr. 1806, 339–40.

Raised near Elgin, Morayshire, in Scotland, Dunbar had been educated in mathematics and astronomy at universities in Glasgow and London before coming to America. "For Science, Probity, and general information," Daniel Clark told Jefferson, "[Dunbar] is the first Character in this part of the World." A. Johnson and Malone, eds., *Dictionary*, 5:507–8 (footnote quotation); DeRosier, "William Dunbar," 165–85.

17. Dunbar could not "sufficiently lament the absence of a good Naturalist particularly a botanist" from the expedition. Dunbar to Dearborn, 15 June 1804, quoted in Rowland, *Life, Letters*, 139. Hunter's career has been covered superbly in McDermott, "Western Journals." This work is the best treatment of the Ouachita probe thus far. The Dunbar-Hunter narrative, redacted by Nicholas King (as is made clear in Jefferson to Dunbar, 12 Jan. 1806, Rowland, *Life, Letters*, 188–89), is available in "Observations Made," *Annals of Congress*, 9th Cong., 2d sess., 1106–46, and also in serialized form in the *National Intelligencer and Washington Adviser* (Washington, D.C.), in the issues of 15, 27, and 31 Oct. and 10 and 12 Nov. 1806. Dunbar's rather obtuse journal of the tour may be found, although without annotation, in Rowland, *Life, Letters*, 216–320. For a variety of reasons, salary evidently the foremost, Hunter declined the Grand Excursion.

18. The letter proffering the appointment to Freeman has not survived but seems to have been mailed soon after Freeman's thought-provoking reply of 13 July 1805, to an earlier Jefferson letter concerning longitude work without a chronometer. See Freeman to Jefferson, 13 July 1805, TJP, first series. Finding a second Meriwether Lewis had not been easy; at least half a dozen

candidates had been considered and rejected before Freeman was approached. See Flores, *Jefferson*, 35–42, 46–48. The other candidates included Peter Walker, James Gillespie, Stephen Minor, Seth Pease, George Davis, and a Mr. Wiley. Details of Thomas Freeman's interesting career are only now being assembled. The most thorough treatments are in D. Jackson, *Thomas Jefferson*, 226–27, 237–38, and Flores, *Jefferson*, 48–54, 313–16. On the survey of the boundary between Florida and the United States, see "Andrew Ellicott," in D. Johnson and Malone, *Dictionary*, 6:90.

19. Constantine Samuel Rafinesque to Jefferson, 27 Nov. 1804, D. Jackson, *Letters*, 1:217–18; Jefferson to Rafinesque, 15 Dec. 1804, TJP; Rafinesque, *Florula Ludoviciana*, iv.

20. Rafinesque to Jefferson, 27 Nov. 1804, D. Jackson, *Letters*, 1:217–18. Inexplicably, Rafinesque writes in his autobiography that, although he knew Alexander Wilson had applied as "Ornithologist or Hunter" for Jefferson's expeditions, "I did not apply." See Rafinesque, "A Life," 305 (footnote quotation).

21. Rafinesque, *Florula Ludoviciana*, iii–iv.

22. Freeman to Jefferson, 25 Nov. 1805, TJP; Robert Patterson to Jefferson, 16 Dec. 1805, TJP, first series. Pendergast served as a surgeon to the New Orleans military in 1806. Seip was a friend of Alexander Wilson and a subscriber to his *American Ornithology*; Wilson held him in "very great esteem." Wilson to Dunbar, 24 June 1810, Rowland, *Life, Letters*, 205–6 (footnote quotation). Both men were interested in the expedition, but Jefferson does not seem to have considered either of them for the position.

23. Freeman to McKee, Nov. 1805, McKee Papers.

24. Jefferson's letter has not survived; the quotation is from Bartram's reply of 6 Feb. 1806 to Jefferson, TJP. This exchange is undoubtedly the source of stories, common in treatments of Bartram's life, that he was asked to go on the Lewis and Clark expedition.

25. See Wilson to Jefferson, Kingsessing, 6 Feb. 1806, in Hunter, ed., *Life and Letters*, 249–51. Bartram to Jefferson, 6 Feb. 1806, TJP. The letter from Wilson, which Bartram said was enclosed, is missing from TJP, and I doubt that Jefferson ever saw it. Wilson's early biographer, George Ord, however, castigated Jefferson for ignoring Wilson's appeal to go on a western expedition. Ord, "Biographical Sketch," 9:xxx–xxxiii. In later years, Dearborn and Jefferson were confused about this incident. Their correspondence is in D. Jackson, ed., *Journals*, 2:391–92, 393–94. Jefferson apparently was unable to recall his 1805–1806 planning of the Red River expedition; the only expedition he could remember for 1806 was the Pike expedition. Wilson's letter is quoted in D. Jackson, *Journals*, 2:389 n. 1.

A modern biographer, similarly confused, charged Wilson with "imprudence" in disclosing a state secret about Pike's military venture. See Cantwell, *Alexander Wilson*, 135. The Pike tour, however, was mounted by James Wilkinson rather than Jefferson and had not even been planned early in 1806. See Wilkinson's letter to Jefferson in D. Jackson, *Journals*, 2:390, and Dearborn's letter to Jefferson, D. Jackson, *Journals*, 2:393–94. This mistake points up the obscurity of the Red River expedition, even among its contemporaries.

26. Information on William Darlington is from an unsigned article in the American Philosophical Society *Proceedings*, 9:330–43. For Frederick Pursh, who wrote *Flora Americae Septentrionales*, see Johnson and Malone, *Dictionary*, 15:271. Sources on Custis's early life include Accomack County Deeds for 1804, 55, 59 (Ocancock Courthouse, Va.), and Nottingham, ed. and comp., *Wills*, 346 (quotation). General information on the Custis family and its connections (including details on Daniel Parke Custis, first husband of Martha Dandridge Washington) may be found in Freeman et al., *George Washington*, especially 2:278–302, and in Upshur, "Hill and Custis," 319–21.

27. Since Custis was a medical student, his specialty in natural history would have been botany. In the Manuscripts Division of the Library of Congress, according to Martin Smallwood, are a student's notes on seventeen consecutive lectures delivered by Barton in 1805, while Custis

was studying under him. These demonstrate that Custis's training was wide ranging, for Barton divided natural history into botany, zoology, geology, mineralogy, hydrography, and meteorology. His lectures covered both ancient and modern work, with particular emphasis upon classification. See Smallwood, *Natural History*, 289–93, for a discussion of Barton's program at Pennsylvania.

28. Jefferson to Dunbar, 12 Jan. 1806, TJP (also in Rowland, *Life, Letters*, 188–89). Custis's official appointment came from Secretary of War Henry Dearborn in a letter dated 14 Jan. 1806. Custis left Philadelphia for Natchez just three days later. See Dearborn to Custis, 14 Jan. 1806, Rowland, *Life, Letters*, 189–90.

29. Thomas Say, professor of natural history at the University of Pennsylvania, was the zoologist on Major Stephen H. Long's expedition to the Rocky Mountains in 1819–20. Edwin James was the botanist, geologist, and surgeon of the expedition. On the return trip the two collected natural history specimens in the Southwest, including Texas and Oklahoma, during the search for the Red River (they descended the Canadian River). See Geiser, *Naturalists*, 276, and Clark A. Elliott, *Biographical Dictionary*, 137, 228.

30. Flores, *Jefferson*, 63–67, 295–96 n. 25.

31. For a discussion of the botanical texts used by Custis, see Conrad Morton, "Account." Both botanical and zoological texts are discussed in Flores, *Jefferson*, 65–66.

Custis's references to published sources clearly demonstrate his familiarity with the three major scientific journals of his day and place: see Flores, *Jefferson*, 240–41 n. 125, for references to *Transactions of the American Philosophical Society* in Custis's natural history catalogues; see Flores, *Jefferson*, 231 n. 94, 271 n. 265, 276 n. 278, 277 n. 280, and 278 n. 285 for his references to Barton's *Philadelphia Medical and Physical Journal*; see Flores, *Jefferson*, 240–41 n. 125, for references to Mitchill's *Medical Repository*.

The texts mentioned include Jefferson, *Notes*; Bartram, *Travels*; Barton, *Fragments* and *Elements*; Marshall, *Arbustum Americanum*; Walter, *Flora Caroliniana*; du Pratz, *History of Louisiana*; Linné, *Systema Naturae* and *Systema Vegetabilium*.

32. See Jefferson to Dunbar, 25 May 1805, and Dunbar's journal entry, Rowland, *Life, Letters*, 269–70. Lewis to Jefferson, 23 Sep. 1806, D. Jackson, *Letters*, 1:320. Dunbar to Dearborn, 18 Mar. 1806, Rowland, *Life, Letters*, 232. Letters on this subject include Jefferson to Freeman, 14 Apr. 1804, TJP, and Jefferson to Dunbar, 25 May 1805, ibid., 174–77; Dunbar to Dearborn, 25 Feb. 1806, ibid., 329–30; Jefferson to Dunbar, 28 Mar. 1806, ibid., 192–93; Dunbar to Dearborn, 18 Mar. 1806, ibid., 331–33.

33. Dunbar's additions to Jefferson's exploring instructions came in a letter to "[Fre]eman Esqr. & his associates," 28 Apr. 1806, 339–40. Dunbar to Dearborn, 6 May 1806, 341; Dunbar to Dearborn, 24 June 1806, 347; Dunbar to Jefferson, 10 Nov. 1805, 187, 188; Dunbar to [Fre]eman Esqr. & his associates," 28 Apr. 1806, 339; Dunbar to Jefferson, 6 July 1805, 154; Dunbar to Dearborn, 13 July 1805, 157; Dearborn to Dunbar, 24 May 1805, 152; all in Rowland, *Life, Letters*.

34. Except where otherwise noted, all of the following details and quotations dealing with the first leg of the exploration are from Custis's first natural history report to the War Department, dated 1 June 1806, and available in manuscript in Letters Received, Unregistered Series, Records of the War Department, Record Group M221, National Archives. Hereafter called Custis, MS report, 1 June 1806. I've rendered the names of species mentioned into modern binomials. All identifications have been checked against standard references: Hall and Kelson, *Mammals*; Lowery, *Louisiana Birds*; Wright and Wright, *Handbook*; Zweifel, *American Amphibians*; Vines, *Trees, Shrubs*; Rickett, *Wild Flowers*; Correll and Johnston, *Manual*; Oberholser, *Bird Life*; Cochran and Goin, *New Field Book*.

35. Flores, *Jefferson*, 99–122.

36. Hall and Kelson, *Mammals*, 1:387. For Custis's fox squirrel, mammalogists do not cite the

published account of the exploration, [Nicholas King], *Account of the Red River*, but instead his description of it in his letter to the editor, "Observations Relative to the Geography, Natural History, &c., of the country along the Red-River, in Louisiana," *Philadelphia Journal*, vol. 2, pt. 2, 47. The fact that Custis saw only fox squirrels, which are ground-foraging parkland squirrels, is a useful bit of information on the forest ecology of the area.

37. Custis, MS report, 1 June 1806; Cochran and Goin, *New Field Book*, 125 (*Alligator mississippiensis*). See Lowery, *Louisiana Birds*, 364–65, for the scientific name of the Carolina parakeet, and pages 415–19 for the ivory-billed woodpecker.

38. Custis, MS report, 1 June 1806; Vines, *Trees, Shrubs*, 8–9 (white cedar), 13–14 (bald cypress), 127–28 (pecan), 293–94 (spicewood), 852 (swamp privet); Morton, "Account," 759 (*Juglans petiolata*). The shrub was identified as swamp privet from Custis's description in his manuscript report. See Flores, *Jefferson*, 109 n. 37.

39. Custis's account in Flores, *Jefferson*, 125; E. James, *Expedition*, pt. 4, 67. The names of the Caddo guides are provided by John Sibley, *Report*, entries for 21 Feb. and 14 Apr. 1807, 13–14, 21; Swanton, *Source Material*, 77; Freeman's account in Flores, *Jefferson*, 131, 134.

40. Custis, MS report, 1 June 1806; Freeman in Flores, *Jefferson*, 131. The best discussion of theories regarding the formation of the Great Raft is in Fisk, *Geology*, 40–42. See also Veatch, "Shreveport Area," 160–74. The date of the raft's formation comes from Clarence Webb to the author, 26 Apr. 1979.

41. Effects of the raft on the environment of the Red River Valley appear in a contemporary letter from Dr. Joseph Paxton to A. H. Sevier, 1 Aug. 1828, U.S. Congress, H. Doc. 78, 1–5, 20th Cong., 2d sess. For modern analyses, see Guardia, "Log Jams," 106–33; and Veatch, "Shreveport Area."

42. The quotation is from Freeman, from his account reproduced in Flores, *Jefferson*, 143. Great Swamp was the Caddo Indian name, according to Freeman (161). In 1806 the swamp stretched from Campti, a small French village, to just below the mouth of Twelve Mile Bayou, within the city limits of modern Shreveport. Log lining was the accepted method for measuring distances on water and river speed at this time.

43. Custis's information on the Great Raft and Great Swamp leg of the exploration, except where otherwise noted, is from his second natural history report to the War Department, dated 1 July 1806, available in manuscript in Letters Received, Unregistered Series, RG M221, National Archives. Hereafter cited as Custis, MS report, 1 July 1806. The three-lobed catalpa occurs only rarely and has never been granted subspecific designation. See Correll and Johnston, *Manual*, 1445; Morton, "Account," 459.

44. Custis, MS report, 1 July 1806. The country referred to includes the present Red River and Bossier parishes of Louisiana. The passage through the Great Swamp took the party through Big Broth Lake (as the Indians called the present Lake Bisteneau) and Bayou Badtka (as Custis rendered the name of the present Bodcau).

45. These Indians were Creek emigrants who had settled, with Caddo permission, on a high bluff of the river, in present Bossier Parish, in 1804. Led by their chief, Echean, they would soon become an important factor in the unfolding of early Red River Valley history. For their history, see Flores, "Red River Branch," 55–72.

Archaeologists in Louisiana excavated these Alabama-Coushatta sites in the mid-1980s, finding Indian-planted bois d'arc trees still living and recovering among the materials a U.S. Artillery 1st Regiment button of a type (1802–10 design) used by one of the regiments that mustered the Red River party's rank-and-file members. See McCrocklin, "Coushatta Indian Villages," 129–78.

46. Relying upon the published account of the exploration, King's *Account of the Red River*, which combined the explorers' journals into a single narrative, Smithsonian ethnologist John R.

Swanton mistakenly credited Freeman with the ethnological data that Custis had assembled. Swanton considered these data, along with the location of several ancient Red River Caddoan villages, which the explorers had fixed by celestial observation, to be extremely important contributions, since the Caddos had almost ceased to exist by the time modern scholars studied them. He reproduced material from these data verbatim in his *Source Material*, 27, 76–81. Indian Claims Commission scholars also relied heavily on the "Freeman Report," twice reproducing the map of the expedition as a key document. See Swanton, *Caddoan Indians*.

47. Hall and Kelson, *Mammals*, 2:868 (black bear), 1,010 (white-tailed deer). Among the medicinal plants noted was the saw palmetto (*Serenoa repens* [Bartr.] Small), "used by the natives to cure *Lues venera* (syphilis), in the form of decoction." Also collected as specimens (which have not survived) were "a Caddo remedy for the convulsions of children [apparently caused by parasites]," an anthelmintic that was evidently the pinkroot (*Spigelia marilandica* L.). Another was a plant used as an emetic decoction at the Alabama-Coushatta Green Corn Dance "previous to taking the Black Drink"; this plant was probably the great blue lobelia (*Lobelia siphilitica* L.), and Custis noted that "it pukes them violently immediately after drinking it." Custis, MS report, 1 July 1806. The Black Drink seems to have been made, in the Red River area, from the yaupon holly (*Ilex vomitoria* Ait.); see C. Brown, *Wildflowers*, 106. Although the purifying effects of the plant were clearly involved with the ceremony the Caddos were about to perform, we're not sure why the Indians would have used multiple emetics. Perhaps the plants had narcotic effects as well or were required by the deities. For additional information regarding yaupon holly, see Vogel, *American Indian Medicine*, 78, 175, 330–32.

48. Custis, MS report, 1 July 1806. There are, of course, no volcanoes on the headwaters of the Red River, which arises on the Llano Estacado and not in mountains. I've been unable to locate Custis's mineralogical specimens, but this one might have been carried to the Red by some previous visitor to the Capulin Volcano region of northeastern New Mexico.

49. Antoine Simon Le Page du Pratz, in the 1720s, was probably the first to collect plants in Louisiana when he "transplanted . . . above three hundred simples [*sic*], with their numbers, and a memorial, which gave a detail of their virtues." Before Custis's collection, some sixty advance specimens had been sent back from the Missouri by Lewis, and some plants collected on the Ouachita River trip had been forwarded by Dunbar to Jefferson and on to Barton. See du Pratz, *History of Louisiana*, 45 (footnote quotation). Cutright, *Lewis and Clark*, 357–58; McDermott, "Western Journals," 121–22; Dunbar to Jefferson, 16 Mar. 1805, Rowland, *Life, Letters*, 147–48; Dunbar to Muhlenberg, 12 May 1808, ibid., 198–204.

50. Custis, MS report, 1 July 1806; Hall and Kelson, *Mammals*, 1:449 (*Geomys bursarius dutcheri*).

51. For the kite's story in subsequent natural history, see my chapter, "Western Exploration," in Bolen and Flores, *Mississippi Kite*, 18–32. Also, Lowery, *Louisiana Birds*, 220–21 (Mississippi kite). Wilson's drawings of the Mississippi kite is considered to be "the most spectacular plate in the *Ornithology*, the most vivid proof of Wilson's curious ability to capture the wildness of living creatures" (Cantwell, *Alexander Wilson*, 229). The plate and accompanying descriptions (evidently rendered with no knowledge of Custis's previous description) were of a bird Wilson had wounded and kept alive during a visit to Dunbar's home in 1810. See Brewer, ed., *Ornithology*, 241–42.

Custis missed an opportunity to describe a third new species, mistaking the then undescribed Louisiana milk snake (*Lampropeltis trangulum amaura* Cope) for the eastern king snake. See K. Williams, *Systematics*.

52. Freeman in Flores, *Jefferson*, 208, 175; Custis, MS report, 1 Oct. 1806. The quotation and descriptions above and in what follows, except where indicated otherwise, are, for the last part of the journey, from Custis's third report dated 1 Oct. 1806, Letters Received, Unregistered Series,

RC M221, National Archives; hereafter cited as Custis, MS report, 1 Oct. 1806, and from Freeman's account, the most complete version of which appears in Flores, *Jefferson*. This version is the most complete reconstruction of Freeman's account that is now possible to assemble. It includes the portions of Freeman's original journal that are preserved in E. James, *Account*, 61–80, along with the material from the King redaction of the original journal, returned to first-person narrative. The original of Freeman's journal has been lost.

53. Freeman in Flores, *Jefferson*, 133, 177; Custis, natural history catalogues, ibid., 264; Vines, *Trees, Shrubs*, 22–23 (*Pinus taeda*), 44 (*Arundinaria gigantea*); Rickett, *Wild Flowers*, 2:194, 3:116 (*Frescaria virginiana*); Stephen J. Pyne, *Fire in America*, 148; and Calvin Martin, "Fire and Forest Structure," 38–42, 54.

54. Custis in Flores, *Jefferson*, 169, 170, 262; Freeman, ibid., 184–89.

The ridge is now known as Boyd Hill and is located about six miles northwest of Lewisville, in Lafayette County, Arkansas, at about 33°28' north latitude. See United States Geological Survey, Boyd Hill (Ark.) Quadrangle. It is remarkable, in light of their uprooting and transculturation, that the Oklahoma Caddos interviewed by James Mooney nearly a century later still remembered this hill and its mythological name, which Mooney rendered Cha'kani'na— "place of crying." See Swanton, *Source Material*, 25, 26 (footnote quotation), 27, 28, 79–80; Dorsey, *Traditions*, 8–9, 12, 18–19. In Dorsey's rendering of the myth, the name is translated as Moon's-Tears-on-the-Mountain.

The lower Kadohadacho village is traditionally remembered as one of the first spots occupied by Caddoan peoples on the Red (and documented as the last they abandoned). Luis de Blanc to Estevan Miró, 27 Mar. 1790, pt. 2, 316. It has never been excavated, since the area has been plowed for at least a century. Several of the ceremonial mounds were worked by Clarence B. Moore, the distinguished archaeologist of the Smithsonian Institution, in 1911. See Moore, "Aboriginal Sites," 584–619.

55. Vines, *Trees, Shrubs*, 27. Today only a few scattered immature trees remain of this magnificent stand. See Flores, "Final Journey." The appearance of this nineteenth-century juniper forest never failed to excite early travelers. "It would be difficult for a person acquainted only with upland cedars, to form a correct idea of the beauty, size, and symmetry of those that grow in the bottoms of Red River," wrote George Paxton, adding that he had not formed an adequate impression of them until actually viewing "with wonder and never-ceasing astonishment, those vast, lofty cedar groves." Paxton to Sevier, 1 Aug. 1828, H. Doc. 78, 20th Cong., 2d sess., 13. Possibly the cutting of these trees by pioneer millmen contributed to the end of the Great Raft; their durability may have contributed greatly to its longevity. For the removal of the Great Raft, see Tyson, *Red River*, 94–101, 150–53.

56. Hall and Kelson, *Mammals*, 2:1025–26 (*Bison bison bison*); Lowery, *Louisiana Birds*, 243–45 (*Falco peregrinus*). The correct name of the post is given in an unpublished paper, "The Location of Le [*sic*] Poste des Cadodoquious," by M. L. Britton. This paper is in my possession.

Using the topographical descriptions and celestial observations of the Freeman and Custis exploration, the well-known Southwestern archaeologist R. King Harris is convinced that he has successfully excavated the site of the Nassonite-upper Kadohadacho village and la Harpe's Post in a prairie about twenty miles northwest of present-day Texarkana. See Miroir et al., "Bernard de la Harpe," 113–67.

57. Custis, MS report, 1 Oct. 1806; Hall and Kelson, *Mammals*, 1:284 (*Lepus californicus melanotis*); Rickett, *Wild Flowers*, 3:406 (*Orobanche*).

Conrad V. Morton has identified Custis's broomrape as *Orobanche Ludoviciana* Nutt. The plant did not represent a new genus (and Barton evidently recognized that), although Custis's description and species name, *Bartonia bracteata*, clearly predate Nuttall's. The plant cannot now be credited to Custis, however, because *bracteata* was assigned to a European *Orobanche* in 1830.

Morton, "Account," 458–59 (footnote quotation). Custis's effort was actually the second try at naming a plant for Barton, Henry Muhlenberg having done it in 1801. In 1815, both Nuttall and Frederick Pursh likewise attempted to honor Barton with a plant name. A discussion of the confusion, without, however, knowledge of Custis's attempt, appears in Pennell, "Benjamin Smith Barton," 120–21.

58. Custis, natural history catalogues in Flores, *Jefferson*, 272, 274, 275; Hall and Kelson, *Mammals*, 2:850 (*Canis lupus nubilus*), 1002–3 (*Cervus merriami*), 1021–23 (*Antipocapra* spp.); Oberholser, *Bird Life*, 282–85, (*Meleagris gallopavo silvestris* Viellot). Custis notes that the native eastern wild turkey was in "the greatest abundance high up the river" and that the birds fed entirely on locusts (Flores, *Jefferson*, 270–71, 278).

In *Jefferson,* I argued that a rattlesnake Custis saw on this final leg of the exploration was a western species—a diamondback (278 n. 283). Alan Tennant's *Snakes of Texas* has modified that opinion. I now believe this snake was a canebrake rattler (*Crotalus horridus atricaudatus* Latrielle) and that another rattlesnake Custis had identified on the lower Red River as *Crotalus durissus* (Flores, *Jefferson*, 236) was actually a western pigmy rattler (*Sistrurus miliarius streckeri* Gloyd). See Tennant, *Snakes of Texas*, 457, 472–78, 514–15; and Wright and Wright, *Handbook*, 2:962, 965, 1058.

59. Flores, *Jefferson*, 75–83. Jefferson's instructions that the party return rather than risk confrontation can be found in Jefferson to Freeman, 14 Apr. 1804, TJP, reproduced ibid., appendix I.

From map work and personal investigation, I have identified the spot where the exploration was terminated as a bluff, known in local folklore (and on subsequent United States Geological Survey maps) as Spanish Bluff, located about two miles downriver from the intersection of Texas Highway 8 and the Red River, between New Boston, Texas, and Foreman, Arkansas. Custis's examination, then, reached the edge of the post-oak savannah. See United States Geological Survey map, Daniels Chapel (Texas)7 5' Quadrangle. The exploration reached to about 94°23'30" west longitude.

A diary kept by Indian trader Anthony Glass two summers later makes it clear that Custis was only about a week's travel from the first large herds of bison and wild mustangs and the most easterly prairie dog towns. See Flores, ed., *Journal.*

60. The preparation for war along the border is described in Flores, *Jefferson*, 281–88; Abernethy, *Burr Conspiracy*; Haggard, "Neutral Ground," 1001–128; Dearborn to Wilkinson, 8 Nov. 1806, Letters Sent, Main Series, Records of the War Department, Record Group M370, National Archives.

Because of the obscurity of the published account of the expedition, *Mus ludovicianus* was never picked up by mammalogists, and the lack of sufficient details (or an extant specimen) makes the identity of this species (or genus) unclear. It could have been the white-footed mouse, the cotton mouse, or still another species. See J. Jones, Flores, and Owen, "*Mus ludovicianus* Custis," 47.

61. Stories of unicorns were old in the Southwest. Jean Baptiste le Moyne de Bienville, governor general of Louisiana, had been told, for example, that the mythical creatures were found on the Ouachita River. Custis's inclusion of this story may have been prompted by a pair of references, in the Bénard de la Harpe journal (which had been discovered by Sibley in Natchitoches in 1805), to unicorns north of the Red. Custis's descriptions of the unicorn can be found in Flores, *Jefferson*, 276–77. La Harpe had founded his post among the Caddos in 1719 and then had traveled beyond the Ouachita Mountains into what is now central Oklahoma. Here la Harpe claims to have seen a common animal with "red hair the color and length of that of goats . . . and in the middle of the forehead a horn without branch, of a half-foot long." He believed he had confirmed Bienville's account of unicorns. R. Smith, ed. and trans., "Bénard de la Harpe," 256, 385 (footnote quotation), 534. Custis's inclusion of this unicorn description may also have been prompted by

Barton's belief that there were two types of American antelope in the West, the least known of which was to be found on the Arkansas River. See Barton, "Miscellaneous Facts," 194–95.

Two other interesting entries from the last report are a "Tyger," evidently a cougar, *Felis concolor stanleyana* Goldman (see Hall and Kelson, *Mammals*, 2:1959) but possibility a jaguar, and large numbers of whooping cranes, probably a rookery, in present southwestern Arkansas.

62. Vines, *Trees, Shrubs*, 220 (*Maclura pomifera*). Custis's completed tree list can be found in Flores, *Jefferson*, 252–60.

63. Custis to Dearborn, 1 Oct. 1806, Letters Received, Unregistered Series, RG M221, National Archives.

64. Generically, Custis's work is reliable, but his specific identifications leave much to be desired. Numerous European and tropical species appear in his lists. This problem can be traced to Barton, who wrote several times in the *Philadelphia Medican and Physical Journal* that the novel species being reported from the West by Jefferson's explorers were identical to Old World species. See Barton, "Miscellaneous Facts," 159–60, where he argues that magpies and prairie dogs in the American West were identical to Eurasian species. Donald Jackson, perusing the garbled published account of the expedition while writing *Stony Mountains*, found Custis "no match for Meriwether Lewis" as a naturalist (233). Morton was much more positive toward Custis and believed that the inadequacy of his texts was Custis's major problem. Morton, "Account," 440–41, 449, 459.

65. Correll and Johnston, *Vascular Plants*, 1208 (*Eustoma grandiflorum* [Raf.] Shinners). "The botanical specimens &c received some wet or dampness from rain on the way from Nachitosh . . ." Dunbar to Dearborn, 6 Sept. 1806, Rowland, *Life, Letters*, 348.

The Barton Herbarium is housed in the Academy of Natural Sciences, Philadelphia. The other specimen from the collection is a medicinal herb, the eastern culver's root (*Veronicastrum virginicum* [L.] Farw.). Custis's attached note describes it as having been collected "about 450 miles up the Red River, in a large prairie." Since Custis's 1 July report does not identify the specimens by name except in a handful of cases, very few of the plants in this twenty-six-item collection can now be identified. One that can be identified is *Yucca louisianensis* Trel., a new species of soapweed native to the middle Red, about which he noted, "The poor people use the root as a substitute for soap."

66. Du Pratz, *History of Louisiana*, 208–9, had mentioned that such an exchange was already taking place in Louisiana as early as the 1720s, but Custis's list of exotics (the identifications of which seem unquestionable) is the first documentation for the phenomenon west of the Mississippi. Before Custis, the only United States botanist to list European exotics was Muhlenberg, in his "Index Florae-Lancastriensis," 157–84, although Rafinesque would soon do the same in "Essay on the Exotic Plants," 330–45.

67. Correll and Johnston, *Vascular Plants*, 1405 (*Datura stramonium* L.) and 1522 (*Lobelia siphilitica* L.). See Freeman in Flores, *Jefferson*, 209–10. Freeman ignored, of course, the equally important role of increasing aridity farther west, but he was far more accurate than the next United States citizen to venture an explanation: Atwater, "Prairies and Barrens," 116–25, postulated that the plains were the remains of former lakes. The controversy over the role that Indian fires played in creating and extending the plains continues to attract scholarly attention. For particularly good discussions, see Sauer, "Grassland Climax," 16–21, and Pyne, *Fire in America*, 71–122.

68. See Rostlund, "Historic Bison," 395–407. For both earlier and later accounts of the Red River area that report very different wildlife circumstances than Custis seems to have found in 1806, see R. Smith, "Bénard de la Harpe," 75–86, 246–59, 371–85, 525–41; la Harpe traversed the Red River country in 1718–19, and Indian agent George Gray of Caddo Prairie Agency was there in the 1820s after the Indian population in the region had filled in. See Gray to Secretary of War James Barbour, 13 June 1827, in Carter, ed., *Territory of Arkansas*, 20:479–81.

69. See Worster, *Nature's Economy,* 205–18; Botkin, *Discordant Harmonies.* Also, Custis in Flores, *Jefferson*, 264; Correll and Johnston, *Vascular Plants*, 356 (*Tillandsia usneoides* [L.] L.), 791–92 (*Cassia occidentalis* L. and *C. obtusifolia* L.).

70. Barton had not included Custis's *Syren quadrupeda* when he published Custis's 1 June report, apparently because he was awaiting further details on it. The name and description did appear, of course, in the King redaction, *Account of the Red River*, 60. See Gray, "Synopsis," 9:109; Salthe, "*Amphiuma tridactylum*," 149.1–149.2.

71. It is not known how many copies of King's, *An Account of the Red River, in Louisiana*, apparently printed in the offices of the *National Intelligencer and Washington Advertiser*, were actually published, but the number must have been very small. If one were done for each member of Congress, about 175 to 200 would have been printed, but the figure may have been much smaller; only ten originals exist in libraries today. Morton, "Account," 436. Morton lists nine copies, but a tenth, at the Yale Library of Western Americana, is not on his list. The copy sent to the Library of Congress is said to have been bound to the back of King's redaction of Pike's 1805 Mississippi River account, under cover of a letter from Dearborn dated 9 Mar. 1807. Streeter, *Bibliography of Texas,* pt. 3, vol. 1, item 1040, 15, 16.

72. Samuel L. Mitchill, one of the active supporters of the tour in the House of Representatives during Jefferson's presidency, reviewed all of the other Louisiana explorations and their accounts in *The Medical Repository*. The Dunbar and Hunter account of the Ouachita was covered in 3:305–8; Pike's Mississippi River account (redacted, like the Dunbar-Hunter and Freeman-Custis accounts, by Nicholas King) in 4:376–89; Patrick Gass's journal of the Lewis and Clark expedition in 5:185–90; and the report of Pike's western expedition in 6:297–300.

C. C. Robin had spent the years 1802 through 1806 examining the flora of the Gulf Coast from Pensacola to New Orleans.

73. I am reconstructing Custis's later life from the following sources: His thesis title is from Louise Coursey, Charles Van Pelt Library, University of Pennsylvania, to Dan Flores, 25 Apr. 1979. His relationship to Barton appears in Custis to Barton, 21 May 1807 and 29 Oct. 1808, in the Barton collection and in Barnhart, "Brief Sketches," 35. His characterization is in the S. Miller Memoir. His first marriage: Notice of marriage, Dr. Peter Custis to Mary Pasteur, in Watson, *New Bern and Craven County*, 323. Custis applied for a license to marry Catherine Carthy on 16 Jan. 1818. See also, Custis Family Bible, New Bern Historical Society. His children and death: Peter Custis Will and Testament (the will lists as his children: Linnaeus, Peter, Sally, Betsey, Pennan, and Park). He made Katherine (his spelling of her name), his second wife, the executrix of his will.

74. Simpson and McAllister, "Alexander Wilson's Southern Tour," 421–76.

Chapter 3. Bison Ecology and Bison Diplomacy Redux

1. Sherow, "Geodialectic," 61–84; Dobak, "Canadian Buffalo," 33–52; Isenberg, *Destruction*; West, "Called Out People," 2–15 and *The Contested Plains*; Krech, *Ecological Indian*; Flores, "Great Contraction," 3–22.

2. Wisart, "Preface," iv.

3. For an excellent discussion of anthropology's three decades of debate over this issue, which has pitted those like Julian Steward and Marvin Harris (both materialists and universalists) against the contemporary defenders of Franz Boas (the cultural relativists) like Marshall Sahlins and Clifford Geertz, see Trigger, "Romantic Versus Rationalist," 1195–215.

4. C. Martin, *Keepers of the Game*. With scant evidence, Martin argued that the Micmacs and other Northeastern groups engaged in the fur trade with Europeans not because of universal

economic considerations but because the new disease epidemics ushered in by contact made them think that beaver and other animals had broken their spiritual pact with the native peoples.

5. See, for example, Geist, *Buffalo Nation*.

6. On this question, see in particular Dobak's "Army and the Buffalo," 197–202, and Flores's, "Review," 160–62. Richard White and Andrew Isenberg are also convinced that market forces are sufficient as an explanation for what happened to Western bison in the nineteenth century. See Isenberg, "Policy of Destruction," 247–84.

7. See Callenbach, *Bring Back the Buffalo*; Isenberg, "Return of the Bison," 179–96; and Peterson, "Bison to Blue Whales."

8. See Jacobo Loyola y Ugarte to Juan Bautista de Anza, one of the lines in which reads: " . . . use all your sagacity and efficiency, making evident to the [Comanche] Captains . . . that the animals they hunt with such effort at sustenance are not at base inexhaustible." See also, A. Thomas, ed., *Forgotten Frontiers*, 69–72, 82.

9. Alfred W. Crosby Jr., *Columbian Exchange* and *Ecological Imperialism,* detailed how the exchange of biological organisms, as well as cultural traits and artifacts, affected both Old and New Worlds. Crosby's work portended a number of significant new works. Henry Dobyns, *Historical Demography* and *Their Number Became Thinned*, revolutionized ideas of pre-Columbian population and the effects of introduced disease on it. Calvin Martin, *Keepers of the Game*, offered a controversial explanation of why some Indians participated in the fur trade. Richard White, *Roots of Dependency*, extended Third World dependency theory to North America to demonstrate how previously self-sufficient Indians became unable to feed themselves. William Cronon, *Changes in the Land*, demonstrated how American landscapes changed ecologically as a consequence of passing from Native American to Euro-American hands. And paleobiologists Paul Martin and Henry Wright Jr., eds., *Pleistocene Extinctions*, and Paul Martin and Richard Klein, eds., *Quaternary Extinctions*, reevaluate Indians' role in the Pleistocene megafaunal extinctions of nine thousand to eleven thousand years ago.

10. See R. White, "American Indians," 101–3, and "Native Americans," 179–204; Vecsey and Venables, eds., *American Indian Environments*; R. White and Cronon, "Indian-White Relations," 4:417–29; and Hughes, *American Indian Ecology*.

11. See R. White, "American Indians," and White and Cronon, "Indian-White Relations."

12. Several earlier scholars have addressed this question. William T. Hornaday, "Extermination," 480–90, 506, was one of the first authors to argue that the horse Indians overhunted bison. James Malin, George Hyde, and Preston Holder agreed with this position without offering anything beyond anecdotal evidence. See Malin, *History and Ecology*, 9, 31–54; Hyde, *Spotted Tail's Folk*, 24; Holder, *Hoe and Horse*, 111, 118. Roe, *The Buffalo*, 500–505, 655–70, and *Indian and the Horse*, 190–91, disputes their claims. The breadth and authority of Roe's books have given him priority in the field.

13. Since he utilizes long-ignored Spanish documents, here I follow Kavanagh, *Comanche Political History*, rather than Wallace and Hoebel, *Comanches*.

14. Wallace and Hoebel, *Comanches*; Shimkin, *Wind River*; Goss, "Shoshonean Ecological Model," 123–27.

15. Binnema, "Common and Contested Ground"; R. White, "Winning of the West," 319–43.

16. Kiowa origin myths set on the Northern Plains are at variance with the linguistic evidence, which ties them to the Tanoan-speakers of the Rio Grande pueblos. Scholars are coming to believe that there is a connection between the mysterious Jumano peoples of the seventeenth- and eighteenth-century New Mexico documents and the later Kiowas. See Hickerson, *The Jumanos*.

17. Brandon, *Indians*, 340.

18. Wallace, "Kiowa, Comanche and Apache Indians."

19. See Kavanagh, "Comanche," 109–28; Thurman, "Comanche Social Organization," 578–79; Gelo and Thurman, critique and response to Thurman, 551–55. For a concise statement of the earlier position that the Comanches are atypical on the plains, see Oliver, *Ecology and Cultural Continuity*, 69–80. On ethnogenesis, see Anderson, *Indian Southwest.*

20. J. McDonald, *North American Bison,* 250–63.

21. Dillehay, "Bison Population Changes," 180–96; Creel et al., "Faunal Record," 55–69.

22. For Great Plains dendrochronology see Weakly, "Record of Precipitation," 816–19; and Schulman, *Dendroclimatic Changes,* 86–88. Douglas Bamforth, *Ecology and Human Organization,* 74, uses meteorological data to argue that climate variability was exponentially greater on the Southern Plains than farther north.

23. Weakly, "Record of Precipitation," 819.

24. Le Grand Powers, comp., Thirteenth Census, vols. 6, 7. My method here has been to compile 1910 cattle, horse, and mule figures for then-existing Plains counties of Texas (119), western Oklahoma (45), New Mexico (10), those below the Arkansas River in Colorado (8), and southwestern Kansas (19). The only way the carrying capacity for a biome such as the Great Plains can be measured is through the use of the county figures. The principal problem with this technique in the past has been overgeneralization of stock numbers through reliance on state totals. It was first used by Ernest Thompson Seton, *Life Histories,* 1:259–63, and more recently by Bill Brown, "Comancheria Demography," 8–12. Range management commonly assigns cows a grazing quotient of 1.0, bulls 1.30, and horses/mules 1.25.

25. Chapman and Feldhamer, eds., *Wild Mammals,* 978, 986, 1001–1002. Greater land-use efficiency and larger herd size on native grass compared to cattle is one of the claims made by modern bison ranchers, but the editors of the above work call for more research into this question. See also, Charles Rehr, "Buffalo Population," 25–27.

26. Tom McHugh's *Time of the Buffalo,* 16–17, uses a different formula (mean potential bovine carrying capacity per acre) but arrives at similar totals, or about 30 million bison on the entire plains. Bamforth, *Ecology,* 74, 78, is reasonably convincing that because of climate variability and less nutritious grasses, population densities of Great Plains bison were lowest on the Southern Plains.

27. Based on a comparison of remembered ethnobotanies for the Shoshones (172 species) and the Comanches (67 species). See Brian Spykerman, "Shoshoni Conceptualizations," and Carlson and Jones, "Some Notes."

28. On women's loss of status see Holder, *Hoe and the Horse.* Kardiner, "Analysis," discusses the loss of Shoshonean birth-control mechanisms among Comanche women.

29. Jean Louis Berlandier, *Indians of Texas,* 119, reported five hundred adopted captives in that decade alone. Estimates on the Euro-American constituency of nineteenth-century Comanche bands approaching 75 percent are probably too high, but 30 percent may not be. On Comanche adoption and captives trade, see Rister, *Border Captives;* and Magnaghi, "Indian Slave Trader." Indian agent Thomas Fitzpatrick was adamant that Comanche raids were for children, "to keep up the numbers of the tribe," in Kardiner, "Analysis," 89.

For general recent discussions of hunter-gatherer carrying capacity see Harris and Ross, *Death, Sex, and Fertility,* 23–26; and Zubrow, *Prehistoric Carrying Capacity.*

30. David Kaplan, "Law of Cultural Dominance," 75–82, explains how this would have worked. George Hyde, *Indians of the High Plains,* 65, 70, 91, explains Apache vulnerability as a result of horticulture. Other explanations include the Spanish refusal to trade guns to the Apaches, and Comanche superiority at horse care. For less monocausal interpretations for Comanche success against the Apaches, see Rathjen, *Texas Panhandle,* 47–48.

31. "Wolf" was rendered from the Comanche language phonetically by Euro-Americans, as

"Isa," "Ysa," "Esa," or sometimes with an "-sh" second syllable. Three of the five Comanche head-men whom George Catlin painted in 1834 had names with the prefix "wolf": Ish-a-ro-yeh (Carries a Wolf), Is-sa-wah-tam-ah (Wolf Tied with Hair), and the principal headman, Ee-shah-ko-nee, which Catlin incorrectly translates as Bow and Quiver. Catlin, *Letters and Notes*, 2:67–69. Ysambanbi (Handsome Wolf) of the Yamparikas was a leading figure on the Llano Estacado in the early nineteenth century. His son was named Isaconoco. Loomis and Nasatir, eds., *Pedro Vial*, 488 n. 22a. Among the Comanche leaders treated by de Anza in the New Mexico peace of 1786 was Sabambipat (perhaps Amangual's Ysambanbi) and Ysaquebera (Long Wolf). In A. Thomas, *Forgotten Frontiers*, 325–27.

32. On Comanche trade with Anglo-Americans see Flores, ed., *Journal,* 3–33 particularly; and T. James, *Three Years,* 191–235. Kavanagh argues in "Comanche Political History" that the Comanches were among the earliest of Plains traders, and that Comanche leadership evolved in a trade/market situation. Anderson, *Indian Southwest* does the same.

33. See Kenner, *History*; and Swagerty, "Indian Trade," 4:351–74; T. Hall, *Social Change*.

34. See especially Hickerson, *The Jumanos*. Kiowa origins are also treated in Boyd, *Kiowa Voices*; and Wunder, *Kiowas*.

35. John, "Earlier Chapter," 379–97.

36. The sources are numerous. See, particularly, Benson, ed., *Pittsburgh,* 327–36.

37. Holder, *Hoe and the Horse*. Also, Medicine and Albers, *Hidden Half*, and Weist, "Plains Indian Women," 255–71.

38. Jablow, *Cheyenne*; Berthrong, *Southern Cheyennes*, 4–18.

39. Loomis and Nasatir, *Pedro Vial,* 256–58.

40. Berthrong, *Southern Cheyennes*, 19–21.

41. Osburn, "Ecological Aspects," 563–91; Berthrong, *Southern Cheyennes,* 25–26; Jablow, *Cheyenne,* 67; Lavender, *Bent's Fort*, 141–54; Phillips, *Chiefs and Challengers*, 42–43; E. Lawrence, "Old Spanish Trail."

42. Berthrong, *Southern Cheyennes,* 76, 93, discusses these intertribal buffer zones. Their function in preserving large bodies of huntable wildlife in other ecosystems has been discussed in H. Hickerson, "Virginia Deer," 43–66.

43. Dasmann, "Future Primitive," 26–31.

44. See particularly Wisart, *Fur Trade;* Ray, *Fur Trade*; and R. White, *Roots of Dependency*, 147–211.

45. Zubrow, *Prehistoric Carrying Capacity,* 8–9.

46. Chapman and Feldhamer, *Wild Mammals*, 980–83; Halloran, "Bison Productivity," 23–26; Shull and Tipton, "Effective Population," 35–41.

47. Data on the modern bison herds on the Great Plains is from the refuge managers and superintendents of the Wichita Mountains National Wildlife Refuge, Theodore Roosevelt National Park, and Wind Cave National Park. The National Bison Refuge in Montana did not respond to my inquiries. Robert Karges to Flores, 18 Mar. 1988; Robert Powell to Flores, 10 Feb., 1988; Ernest Ortega to Flores, 11 Feb. 1988.

48. See Caughley, "Ungulate Populations," 53–72, a study widely cited in wildlife ecology as evidence that starvation rather than predation is often the key to regulating natural population eruptions. The only documentary evidence I have seen for starvation of bison on the Southern Plains is an account by Charles Goodnight, who claimed to have seen "millions" of starved bison along a front twenty-five miles wide and a hundred miles long between the Concho and Brazos Rivers. This was in 1867, after bison migration patterns had been disrupted by settlements. Haley, *Charles Goodnight,* 161. I suspect a disease cause.

49. The documentary evidence from the nineteenth-century Plains assigns wolves three roles with respect to bison: as scavengers of bison killed by other agents, as cullers of weak, sick, and

old animals, and as predators of bison calves. It is the last that I believe best expresses the regulatory effect wolves would have had on Plains bison population dynamics. Documents for wolf predation on calves include Moulton, ed., *Journals,* 4:62–63; D. Jackson and Spence, eds., *John Charles Fremont,* 1:190–91; Boller, *Among the Indians,* 270–71; Audubon and Coues, eds., *Audubon,* 1:49; Hollon, ed., *William Bollaert's Texas,* 255. There are many others, including descriptions by John Kirk Townshend and J. A. Allen. Many of these are quoted in Young and Goldman, *Wolves of North America,* 1:50, 218, 224–31.

50. Spielman, "Late Prehistoric Exchange," 257–79. Bamforth, *Ecology,* argues that the availability of essential plant resources from this trade ended a nutrition "bottleneck" that allowed the build-up of much larger human populations on the Southern Plains, 8.

51. Levy, "Ecology," 18–25.

52. B. Brown, "Comancheria Demography," 10–11.

53. Thompson, "Technique," 417–24.

54. Fowler, *Journal,* 59, 61.

55. Wallace and Hoebel, *Comanches,* 31–32. I should point out that the anthropological literature tends to set Comanche population much more conservatively, most often at no more than seven thousand (see, for example, Bamforth, *Ecology,* 104–14). Figures this low ignore eyewitness accounts of localized Comanche aggregations of several thousand. I have a historian's bias in favor of the documentary evidence for estimating human populations; Plains observers computed village sizes relatively easily by counting the number of tents.

56. Berthrong, *Southern Cheyennes,* 78, 92, 107. The Kiowas and Kiowa-Apaches seem to have averaged about twenty-five hundred to three thousand in the middle quarter of the nineteenth century, and the Prairie Caddoans perhaps two thousand, shrinking to a thousand by midcentury. Gregg, "Report," 431–32, 432 n. 3.

57. Because of the toughness of the meat and the thick hides that made soft tanning difficult, Indians (and whites hunting for meat) rarely killed bison bulls. See Roe, *North American Buffalo,* 650–70, and Barsness, *Heads, Hides, and Horns,* 96–98.

58. Medin and Anderson, *Colorado Mule Deer.*

59. Whether anything like sixty thousand hunters ever worked the Southern Plains in pre-contact times is unknowable at present, but there is the intriguing statement by Coronado's chronicler, Castañeda, that there were more people on the plains in 1542 than there were living in the Rio Grande pueblos. Castañeda, "Narrative," 362. Simmons, "Pueblo-Spanish Relations," 185 (table 1) shows a seventeenth-century population in the Rio Grande pueblos then of about 30,500, down from some 60,000.

60. Berthrong, *Southern Cheyennes,* 124.

61. English traveler William Bollaert mentions that the Texas Comanches were supposed to have eaten twenty thousand mustangs in the late 1840s. Hollon, *William Bollaert's Texas,* 361. Haley, "Comanchero Trade," 157–76, describes the escalating nature of stock raids and trade to New Mexico beginning in the 1840s. So does Kenner, in *History,* 78–97, 155–200. Haley generally ascribes the situation to Comanche barbarity and Hispanic lack of respect for Lockean private property rights.

62. See Mooney, *Calendar History,* 287–95; Levy, "Ecology," 19. The trend toward fewer bison was becoming noticeable as early as 1844, two years before the 1846–57 drought set in. See Sublette Papers. In 1845 trader James Webb and his party traveled the entire route from Bent's to Missouri without killing a single bison. Webb, "Memoirs," 69.

63. According to Ewers, *Horse in Blackfoot Culture.* One interesting recent study of the environmental effects of horses on Southern Plains tribes is John Moore's, *Cheyenne Nation,* 127–75, a systematic assessment of the effects of horses on seasonal band size, camps, and resources. Another is James Sherow's, "Geodialectic," which argues for a dynamic rather than a static horse

ecology. Clyde Wilson's, "Inquiry," 355–69, is an older work demonstrating that horses were making the Southern Plains people nomadic pastoralists who hunted.

64. Dobie, *Mustangs*, 108–9. Dobie's estimate, he is quick to point out, is only a guess, but my work in the agricultural censuses indicates that it was a good guess. On horse/bovine dietary overlap see Krysl et al., "Horses and Cattle," 72–76. On dendrochonological data for a swing to a drier climate on the Plains between 1848 and 1874, see Weakly, "Tree-Ring Record," 817, 819; Stahle and Cleaveland, "Texas Drought History," 59–74; and Levy, "Ecology," 19.

65. I follow Chapman and Feldhamer, *Wild Mammals*, 991–94, who review the recent literature on bison diseases, but more especially, Witter, "Brucellosis," 280–87; Chouquette and Broughton, "Anthrax," 288–96; Thoen and Himes, "Tuberculosis," 263–74, all in Davis et al., *Infectious Diseases*. Also, Meagher and Meyer, "Origin of Brucellosis," 645–53. There is, of course, continuing debate about the effects of brucellosis on bison reproductivity, and about the transmission of the disease from bison to cattle, particularly in the Greater Yellowstone Ecosystem and at Wood Buffalo National Park in Alberta.

66. McHugh, *Time of the Buffalo*, 226–27. I make no effort to review here the literature on wolf predation, since no examples exist that can be transliterated into the bison/wolf relationship on the Great Plains. David Mech's *The Wolf* is the best scientific discussion of predation by wolves on large ungulates; see also Chapman and Feldhamer, *Wild Mammals*, 994–96, who discuss wolf predation at Wood Buffalo National Park in Alberta. Predation experts polled in a prewolf-recovery Yellowstone study estimated that once wolves learn how to prey on bison, the reintroduction of wolves to Yellowstone is likely to reduce the bison herd there between 5 percent and 20 percent. Koth, Lime, and Vlaming, "Restoring Wolves," 4–71, 4–72, and the computer simulation of possible wolf predation of Yellowstone bison on 3–31.

67. Young and Goldman, *Wolves of North America*, 2:327–33.

68. Schulman, *Dendroclimatic Data*, fig. 22; Weakly, "Tree-Ring Record," 817, 819.

69. Bamforth, "Historical Documents," 1–16, argues for much disruption by whites. On the Ciboleros see Kenner, *History*, 115–17.

70. Jablow, *Cheyenne*, 72.

71. Jablow's interpretation of the great 1840 alliance of the Southern Plains tribes has been very influential on my treatment here.

72. Levy, "Ecology," 19; Mooney, *Calendar History*, 276–346.

73. Whitfield Report. Letters between the principals at Bent's Fort make it clear that the Comanche trade in robes was Bent and St. Vrain's chief hope for economic solvency in the early 1840s. See Drips Papers, W. D. Hodgkiss to Andrew Drips, 25 Mar. 1843.

74. There are a few spotty figures for the Comanches, but records on the robe trade are at best fragmentary and frequently at odds with one another. But as an example of the volume, 199,870 bison robes arrived in New Orleans in 1828. The robe trade reached its peak in the 1840s, when eighty-five thousand to a hundred thousand cow robes a year were arriving in St. Louis from the upper Missouri and the Hudson's Bay Company trade in Canada reached some forty thousand a year. It dropped off sharply after 1847, more evidence that midcentury serves as a kind of watershed for bison in the West. See Burlingame, in "Buffalo in Trade and Commerce," 262–91; and Baker, "Buffalo Robe Trade."

75. See Ray, *Fur Trade and the Indian*, 228.

76. Berlandier, *Indians of Texas*, 84–85; Dobyns, *Their Number Became Thinned*, 15–20, lists thirteen epidemics and pandemics that would have affected the Comanches between 1750 and 1864. On the abandonment of Bent's first Arkansas River post, see Lavender, *Bent's Fort*, 338–39.

77. Ewers, "Influence of Epidemics," 106. Ewers bases his decline on an estimated early nineteenth-century Comanche population of only seven thousand. My figures would indicate a Comanche population decline of more than 90 percent.

78. Abert, *Journal*, 15–16, and "Report," 5–6.

79. The statement was that of Richard I. Dodge, *Our Wild Indians*, 286. In various forms the idea has lingered in the preserved mythologies of tribes from all over the Plains, from the Kiowas to the Lakota and the Blackfeet. For example, see J. Brown, *Animals of the Soul*. In 1881, representatives of many of the Southern Plains tribes assembled on the North Fork of the Red River for the Kiowa Sun Dance, where a Kiowa shaman, Buffalo Coming Out, called on the herds to reemerge from the ground. The Kiowas believed the bison had gone underground in "Hiding Mountain" in the Wichita Range. According to Old Lady Horse's account, "Hiding Mountain" was Mount Scott, the highest peak in the Wichitas. See Mariott and Rechlin, *Plains Indian Mythology*, 140. Buffalo Coming Out's story is in Powell, *Sweet Medicine*, 1:281–82, and Old Lady Horse, 241–42. Elliott Canonge's *Comanche Texts*, contains no mention of this idea, but is far from a complete study of Comanche mythology.

80. See Marcy, *Report*, Marcy's quadruped list, 78–81.

81. Wallace and Hoebel, *Comanches*, 32.

82. According to R. Dodge, *Plains of North America*, 155–57. See Roe, *North American Buffalo*, 440–41 for a discussion of these figures.

Chapter 4. Dreams and Beasts

1. Thoreau, *Heart of Thoreau's Journals*, 238–39.
2. D. Brown, *Grizzly in the Southwest*, 177–88; Thomas McNamee, "A Wild Bear Chase," 10.
3. See Dunlap, *Saving America's Wildlife*.
4. D. H. Lawrence, "Form and Spirit in Art."
5. P. Shepard, *The Others*, 72.
6. Murray, *Great Bear*, 6–7.
7. Hall and Kelson, *Mammals of North America*, map, 870.
8. Seton, *Lives of Game Animals*, vol. 1, pt. 1, 258–65; vol. 2, pt. 1, 21.
9. Geist, "Large Predators."
10. See particularly P. Shepard, *Sacred Paw*.
11. Moulton, *Journals*.
12. Flaherty, *Wild Animals*, 27.
13. Fowler, *Journal*, 46–49.
14. Victor, *River of the West*, 90.
15. Clark and Casey, *Tales of the Grizzly*, xiii.
16. Ibid., xviii.
17. Grumbine, *Ghost Bears*, 67.
18. Cartmill, *View to Death*, 119.
19. Roosevelt, *Hunting the Grisly*, 99, 109.
20. Mighetto, *Wild Animals*, 9–26.
21. Quoted in ibid., 9.
22. The bear was known in Wyoming as "Wab," however, Seton changed the spelling in his book to "Wahb."
23. For use of the grizzly bear and its range needs in defining the Greater Yellowstone, see the various papers in Keiter et al., eds., *Greater Yellowstone Ecosystem*.
24. Nash, *Rights of Nature*, chaps. 1, 6.
25. T. Wilkinson, "Grizzly War," 1, 10–14; U.S. Department of Interior, *Reintroduction*.
26. See J. Brown, *Animals of the Soul*.
27. For an argument contrary to my position, once again Paul Shepard's views stand out. See

his chap. 23 (304–20) in *The Others* for his articulation of why individualization of animals is a "neurotic zeal," as he puts it.

28. I am relying particularly here on an unpublished paper, Minette Johnson's "The Spiritual Significance of the Bear to the Indians of the Great Plains."

29. Rockwell, *Giving Voice,* 116–37.

30. After being federally listed as endangered in 1992, black bears are recovering in Louisiana at the beginning of the century, with an estimated 425 in the state, and bear-sighting reports from half of Louisiana's parishes. Perhaps three hundred black bears are now in the Arkansas/East Texas/SE Oklahoma/NW Louisiana region drained by the Sulphur River. Telephone interview with Paul Davision, Executive Director of the Black Bear Conservation Committee, 13 Nov. 1998.

31. See Hauser, *Wild Minds,* and Linden, *Parrot's Lament,* the most recent works in a growing literature on the similarities in human and nonhuman cognition.

Chapter 5. Place

1. Tobin, "Walter Prescott Webb," 713–29, and *Great Plains.*

2. Shannon, "Appraisal." Webb's response and the comments of Schlesinger, Wissler, Colby, and Dale are summarized on 12–27.

3. See Tobin, "Walter Prescott Webb."

4. Cronon, "Vanishing Frontier," 157–76. Howard Lamar has observed more recently that within the past decade, a survey of historians of the American West indicated that it was Webb's ideas rather than Turner's that they found most stimulating. Lamar, "Regionalism," 25.

5. Worster, "New West, True West," 23–24. Webb's assertion that the West is place rather than process is perhaps one point on which the new Western historians and traditional Western historians might agree. Even Frederick Jackson Turner, endlessly associated with the idea of frontier as process, late in his career accepted that the West actually consisted of four regions—the Southwest, Great Plains, Mountain states, and Pacific Coast. See Steiner, "Turner's Sectional Thesis," 437–66.

6. Flores, *Caprock Canyonlands* and *Horizontal Yellow.*

7. On the continuing relevance of place in America, see works like Garreau, *Nine Nations;* Hays, *Beauty, Health, and Permanence,* 36–9; J. Wright, *Rocky Mountain Divide;* Parsons, "Bioregionalism," 1–5; C. Wilkinson, *Crossing the Next Meridian.* Numerous other modern works on place are cited below.

8. For a particularly good account of the range of 1930s regionalism in the West, see Etulain, *Re-Imagining,* pt. 2, 79–139.

9. Bevis, "Region, Power, Place," 21; Worster, *Dust Bowl,* chap. 11.

10. Kevin Lynch argued in *Managing the Sense of a Region,* that Americans actually see themselves as the inhabitants of 295 different regions. See also, Wrobel and Steiner, *Many Wests.*

11. See Shields, *Places on the Margin;* Entrikin, *Betweenness of Place;* Lefebvre, *Production of Space;* Soja, *Postmodern Geographies.*

12. As reported in a trio of *USA Today* articles (21 and 27 Nov., 4 Dec. 1997).

13. Geographer David Demeritt in fact argues that environmental history's overriding conviction that places and landscape ecologies are "real" historical actors rather than "texts" is what most distinguishes it from geography. See Demeritt, "Nature of Metaphors," 163–85.

14. Limerick, "Unleashing," 72.

15. Kemmis, "Last Best Place," and Guerin-Gonzalez, "Freedom Comes from People."

16. To aridity, the causative factor in American Western history for John Wesley Powell, Webb, and Wallace Stegner, contemporary historians have added the others I mention in the text. All these are singled out to explain Western homogeneity in the articles in *Trails*. See, particularly, Limerick, "Unleashing," 70–71; West, "Longer, Grimmer," 103–11; Malone, "Beyond the Last Frontier," 139–60. Also, Emmons, "Constructed Province," and Neel, "Place of Extremes," 105–24.

17. Parsons, "Bioregionalism," 1–5; Foreman, *Confessions,* 43–50; Stephanie Mills's lecture on bioregionalism. For a good introduction to evolving bioregional thought, see the essays in Andruss et al., *Home: A Bioregional Reader*, and McGinnis et al., *Bioregionalism*.

18. Berg, "Strategies," 2.

19. Parsons, "Bioregionalism," 2, 5.

20. While Webb argued that his book was about the Great Plains, and he offered semiaridity, treelessness, and lack of topographical relief as the defining characteristics of the Plains, many readers have observed that his maps implied that virtually all of North America west of the 98th meridian belonged to the Plains province, while most of his historical examples came from Texas. See Webb, *Great Plains*, map 1, frontispiece.

21. U.S. Geological Survey, "Arid Region." I am indebted to Alex Philp for ferreting out this elusive map. See also, Worster, *Unsettled Country,* 15–16.

22. Atwood, *Physiographic Provinces*. Also, S. Jones, "Boundary Concepts," 241–55.

23. R. Bailey, *Ecoregions* and *Descriptions of Ecoregions*.

24. Montana Environmental Quality Council. On the more recent ecosystem bioregions in the Northern Rockies, see C. Wilkinson, "Yellowstone Ecosystem," in *Eagle Bird,* 162–86. On Texas bioregions, see Kingston, ed., *Texas Almanac,* 94.

25. Tuan, *Space and Place,* 4–6.

26. Webb, *Great Plains*, 85–139.

27. See the various essays in Malin's *History and Ecology*, especially "Space and History" and "Webb and Regionalism"; Berkhofer, "Space, Time, Culture," 21–30.

28. As Worster points out in "Doing Environmental History," 289–307, this has been one of three major avenues of environmental history inquiry, and one that Roderick Nash and others have made especially influential in American environmental history.

29. See Odum, "Strategy," 262–70, and *Fundamentals*. A good overview and introduction to the various systems models devised for human societies—modernization theory, dependency theory, world-systems theory—may be found in T. Hall's *Social Change,* 11–32.

30. See Winterhalder, "Concepts in Historical Ecology," 27–30.

31. Butzer, "Civilizations," 517–24. In light of James Lovelock's Gaia hypothesis, Butzer's conception has some special interest.

32. Rappaport, "Maladaptation," 69–71. In the same volume, see Whyte, "Systems as Perceived," 73–8, and Rappaport, "Normative Modes," 79–88; Hardesty, "Rethinking Cultural Adaptation," 11–18.

33. For example, Howard Lamar points out the striking differences in the Canadian and American responses to the Dust Bowl. Lamar, "Regionalism," 25–44. On North American cultural regions, see Kroeber, *Cultural and Natural Areas*; Gastil, *Culture Regions*; and Garreau, *Nine Nations*.

34. Rothman, "Environmental History," 8–9.

35. See especially Worster's three essays, "Shaky Ground," "Order and Chaos," and "Restoring a Natural Order," 142–83, wherein Worster argues hopefully (181) that ecology "will eventually come back with renewed confidence" to the older models.

36. Botkin, *Discordant Harmonies*, 62. See also, Winterhalder, "Concepts in Historical Ecology," 29–30.

37. Flores, "Bison Ecology," 465–85. What *longue durée* history implies, of course, is that bioregional historians have a sound grasp of paleontology and archaeology, as well as ecology and climate study.

38. See Ingerson, "Tracking and Testing," 43–66.

39. On human evolutionary psychology and sociobiology, see Diamond, *Third Chimpanzee*; Dawkins, *Selfish Gene*; Ackerman, *Natural History*.

   The best recent introduction to biophilia and biophobia is contained in the essays collected in Kellert and Wilson, *Biophilia Hypothesis*. For my points in the text, see, especially, Kellert's "Biological Basis," 42–69; Ulrich, "Biophilia, Biophobia," 73–137; and Heerwagen and Orians, "Humans, Habitats, and Aesthetics," 139–72. Ulrich concludes that genetic biophilias and biophobias may be 20–40 percent determinative, but probably have to be triggered by learning (125).

40. I derive the term "captured knowledge" from Gunn, "Global Climate," 86–90. For examples of this kind of approach, see the anthology, McDonnell and Pickett, eds., *Humans as Components*.

41. Riebsame, "Sustainability," 133–51.

42. Cronon has appropriated the term "second nature" to describe these culturally altered settings, but I think I would have to insist that for the last eleven thousand years, very few human societies have interacted with anything else. See Cronon's *Nature's Metropolis,* 266–67. On the human shaping of North America before the arrival of Europeans, the best general discussion I have seen is Denevan, "The Pristine Myth," 369–85.

43. See Gallagher, *Power of Place*; Flores, "Spirit of Place," 6–10.

44. Merchant, *Ecological Revolutions,* 2–3. Clive Ponting prefers the term ratcheting. See his *Green History,* 38.

45. A summary of a classic and useful comparative study of cultural values in the context of environmental choice in a bioregion (in this case Pueblos, Navajos, Mormons, Texans, and Hispanics in the Southwest) is Vogt and Roberts, "Study of Values," 25–30. On bioregional art, see the various essays in Norwood and Monk, eds., *The Desert Is No Lady*. And for an older piece that essentially denies a connection between art and place, Richardson, "Regionalism in American Painting," 261–72. On literature, Howarth, "Literature of Place," 167–73. A particularly fine collection of place literature—using state borders as its perimeters, however—is Kittredge and Smith, *Last Best Place*.

   I might note that Marvin Harris, in *Cultural Materialism*, sees values and ideologies as interesting, but secondary, explanations for cultural change in place.

46. Bioregional historians who properly seek to bring their work to life by interweaving the stories of individuals should be aware, to quote Amos Hawley, that the "basic assumption of human ecology . . . is that adaptation is a collective rather than an individual process. And that in turn commits the point of view to a macrolevel approach." Hawley, *Human Ecology,* 126.

47. Tuan, *Topophilia*, 93–112.

48. Conversation with Richard White, 9 Apr., Missoula, Montana.

49. An effective model for river-valley studies in the West, although written in social science language, is the article-length study by Wyckoff and Hansen, "Settlement, Livestock," 45–72.

50. The quotation is in Swierenga's introduction (129) to Malin's chapter titled "On the Nature of the History of Geographical Area" in *History and Ecology*, 129–43. Malin goes on in this essay to assert that "The study of the history of the western United States as a geographical area is *not* the study of 17, 20, or 22 separate *states* that lie within that area" (130). (Emphasis added.)

   I would be remiss if I did not mention that Donald Worster has described something like the history I am calling for in a 1984 essay titled "History as Natural History." It is reprinted in Worster, *Wealth of Nature*, 30–44.

Chapter 6. Islands in the Desert

1. Worster, "John Wesley Powell," 1–30.

2. Stegner, "Living Dry," 8–9.

3. Price, *Mountains and Man,* 62; Vale, "Mountains and Moisture," 141–65.

4. For examples of how we've conceptualized mountains, see Tobias, "Dialectical Dreaming," 183–200.

5. See the special issue of *Human Ecology* edited by Stephen Brush on mountain cultures worldwide, vol. 4 (Apr. 1976), along with his "Introduction," 125–33.

6. Price, *Mountains and Man,* 57–125; Goldstein and Messerschmidt, "Significance of Latitudinality," 117–34.

7. McKelvey, *Botanical Exploration,* 205–49; LaMarche and Mooney, "Altithermal Timberline," 980–82.

8. Merriam, *Life-Zones.*

9. J. Brown, "Mammals on Mountaintops," 467–78; J. Brown and Gibson, *Biogeography*; MacArthur, *Island Biogeography*.

10. Trimble, *Sagebrush Ocean,* 51. See also, Daubenmire, "Vegetational Zonation," 325–93.

11. Daubenmire, "Vegetational Zonation," 325–93.

12. See chapter 10 for details.

13. Paleolithic and Archaic mountain traditions are a special focus of Stanford and Day, eds., *Ice-Age Hunters.* See, particularly, Frison, "Foothills-Mountains," 323–42; Benedict, "Paleoindian Subsistence Strategies," 349–59, and "Paleoindian Archeology," 359–73. See also, Husted, "Prehistoric Occupation"; and Frison and Bonnichsen, "Pleistocene-Holocene Transition." Clark Wissler prepared the first Indian "culture area" maps for North America; since Alfred Kroeber reworked them in the 1930s, they have undergone very little revision. See Kroeber, *Cultural and Natural Areas*.

14. On the Mountain Crows, see Loendorf, "Remnants," 22–29. For a history of the interior "Flatheads" or Salish, one of the most pure mountain-dwelling Indian groups in historic times, occupying the Bitterroot Valley of western Montana, see Fahey, *Flathead Indians*, and Peterson, *Sacred Encounters.* On the lumping of historic mountain-living tribes like these (along with the Nez Perce, Kutenais, and Utes) into the Great Plains Culture Area, see Gunther, "Westward Movement," 174–80, and for more recent work, Osburn, "Ecological Aspects," 563–91, and Spence, *Dispossessing the Wilderness*.

15. See Gastil, *Culture Regions*, which locates three culture areas within the modern Rockies: Southwestern, Mormon, and Rocky Mountain. Garreau's *Nine Nations* refers to the Mountain West as a single region but calls it the "Empty Quarter."

16. For evidence that scholars failed to recognize a Rocky Mountain regional literature, see Howarth, "Literature of Place," 167–73. More recently, however, see the Western Literature Association, *Updating the Literary West*, frontispiece map, "The Literary West," and sec. 6, "The Rocky Mountains," 731–862. Northern New Mexico is included here in the Southwest section, however.

17. See Tobias, *Mountain People*, divided into six parts: the United States, South America, Africa and the Middle East, Central Asia, East Asia, Southeast Asia.

18. On valley importance, see Tuan, *Topophilia,* 122.

19. Lao Tzu, *Tao Te Ching*, 2.

20. Capra, *Tao of Physics*, 106.

21. Schama, *Landscape and Memory*, 407–8.

22. Van Slyke, *Yangtze,* 176–80.

23. Tyler, "Japanese Mountains," 153–55.

24. See Scully, *Greek Sacred Architecture*, who describes the religious role of mountains thus:

> First an enclosed valley of varying size in which the palace is set . . . second, a gently mounded or conical hill, on axis with the palace to north or south; and lastly a higher, double-peaked or cleft mountain some distance beyond the hill but on the same axis. . . . The double peaks or notched cleft seems essential to it. These features create a profile which is basically that of a pair of horns, but it may sometimes suggest the female cleft, or even, at some sites, a pair of breasts. . . . [T]he one would appear to have been seen as the earth's motherly form, the horns as the symbol of its active power. . . . [T]he horned mountain itself defined the consecrated site. (10–11)

25. The major work on this subject is Nicolson's *Mountain Gloom*. But see also Nash, *Wilderness*, 45.

26. I am generally following Schama's interpretation in *Landscape and Memory*, chaps. 7 and 8, and Nicolson's in *Mountain Gloom*.

27. See Nash, *Wilderness and the American Mind*.

28. Ruskin, *Modern Painters*, 4:427.

29. Thoreau's passages atop Mount Ktaadn as quoted in Oelschlaeger, *Idea of Wilderness*, 148–49.

30. See Novak, *Nature and Culture*; and Trenton and Hassrick, *Rocky Mountains*.

31. Trenton and Hassrick, *Rocky Mountains*.

32. Bierstadt's and Moran's images of the Rockies are widely available in works such as Novak, *Nature and Culture*, and Hassrick and Trenton, *Rocky Mountains*, along with Henricks, *Albert Bierstadt,* and Kinsey, *Thomas Moran*. See also, N. Anderson's " 'Curious Historical Artistic Data': Art History and Western American Art," and Sandweiss, "The Public Life of Western Art" in Prown et al., *Discovered Lands*, 1–36, 117–34.

33. See Runte, *National Parks*.

34. The quotations that follow are from Marsh, *Earth as Modified By Human Action*, 43, 247–54.

35. Ibid., 254.

36. Ibid., 263, 326–27.

37. The literature on mountain forests and the protection of streams as the initial reason for the creation of the national forests is vast. For introductions, see Dodds, "Stream-Flow Controversy," 59–69; Rakestraw, "Uncle Sam's Forest Reserves," 145–51.

38. See Wyckoff and Dilsaver's introduction, "Defining the Mountainous West," 1–59, for their particular list of Mountain West characteristics. I do not entirely agree with it and offer here my own version.

39. Van Slyke, *Yangtze*, 65–80, 184–90. On the environmental history of Western America's hydraulic empire, see Worster's *Rivers of Empire*.

40. See Runte, *The National Parks*, a book predicated in part around the wastelands idea. The notion that the Rockies were almost worthless was widespread in the nineteenth century. John Mullan, for example, exploring the Bitterroot Mountains for the Pacific Railroad Survey in the 1850s, wrote that "From the head of Lo-Lo's Fork to the Clearwater the country is one immense bed of rugged, difficult, pine-clad mountains that can never be converted to any purpose for the use of man." In Mullan, "Reports of Explorations," 518–19. On the railroad's ad campaigns, see Wyckoff and Dilsaver, "Promotional Imagery."

41. Graber, *Wilderness as Sacred Space*; Worster, "Wilderness Ideal."

42. Muir, "Wild Parks," 16–17.

43. See chapter 8, where I provide additional details (and citations) on this feature of mountain life.

44. See T. Alexander, "Synthetic Interpretation," 202–6; Flores, "Rocky Mountain West," 46–56.

45. Such is the conclusion of the special issue on mountain adaptations in *Human Ecology*. See, for example, Brush, "Introduction," 130–31, and "Man's Use," 143–49; Netting, "Alpine Peasants," 140–41; Messerschmidt, "Ecological Change," 177.

High mountain zones join swamplands and high altitude grasslands as the trio of landforms most often left as commons around the world because their resources are either diffuse or low in yield. See McKay and Acheson, "Human Ecology," 1–34.

Chapter 7. Zion in Eden

1. L. White, "Historical Roots," 1203–7; Nash, *Wilderness and the American Mind*, 13–20. See also, essays by Barr, "Man and Nature," and Dubos, "Franciscan Conservation."

2. Hargrove, "Anglo-American Land-Use," 121–48.

3. See especially Worster's *Dust Bowl*, but also more recent Worster works, such as the essay collection, *Wealth of Nature*.

4. Commoner, *Closing Circle*, 253–59

5. Grassroots environmentalism's embrace of decentralization and community control—while the mainstream movement continues to endorse federal management especially in the case of the West—is analyzed in Petulla, *American Environmentalism*, and Paehlke, *Environmentalism*.

6. Chase, *Rich Land, Poor Land*; Robbins, *Our Landed Heritage*.

7. Arrington, "Mormon Economic Policies," 96–97. The best survey study of Mormon cooperation is Arrington, Fox, and May, *Building the City*.

8. "If ye are not equal in earthly things ye cannot be equal in obtaining heavenly things." *Doctrine and Covenants*, 76:6.

9. Young's quotations here are from the Mormon *Journal of Discourses*, 20:233, 19:60. On the absolute centrality of this landscape transformation in Mormon history in the West, see also J. Kay, "Mormons and Mountains," 369–95; Worster's section, "Lord's Beavers," chap. 3, 74–83; T. G. Alexander, "Stewardship and Enterprise," 341–66; and Bowden, "Invention," 3–26.

10. D. Jackson and Spence, eds., *Expeditions*, 1:695.

11. R. Jackson has shown in his fine dissertation, "Myth and Reality," that, contrary to Mormon mythology, both Young and Smith had carefully studied the records of early trappers and explorers in the Rockies. Brigham Young knew the Wasatch Front was "the place" long before the migration of 1847. See Jackson, 56–86.

12. For the geologic history of the central Rockies, see P. King, *Evolution*, 90–128.

13. W. Coffman, "Utah Valley Crescent," 10, 24; Wasatch Front Regional Council, *Historical Settlement*, 1–2; Stegner, "Dead Heart," 56–59.

14. W. Coffman, "Utah Valley Crescent," 34–35, 40; Wasatch Front Regional Council, *Historical Settlement*, 4; R. Bailey, "Utah's Watersheds," 24–25, 36.

15. Roth, "A Graphic Summary," and the Utah Agriculture Experiment Station, *Report of Utah Flood Survey*; R. Bailey, Forsling, and Becraft, "Floods."

16. Carley et al., "Soil Survey"; "Report of the Secretary of the Interior," 546–47.

17. I rely generally here on Trimble, *Sagebrush Ocean*, 144–202. But on place-specific Utah historical ecology, see also: Christensen and Hutchinson, "Historical Observations," 90–105; Hull and Hull, "Pre-settlement Vegetation," 27–29; Cottam, "Ecological Study"; Guymon, "Ecological History"; H. Hall, "Impact of Man"; and Wakefield, "Study of Plant Ecology."

18. See Christensen and Hutchinson, "Historical Observations," 99–103; and, for original ranges of the faunal subspecies herein indicated, Hall and Kelson, *Mammals of North America*. For both floral and faunal climax dominants, see Shelford, *Ecology of North America*, 152–68.

19. Jennings, *Prehistory,* 183, 264, 274–76; Jennings and Norbeck, eds., *Prehistoric Man,* 162; Gunnerson, "Plateau Shoshonean Prehistory," 44; Madsen et al., "Man, Mammoth"; Christensen, "On the Prehistory," 101–9; Chamberlain, "Man and Nature," 3–22.

20. Cottam, "Impact of Man." Cottam cites primary documents on Indian fire ecology, pointing out the fact that both big sagebrush and Utah juniper are fire intolerant.

21. Arrington, *Great Basin Kingdom,* 18.

22. Woodruff, "Journal," in R. Jackson, "Myth and Reality," 168. For a discussion, see 151–73.

23. *Journal of Discourses,* 2:348. Mere subsistence obviously was not the goal of this cooperation: "If we will work unitedly, we can work ourselves into wealth, health, prosperity and power ..." ibid., 12:376.

24. See *Doctrine and Covenants,* 104:13–18, 55–56. Young's pronouncements were consistent with those of Smith on stewardship and cooperation: "There is any amount of property, and gold and silver in the earth ... and the Lord gives to this one and that one ... but it all belongs to him ... No person on earth can truly call anything his own ..." And on cooperation: "This co-operative movement is only a stepping stone to what is called the Order of Enoch, but which is in reality the Order of Heaven." *Journal of Discourses,* 16:10; 9:106; 13:2.

25. Arrington, "Property," 345; Fox, "Mormon Land System."

26. G. Thomas, *Development of Institutions,* 27

27. B. Roberts, *Comprehensive History,* 269.

28. Arrington, "Property," 348. The Territorial Ordinance of 1850, signed by Governor Brigham Young, is reprinted in G. Stewart, "Utah's Biological Heritage," 7–8. See also, Knowlton, *Highway Development,* 24. At first, Young also determined that his constituency should use dead wood for fuel so as "to foster the growth of timber." B. Roberts, *Comprehensive History,* 3:269. This must have become impractical rather quickly.

29. Arrington, "Mormon Economic Policies," 178.

30. Works Progress Administration, "History of Grazing." Also see *Deseret News,* 16 Nov. 1865.

31. Nelson, *Mormon Village,* xv, 11, 26–27, 38–40, 53; Ricks, *Forms and Methods*; Rosenvall, "Defunct Mormon Settlements," 60.

32. *Journal of Discourses,* 12:153. On United Order settlements, see Arrington, *Orderville, Utah,* and Fox, *Experiments.*

33. Larson, *"Americanization,"* introduction, 35.

34. Arrington, "Mormon Economic Policies," 178. Wahlquist, "Population Growth," has worked out a population schedule for Utah, which he believes to be more accurate than the Census Reports (table 2). Between 1848 and 1883, he estimates that the Mormons had to provide homes for some 72,551 who emigrated to Zion from abroad (table 5).

35. *Deseret News,* 16 Nov. 1865.

36. The quotation is Albert Potter's, in Peterson, "Albert F. Potter," 249. See also, USGS, "Forest Reserves," 22; "Report on the Forests," 13:567–69.

37. Barnes, "Story of the Range," Box 6, folder 11; Box 15, folder 2; Box 7, folder 3. In addition, Walker, "Cattle Industry," 34; Arrington and Alexander, *Dependent Commonwealth,* 16; N. Roberts and Gardner, "Livestock," 286; *U.S. Census Report,* 1880, 144–76. For a fuller discussion of altitudinal grazing migrations and the mountain environment, see Flores, "Islands," 404–10.

38. Christensen and Hutchinson, "Historical Observations," 98; Cottam "Impact of Man," 9. Of what is now the Manti/La Sal National Forest in southeastern Utah, Cottam says: "Local history and ecological data regarding Mountain Meadows establish a record of almost complete change in vegetation since settlement in 1862." Cottam and Stewart, "Plant Succession," 31. For a species and habits breakdown of the Chenopodiaceae, or "pigweeds," which have replaced the native grasses in many areas of Utah and the West, see Rickett, *Central Plains,* 6:110.

39. Powell, *Report on the Lands*. For a laudatory assessment of Powell's plan, based on local and collectivist "grazing and water districts" and (later) legal rights and institutional lines conforming with natural drainage, consult Stegner, *Hundredth Meridian*. A major flaw of Powell's plan was his seeming failure to recognize the link between the mountain forests and streamflow regulation. His 1878 plan would have put Rocky Mountain forests under private ownership, in the hands of lumber firms (in his words, "woodsmen"). See Flores, "Islands," 283–89, for a more critical analysis of Powell's land-use plan.

40. "Every civilized government," Fernow wrote, "must in time own or control the forest cover of the mountains in order to secure desirable water conditions." Fernow, "Forestry Investigations," 316. Marsh had opened this debate in America with his *Man and Nature*. By 1891, among the eight European nations that had already had moved to public ownership of their mountains, was Germany, Fernow's homeland.

41. Lands Committee chairman John Payson of Illinois implied in the House that the reserves might be "temporary," but were necessary for "conserving the general good by preserving the watersheds . . ." William McRae of Arkansas noted prophetically that "we shall hear from it [the reservation clause] in the future." *Congressional Record*, 3613–16. Bills to establish such a mountain reserve system in the West had been introduced in every session of Congress beginning in 1882. In 1890 both the American Association for the Advancement of Science and the National Academy of Science lobbied for the idea, the National Academy opining that "no other problem confronting the government of the United States is equal in importance to that offered by the present condition and future fate of the forests of western North America." Quoted in Robbins, *Our Landed Heritage*, 312.

42. T. G. Alexander, "Senator Reed Smoot," 245–64; Peterson, "Albert F. Potter," 249–53. Smoot was one of the few Western legislators who also supported the Pettigrew Amendment, which opened the reserves to multiple use and to the fee and permit system later implemented by Pinchot. The question of support for the National Forest system was not, we now know, the clear-cut "people vs. special interests" confrontation of Progressive rhetoric. Generally speaking, farmers and urban dwellers in the West were supportive of the system, as was the National Forestry Association and some of the individual timbermen and cattlemen. The most vehement opponents were the sheepmen, the mining industry, and the majority of cattlemen. See Rakestraw, "Uncle Sam's Forest Reserves," 145–46, and "West, States' Rights," 89–99.

43. Again contrary to popular impression, not all Eastern government scientists supported the rationale of the forest system. In addition to the two entities mentioned, Hiram M. Chittenden of the reservoir survey also expressed doubts regarding the beneficial effects of vegetation upon streamflow. See Dodds, "Stream-flow Controversy," 56–59. Also Thomas Alexander, "Sylvester Q. Cannon," who points out that Cannon pushed for Utah's acquisition of watersheds not already in the federal system during the 1920s and 30s.

44. Reynolds, "Grazing and Floods." Of a total of forty-three Mormon settlements that were abandoned because of environmental factors, the highest number of failures (sixteen) was due to flooding. All but three of these were located in southern Utah, in the Colorado Plateau country. Rosenvall, "Defunct Mormon Settlements," table 2, 60–61.

45. The point of the Weather Service that bared slopes yield more runoff than vegetated ones was ably documented in Utah, where some studies indicated that as much as sixty-two times the amount of water came from cleared slopes. But the Utah experiences made the further point that without vegetation, mountains shed their soil, boulders, and other debris along with the water, in destructive and erosive floods. In government tests, *bare slopes averaged 110 cubic feet per acre soil loss during heavy storms*. Further, the rapid runoff of degraded mountain slopes interfered with water percolation, causing streams to dry up prematurely. In one of the 1920s floods, gullies

were cut seventy-five feet deep to bedrock, rock and debris covered the ground to a depth of eight feet at the mouths of the canyons, and boulders of three hundred tons weight rolled through towns and irrigation systems. Sixty years later, these gullies are still etched into the slopes.

Utah ecologists proved that they could revegetate a slope and stop floods in no more that a decade, but when flood fears subsided, the ecologists found the public apathetic to their arguments that use ought to be severely curtailed. For several scores of high-quality, black-and-white photographs that graphically illustrate the seriousness of this mountain lands collapse, see Utah Agricultural Experiment Station, *Report*. Other major studies documenting the relationship between watershed abuse and ecological collapse in Utah include: Forsling, "Herbaceous Plant Cover"; Baily, Forsling, and Becraft, "Floods and Accelerated Erosion"; Marston, "Effect of Vegetation"; Buhler, "Forest and Watershed"; Zon, "Forests and Water."

46. Stewart, "Utah's Biological Heritage," 14; Craddock, "Salt Lake City Flood," 51–61.

47. Cottam, "Influence of Man," 10; Christensen and Hutchinson, "Historical Observations."

48. *U.S. Census Report*, 1900; Stewart, "Utah's Biological Heritage," 7; Knowlton, "Our Resources," 39; Peterson, "Americanization," 109–25; Lamborn, "Dry Farming in Utah." For early reservoir development, see T. G. Alexander, "Investment in Progress," 286–304. Mining also had an adverse impact on the Utah environment. Poisoning of stock and crops emerged as a major problem around 1900. See Widtsoe, "Smelter Smoke." I also wish to thank John Lamborn of the Special Collections Library at Utah State University for allowing me to peruse Lamborn's unpublished paper, "The Smelter Cases of 1904 and 1906."

49. Utah's literary figures need no introduction, but the scientists may. Cottam and Paul were both long-time professors of natural sciences at the University of Utah. For an example of their mid-twentieth-century efforts to turn Utah in an environmentalist direction, see Cottam's "General Plan for Conservation," 69–70. Becraft was professor of Range Management at Utah State, Bailey for years the director of the Intermountain Forest and Range Experiment Station at Ogden, and Forsling a research ecologist in the Forest Service, Intermountain Region. On the 1960s conference, see Treshow and Gilmour, eds., *Proceedings*.

50. Hatch's quotation is in *High Country News*, 30 Sep. 1996.

51. The quotation is Don Snow's "Squeezing the Daylights," 5–6.

52. See Runte, *National Parks*, 112–13.

53. Harvey, *Symbol of Wilderness*.

54. Roth, "Graphic Summary," pt. 1, 1–6; U.S. Forest Service, *Draft Environmental Impact*; U.S. Bureau of Land Management, *Final Environmental Impact*, I-1–I-10; D. Bailey, "Economic Impacts."

Chapter 8. The Rocky Mountain West

1. Emerson, "On Nature," 400.

2. Emerson, "Young American," 216.

3. Kemmis, "Last Best Place," 84. See also Kemmis's similar arguments in *Community*, 125–28.

4. Guerin-Gonzalez, "Freedom," 194–95.

5. Fairfax, "Lands, Natural Resources," 196–205.

6. Nugent, "American West," 2–23; Emmons, "Constructed Province"; Worster, "New West, True West," 141–56.

7. See Tuan, *Space and Place*; Flores, "Spirit of Place," 6–10.

8. Cronon, "Vanishing Frontier," 157–76.

9. Webb, *Great Plains*. See also, Billington, "Frederick Jackson Turner," 89–113.

10. See Tobin, "Walter Prescott Webb," 713–29. Howard Lamar observes that within the past decade, a survey of Western historians indicated that it was Webb, rather than Turner, whose ideas they found most influential. Lamar, "Regionalism," 25.

11. See Malin, *Grasslands,* and "Webb and Regionalism," 85–104; Worster, "Grassland Follies"; and Berkhofer, "Space, Time," 21–30.

12. See Flores, "Islands," for a general discussion. Also, Jordan, *Cattle-Ranching,* 298–307; Kilpinen, "Material Folk Culture"; Crowley, "Ranching," 445–60; John Alwin, "Montana's Beaverslide Hay Stacker," 42–50; MacKenzie with Maunder, "Logging Equipment," 30–35; Best, *Snowplow*; Cole, "Transmountain Water Diversion," 49–65, 130–48; Rodman, "Colorado," 34–50; Hereford, *Rotary Snowplows.*

13. Jordan, Kilpinen, and Gritzner, *Mountain West,* 128; Kilpinen, "Front-Gabled Log Cabin," 19–31.

14. Braudel, *Civilization*; Wallerstein, *Modern World System,* and *Modern World System II*; Emmons, "Constructed Province." Perhaps the most effective examination of this process so far in Western historiography is T. Hall's *Social Change.*

15. Rappaport, "Maladaptation," 49–71; Whyte, "Systems," 73–78; Rappaport, "Normative Modes," 79–88; Butzer, "Civilizations," 517–24; Hardesty, "Rethinking Cultural Adaptation," 11–18.

On the technological response to the Dust Bowl as a possible maladaptation, see Riebsame, "Sustainability," 133–51. Howard Lamar offers an interesting comparison of the Southern and Northern Plains and Canadian plains in their Dust Bowl responses that seems to me to bear out Riebsame's argument. Lamar, "Regionalism," 25–44.

16. See Stanford and Day, eds., *Ice Age Hunters*, especially Frison's "Foothills-Mountains," 323–42, and Benedict's "Along the Great Divide," 359–73. Also, Husted, "Prehistoric Occupation."

17. On the Anasazi collapse, see Frazier, *People of Chaco*; Samuels and Betancourt, "Modeling," 505–15; Cordell, *Prehistory*. On the Pueblos, see Josephy, *Now That the Buffalo's Gone*, 94–99; and Tuan, *Topophilia*, 79–83, and *Space and Place*, 91–93.

18. See deBuys, *Enchantment and Exploitation,* 67, 80.

19. DeBuys, *Enchantment and Exploitation*; deBuys and Harris, *River of Traps*; Rothman, *On Rims and Ridges*; MacCameron, "Environmental Change," 17–39. See also, T. Hall, *Social Change* and the essays in *Land, Water, and Culture*.

20. My information here is mostly from research in the Spanish Archives of New Mexico, Joseph Halpin Records Center and Archives, Santa Fe, New Mexico. Among indispensable secondary works, however, see Nostrand, *Hispano Homeland*; Quintana, *Pobladores*; Chavez, *My Penitente Land*; Westphall, *Mercedes Reales*; Ebright, *Land Grants*; Kutsch and Van Ness, *Cañones*; Van Ness, "Hispanic Land Grants," 141–214.

21. See Powell, "Institutions," 111–16.

22. Rudnick, "Re-Naming the Land," 10–26. Along with Edgar Hewitt, Austin was somewhat unusual in this regard. Most of the Anglo artists and writers looked to the Pueblos rather than the Hispanics as models for what D. H. Lawrence called the American "Future-Primitive." See Rudnick, *Mabel Dodge Luhan,* chaps. 5–6 especially.

23. Quintana, *Pobladores*, 213–14; Peña, "Spanish-Mexican Land Grants."

24. On Mexican environmental history, see Rangel and Canales, "Habitat Preservation," 19–21; Simonian, *Defending the Land*; Melville, *A Plague of Sheep.*

25. In the Sandoval Case of 1897, the Supreme Court argued that the Spanish *government* had owned the common lands of the grants. According to Malcolm Ebright this was a flawed decision "based on scanty Spanish legal authorities." Ebright thinks, instead, that "the New Mexico community land grant itself owned the common lands." See Ebright, *Land Grants,* chap. 5; and Westphall, *Mercedes Reales.*

Spanish tradition featured several commons:

Monte (mountains) used for wood

Prado (meadow) high-quality pasture, often irrigated

Debesa (enclosed) fenced pasture

Ejido (exit) multipurpose lands near the towns, often used for dumping, herding stray
  animals, etc.

In New Mexico commons were almost all called ejidos, although they were given as *mercedes* (community grants).

I'd like to thank Spanish visiting scholar Juan Diego Perez Cebada for his help with the above.

26. See deBuys, *Enchantment and Exploitation*, 195, 215–47, for the best account of the details of this Southern Rockies collapse.

27. Leopold, "Pioneers and Gullies," 106–13, and "Vegetation of Southwestern Watersheds," 295–316.

28. Leopold, "Vegetation of Southwestern Watersheds," 295–316.

29. Kutsch and Van Ness, *Cañones*, 46.

30. See Atencio, "Human Dimensions," 45–46. Kutsch and Van Ness, in *Cañones*, 146, downplay *fatalismo*, asserting that if it exists at all, it's superficial, less a "shrug" of passive acceptance than "an unwillingness to get ulcers from frustration."

31. DeBuys, *Enchantment and Exploitation*; Rothman, *On Rims and Ridges*; MacCameron, "Environmental Change."

32. The quotation is from Peña, "Spanish-Mexican Land Grants." See also, Peña's "Los Animalites," 49–50, and Peña and Martinez, "Critique of Recent Southwestern Environmental History," 149–62, 164, 171, both in Peña, ed., *Chicano Culture, Ecology, Politics*.

33. Tuan, "New Mexican Gullies," 573–82; Denevan, "Livestock Numbers," 691–703.

34. Powell, *Report*, 89. One of the classic studies of cultural regionalism done on the Mormons is Donald Meinig's "Mormon Culture Region," 191–220.

35. For recent treatments of Mormon environmental history, see J. Wright, *Rocky Mountain Divide*, chaps. 14 and 15, and T. Alexander, "Stewardship and Enterprise," 341–64. See also, Utah Agricultural Experiment Station, *Report*; Rosenvall, "Defunct Mormon Settlements," 60.

36. Jordan et al., *Mountain West*, 123–24.

37. Howard, *Montana*; Toole, *Montana* and *Twentieth-Century Montana*; Emmons, "The Price of 'Freedom,'" 66–73.

38. See T. Alexander, "Synthetic Interpretation," 202–6. Also, M. L. Wilson, "Evolution of Montana Agriculture," 429–40; Reynolds, "Some Chapters"; Biggar, "Lower Flathead Valley"; Isch, "Upper Flathead." On Powell in Montana, see Stegner, *Hundredth Meridian*, 315–16.

39. In addition to the Clark Fork River downstream of Butte, currently the largest Superfund cleanup site in the United States, the Blackfoot River (of *A River Runs through It*) was listed by American Rivers in 1993 as the tenth most endangered river in the country. The state is believed to have 1,118 miles of mine-polluted streams and rivers. *Missoulian*, 5 Apr. 1993.

40. The original Bitterroot Report was University of Montana, "University View." See also, Bolle, "Bitterroot Revisited," 1–18, and Oral History File 249. On Montana's high ranking on environmental awareness (in the 1970s and 1980s Montana led League of Conservation Voter state rankings in the Rockies with a 55; the median mountain West ranking was 32.9) see Hays, *Beauty, Health*, 40–48. On land trusts to conserve open space, Montana currently has five, New Mexico (with more than twice the population) five, Utah one (J. Wright, *Rocky Mountain Divide*, 263–64). The application of the precepts of conservation biology and the tendency to think of landscapes in terms of ecosystems is also more developed in Rocky Mountain Montana than elsewhere in the Mountain West. See Keiter, ed., *Greater Yellowstone Ecosystem*.

41. On replacement of the Blackfeet land-use strategy in Montana, see Warren, *Hunter's Game*, and Spence, "Crown of the Continent," 29–49.

42. Clifford, "Timber Fight," *Missoulian*, 6 Sep. 1998; Ebright, *Land Grants*.

43. See Wilkinson, *Eagle Bird*, 132–61, on the Hispanic response to the Rio Arriba County (Chama) controversy in the middle 1980s over water diversions for a new ski resort and guest ranch; deBuys, *Enchantment and Exploitation*, 255–77; Bustamante, "Human Element," 75–77; Rodriguez, "Land, Water," 313–403, and "Tourist Gaze," 105–26.

44. Larson, *"Americanization"*; Snow, "Squeezing the Daylights," *High Country News*, 25 July 1980, 5–6; M. L. Wright, *Rocky Mountain Divide*, 181, 186.

45. William Cronon calls this new product "second nature." See Cronon, *Nature's Metropolis*, 266–67.

46. See Lowitt, *New Deal*; and Nash, *American West Transformed*. Montana is strikingly absent from the trends Nash, in particular, discusses for the rest of the West. With few centers of population and remote in terms of transportation, the state ended up garnering very little of the defense spending that created population growth and high-tech economic development across the region as a whole.

47. J. Wright, *Montana Ghost Dance*, 15.

48. Such is the conclusion of the special issue on mountain adaptations in *Human Ecology*. See, for example, Brush, "Introduction," 130–31; Netting, "Alpine Peasants," 140–41; Messerschmidt, "Ecological Change," 177; Brush, "Man's Use of an Andean Ecosystem," 143–49.

High mountain zones, swamplands, and high altitude grasslands have remained in commons around the world in part because of their environmental fragility. See McKay and Acheson, "Human Ecology," 1–34.

49. Guthrie, *Big Sky, Fair Land*, 91.

Chapter 9. A Long Love Affair

1. U.S. Department of the Census, 1990; Popper and Popper, "Daring Proposal," 12–18; Matthews, *Where the Buffalo Roam*, 19–20, 179; *Missoulian*, 26 Jan. 1995; Long, "Colorado's Front Range," 86–103.

2. Kittredge and Smith, eds., *Last Best Place*; Matthews, *Where the Buffalo Roam*, xi–xii; Riebsame, "United States Great Plains," chap. 34.

3. The two earliest Spanish reactions to the Great Plains come from the entradas of Cabeza de Vaca and Coronado in the sixteenth century. They are widely available in several translations, perhaps most accessibly in Cabeza de Vaca, "Relation," 1–123, and "Narrative," 273–384.

4. Dunbar, "Journal of a Voyage," 78–79.

5. Haley, *Albert Pike's Journeys*; Whitman, *Leaves of Grass*; Bloemink, *Georgia O'Keeffe*; Flores, "Plains and the Painters," 19–28; F. Turner, *Spirit of Place*.

6. Pike, *Journals*; E. James, *Account of an Expedition*.

7. H. Smith, *Virgin Land*, offers the classic statement of this idea. See also, Blouet and Lawson, *Images of the Plains*.

8. See Webb, *Great Plains*, especially chap. 1. The best examples of Malin's ruminations on Great Plains deficiencies (and his attempts to reverse such notions) appear in a variety of forms in his essays and book excerpts in: Malin, *History and Ecology*.

9. See, particularly, these works: Runte, *National Parks*; Nash, *Wilderness and the American Mind*; Novak, *Nature and Culture*.

10. Evernden, "Beauty and Nothingness," 3–6; Riebsame, "United States Great Plains."

11. See Broach, "Angels, Architecture," 2–15; Flores and Winton, *Canyon Visions*; Flores, "Plains and the Painters."

12. Wallach, "Return of the Prairie," 1–5.

13. Gould, *Wonderful Life*.

14. Madole, "Stratigraphic Evidence," 483–86; Riebsame, "Sustainable Development"; Finley, "Desert's Return," *Denver Post*, 22 July 1990.

15. Cabeza de Vaca, "Relation," 67. See Denevan, "Pristine Myth," 369–85, for the general anthropogenic argument, but more specifically Pyne's *Fire in America*, with its several chapters on the history of Plains fire ecology. Sauer's old argument about the Plains, in other words, has been settled in his favor. See Flores, "Essay: The Great Plains 'Wilderness.'"

16. Ponting, *Green History*, 12–48; P. Martin, "Prehistoric Overkill," 354–403.

17. The two major collections of scientific papers on the issue of the Pleistocene extinctions are P. Martin and Wright, *Pleistocene Extinctions*; and P. Martin and Klein, *Quaternary Extinctions*.

18. The best survey of the archeological record on bison hunting on the Northern Plains is Bryan, *Buffalo People*. On the Southern Plains during the Altithermal, see E. Johnson, ed., *Lubbock Lake*.

19. Wedel, "Some Aspects of Human Ecology," 409–513.

20. Worster, "Cowboy Ecology," 34–52.

21. Box, "Range Deterioration," 39–45; Jordan, *Cattle Ranching Frontiers*, 10–11.

22. See the following collections especially: Hester, ed., *The Texas Archaic*; Schlesier, ed., *Plains Indians*.

23. Adaptation to nature rather than to the market has long been emphasized in history and geography of Great Plains studies. Half a century ago Carl Kraenzel pointed to adaptation in his chapters "The Need to Adapt or Get Out," 21, and "Keys for Survival," 24. See Kraenzel, *Great Plains in Transition*.

24. Worster, *Dust Bowl*; Riebsame, "Dust Bowl," 127–36.

25. Riebsame, "Sustainable Development."

26. Green, *Land of the Underground Rain*; High Plains Associates, *Ogallala Aquifer*; Worster, "Warming of the West," 91–120. More optimistic than the above are Kromm and White, *Conserving the Ogallala*, and Kromm and White, eds., *Groundwater Exploitation*.

27. Samson and Knopf, "Prairie Conservation"; Lesica, "Endless Sea of Grass," 1, 9.

28. Flores, *Caprock Canyonlands*, 45.

29. J. Mitchell, *Conservation Reserve Program*.

30. Samson and Knopf, "Prairie Conservation in North America." See also, Northern Great Plains Planning Team, *Northern Great Plains Management Plans Revision*.

31. Catlin, *Letters and Notes*, 2:423.

32. K. Miller, "Natural Protected Areas," 17–22.

33. I assembled this story from the records of the NPS; in Flores, *Caprock Canyonlands*; see especially 160–65.

34. Shepard, "Singing out of Tune."

35. Shelford, "Preservation," 240–45.

36. Flores, "Grand Canyon of Texas," 4–14; Tolson, Christianson et al., "Investigative Report."

37. Flores, *Caprock Canyonlands*, 160–65; "Proposed National Parks."

38. K. Miller, "Natural Protected Areas"; Friesen, *Canadian Prairies*.

39. E. R. Hall, "Prairie National Park," 1–6; Shepard, "Singing out of Tune."

40. See the Sierra Club's ecoregions website (http://www.sierraclub.org/ecoregions/prairie.html) for details of their plans for more public lands on the Great Plains.

41. The original quotation appeared front and center in the Poppers' "Daring Proposal," 14. See also Popper and Popper, "Fate of the Plains," 15–19.

42. The McCook incident is described in Matthews, *Where the Buffalo Roam*, 49–54. The Poppers' reception in Billings is treated on 143–53.

43. Riebsame, "Sustainability," 133–51; Worster, *Dust Bowl*, especially chapters 9–11 on Haskell County, Kansas.

44. Worster, "Warming of the West"; Glanz and Ausubel, "Ogallala Aquifer," 123–31. Schmidt, "Mega-Chihuahuan Desert," 105–15.

45. Shepard, Boggs, Higgs, and Burgess, *New Vision*.

46. W. Jackson, *New Roots*; W. Jackson, Berry, and Colman, *Meeting the Expectations*.

47. Callenbach's *Bring Back the Buffalo*, 65–86, tells a version of the story of the ITBC through the middle 1990s. Also, interview with Baker, Crow Agency. My recent information is from the ITBC site on the World Wide Web (http://www.intertribalbison.crst.htm), which notes that in 1992 the Ft. Sill Apache of the Southern Plains were members of the ITBC before deciding they lacked a sufficient land base to participate.

48. Interview with M. Johnson.

Chapter 10. The West That Was

1. Thoreau, *Heart of Thoreau's Journals*, 238–39.

2. Plenty Coups, "Vision," 223–29.

3. Brown and Felton, *Before Barbed Wire*, 5.

4. Thoreau, *Heart of Thoreau's Journals,* 239.

5. On bison in the Bitterroot Valley, see Roe's discussion in his *Buffalo*. On 267–70, Roe analyzes the fur-era accounts of the 1820s to the 1840s (primarily Alexander Ross, John Work, William Ashley, and Father DeSmet) to conclude that there were still "immense herds" on the Bitterroot and Salmon Rivers in the 1820s. By 1831, however, bison seldom visited the valley of the Bitterroot. In the 1840s, despite one report of a valley in present western Montana/Idaho "clouded with buffalo," the animals were scarcely ever seen there. In fact, the cool-season bunch grasses west of the Continental Divide lose their nutritional value by midsummer, a key reason the bison were not full-time residents there. See also, Daubenmire's "Western Limits," 622–24.

6. For Salish grizzly stories, see Rockwell, *Giving Voice to Bear,* 91–93. Lewis and Clark also found a *sumes* medicine place, an Indian shrine to the grizzly, on Lolo Creek in the Bitterroot in 1805 (see chap. 4). On subsequent grizzly history in the valley, I have relied on M. Johnson, of Defenders of Wildlife, "Grizzly Bears in the Bitterroot."

7. Stegner, "Wilderness Letter," 328–33.

8. See, particularly, his interviews with Richard Etulain, in Stegner and Etulain, *Conversations*, especially the "After Ten Years" essay in the revised edition, ix–xxix.

9. See Marsh, *Earth as Modified by Human Action.*

10. See Rothman, *Greening of America,* 53–54.

11. Seton, *Lives of Game Animals*, vol. 1, pt. 1, 258–65; vol. 2, pt. 1, 21; vol. 4, pt. 2, 447–48. Worster, "Other People, Other Lives," 66–71; Clark and Casey, *Tales of the Grizzly,* xiii; Grumbine, *Ghost Bears,* 67.

12. Wagner, "Livestock Grazing," 133–35.

13. Hall and Kelson, *Mammals of North America*, map, 870.

14. Seton, *Lives of Game Animals*, vol. 2, pt. 1, 21.

15. This is a general trend informing the ecology Trimble describes in *Sagebrush Ocean*, 47–54.

16. Phelan, *Texas Wild,* 123–45.

17. See V. Bailey, *Biological Survey of Texas.*

18. Moulton, *Journals.*

19. See Grumbine, *Ghost Bears*; Callenbach, *Bring Back the Buffalo,* 118.

20. A. Leopold, "The Virgin Southwest," 106–13, and "Pioneers and Gullies," 173–80.

21. See especially Cronon's introductory pair of essays, "In Search of Nature" and "The Trouble with Wilderness," 23–90.

22. Denevan, "Pristine Myth," 369–85. On Indian population see Dobyns, "Estimating," 395–416, wherein Dobyns estimates 90 million to 112.5 million for the hemisphere and 9.8 million to 12.25 million in what is now the United States and Canada. See also, W. Jacobs, *Fatal Confrontation*, especially his chapter, "Tip of an Iceberg," 77–89.

23. P. Martin, "Prehistoric Overkill," 354–403; Owen-Smith, "Pleistocene Extinctions," 351–62.

24. In several articles, among them "Indian Fires," (Barrett and Arno) 641–53, Steven Barrett has shown how even at high elevations in the Rockies, fire frequency accelerated dramatically some two-to-four millennia ago, when Indians began inhabiting the region.

25. McCann, "Before 1492," 23.

26. See P. Martin, "Prehistoric Overkill."

27. G. Morgan, "Beaver Ecology/Beaver Mythology." Her argument is that the aversion to killing beavers, judging by their paucity in the archeological record, is ancient, and sprang from the foot nomad background of the Plains people such as Blackfeet, Gros Ventres, and Plains Assiniboine. These people found that beaver populations conserve and stabilize surface water in select habitats, usually large tributaries, on the plains. On "Optimal Foraging Theory" among native peoples, see E. A. Smith, "Anthropological Applications," 628–32; and Hames, "Game Conservation," 92–120.

28. See as an example of the literature, N. Williams and Hunn, eds., *Resource Managers.*

29. Hickerson, "Virginia Deer," 43–61.

30. R. White, *Roots of Dependency,* 10–11.

31. W. Clark, entry for Friday, 29 August 1806, in Moulton, ed., *Journals,* 8:38.

32. P. Martin and Szuter, "War Zones and Game Sinks."

33. Campbell and Twining, *Reports,* 63–64

34. Dodge, *Plains of the Great West,* 130–31

35. Marcy, *Thirty Years,* 144; Mollhausen, *Diary of a Journey,* 1:224; E. James, *Account of an Expedition,* 3:228.

36. For a good, recent guide to the past thirty years of revisionist literature on estimates of precontact Native American populations—which emerged after scholars recognized the profound effects of Virgin Soil Epidemics—see Wilbur Jacobs's essay, "Tip of an Iceberg," 77–89. The critical works in the field have been Dobyns, *Their Number Became Thinned* and "Estimating," 395–416. See also, Flores, "Essay," and chapter 1 in Flores, *Horizontal Yellow,* for estimates of Southern Plains population.

37. Denevan, "Pristine Myth."

38. Bowden, "Invention of American Tradition," 3–26.

39. Rostlund, "Geographical Range," 395–407.

40. C. Kay's book, *Aboriginal Overkill,* is soon to be released from Oxford University Press. See also his "Aboriginal Overkill," 141–64, and "Ecosystems Then and Now," 79–87. Also, Burkhardt, "Herbivory in the Intermountain West," 4–15; Laycock, "Stable States," 427–33.

41. Botkin, *Discordant Harmonies.*

42. E. Wilson, *Consilience,* 278.

43. *Conserving Prairie Dog Ecosystems.*

44. That "unhappiness" is ably documented in A. Matthews, *Where the Buffalo Roam.*

45. Quoted in Callenbach, *Bring Back the Buffalo.*

46. U.S. Department of Agriculture, *America's Private Land.*

47. My information on the extent of the cheatgrass spread as of the 1990s is from a letter in *High Country News*, 3 Aug. 1998, by Eric Lane, Colorado Weed Coordinator for the state's Department of Agriculture.

48. T. Williams, "Killer Weeds," 24–31; Ewing, *The Range*, 228–29.

49. See especially Whitehouse's *Journal,* 11:304–11.

50. Mullan, "Report of the Pacific Railroad Surveys," 169.

51. See Barrett and Arno, "Indian Fires," 641–53; and Barrett, "Relationship."

52. Mullan, "Report of the Pacific Railroad Surveys," 169. On the general difficulty of raising horses on the Northern Plains and the lucrative qualities of the Bitterroot Valley in contrast, see Binnema, "Common and Contested Ground," chap. 7.

53. See W. Mitchell, "An Ecological Study." The observer was Albert Groff, in the Groff Family Collection.

54. See Richey, "Valley of Troubles."

55. Spotted knapweed produces an allelopathic compound called cnicin that suppresses growth in surrounding grasses and forbs.

56. A moth (*Agapeta zoegana*), a European species that coevolved with knapweed and lays its eggs in knapweed roots was test released in the Bitterroot Valley in 1997. Two species of gallflies that eat knapweed flowerheads were released in the 1980s with limited results. *Missoulian*, 17 July 1998.

57. North et al., "Changing Climate of Texas," 24–49.

BIBLIOGRAPHY

Primary Documents

Abert, James W. *The Journal of Lieutenant J. W. Abert from Bent's Fort to St. Louis in 1845.* Edited by H. Bailey Carroll. Canyon, Tex.: West Texas Historical Association, 1941.

American Philosophical Society. *Proceedings* 9 (1863–64).

Atwater, Caleb. "On the Prairies and Barrens of the West." *American Journal of Science ... [and] Arts* 1 (1818): 116–25.

Barnhart, John Hendley. "Brief Sketches of Some Collectors of Specimens in the Barton Herbarium." *Proceedings of the Philadelphia Botanical Club* 9 (1926): 35.

Barton, Benjamin Smith. Collection. Library of the American Philosophical Society. Philadelphia.

———. "A Discourse on Some of the Principal Desiderata in Natural History, and on the Best Means of Promoting the Study of This Science, in the United States." In *Contributions to the History of American Natural History,* compiled by Keir Sterling. New York: Garland, 1974.

———. *Elements of Botany.* Philadelphia, printed for the author, 1803.

———. *Fragments of the Natural History of Pennsylvania, Part First.* Philadelphia, 1799.

———. "Miscellaneous Facts and Observations." *Philadelphia Medical and Physical Journal* 2 (1806): 159–60.

———. "Miscellaneous Facts and Observations." *Second Supplement to the Philadelphia Medical and Physical Journal* (1807): 194–95.

Bartram, William. *Travels through North and South Carolina, Georgia, East and West Florida ... .* Philadelphia: printed by James and Johnson, 1791.

Bexar Archives (Spanish Archives of Texas). Eugene C. Barker Texas History Collection, the University of Texas, Austin.

Bolle, Arnold. Oral History File 249. Mansfield Library Archives. University of Montana.

Boller, Henry. *Among the Indians: Four Years on the Upper Missouri, 1858–1862.* Edited by Milo Milton Quaife. Lincoln: University of Nebraska Press, 1972.

Britton, M. L. "The Location of Le [*sic*] Poste des Cadodoquious." Possession of author.

Byron, Lord. *Childe Harold's Pilgrimage.* In *The Complete Poetical Works,* edited by Jerom J. BcGann. 2 vols. Vol. 1, 174–204. Oxford: The Clarendon Press, 1980.

Cabeza de Vaca, Álvar Núñez. "Relation that Alvar Nunez Cabeza de Vaca Gave ... from the Year 1527 to the Year 1536 [1537]." In *Spanish Explorers in the Southern United States, 1528–1543,* edited by Frederick W. Hodge and Theodore H. Lewis. Austin: The University of Texas Press, 1984.

Castañeda, Pedro de. "The Narrative of the Expedition of Coronado." In *Spanish Explorers in the Southern United States, 1528–1543,* edited by Frederick W. Hodge and Theodore H. Lewis. Austin: The University of Texas Press, 1984.

Catlin, George. *Letters and Notes on the Manners, Customs, and Conditions of North American Indians.* 2 vols. New York: Dover Press, 1973.

Church of Jesus Christ of Latter-Day Saints. *Journal of Discourses.* 26 vols. Liverpool: F. D. Richards, 1852–86.

"Concerning Philip Nolan." *Quarterly of the Texas State Historical Association* 7 (Apr. 1904): 314.

Cox, Isaac Joslin. "General James Wilkinson and His Later Intrigues with the Spaniards." *American Historical Review* 19 (July 1914): 789n.

Craven County Marriage Bonds. 16 Jan. 1818. North Carolina State Archives, Raleigh, N.C.

Custis Family Bible. New Bern, N.C.: New Bern Historical Society, Custis Family Collection.

Custis, Peter. Certificate of Death. 1 May 1842. Craven County, N.C., Superior Court. "Will Book D," 54–55.

———. Ms. reports. 1 June 1806, 1 July 1806, 1 Oct. 1806. Letters Received, Unregistered Series. Records of the War Department. RG M221. National Archives.

———. Notice of marriage to Mary Pasteur. 20 Apr. 1809. *Raleigh Register* 27 Apr. 1809.

———. "Observations Relative to the Geography, Natural History, &c., of the Country along the Red-River, in Louisiana." *The Philadelphia Medical and Physical Journal* 2, pt. 2 (1806): 47.

———. "Will and Testament." 13 June 1840. Craven County Original Wills. North Carolina State Archives, Raleigh, N.C.

Cuvier, Georges, et al., eds. *The Animal Kingdom: Arranged in Conformity with Its Organization.* 16 vols. London: printed for G. B. Whittaker, 1827–35.

De Blanc, Luis. "Letter to Estevan Miro, March 27, 1790." In *Spain in the Mississippi Valley, 1765–1794,* edited by Lawrence Kinnaird, vol. 2, 316. Washington, D.C.: Government Printing Office, 1946.

Deseret News, 16 Nov. 1865.

Doctrine and Covenants of the Church of Jesus Christ of Latter-Day Saints. Salt Lake City: Church of Jesus Christ of Latter-Day Saints, 1921.

Dodge, Richard. *Our Wild Indians.* Freeport, N.Y.: Books for Libraries Press, 1970.

———. *The Plains of the Great West and Their Inhabitants, Being a Description of the Plains, &c. of the Great North American Desert.* 1877. Reprint, New York: Archer House, 1959.

———. *The Plains of North America and Their Inhabitants.* Edited by Wayne Kime. Newark: University of Delaware Press, 1989.

Drips, Andrew. Papers. Archives of the Missouri State Historical Society, St. Louis, Missouri.

Dunbar, William. "Journal of a Voyage up the Washita River, in Louisiana, in the Years 1804–5." In *Message from the President of the United States Communicating Discoveries Made in Exploring the Missouri, Red River, and Washita,* Thomas Jefferson. 78–79. New York: Hopkins and Seymour, 1806.

———. "Observations Made in a Voyage Commencing at St. Catharine's Landing ... ." *National Intelligencer and Washington Advertiser.* Washington, D.C.: 15, 27, 31 Oct. and 10, 12 Nov. 1806.

Du Pratz, Antoine Simon Le Page. *The History of Louisiana, or of the Western Parts of Virginia and Carolina.* Introduction by Henry C. Dethloff. 1774. Reprint, Baton Rouge, La.: Claitor's Publishing Division, 1972.

Flores, Dan, ed. *Jefferson & Southwestern Exploration: The Freeman and Custis Accounts of the Red River Expedition of 1806.* Norman: University of Oklahoma Press, 1984.

———, ed. *Journal of an Indian Trader: Anthony Glass & the Texas Trading Frontier, 1790–1810.* College Station: Texas A&M University Press, 1985.

Force, Peter. Collection. Manuscripts Division. Library of Congress.

Fowler, Jacob. *The Journal of Jacob Fowler: Narrating an Adventure from Arkansas through the Indian Territory, Oklahoma, Kansas, Colorado, and New Mexico, to the Sources of the Rio Grande del Norte.* Edited by Elliott Coues. New York: F. P. Harper, 1898.

Gray, J. E. "A Synopsis of the Species of the Class Reptilia." In *The Animal Kingdom: Arranged in Conformity with Its Organization,* edited by Georges Cuvier, et al. 16 vols. Vol. 9, 109. London: printed for G. B. Whittaker, 1827–35.

Gregg, Josiah. "Report, Commissioner of Indian Affairs, 1842." In *Commerce of the Prairies,* edited by Max Moorhead. Norman: University of Oklahoma Press, 1964.

Groff Family Collection. Bitterroot Valley Historical Society. File SC 1053. Montana State Historical Society, Helena, Montana.

Haley, J. Evetts, ed. *Albert Pike's Journeys in the Prairie, 1831–1832.* Canyon, Tex.: Panhandle-Plains Historical Society, 1969.

Harshberger, John W. *The Botanists of Philadelphia and Their Work.* Philadelphia: T. C. Davis and Sons, 1899.

Hornaday, William T. "The Extermination of the American Bison, with a Sketch of Its Discovery and Life History." Smithsonian Report 1887. Washington, D.C., 1889.

Hunter, Clark, ed. *The Life and Letters of Alexander Wilson.* Philadelphia: American Philosophical Society, 1983.

Jackson, Donald, ed. *Letters of the Lewis and Clark Expedition, with Related Documents, 1783–1854.* 2d ed. 2 vols. Urbana: University of Illinois Press, 1978.

———, ed. *The Journals of Zebulon Montgomery Pike, with Letters and Related Documents.* 2 vols. Norman: University of Oklahoma Press, 1966.

Jackson, Donald, and Mary Lee Spence, eds. *The Expeditions of John Charles Fremont.* 5 vols. Urbana: University of Illinois Press, 1970–84.

James, Edwin. "Account of an Expedition from Pittsburgh to the Rocky Mountains Performed in the Years 1819, 1829." In *Early Travels,* edited by Reuben Gold Thwaites. Vol. 17. Cleveland, Ohio: Arthur H. Clark, 1906.

James, Thomas. *Three Years among the Indians and Mexicans.* Edited by Walter Douglas. St. Louis: Missouri Historical Society, 1916.

"Jefferson the President: Second Term, 1805–1809." *The Louisiana Gazette* (New Orleans), 16 May 1811.

Jefferson, Thomas. "The Limits and Bounds of Louisiana." In *Documents Relating to the Purchase and Exploration of Louisiana.* Boston, 1904.

———. *Message from the President of the United States Communicating Discoveries Made in Exploring the Missouri, Red River, and Washita.* New York: Hopkins and Symour, 1806.

———. "Notes on the State of Virginia, Written in the Year 1781, Somewhat Corrected and Enlarged in the Winter of 1782 ... ." London: J. Stockdale, 1787.

[King, Nicholas]. *An Account of the Red River, in Louisiana ... .* Washington, D.C.: [*The National Intelligencer*], 1807.

Linné, Caroli A. [Carolus Linnaeus]. *Systema Naturae per Regna Tria Naturae.* Edited by J. F. Gmelin. 4 vols. London, 1789.

———. *Systema Vegetabilium.* 14th ed. Edited by J. Andrea Murray. Göttingen, Germany: J. C. Dieterich, 1784.

Marcy, Randolph. *A Report on the Exploration of the Red River, in Louisiana.* Washington, D.C.: A. O. P. Nicholson, Public Printer, 1854.

———. *Thirty Years of Army Life on the Border.* 1866. Reprint, Philadelphia: J. B. Lippincott, 1963.

Marshall, Humphrey. *Arbustum Americanum: The American Grove; or an Alphabetical Catalogue of Forest Trees and Shrubs ... .* Philadelphia, 1785.

McDermott, John Francis, ed. "The Western Journals of Dr. George Hunter, 1796–1805." *Transactions of the American Philosophical Society* 53 (1963): 12.

McKee, John. Papers. Manuscript Division. Library of Congress, Washington, D.C.

Michaux, Andre. *Flora Boreali-Americana ... .* Paris, 1803.

Miller, Stephen. Memoir. Collection no. 371. Recollections of Physicians in early North Carolina. East Carolina Manuscript Collection. J. Y. Joyner Library. East Carolina University, Greenville, North Carolina.

Mitchill, Samuel L., ed. *The Medical Repository.*

Mollhausen, Heinrich. *Diary of a Journey from the Mississippi to the Coasts of the Pacific.* 2 vols. New York: Johnson Reprint Corp., 1969.

Moorhead, Max, ed. *Commerce of the Prairies.* Norman: University of Oklahoma Press, 1964.

Morton, Conrad. "Freeman and Custis' Account of the Red River Expedition of 1806: An Overlooked Publication of Botanical Interest." *Journal of the [Harvard] Arnold Arboretum* 48 (1967): 431–59.

Moulton, Gary, ed. *The Journals of the Lewis and Clark Expedition.* 11 vols. Lincoln: University of Nebraska Press, 1984–97.

Muhlenberg, Henry. "Index Florae-Lancastriensis." *Transactions of the American Philosophical Society* 3 (1793): 157–84.

Northern Great Plains Planning Team. *Summary of the Draft Environmental Impact Statement for the Northern Great Plains Management Plans Revision, July 1999* Chadron, Neb.: USDA Forest Service, 1999.

Nottingham, Stratton, ed. and comp. *Wills and Administrations, Accomack County, Virginia, 1663–1800.* Cottonport, Va.: Polyanthos, 1973.

Pammel, Louis. Papers. "Note on the Death of Edwin James." University Archives. Iowa State University Library, Ames, Iowa.

"Proposed National Parks." Files. *Records of the National Park Service.* National Archives. RG 79.

Rafinesque, Constantine Samuel. "An Essay on the Exotic Plants, Mostly European, Which Have Been Naturalized and Now Grow Spontaneously in the Middle States of North America." *The Medical Repository,* 8 (1811): 330–45.

———. *Florula Ludoviciana; or A Flora of the State of Louisiana.* Introduction by Joseph Ewan. 1817. Facsimile reprint, New York: Hafner, 1967.

———. "A Life of Travels." *Chronica Botanica: An International Collection of Studies in the Method and History of Biology and Agriculture* 7 (spring 1944): 305.

Records of the War Department. Letters Sent, Main Series. National Archives. RG M370.

Rowland, Eron Dunbar. *Life, Letters and Papers of William Dunbar ... .* Jackson, Miss.: Press of the Mississippi Historic Society, 1930.

Sibley, John. "A Report from Natchitoches in 1807." Edited by Annie Heloise Abel. New York: Museum of the American Indian, 1922.

Smith, Ralph A., ed. and trans. "Account of the Journey of Bénard de La Harpe: Discovery Made by Him of Several Indian Nations Situated in the West." *Southwestern Historical Quarterly* 62 (July 1958–Oct. 1959): 75–86, 246–59, 371–85, 525–41.

Spanish Archives of New Mexico. Joseph Halpin Records Center and Archives, Santa Fe, New Mexico.

Sublette Papers. "Soloman Sublette to William Sublette, Feb. 2, and May 5, 1844." Archives of the Missouri State Historical Society, St. Louis, Missouri.

Thomas Jefferson Papers. Manuscripts Division. Library of Congress, Washington, D.C.

Thoreau, Henry David. *The Heart of Thoreau's Journals.* Edited by Odell Shepard, 23 Mar. 1856 entry. Boston and New York: Houghton Mifflin, 1906.

Thwaites, Reuben Gold, ed. *Early Western Travels, 1748–1846.* Cleveland, Ohio: Arthur H. Clark, 1906.

Von Humboldt, Baron Alexander. *Carte generale du royaume de la Nouvelle Espagne.* University of Illinois, Urbana-Champaign, Library. Photocopy in author's possession.

Walter, Thomas. *Flora Caroliniana, Secundum Systema Vegetabilium Perillustris Linnaei Digesta.* London: Sumtipbus J. Fraser, 1788.

Webb, James J. "Memoirs of James J. Webb, Merchant in Santa Fe, N.Mex., 1844." Archives of the Missouri State Historical Society, St. Louis, Missouri.

Whitehouse, Joseph. *The Journals of the Lewis and Clark Expedition.* Edited by Gary Moulton. 11 vols. Vol. 11, *The Journal of Joseph Whitehouse.* Lincoln: University of Nebraska Press, 1997.

Whitfield, James. Report. "Census of the Cheyenne, Comanche, Arapaho, Plains Apache, and the

Kiowa of the Upper Arkansas Agency, 15 August 1855." U.S. Department of the Interior, Bureau of Indian Affairs. Letters received by the office of Indian Affairs, 1824–81. National Archives. RG 75, M234.

Woodruff, Wilford. "Journal." 24 July 1847. In "Myth and Reality: Environmental Perceptions of the Mormons, 1840–1865, An Historical Geosophy," Richard H. Jackson. Ph.D. diss., Clark University, Worcester, Mass., 1970.

Works Progress Administration. "History of Grazing Collection, 1690–1941." Box 15, folder 2; Box 6, folder 11; Box 7, folder 3. Special Collections. Milton R. Merrill Library. Utah State University, Logan.

Government Publications

Abert, J. W. "Report of Lieut. J. W. Abert of his Examination of New Mexico in the Years 1846–1847." Cong., 1st sess., Senate Exec. Doc. No. 23.

Accomack County Deeds for 1804. Ocanock Courthouse, Va.

Annals of Congress of the United States, 1789–1824. 42 vols. 8th Cong.

Annals of Congress, 9th Cong.

Bailey, Reed, C. L. Forsling, and R. J. Becraft. "Floods and Accelerated Erosion in Northern Utah." U.S. Department of Agriculture Misc. Publication 196. Washington, D.C.: Government Printing Office, 1934.

Bailey, Robert. *Description of the Ecoregions of the United States* (and map). Washington, D.C.: Department of Agriculture. United States Forest Service. Misc. Publication No. 1391. 2d ed. Washington, D.C., 1995.

Bailey, Vernon. *Biological Survey of Texas.* Washington, D.C.: Government Printing Office, 1905.

Barnes, Will C. "The Story of the Range." WPA Grazing Collection. Special Collections. Milton R. Merrill Library. Utah State University, Logan.

Buhler, Ernest O. "Forest and Watershed Fires in Utah." *Utah Agricultural Experiment Station Circular 115.* Logan: Utah Department of Agriculture, 1940.

Cambell, Archibald, and W. J. Twining. *Reports upon the Survey of the Boundary between the Territory of the United States and the Possessions of Great Britain from the Lake of the Woods to the Summit of the Rocky Mountains.* Washington, D.C.: Government Printing Office, 1878.

Carley, James, et al. "A Soil Survey and Soil Interpretations of Ogden Valley." *Utah Agricultural Experiment Station Research Reports.* No. 14. Logan: Utah Department of Agriculture, 1973.

Carter, Clarence, ed. *The Territorial Papers of the United States.* 28 vols. Washington: Government Printing Office, 1933–.

———, ed. *The Territory of Arkansas, 1819–1836.* Vol. 20, *Territorial Papers.* Washington: Government Printing Office, 1933–.

Congressional Record. 51st Cong., 2nd sess. Vol. 22. 1 Dec. 1890. Pt. 1. 8 Jan. 1891.

Fernow, B. E. "Report upon the Forestry Investigations of the U.S. Department of Agriculture, 1877–1898." 55th Cong., 3d sess., 1899. House Doc. 181.

Forsling, C. L. "A Study of Herbaceous Plant Cover and Soil Erosion in Relation to Grazing on the Wasatch Plateau in Utah." *U.S. Department of Agriculture Experiment Station Circular 92.* Logan, Utah, 1931.

Merriam, C. Hart. *Life-Zones and Crop-Zones of the United States.* Washington, D.C.: USDA. Division of Biological Survey. Bulletin 10, 1898.

Mitchell, J. E. *Conservation Reserve Program in the Great Plains.* Fort Collins, Col.: USDA Forest Service, 1988.

Montana Environmental Quality Council. *Fourth Annual Report.* Helena: State of Montana, 1975.

Mooney, James. *Calendar History of the Kiowa Indians.* Washington, D.C.: Smithsonion Institution Press, 1979.

Mullan, John. "Report of Explorations and Surveys." 33d. Cong., 2d sess., 1853. House Exec. Doc. 91.

———. "Report of the Pacific Railroad Surveys, Stevens Report." 36th Cong., 1st sess., 1859. House Doc. 56. Vol. 12, sec. 2.

Paxton, Joseph. Letter to A. H. Sevier. 20th Cong., 2d sess., 1 Aug. 1828. House Document 78.

Powell, John Wesley. *Report on the Lands of the Arid Region of the United States, with a More Detailed Account of the Lands of Utah.* Washington, D.C.: Government Printing Office, 1878.

Powers, Le Grand, comp. Thirteenth Census of the United States taken in the Year 1910. Agriculture. Pt. 1. Vol. 5, Farms, Livestock and Animal Products; and Pt. 2. Vol. 6, Crops and Irrigations. Washington, D.C.: Government Printing Office, 1913.

"Report of the Secretary of the Interior." 34th Cong., 3d sess., 1855. House Exec. Doc. No. 1.

Report of the Utah Flood Survey, 1931, 1932. Washington, D.C.: Government Printing Office, 1933. Special collections, Milton R. Merrill Library, Utah State University, Logan, Utah.

"Report on the Forests." 47th Cong., 2d sess., 1882. Vol. 13, pt. 9. House Misc. Doc. 1

Reynolds, Robert V. R. "Grazing and Floods: A Study of Conditions in the Manti National Forest, Utah." *U.S. Department of Agriculture Forest Service Bulletin 91.* Washington, D.C.: Government Printing Office, 1911.

Roth, Arthur H., Jr. "A Graphic Summary of Grazing on the Public Lands of the Intermountain Region." *U.S. Department of Agriculture, U.S. Forest Service, and Intermountain Forest and Range Experiment Station Project 3298.* Washington, D.C.: Government Printing Office, 1940.

Tolson, Hillory, et al. "Investigative Report on Proposed Palo Duro National Monument Texas." Washington, D.C.: National Park Service Report, 1939. In "Proposed National Parks" files. Records of the National Park Service. National Archives. RG 79.

Ugarte, Jacobo Loyola y. Letter to Juan Bautista de Anza, Chihuahua, 5 Oct. 1786. Spanish Archives of New Mexico II. Microfilm Roll 10. New Mexico State Archives, Santa Fe, New Mexico.

University of Montana. "A University View of the Forest Service." 91st Cong., 2d sess., Dec. 1970. Senate Docs. 91–115.

U.S. Bureau of Land Management. *Final Environmental Impact Statement: Livestock Grazing Management of National Resource Lands.* Washington, D.C.: Government Printing Office, 1974.

U.S. Census Report. 1880. Agriculture: 144–76.

U.S. Census Report. 1900. Agriculture.

U.S. Department of Agriculture. *America's Private Land: A Geography of Hope.* Washington, D.C.: Government Printing Office, 1997.

U.S. Department of the Interior. Fish and Wildlife Service. *Reintroduction of the Mexican Wolf within Its Historic Range in the Southwestern United States: Final Environmental Impact Statement.* Albuquerque, N.Mex.: U.S. Fish and Wildlife Service, 1996.

U.S. Forest Service, Intermountain Region. *Draft Environmental Impact Statement and Proposed Land Management Plan: Wasatch National Forest, Utah.* Ogden, Utah: USDA Forest Service Inter-Mountain Region, 1977.

U.S. Geological Survey. "Arid Regions of the United States, Showing Drainage Districts." *Annual Report, 1889–90, Irrigation Survey.* Pt. 2. Washington, D.C.: Government Printing Office, 1891.

U.S. Geological Survey. "Forest Reserves." *19th Annual Report of the U.S. Geological Survey.* Washington, D.C.: Government Printing Office, 1898.

U.S. Geological Survey Map. Boyd Hill (Ark.) 7.5' Quadrangle.

U.S. Geological Survey Map. Daniels Chapel (Tex.) 7.5' Quadrangle.

Utah Agricultural Experiment Station. *Report of Utah Flood Survey, 1931, 1932.* Pamphlet. Special Collections. Merrill Library. Utah State University, Logan, Utah.

[Walker, Francis, and Chas. Seaton, Superintendents of the Census Office]. Report on the Productions of Agriculture. Vol. 3. As returned at the Tenth Census (1 June 1880). Washington, D.C.: Government Printing Office, 1883.

Wallace, Ernest. "The Habitat and Range of the Kiowa, Comanche and Apache Indians before 1867." Prepared for the U.S. Dept. of Justice for Case No. 257 before the Indian Claims Commission, 1959. Southwest Collection. Texas Tech University, Lubbock, Tex.

Zon, Raphel. "Forests and Water in Light of Scientific Evidence." 62d Cong., 2d sess., 1913 Sen. Doc. 469

Letters and Interviews

Baker, Gerard, Superintendent of the Little Bighorn Battlefield National Monument, Crow Agency, Montana. Interview by author. 8 Sep. 1997. Notes in author's possession.

Cebada, Juan Diego Perez. Visiting scholar, University of Montana. Interview by author. 10 Apr. 1997, Missoula. Notes in author's possession.

Coursey, Louise. Letter to author. 25 Apr. 1979. Charles Van Pelt Library, University of Pennsylvania.

Davison, Paul. Executive Director of the Black Bear Conservation Committee. Telephone interview. 13 Nov. 1998. Notes in author's possession.

Johnson, Minette. Program Associate, Northern Rockies Office, Defenders of Wildlife. Interview by author. 10 Aug. 1998, Missoula, Mont. Notes in author's possession.

Karges, Robert. Letter to author. 18 Mar. 1988. Letter in author's possession.

Oelschlaeger, Max. Conversation with author. 6 Apr. 1996.

Ortega, Ernest. Letter to author. 11 Feb. 1988. Letter file in author's possession.

Powell, Robert. Letter to author. 10 Feb. 1988. Letter file in author's possession.

White, Richard. Conversation with author. 9 Apr. 1994.

Secondary Works

Abernethy, Thomas Perkins. *The Burr Conspiracy.* New York: Oxford University Press, 1954.

Ackerman, Diane. *A Natural History of the Senses.* New York: Random House, 1990.

Adams, Charles. *Origin and Development of the Pueblo Katsina Cult.* Tucson: University of Arizona Press, 1991.

Alexander, Thomas G. "An Investment in Progress: Utah's First Federal Reclamation Project, The Strawberry Valley Project." *Utah Historical Quarterly* 39 (summer 1971): 286–304.

———. "Senator Reed Smoot and Western Land Policy, 1905–1920." *Arizona and the West* 13 (autumn 1971): 245–64.

———. "Stewardship and Enterprise: The LDS Church and the Wasatch Oasis Environment, 1847–1930." *Western Historical Quarterly* 25 (autumn 1994): 341–66.

———. "Sylvester Q. Cannon and the Revival of Environmental Consciousness in the Mormon Community." *Environmental History* 3 (Oct. 1998): 488–507.

———. "Toward a Synthetic Interpretation of the Mountain West: Diversity, Isolation, and Cooperation." *Utah Historical Quarterly* 39 (summer 1971): 202–206.

Alwin, John. "Montana's Beaverslide Hay Stacker." *Journal of Cultural Geography* 3 (1982): 42–50.

Anderson, Gary. *The Indian Southwest, 1580–1830.* Norman: University of Oklahoma Press, 1999.

Andruss, Van, et al., eds. *Home: A Bioregional Reader.* Santa Cruz: New Society Publishers, 1990.

Arrington, Leonard J. *Great Basin Kingdom: An Economic History of the Latter-Day Saints, 1830–1900.* Cambridge: Harvard University Press, 1958.

———. "Mormon Economic Policies and Their Implementation on the Western Frontier, 1847–1900." Ph.D. diss., University of North Carolina, Chapel Hill, 1952.

———. *Orderville, Utah: A Pioneer Mormon Experiment in Economic Organization.* Logan: Utah State University Press, 1954.

———. "Property among the Mormons." *Rural Sociology* 18 (Dec. 1951): 345–48.

Arrington, Leonard J., and Thomas G. Alexander. *A Dependent Commonwealth: Utah's Economy from Statehood to the Great Depression.* Edited by Dean May. Provo, Utah, 1974.

Arrington, Leonard J., Feramorz Y. Fox, and Dean May. *Building the City of God.* Salt Lake City: Deseret, 1976.

Atencio, Tómas. "The Human Dimensions in Land Use and Land Displacement in Northern New Mexican Villages." In *Indian and Spanish American Adjustments to Arid and Semiarid Environments,* edited by Clark Knowlton. Lubbock: Texas Technological College, 1964.

Atwood, Wallace. *The Physiographic Provinces of North America.* Boston: Ginn, 1940.

Audubon, Maria, and Elliott Coues, eds. *Audubon and His Journals.* Vol. 2. 1897. Reprint, New York: Dover Press, 1986.

Bailey, Deevon. "Economic Impacts of Public Grazing Reductions in the Livestock Industry with Emphasis on Utah." Master's thesis, Utah State University, Logan, 1980.

Bailey, Reed. "Utah's Watersheds." *Proceedings.* Utah Academy of Sciences, Arts and Letters 25 (1947–48): 22–39.

Baker, T. Lindsay. "The Buffalo Robe Trade in the 19th-Century West." Paper presented at the Center for the American Indian, Oklahoma City, Apr. 1989. Paper in author's possession.

Bamforth, Douglas. *Ecology and Human Organization on the Great Plains.* New York: Plenum Press, 1988.

———. "Historical Documents and Bison Ecology on the Great Plains." *Plains Anthropologist* 32, no. 115 (Feb. 1987): 1–16.

Barr, James. "Man and Nature: The Ecological Controversy and the Old Testament." In *Ecology and Religion in History,* edited by David Spring and Eileen Spring. New York: Harper and Row, 1974.

Barrett, Stephen. "Relationship of Indian-Caused Fires to the Ecology of Western Montana Forests." Master's thesis, University of Montana, Missoula, 1981.

Barrett, Stephen, and S. F. Arno. "Indian Fires as an Ecological Influence in the Northern Rockies." *Journal of Forestry* 80 (1982): 641–53.

Barsness, Larry. *Head, Hides, and Horns: The Compleat Buffalo Book.* Fort Worth: Texas Christian University Press, 1974.

Bell, Robert, and Nancy Bell, eds. *Sociobiology and the Social Sciences.* Lubbock: Texas Tech University Press, 1989.

Benedict, James. "Along the Great Divide: Paleoindian Archeology of the High Colorado Front Range." In *Ice-Age Hunters of the Rockies,* edited by Dennis Stanford and Jane Day, 359–73. Niwot: University of Colorado Press, 1992.

———. "Along the Great Divide: Paleoindian Subsistence Strategies between Two Ecosystems." In *Ice-Age Hunters of the Rockies,* edited by Dennis Stanford and Jane Day, 349–59. Niwot: University of Colorado Press, 1992.

Benson, Maxine, ed. *From Pittsburg to the Rocky Mountains: Major Stephen Long's Expedition, 1819–1820.* Golden, Colo.: Fulcrum, 1988.

Berg, Peter. "Strategies for Reinhabiting the Northern California Bioregion." *Seriatim: The Journal of Ecotopia* 3 (1977): 2.

Berkhofer, Robert. "Space, Time, Culture and the New Frontier." *Agricultural History* 38 (Jan. 1964): 21–30.

Berlandier, Jean Louis. *The Indians of Texas in 1830,* edited by John C. Ewers. Washington, D.C.: Smithsonian Institution Press, 1969.

Berthrong, Donald. *The Southern Cheyennes.* Norman: University of Oklahoma Press, 1963.

Best, Gerald. *Snowplow: Clearing Mountain Rails.* Berkeley and Los Angeles: University of California Press, 1966.

Bevis, Bill. "Region, Power, Place." In *Reading the West: New Essays on the Literature of the American West,* edited by Michael Kowalewski, 15–28. New York: Cambridge University Press, 1996.

Biersack, Aletta, ed. *Clio in Oceania: Toward a Historical Anthropology.* Washington, D.C.: Smithsonian Institution Press, 1991.

Biggar, Hugh. "The Development of the Lower Flathead Valley." Master's thesis, Montana State University, Bozeman, 1948.

Billington, Ray Allen. "Frederick Jackson Turner and Walter Prescott Webb: Frontier Historians." In *Essays on the American West,* edited by Harold Hollingsworth and Sandra Myres, 89–113. Austin: The University of Texas Press, 1969.

Binnema, Ted. "The Common and Contested Ground: A History of the Northwestern Plains from A.D. 200 to 1806." Ph.D. diss., University of Alberta, 1998.

Bloemink, Barbara. *Georgia O'Keeffe: Canyon Suite.* New York: George Braziller, 1995.

Blouet, Brian, and Merlin Lawson. *Images of the Plains: The Role of Human Nature in Settlement.* Lincoln: University of Nebraska Press, 1975.

Blum, Deborah. *Sex on the Brain: The Biological Differences between Men and Women.* New York: Viking Press, 1997.

Bolen, Eric, and Dan Flores. *The Mississippi Kite.* Austin: The University of Texas Press, 1993.

Bolle, Arnold. "The Bitterroot Revisited: A University Review of the Forest Service." *Public Land Review* 10 (1989): 1–18.

Botkin, Daniel. *Discordant Harmonies: A New Ecology for the 21st Century.* New York: Oxford University Press, 1990.

Bowden, Martyn. "The Invention of American Tradition." *Journal of Historical Geography* 18 (Jan. 1992): 3–26.

Box, Thadis. "Range Deterioration in West Texas." *Southwestern Historical Quarterly* 71 (1967): 39–45.

Boyd, Maurice. *Kiowa Voices: Ceremonial Dance, Ritual and Songs.* 2 vols. Fort Worth: Texas Christian University Press, 1981.

Brandon, William. *Indians.* Boston: Houghton-Mifflin, 1987.

Braudel, Fernand. *Civilization and Capitalism: 15th–18th Centuries.* 3 vols. New York: Harper and Row, 1971–84.

Brewer, T. M., ed. *Wilson's American Ornithology.* 1840. Reprint, New York: Arno Press, 1970.

Briggs, Charles, and John Van Ness, eds. *Land, Water, and Culture: New Perspectives on Hispanic Land Grants.* Albuquerque: University of New Mexico Press, 1987.

Brightman, Robert. "Conservation and Resource Depletion: The Case of the Boreal Forest Algonquians." In *The Question of the Commons: The Culture an Ecology of Communal Resources,* edited by Bonnie McKay and James Acheson, 121–41. Tucson: University of Arizona Press, 1987.

Broach, Elise. "Angels, Architecture, and Erosion: The Dakota Badlands as Cultural Symbol." *North Dakota History* 59 (1992): 2–15.

Brokaw, Howard, ed. *Wildlife in America.* Washington, D.C.: Council on Environmental Quality, 1978.

Brown, Bill. "Comancheria Demography, 1805–1830." *Panhandle-Plains Historical Review* 59 (1986): 8–12.

Brown, Clair A. *Wildflowers of Louisiana and Adjoining States.* Baton Rouge: Louisiana State University Press, 1972.

Brown, David. *The Grizzly in the Southwest.* Norman: University of Oklahoma Press, 1985.

Brown, James. "Mammals on Mountaintops: Nonequilibrium Insular Biogeography." *American Naturalist* 105 (1971): 467–78.

Brown, James, and Arthur Gibson. *Biogeography.* St. Louis: C. V. Mosby, 1983.

Brown, Joseph Epes. *Animals of the Soul: Sacred Animals of the Oglala Sioux.* Rockport, Mass.: Element Press, 1992.

Browne, Kingsley. *Divided Labors: An Evolutionary History of Women at Work.* New Haven: Yale University Press, 1999.

Brown, Mark, and W. R. Felton. *Before Barbed Wire: L. A. Huffman, Photographer on Horseback.* New York: Bramhall House, 1956.

Brush, Stephen. "Introduction: Cultural Adaptations to Mountain Ecosystems." *Human Ecology* 4 (Apr. 1976): 130–31.

———. "Man's Use of an Andean Ecosystem." *Human Ecology* 4 (Apr. 1976): 143–49.

Bryan, Liz. *The Buffalo People: Prehistoric Archeology on the Canadian Plains.* Edmonton: University of Alberta Press, 1991.

Burkhardt, Wayne. " Herbivory in the Intermountain West." In *Herbivory in the Intermountain West: An Overview of Evolutionary History, Historic Cultural Impacts and Lessons from the Past,* edited by Wayne Burkhardt et al., 4–15. Walla Walla, Wa.: Interior Columbia Basin Ecosystem Management Project, 1994.

Burlingame, Merrill. "The Buffalo in Trade and Commerce." *North Dakota Historical Quarterly* 3 (July 1929): 262–91.

Bustamante, Adrian. "The Human Element in the West: Contradictions, Contradictions, Contradictions." In *A Society to Match the Scenery: Personal Visions of the Future of the American West,* edited by Gary Holthaus, 75–77. Niwot: University of Colorado Press, 1991.

Butzer, Karl. "Civilizations: Organisms or Systems?" *American Scientist* 68 (Sep.–Oct. 1980): 517–24.

———. "Environment, Culture, and Human Evolution." *American Scientist* 65 (1977): 572–84.

Callenbach, Ernest. *Bring Back the Buffalo! A Sustainable Future for American's Great Plains.* Washington, D.C.: Island Press, 1995.

Canonge, Elliott. *Comanche Texts.* Norman: University of Oklahoma Press, 1958.

Cantwell, Robert. *Alexander Wilson, Naturalist and Pioneer … .* Philadelphia: Lippincott, 1961.

Carlson, Gustav, and Volney H. Jones, "Some Notes on the Uses of Plants by the Comanche Indians," *Papers of the Michigan Academy of Sciences, Arts, and Letters* 25 (1940): 517–42.

Carpra, Fritjof. *The Tao of Physics.* Boulder: Shambhala Press, 1975.

Cartmill, Matt. *A View to Death in the Morning: Hunting and Nature through History.* Chap. 1. Cambridge: Harvard University Press, 1993.

Caughley, Graeme. "Eruption of Ungulate Populations, with Emphasis on Himalayan Thar in New Zealand." *Ecology* 51, no. 1 (winter 1970): 53–72.

Chamberlain, Ralph V. "Man and Nature in Early Utah." *Proceedings.* Utah Academy of Science, Arts and Letters 24 (1946–47): 3–22.

Chapman, Joseph, and George Feldhamer, eds. *Wild Mammals of North America: Biology, Management, and Economics.* Baltimore: Johns Hopkins University Press, 1982.

Chase, Stuart. *Rich Land, Poor Land: A Study of Waste in the Natural Resources of America.* New York: Whittlesey House, 1936.

Chavez, Fray Angelico. *My Penitente Land: Reflections on Spanish New Mexico.* Santa Fe: Museum of New Mexico Press, 1993.

Chouquette, P. E., and E. Borughton. "Anthrax." In *Infectious Diseases of Wild Mammals,* edited by J. W. Davis et al., 288–96. 2d ed. Ames: Iowa State University Press, 1981.

Christensen, Ross T. "On Prehistory of Utah Valley." *Proceedings.* Utah Academy of Science, Arts and Letters 25 (1947–48): 101–9.

Christiansen, Early, and Myrtis A. Hutchinson. "Historical Observations on the Ecology of Rush and Tooele Valleys, Utah." *Utah Academy Proceedings* 42 (1965).

Clark, Tim, and Denise Casey. *Tales of the Grizzly: Thirty-Nine Stories of Grizzly Bear Encounters in the Wilderness.* Moose, Wy.: Homestead Publishing, 1991.

Clews, Elsie Parsons. *Pueblo Indian Religion.* 2 vols. Chicago: University of Chicago Press, 1939.

Clifford, Frank. "Timber Fight Is Clash of Cultural, Land Values." *Los Angeles Times,* 6 Sep. 1998.

Clutton-Brock, Janet, ed. *The Walking Larder.* London: Unwin-Hyman, 1989.

Cochran, Doris M., and Coleman J. Goin. *The New Field Book of Reptiles and Amphibians.* New York: G. P. Putman's Sons, 1970.

Coffman, Elmo. "The Geography of the Utah Valley Crescent." Ph.D. diss., Ohio State University, Columbus, 1944.

———. "Our Resources." *Proceedings.* Utah Academy of Sciences, Arts and Letters 25 (1947–48).

Cole, Donald. "Transmountain Water Diversion in Colorado." *Colorado Magazine* 25 (Mar. and May 1948): 49–65, 130–48.

Commoner, Barry. *The Closing Circle: Nature, Man, and Technology.* New York: Knopf, 1971.

Coniff, Richard. "The Natural History of Art." *Discover* 20 (November 1999): 94–101.

Conserving Prairie Dog Ecosystems on the Northern Plains. Bozeman, Mont.: Predator Project, 1997.

Cordell, Linda. *Prehistory of the Southwest.* Orlando: Academic Press, 1984.

Correll, Donovan Stewart, and Marshall Conring Johnston. *Manual of Vascular Plants of Texas.* Renner, Tex.: Texas Research Foundation, 1970.

Cottam, Walter. "An Ecological Study of the Flora of Utah Lake, Utah." Ph.D. diss., University of Chicago, 1926.

———. "General Plan for Conservation." *Proceedings.* Utah Academy of Science, Arts and Letters 25 (1947–48): 69–70.

———. "The Impact of Man on the Flora of the Bonneville Basin." Pamphlet. Salt Lake City, 1961. Special Collections, Milton R. Merrill Library. Utah State University, Logan, Utah.

Cottam, Walter, and George Stewart. "Plant Succession as a Result of Grazing and of Meadow Desiccation by Erosion since Settlement in 1862." *Journal of Forestry* 38 (Aug. 1940): 31.

Cox, Isaac J. "The Early Exploration of Louisiana." Ph.D. diss., University of Pennsylvania, Philadelphia, 1906.

———. "The Explorations of the Louisiana Frontier, 1803–1806." *Annual Report of the American Historical Association for the Year 1904.* 151–74. Washington, D.C.: 1905.

———. "General James Wilkinson and His Later Intrigues with the Spaniards." *American Historical Review,* 19 (July 1914): 794–812.

Craddock, George W. "Salt Lake City Flood, 1945." *Proceedings.* Utah Academy of Science, Arts and Letters 23 (1945–46): 51–61.

Creel, Darrell, et al. "A Faunal Record from West-Central Texas and Its Bearing on Late Holocene Bison Population Changes in the Southern Plains." *Plains Anthropologist* 35, no. 127 (Apr. 1990): 55–69.

Cronon, William. *Changes in the Land: Indians, Colonists, and the Ecology of New England.* New York: Hill and Wang, 1983.

———. *Nature's Metropolis: Chicago and the Great West.* Oxford: Cambridge University Press, 1991.

————. "Revisiting the Vanishing Frontier: The Legacy of Frederick Jackson Turner." *Western Historical Quarterly* 18 (Apr. 1987): 157–76.

————. "The Trouble with Wilderness." *New York Times Magazine* (13 Aug. 1995): 42–45.

————. "The Uses of Environmental History." *Environmental History Review* 18 (spring 1994): 1–18.

————, ed. *Uncommon Ground: Toward Reinventing Nature.* New York: W. W. Norton, 1995.

Crosby, Alfred W., Jr. *The Columbian Exchange: Biological Consequences of 1492.* Westport, Conn.: Greenwood Press, 1972.

————. *Ecological Imperialism: The Biological Expansion of Europe, 900–1900.* New York, 1986.

Crowley, John. "Ranching in the Mountain Parks of Colorado." *Geographical Review* 65 (Oct. 1975): 445–60.

Crumley, Carole, ed. *Historical Ecology: Cultural Knowledge and Changing Landscapes.* Santa Fe: School of American Research Press, 1994.

Cutright, Paul Russell. *Lewis and Clark: Pioneering Naturalists.* Urbana: University of Illinois Press, 1969.

Darwin, Charles. *The Descent of Man and Selection in Relation to Sex.* New York: A. L. Burt, 1874.

————. *The Expression of Emotions in Man and Animals.* London: Watts, 1872.

Dasmann, Raymon. "Future Primitive." *The Coevolution Quarterly* 11 (1976): 26–31.

Daubenmire, Rexford. "Vegetational Zonation in the Rocky Mountains." *Botanical Review* 9 (June 1943): 325–93.

————. "The Western Limits of the Range of the American Bison." *Ecology* 66 (Apr. 1985): 622–24.

Davis, J. W., et al., eds. *Infectious Diseases of Wild Mammals.* 2d ed. Ames: Iowa State University Press, 1981.

Dawkins, Richard. *The Selfish Gene.* New York: Oxford University Press, 1976.

DeBuys, William. *Enchantment and Exploitation: The Life and Hard Times of a New Mexico Mountain Range.* Albuquerque: University of New Mexico Press, 1985.

DeBuys, William, and Alex Harris. *River of Traps: A Village Life.* Albuquerque: University of New Mexico Press, 1990.

Del Baso, Eric. "Paradigm of the Homeland Commons: Local Ecosystem Stewardship in the Upper Rio Grande." In *Social Justice and the Environment,* edited by Richard Hofrichter et al., 121–41. Washington, D.C.: Island Press, 1995.

Demeritt, David. "The Nature of Metaphors in Cultural Geography and Environmental History." *The Journal of Historical Geography* 20 (1994): 163–85.

Denevan, William. "Carl Sauer and Native American Population Size." *The Geographical Review* 86 (July 1996): 385–97.

————. "The Pristine Myth: The Landscapes of the Americas in 1492." *Transactions of the Association of American Geographers* 82 (Sep. 1992): 369

DeRosier, Arthur H., Jr. "William Dunbar, Explorer." *Journal of Mississippi History* 25 (July 1963): 165–85.

De Waal, Frans. *Good Natured: The Origins of Right and Wrong in Humans and Other Animals.* Cambridge: Harvard University Press, 1995.

Diamond, Jared. *Guns, Germs, and Steel: The Fates of Human Societies.* New York: W. W. Norton, 1997.

————. "Man the Exterminator." *Nature* 298 (1982): 787–89.

————. *The Third Chimpanzee: The Evolution and Future of the Human Animal.* New York: Harper Collins, 1992.

Dillehay, Tom. "Late Quaternary Bison Population Changes on the Southern Plains." *Plains Anthropologist* 19, no. 65 (Aug. 1974): 180–96.

Dobak, William. "The Army and the Buffalo: A Demur—A Response to David D. Smit's 'The

Frontier Army and the Destruction of the Buffalo: 1865–1883.'" *Western Historical Quarterly* 26 (summer l995): 197–202.

———. "Killing the Canadian Buffalo, 1821–1871." *Western Historical Quarterly* 27 (spring 1996): 33–52.

Dobie, J. Frank. *The Mustangs.* New York: Bramhill House, 1934.

Dobyns, Henry. "Estimating Aboriginal American Population: An Appraisal of Techniques with a New Hemispheric Estimate." *Current Anthropology* 7 (1966): 395–416.

———. *Native American Historical Demography.* Bloomington: Indiana University Press, 1976.

———. *Their Number Become Thinned: Native American Population Dynamics in Eastern North America.* Knoxville: University of Tennessee Press, 1983.

Dodds, Gordon B. "The Stream-flow Controversy: A Conservation Turning Point." *Journal of American History* 56 (June 1969): 56–69.

Dodge, Richard. *Our Wild Indians.* Freeport, N.Y.: Books for Libraries Press, 1970.

Dorsey, George A. *Traditions of the Caddo.* Washington, D.C.: Carnegie Institution of Washington, 1905.

Dubos, Rene. "Franciscan Conservation versus Benedictine Stewardship." In *Ecology and Religion in History,* edited by David Spring and Eileen Spring, 101–20. New York: Harper and Row, 1974.

Dunlap, Thomas. *Saving America's Wildlife.* Princeton: Princeton University Press, 1984.

Ebright, Malcolm. *Land Grants and Lawsuits in Northern New Mexico.* Albuquerque: University of New Mexico Press, 1994.

Ehrlich, Paul, and Robert Ornstein. *New World, New Mind.* New York: Doubleday, 1989.

Elliott, Clark A. *Biographical Dictionary of American Science: The Seventeenth through Nineteenth Centuries.* Westport, Conn.: Greenwood Press, 1979.

Emerson, Ralph Waldo. "On Nature." In *Essays by Ralph Waldo Emerson*, edited by Irwin Edman, 196–201. 1926. Reprint, New York: Harper and Row, 1988.

———. "The Young American." In *Essays and Lectures,* edited by Joel Porte, 213–22. New York: Library of America, 1983.

Emmons, David M. "Constructed Province: History and the Making of the American West." *Western Historical Quarterly* 25, no. 4 (winter 1994): 437–59.

———. "The Price of 'Freedom': Montana in the Late and Post-Anaconda Era." *Montana, the Magazine of Western History* 44 (autumn 1994): 66–73.

Entrikin, J. Nicholas. *The Betweeness of Place: Towards a Geography of Modernity.* Baltimore: Johns Hopkins University Press, 1991.

Essock, Susan, and Michael McGuire. "Social and Reproductive Histories of Depressed and Anxious Women." In *Sociobiology and the Social Sciences,* edited by Robert Bell and Nancy Bell, 105–18. Lubbock: Texas Tech University Press, 1989.

Etulain, Richard. *Conversations with Wallace Stegner on Western History and Literature.* Salt Lake City: University of Utah Press, 1983.

———. *Re-Imagining the Modern American West: A Century of Fiction, History, and Art.* Tucson: University of Arizona Press, 1996.

Evernden, Neil. "Beauty and Nothingness: Prairie as Failed Resource." *Landscape* 27 (1983): 3–6.

Ewers, John C. *The Horse in Blackfoot Culture.* Washington, D.C.: Smithsonian Institution Press, 1955.

———. "The Influence of Epidemics on the Indian Populations and Cultures of Texas." *Plains Anthropologist* 18, no. 60 (May 1973): 106.

Ewing, Sherm. *The Range.* Missoula, Mont.: Mountain Press, 1990.

Fahey, John. *The Flathead Indians.* Norman: University of Oklahoma Press, 1974.

Fairfax, Sally. "The Lands, Natural Resources, and Economy of the West." In *A Society to Match the Scenery: Personal Visions of the Future of the American West,* edited by Gary Holthaus et al., 196–205. Niwot: University of Colorado Press, 1991.

Feit, Harvey. "The Ethno-Ecology of the Wasanipi Cree; or, How Hunters Can Manage Their Resources," in *Cultural Ecology*, Bruce Cox, comp., 115–25. Toronto: University of Toronto Press, 1978.

Fisk, H. N. "Geology of Avoyelles and Rapides Parishes." *Geological Bulletin No. 18.* New Orleans, 1940.

Flaherty, Eugene. *Wild Animals and Settlers on the Great Plains.* Norman: University of Oklahoma Press, 1995.

Flores, Dan. "Bison Ecology and Bison Diplomacy: The Southern Plains from 1800 to 1850." *Journal of American History* 78 (Sep. 1991): 465–85.

———. *Caprock Canyonlands: Journeys into the Heart of the Southern Plains.* Austin: The University of Texas Press, 1997.

———. "Essay: The Great Plains 'Wilderness' As a Human-Shaped Environment." *Great Plains Research* 9 (fall 1999): 343–55.

———. "A Final Journey down the Wild Red." Shreveport, *Times Sunday Magazine.* 14 Aug. 1977.

———. "The Grand Canyon of Texas: How Palo Duro Just Missed Becoming Texas's Third Great National Park." *Texas Parks and Wildlife Magazine* 51 (1993): 4–14.

———. "The Great Contraction: Bison and Indians in Northern Plains Environmental History." In *Legacy: New Perspectives on the Battle of Little Bighorn,* edited by Charles Rankin, 3–22. Helena: Montana Historical Society Press, 1996.

———. "Islands in the Desert: An Environmental Interpretation of the Rocky Mountain Frontier." Ph.D. diss., Texas A&M University, College Station, 1978.

———. "Place: An Argument for Bioregional History." *Environmental History Review* 18 (winter 1994): 1–18.

———. "The Plains and the Painters: Two Centuries of Landscape Art from the Llano Estacado." *Journal of American Culture* 14 (1991): 19–28.

———. "The Red River Branch of the Alabama-Coushatta Indians: An Ethnohistory." *Southern Studies Journal: An Interdisciplinary Journal of the South* 16 (spring 1997): 55–72.

———. "Review of Valerius Geist's *Buffalo Nation.*" *Annals of Iowa* 57 (spring 1998): 160–62.

———. "The River That Flowed from Nowhere." In *Horizontal Yellow: Nature and History in the Near Southwest,* 37–79. Albuquerque: University of New Mexico Press, 1999.

———. "The Rocky Mountain West: Fragile Space, Diverse Place." *Montana, the Magazine of Western History* 45 (winter 1995): 46–56.

———. "Spirit of Place and the Value of Nature in the American West." *Yellowstone Science* 3 (spring 1993): 6–10.

———. "Zion in Eden: Phases of the Environmental History of Utah." *Environmental Review* 7 (winter 1983): 325–44.

Flores, Dan, and Amy Winton. *Canyon Visions: Photographs and Pastels of the Texas Plains.* Lubbock: Texas Tech University Press, 1989.

Foreman, Dave. *Confessions of an Eco-Warrior.* New York: Harmony Books, 1991.

Fowler, Don D., ed. *Great Basin Cultural Ecology: Symposium.* Reno: University of Nevada Press, 1972.

Fox, Feramorz Y. *Experiments in Cooperation and Social Security among the Mormons: A Study of Joseph Smith's Order of Stewardship and Consecration, and Brigham Young's United Order.* Salt Lake City: University of Utah Press, 1937.

———. "The Mormon Land System: A Study of the Settlement and Utilization of Land under the Direction of the Mormon Church." Ph.D. diss., Northwestern University, Chicago, 1937.

Fox, Warwick. "The Deep Ecology-Ecofeminism Debate and Its Parallels." In *Deep Ecology and the 21st Century*, ed. George Sessions, 269–89. Boston: Shambhala, 1995.

Fradkin, Philip. *A River No More: The Colorado River and the West.* Rev. ed. Berkeley and Los Angeles: University of California Press, 1995.

Francaviglia, Richard, and David Narrett, eds. *Essays on the Changing Images of the Southwest.* College Station: Texas A&M University Press, 1994.

Frazier, Kendrik. *People of Chaco: A Canyon and Its Culture.* New York: Norton, 1986.

Freeman, Douglas Southall, et al. *George Washington: A Biography.* 7 vols. New York: Charles Scribner's Sons, 1948–57.

Freud, Sigmund. *Civilization and Its Discontents.* Translated by James Strachey. New York: W. W. Norton, 1961.

Friedman, J., and M. J. Rowlands, eds. *Evolution of Social Systems.* London: Duckworth, 1977.

Friesen, Gerald. *The Canadian Prairies: A History.* Toronto: University of Toronto Press, 1985.

Frison, George. "The Foothills-Mountains and the Open Plains: The Dichotomy in Paleoindian Subsistence Strategies between Two Ecosystems." In *Ice-Age Hunters of the Rockies,* edited by Dennis Stanford and Jane Day, 323–42. Niwot: University of Colorado Press, 1992.

Frison, George, and Paul Bonnichsen. "The Pleistocene-Holocene Transition on the Plains and Rocky Mountains of North America." In *Humans at the End of the Ice Age,* edited by Lawrence Straus et al., 303–15. New York: Plenum Press, 1996.

Gallagher, Winnifred. *The Power of Place: How Our Surroundings Shape Our Thoughts, Emotions, and Actions.* New York: Poseidon, 1993.

Garfield, Viola, ed. *Symposium: Patterns of Land Use and Other Papers.* Seattle: University of Washington Press, 1961.

Garreau, Joel. *The Nine Nations of North America.* Boston: Houghton-Mifflin, 1981.

Gastil, Raymond. *Culture Regions of the United States.* Seattle: University of Washington Press, 1975.

Geiser, Samuel Wood. *The Naturalists of the Frontier.* 2d ed. Dallas: Southern Methodist University Press, 1948.

Geist, Valerius. *Buffalo Nation: History and Legend of the North American Bison.* Stillwater, Minn.: Voyageur Press, 1996.

———. "Did Large Predators Keep Humans Out of North America?" In *The Walking Larder,* edited by Janet Clutton-Brock, 128–40. London: Unwin-Hyman, 1989.

Gelo, Daniel, and Melburn D. Thurman. "Critique" and "Response" to Thurman's, "On a New Interpretation of Comanche Social Organization." *Current Anthropology* 28, no. 4, (Aug.–Oct. 1987): 551–55.

Glanz, Michael, and Jesse Ausubel. "The Ogallala Aquifer and Carbon Dioxide: Comparison and Convergence." *Environmental Conservation* 2 (1984): 123–31.

Goldstein, Melvyn, and Donald Messerschmidt. "The Significance of Latitudinality in Himalayan Mountain Ecosystems." *Human Ecology* 8 (1980): 117–34.

Goss, James A. "Basin-Plateau Shoshonean Ecological Model." In *Great Basin Cultural Ecology: Symposium,* edited by Don D. Fowler, 6–12. Reno: University of Nevada Press, 1972.

Gould, Stephen Jay. *Wonderful Life.* New York: Pantheon, 1991.

Graber, Linda. *Wilderness as Sacred Space.* Madison: University of Wisconsin Press, 1976.

Green, Donald. *Land of Underground Rain: Irrigation on the Texas High Plains, 1910–1970.* Austin: The University of Texas Press, 1973.

Grumbine, R. Edward. *Ghost Bears: Exploring the Biodiversity Crisis.* Washington, D.C.: Island Press, 1992.

Guardia, J. E. "Some Results of Log Jams in the Red River." *Bulletin of the Geographical Society of Philadelphia* 31 (July 1933): 106–33.

Guerin-Gonzalez, Camille. "Freedom Comes from People, Not Place." In *A Society to Match the Scenery: Personal Visions of the Future of the American West,* edited by Gary Holthaus et al., 194–95. Niwot: University of Colorado Press, 1991.

Gunn, Joel. "Global Climate and Regional Bio-Cultural Diversity." In *Historical Ecology: Cultural*

Knowledge and Changing Landscapes, edited by Carole Crumley, 86–90. Santa Fe: School of American Research Press, 1994.

Gunnerson, James H. "Plateau Shoshonean Prehistory: A Suggested Reconstruction." *American Antiquity* 28 (July 1962): 44.

Gunther, Erna. "The Westward Movement of Some Plains Traits." *American Anthropologist* 52 (Apr.–June 1950): 174–80.

Guthrie, A. B., Jr. *Big Sky, Fair Land: The Environmental Essays of A. B. Guthrie Jr.* Edited by David Peterson. Flagstaff: Northland Press, 1988.

Guymon, Richard D. "Ecological History and Biological Resources of San Juan County, Utah." Master's thesis, University of Utah, Salt Lake City, 1964.

Haggard, J. Villasana. "The Neutral Ground between Louisiana and Texas, 1806–1821." *Louisiana Historical Quarterly* 28 (1945): 1001–128.

Haley, J. Evetts. *Charles Goodnight, Cowman and Plainsman.* Norman: University of Oklahoma Press, 1949.

———. "The Comanchero Trade." *Southwestern Historical Quarterly* 38, no. 3 (Jan. 1935): 157–76.

Hall, Heber H. "The Impact of Man on the Vegetation and Soil of the Upper Valley Allotment, Garfield County, Utah." Master's thesis, University of Utah, Salt Lake City, 1954.

Hall, Raymond E. "The Prairie National Park." *National Parks Magazine* 41 (1962): 1–6.

Hall, Raymond E., and Keith R. Kelson. *The Mammals of North America.* 2 vols. New York: The Ronald Press, 1959.

Hall, Thomas. *Social Change in the Southwest, 1350–1880.* Lawrence: University of Kansas Press, 1989.

Halloran, Arthur. "Bison (Bovidae) Productivity on the Wichita Mountains Wildlife Refuge, Oklahoma." *The Southwestern Naturalist* 13, no. 1 (May 1968): 23–26.

Hames, Raymond. "Game Conservation or Efficient Hunting." In *The Question of the Commons: The Culture an Ecology of Communal Resources,* edited by Bonnie McKay and James Acheson, 92–120. Tucson: University of Arizona Press, 1987.

Hamilton, Annette. "Reflections on Economic Forms and Resource Management." In *Resource Managers: North American and Australian Hunter-Gatherers,* edited by Nancy Williams and Eugene Hunn, 240. Boulder: Westview Press, 1982.

Hanley, Wayne. *Natural History in America: From Mark Catesby to Rachel Carson.* New York: Demeter Press, 1977.

Hardesty, Donald. "Rethinking Cultural Adaptation." *The Professional Geographer* 38 (Feb. 1986): 11–18.

Hargrove, Eugene. "Anglo-American Land-Use Attitudes." *Environmental Ethics* 2 (summer 1980): 121–48.

Harper, Francis. Introduction to *The Travels of William Bartram.* New Haven: Yale University Press, 1958.

Harris, Gilbert D., and Authur C. Veatch. *A Preliminary Report on the Geology of Louisiana.* Baton Rouge: Louisiana State University and the State Office of Experiment Stations, 1899.

Harris, Marvin. *Cultural Materialism: The Struggle for a Science of Culture.* New York: Random House, 1979.

Harris, Marvin, and Eric Ross. *Death, Sex, and Fertility: Population Regulation in Preindustrial and Developing Societies.* New York: Columbia University Press, 1987.

———, eds. *Food and Evolution.* Philadelphia: Temple University Press, 1987.

Hauser, Marc. *Wild Minds: What Animals Really Think.* New York: Henry Holt, 2000.

Harvey, Mark. *A Symbol of Wilderness: Echo Park and the American Conservation Movement.* Albuquerque: University of New Mexico Press, 1994.

Hays, Samuel. *Beauty, Health, and Permanence: Environmental Politics in the U.S., 1955–1985.* New York: Cambridge University Press, 1987.

Heerwagen, Judith, and Gordon Orians. "Humans, Habitats, and Aesthetics." In *The Biophilia Hypothesis,* edited by Stephen Kellert and E. O. Wilson, 150–53. Washington, D.C.: Island Press, 1993.

Hereford, Joseph. *Rotary Snowplows on the Cumbres and Toltec Scenic Railroad.* Albuquerque: University of New Mexico Press, 1998.

Hesse, Herman. *Steppenwolf.* Translated by Basil Creighton. London: AllenLane, 1974.

Hester, Thomas, ed. *The Texas Archaic: A Symposium.* San Antonio: Center for Archaeological Research, The University of Texas at San Antonio, 1976.

Hickerson, Harold. "The Virginia Deer and Intertribal Buffer Zones in the Upper Mississippi Valley." In *Man, Culture, and Animals,* edited by Anthony Leeds and Andrew Vayda, 43–66. Washington, D.C.: American Association of the Advancement of Science, 1965.

Hickerson, Nancy. *The Jumanos: Traders of the Southwestern Plains.* Austin: The University of Texas Press, 1994.

High Country News. 30 Sep. 1996.

High Plains Associates. *Six State High Plains Ogallala Aquifer Regional Resources Study.* Austin: High Plains Associates, 1982.

Hofrichter, Richard, et al., eds. *Social Justice and the Environment.* Washington, D.C.: Island Press, 1995.

Holder, Preston. *The Hoe and the Horse on the Plains.* Lincoln: University of Nebraska Press, 1970.

Hollingsworth, Harold, and Sandra Myres, eds. *Essays on the American West.* Austin: The University of Texas Press, 1969.

Hollon, William Eugene, ed. *William Bollaert's Texas.* Norman: University of Oklahoma Press, 1989.

Holthaus, Gary, et al., eds. *A Society to Match the Scenery: Personal Visions of the Future of the American West.* Niwot: University of Colorado Press, 1991.

Howard, Joseph Kinsey. *Montana: High, Wide, and Handsome.* New Haven: Yale University Press, 1943.

Howarth, Bill. "Literature of Place, Environmental Writers." *Isle: Interdisciplinary Studies in Literature and Environment* 1 (spring 1993): 167–73.

Hughes, Donald J. *American Indian Ecology.* El Paso: Texas Western Press, 1983.

Hull, A. C., Jr., and Mary Kay Hull. "Pre-settlement Vegetation of Cache Valley, Utah and Idaho." *Journal of Range Management* 27 (Jan. 1974): 27–29.

Hurtado, Albert, and Peter Iverson, eds. *Major Problems in American Indian History.* Lexington, Mass.: D. C. Heath, 1994.

Husted, Wilfred. "Prehistoric Occupation of the Alpine Zone in the Rocky Mountains." In *Arctic and Alpine Environments,* edited by Jack Ives and R. G. Barry, 38–51. London: Methuen, 1974.

Hyde, George E. *Indians of the High Plains: From the Prehistoric Period to the Coming of Europeans.* Norman: University of Oklahoma Press, 1975.

———. *Spotted Tail's Folk.* Norman: University of Oklahoma Press, 1961.

Ingerson, Alice. "Tracking and Testing the Nature-Culture Dichotomy." In *Historical Ecology: Cultural Knowledge and Changing Landscapes,* edited by Carol Crumley, H3–66. Santa Fe: School of American Research Press, 1994.

Isenberg, Andrew. *The Destruction of the Bison: An Environmental History, 1750–1920.* New York: Cambridge University Press, 2000.

———. "The Return of the Bison: Nostalgia, Profit, and Preservation." *Environmental History* 2 (Apr. 1997): 179–96.

———. "Toward a Policy of Destruction: Buffaloes, Law, and the Market, 1903–1983." *Great Plains Quarterly* 12 (fall 1992): 227–41.

Ives, Jack. "The Future of the Earth's Mountains." In *Mountain People,* edited by Michael Tobias, 3–15. Norman: University of Oklahoma Press, 1986.

Ives, Jack, and R. G. Barry, eds. *Arctic and Alpine Environments.* London: Methuen, 1974.

Jablow, Joseph. *The Cheyenne in Plains Indian Trade Relations, 1795–1840.* Seattle: University of Washington Press, 1950.

Jackson, Donald. *Thomas Jefferson and the Stony Mountains: Exploring the West from Monticello.* Urbana: University of Illinois Press, 1981. Reprint, Norman: University of Oklahoma Press, 1993.

———. *Valley Men: A Speculative Account of the Arkansas River Expedition of 1807.* New Haven: Yale University Press, 1983.

Jackson, Richard, ed. *The Mormon Role in Settlement of the West.* Provo, Utah: Brigham Young University Press, 1978.

———. "Myth and Reality: Environmental Perceptions of the Mormons, 1840–1865, An Historical Geosophy." Ph.D. diss., Clark University, Worcester, Mass., 1970.

Jackson, Wes. *New Roots for Agriculture.* Lincoln: University of Nebraska Press, 1980.

Jackson, Wes, Wendell Berry, and Bruce Colman, eds. *Meeting the Expectations of the Land: Essays in Sustainable Agriculture and Stewardship.* San Francisco: North Point Press, 1984.

Jacobs, Wilbur. "The Tip of an Iceberg: Pre-Columbian Indian Demography and Some Implications for Revisionism." In Wilbur Jacobs, *The Fatal Confrontation: Historical Studies of American Indians, Environment, and Historians.* Albuquerque: University of New Mexico Press, 1996.

Jennings, Jesse D. *Prehistory of North America.* New York: McGraw-Hill, 1968.

Jennings, Jesse D., and Edward Norbeck, eds. *Prehistoric Man in the New World.* Chicago: University of Chicago Press, 1964.

John, Elizabeth A. H. "An Earlier Chapter of Kiowa History." *New Mexico Historical Review* 60, no. 4 (1985): 379–97.

Johnson, Allen, and Dumas Malone, eds. *Dictionary of American Biography.* 20 vols. New York: Scribner, 1928–36.

Johnson, Eileen, ed. *Lubbock Lake: Late Quaternary Studies on the Southern High Plains.* College Station: Texas A&M University Press, 1987.

Johnson, Minette. "Grizzly Bears in the Bitterroot." Paper prepared for Defenders of Wildlife. Paper in author's possession.

———. "The Spiritual Significance of the Bear to the Indians of the Great Plains." Paper prepared for Defenders of Wildlife. Paper in author's possession.

Jones, J. Knox, Dan Flores, and Robert Owen. "The Taxonomic and Nomenclatorial Status of *Mus ludovicianus* Custis." *Southwest Naturalist* (spring 1986): 47.

Jones, Stephen. "Boundary Concepts in the Setting of Place and Time." *Annals of the Association of American Geographers* 49 (Sep. 1959): 241–55.

Jordan, Terry. *North American Cattle-Ranching Frontiers: Origins, Diffusion, and Differentiation.* Albuquerque: University of New Mexico Press, 1993.

Jordan, Terry, Jon Kilpinen, and Charles Gritzner. *The Mountain West: Interpreting the Folk Landscape.* Baltimore: Johns Hopkins University Press, 1997.

Josephy, Alvin. *Now That the Buffalo's Gone: A Study of Today's American Indians.* Norman: University of Oklahoma Press, 1983.

Kaplan, David. "The Law of Cultural Dominance." In *Evolution and Culture,* edited by Marshall Sahlins and Elman Service, 75–82. Ann Arbor: University of Michigan Press, 1960.

Kardiner, Abraham. "Analysis of Comanche Culture." In *The Psychological Frontiers of Society,* Abraham Kardiner et al., 86–101. New York: Columbia University Press, 1945.

Kavanagh, Thomas. "The Comanche: Paradigmatic Anomaly or Ethnographic Fiction." *Haliksa'i* 4 (1985): 109–28.

———. *Comanche Political History: An Ethnohistorical Perspective, 1706–1875.* Lincoln: University of Nebraska Press, 1996.

Kay, Charles. *Aboriginal Overkill.* Oxford: Oxford University Press, forthcoming.

———. "Aboriginal Overkill and the Biogeography of Moose in Western North America." *Alces* 33 (1997): 141–64.

Kay, Jeanne. "Mormons and Mountains." In *The Mountainous West: Explorations in Historical Geography,* edited by William Wyckoff and Lary Dilsaver, 369–95. Lincoln: University of Nebraska Press, 1995.

Keiter, Robert, et al., eds. *The Greater Yellowstone Ecosystem: Redefining America's Wilderness Heritage.* New Haven: Yale University Press, 1991.

Kellert, Stephen. "The Biological Basis for Human Values of Nature." In *The Biophilia Hypothesis,* edited by Stephen Kellert and E. O. Wilson, 42–69. Washington, D.C.: Island Press, 1993.

Kellert, Stephen, and E. O. Wilson, eds. *The Biophilia Hypothesis.* Washington, D.C.: Island Press, 1993.

Kemmis, Dan. *Community and the Politics of Place.* Norman: University of Oklahoma Press, 1990.

———. "The Last Best Place: How Hardship and Limits Build Community." In *A Society to Match the Scenery: Personal Visions of the Future of the American West,* edited by Gary Holthaus et al., 84–85. Niwot: University of Colorado Press, 1991.

Kenrik, Douglas. "Bridging Social Psychology and Sociobiology: The Case of Sexual Attraction." In *Sociobiology and the Social Sciences,* edited by Robert Bell and Nancy Bell, 5–24. Lubbock: Texas Tech University Press, 1989.

Kenner, Charles. *A History of New Mexican-Plains Indian Relations.* Norman: University of Oklahoma Press, 1969.

Kilpinen, Jon. "The Front-Gabled Log Cabin and the Role of the Great Plains in Formation of the Mountain West's Built Landscape." *Great Plains Quarterly* 15 (winter 1995): 19–31.

———. "Material Folk Culture in the Adaptive Strategy of the Rocky Mountain Valley Ranching Frontier." Master's thesis, The University of Texas, Austin, 1990.

King, Philip. *Evolution of North America.* Princeton: Princeton University Press, 1959.

Kingston, Mike, ed. *The Texas Almanac, 1994–1995.* Dallas: Dallas Morning News, 1994.

Kittredge, William, and Annick Smith, eds. *The Last Best Place: A Montana Anthology.* Seattle: University of Washington Press, 1988.

Knowlton, Ezra C. *History of Highway Development in Utah.* Salt Lake City, 1967.

———, ed. *Indian and Spanish American Adjustments to Arid and Semiarid Environments.* Lubbock: Texas Technological College, 1964.

Knowlton, George F. "Our Resources—Beneficial Insects." *Proceedings.* Utah Academy of Science, Arts and Letters, 25 (1947–48): 39.

Koth, Barbara, David Lime, and Jonathan Vlaming. "Effects of Restoring Wolves on Yellowstone Area Big Game and Grizzly Bears: Opinions of Fifteen North American Experts." In *Wolves for Yellowstone?* Yellowstone National Park, 4–71, 4–72, computer simulation, 3–31. N.p., 1990.

Kowalewski, Michael, ed. *Reading the West: New Essays on the Literature of the American West.* New York: Cambridge University Press, 1996.

Kraenzel, Carl. *The Great Plains in Transition.* Norman: University of Oklahoma Press, 1955.

Krech, Shepard, III. *The Ecological Indian: Myth and History.* New York: W. W. Norton, 1999.

Kroeber, Alfred. *Cultural and Natural Areas of Native North America.* Berkeley and Los Angeles: University of California Publications in American Archaeology and Ethnology, 1939.

Kromm, David, and Stephen White. *Conserving the Ogallala: What Next?* Manhattan: Kansas State University, 1985.

Kromm, David, and Stephen White, eds. *Groundwater Exploitation in the High Plains.* Lawrence: University of Kansas Press, 1994.

Krysl, L. J., et al. "Horses and Cattle Grazing in the Wyoming Red Desert, I. Food Habits and Dietary Overlap." *Journal of Range Management* 37, no. 1 (Jan. 1984): 72–76.

Kutsch, Paul, and John Van Ness. *Cañones: Values, Crisis, and Survival in a Northern New Mexico Village.* Albuquerque: University of New Mexico Press, 1981.

Lamar, Howard. "Regionalism and the Broad Methodological Problem." In *Regional Studies: The Interplay of Land and People,* edited by Glen Lich, 19–32. College Station: Texas A&M University Press, 1992.

LaMarche, Valmore, and H. A. Mooney. "Altithermal Timberline Advance in Western United States." *Nature* 213 (1967): 980–82.

Lamborn, John E. "A History of the Development of Dry Farming in Utah and Southern Idaho." Master's thesis, Utah State University, Logan, Utah, 1978.

———. "The Smelter Cases of 1904 and 1906." Unpublished paper in author's possession.

Lane, Eric. Letter to the editor. *High Country News,* 3 Aug. 1998.

Larson, Gustave O. *The Americanization of Utah for Statehood.* San Marino, Calif.: Huntington Library, 1971.

Lavender, David. *Bent's Fort.* Lincoln: University of Nebraska Press, 1954.

Lawrence, D. H. "Spirit of Place." In *Studies in Classic American Literature,* edited by Edward McDonald, 8–9. New York: Viking, 1961.

Lawrence, Eleanor. "The Old Spanish Trail from Santa Fe to California." Master's thesis, University of California, Berkeley, 1930.

Laycock, W. A. "Stable States and Thresholds of Range Condition on North American Rangelands: A Viewpoint." *Journal of Range Management* 44 (1991): 427–33.

Leakey, Richard, and Roger Lewin. *Origins Reconsidered: In Search of What Makes Us Human.* New York: Doubleday, 1992.

Lee, Richard, and Irven Devore, eds. *Man the Hunter.* New York: Aldine de Gruyter, 1968.

Lefebvre, Henri. *The Production of Space.* Translated by Donald Nicholson-Smith. Oxford: Basil Blackwell, 1991.

Leopold, Aldo. "Pioneers and Gullies." In *The River of the Mother of God and Other Essays by Aldo Leopold,* edited by Susan Flader and Baird J. Callicott, 106–13. 1924. Reprint, Madison: University of Wisconsin Press, 1991.

———. "The Virgin Southwest." In *The River of the Mother of God and Other Essays by Aldo Leopold,* edited by Susan Flader and Baird J. Callicott, 173–80. 1933. Reprint, Madison: University of Wisconsin Press, 1991.

Leopold, Luna. "Vegetation of Southwestern Watersheds in the Nineteenth Century." *The Geographical Review* 41 (Apr. 1951): 295–316.

Lesica, Peter. "Endless Sea of Grass—No Longer." *Kelseya* 8 (1995): 1–9.

Levy, Jerold. "Ecology of the South Plains." In *Symposium: Patterns of Land Use and Other Papers,* edited by Viola Garfield, 18–25. Seattle: University of Washington Press, 1961.

Limerick, Patricia Nelson. "The Unleashing of the Western Public Intellectual." In *Trails: Toward a New Western History,* edited by Patricia Nelson Limerick, Clyde Milner, and Charles Rankin, 59–77. Lawrence: University of Kansas Press, 1991.

Linden, Eugene, *The Parrot's Lament.* New York: E. P. Dutton, 1999.

Loendorf, Lawrence. "Remnants of the Mountain Crow in Montana and Wyoming." In *Mountain People,* edited by Michael Tobias, 22–29. Norman: University of Oklahoma Press, 1986.

Long, Michael. "Colorado's Front Range." *National Geographic* 190 (Nov. 1996): 86–103.

Loomis, Noel M. "Philip Nolan's Entry into Texas in 1800." In *The Spanish in the Mississippi River Valley, 1762–1804,* edited by John Francis McDermott, 100–119. Urbana: University of Illinois Press, 1974.

Loomis, Noel M., and Abraham Nasatir, eds. *Pedro Vial and the Roads to Santa Fe.* Norman: University of Oklahoma Press, 1967.

Lopreato, Joseph. "The Maximization Principle: A Cause in Search of Conditions." In *Sociobiology and the Social Sciences,* edited by Robert Bell and Nancy Bell, 119. Lubbock: Texas Tech University Press, 1989.

Low, Bobbi. *Why Sex Matters: A Darwinian Look at Human Behavior.* Princeton: Princeton University Press, 2000.

Lowery, George H., Jr. *Louisiana Birds.* 3d ed. Baton Rouge: Louisiana State University, 1974.

Lowitt, Richard. *The New Deal and the West.* Bloomington: Indiana University Press, 1984.

Lynch, Kevin. *Managing the Sense of a Region.* Cambridge: MIT Press, 1976.

MacArthur, Robert. *Theory of Island Biogeography.* Princeton: Princeton University Press, 1967.

MacCameron, Robert. "Environmental Change in Colonial New Mexico." *Environmental History Review* 18 (summer 1994): 17–39.

Mace, Ruth. "Why Do We Do What We Do?" *Trends in Ecology and Evolution* 10 (Jan. 1995): 4–5

MacKenzie, Donald, with Elwood Maunder. "Logging Equipment Development in the West." *Forest History* 16 (Oct. 1972): 30–35.

Maclean, Norman. *A River Runs through It.* Chicago: University of Chicago Press, 1987.

Madole, Richard. "Stratigraphic Evidence of Desertification in the West-Central Great Plains within the Past 1000 Years." *Geology* 22 (1994): 483–86

Madsen, David, et al. "Man, Mammoth, and Lake Fluctuations in Utah." Selected Papers, no. 5. University of Utah Antiquities Section, 1977.

Magnaghi, Russell. "The Indian Slave Trader: The Comanche, a Case Study." Ph.D. diss., St. Louis University, St. Louis, Missouri, 1970.

Malin, James. *The Grassland of North America: Prolegomena to Its History, with Addenda and Postscript.* Gloucester, Mass.: Peter Smith, 1967.

———. *History and Ecology: Studies of the Grasslands.* Edited by Robert Swierenga. Lincoln: University of Nebraska Press, 1984.

———. "Webb and Regionalism." In *History and Ecology: Studies of the Grasslands,* edited by Robert Swierenga, 85–104. Lincoln: University of Nebraska Press, 1984.

Malone, Dumas. *Jefferson and His Time.* 6 vols. Boston: Little, Brown, 1948–81.

Mariott, Alice, and Carol Rechlin. *Plains Indian Mythology.* New York: Crowell, 1975.

Marsh, George Perkins. *The Earth as Modified by Human Action: A New Edition of Man and Nature.* 1864. Reprint, New York: Arno and the New York Times, 1874.

Marston, Richard. "Effect of Vegetation on Rainstorm Runoff." *Proceedings.* Utah Academy of Science, Arts and Letters 26 (1948–49).

Martin, Calvin. "Fire and Forest Structure in the Aboriginal Eastern Forest." *Indian Historian* 6 (fall 1973): 38–42, 54.

———. *Keepers of the Game: Indian-Animal Relations and the Fur Trade.* Berkeley and Los Angeles: University of California Press, 1979.

Martin, Paul. "40,000 Years of Extinctions on the 'Planet of Doom.'" *Palaeography, Palaeoclimatology, Palaeoecolgy* 82 (1990): 187–201.

Martin, Paul, and Henry Wright Jr., eds. *Pleistocene Extinctions: The Search for a Cause.* New Haven: Yale University Press, 1967.

Martin, Paul, and Richard Klein, eds. *Quaternary Extinctions: A Prehistoric Revolution.* Tucson: University of Arizona Press, 1985.

Martin, Paul, and Christine Szuter. "War Zones and Game Sinks in Lewis and Clark's West." *Conservation Biology* 13 (winter 1999): 36–45.

Matthews, Anne. *Where the Buffalo Roam: The Storm over the Revolutionary Plan to Restore America's Great Plains.* New York: Grove Press, 1992.

McCann, Joseph, "Before 1492: The Making of the Pre-Columbian Landscape. Part I: The Environment." *Ecological Restoration* 17 (spring/summer 1999): 15–30.

McCrocklin, Claude. "The Red River Coushatta Indian Villages." *Louisiana Archaeology* 12 (1985): 129–78.

McDermott, John Francis, ed. *The Spanish in the Mississippi River Valley, 1762–1804.* Urbana: University of Illinois Press, 1974.

McDonald, David. "Food Taboos: A Primitive Environmental Protection Agency (South America)." *Anthropos* 72 (1977): 734–48.

McDonald, Jerry. *North American Bison: Their Classification and Evolution.* Berkeley and Los Angeles: University of California Press, 1981.

McDonnell, Mark, and Stewart Pickett, eds. *Humans as Components of Ecosystems.* New York: Springer-Verlag, 1993.

McGinnis, Michael, ed. *Bioregionalism.* London and New York: Routledge, 1999.

McHugh, Tom. *The Time of the Buffalo.* New York: Alfred Knopf, 1972.

McKay, Bonnie, and James Acheson. "Human Ecology of the Commons." In *The Question of the Commons: The Culture and Ecology of Human Resources,* edited by Bonnie McKay and James Acheson, 1–34. Tucson: University of Arizona Press, 1987.

McKelvey, Susan Delano. *Botanical Exploration of the Trans-Mississippi West, 1790–1850.* Corvallis: Oregon State University Press, 1991.

McNamee, Thomas. "A Wild Bear Chase." Review of Rick Bass's, *The Lost Grizzlies: A Search for Survivors in the Wilderness of Colorado. New York Times Book Review* (26 Nov. 1995): 10.

McNeely, Jeffry, and Kenton Miller, eds. *National Parks: Conservation and Development: The Role of Protected Areas in Sustaining Society.* Washington, D.C.: Smithsonian Institution Press, 1984.

Meagher, Mary, and Margaret Meyer. "On the Origin of Brucellosis in Bison of Yellowstone National Park: A Review." *Conservation Biology* 8 (Sep. 1994): 645–53.

Mech, David. *The Wolf: The Ecology and Behavior of an Endangered Species.* Garden City, N.Y.: Natural History Press, 1970.

Medicine, Bea, and Pat Albers. *The Hidden Half: Studies of Plains Indian Women.* Washington, D.C.: University Press of America, 1983.

Medin, Dean E., and Allen E. Anderson. *Modeling the Dynamics of a Colorado Mule Deer Population.* Fort Collins: USDA Forest Service, 1979.

Meinig, Donald. "The Mormon Culture Region: Strategies and Patterns in the Geographies of the American West, 1847–1964." *Annals of the Association of American Geographers* 55 (1965): 191–220.

Melville, Elinor. *A Plague of Sheep: Environmental Consequences of the Conquest of Mexico.* New York: Cambridge University Press, 1994.

Merchant, Carolyn. *Ecological Revolutions: Nature, Gender, and Science in New England.* Chapel Hill: University of North Carolina Press, 1989.

———. "Gender and Environmental History." *Journal of American History* 76 (Mar. 1990): 1117–21.

Messerschmidt, Donald. "Ecological Change and Adaptation among the Gurungs of the Nepal Himalaya." *Human Ecology* 4 (Apr. 1976): 177.

Mighetto, Lisa. *Wild Animals and American Environmental Ethics.* Tucson: University of Arizona Press, 1991.

Miller, Kenton. "The Natural Protected Areas of the World." In *National Parks: Conservation and Development: The Role of Protected Areas in Sustaining Society,* edited by Jeffry McNeely and Kenton Miller, 17–22. Washington, D.C.: Smithsonian Institution Press, 1984.

Mills, Stephanie. Lecture on bioregionalism. University of Montana-Missoula, 16 Nov. 1993.

Milner, Clyde, ed. *For a New Significance: Re-Envisioning the History of the American West.* New York: Oxford University Press, 1996.

Milner, Clyde, et al., eds. *The Oxford History of the American West.* New York: Oxford University Press, 1994.

Miroir, M. P., et al. "Bernard de la Harpe and the Nassonite Post." *Bulletin of the Texas Archeological Society* 44 (1973): 113–67.

Missoulian, 5 Apr. 1993.

Missoulian, 26 Jan. 1995.

Missoulian, 17 July 1998.

Mitchell, William. "An Ecological Study of the Grasslands in the Region of Missoula, Montana." Master's thesis, Montana State University, Bozeman, 1958.

Moore, Clarence B. "Some Aboriginal Sites on the Red River." *Journal of the Academy of Natural Sciences of Philadelphia* 14 (1912): 584–619.

Moore, John. *The Cheyenne Nation: A Social and Demographic History.* Lincoln: University of Nebraska Press, 1987.

Muir, John. "The Wild Parks and Forest Reservations of the West." In *Our National Parks.* 1911. Reprint, Madison: University of Wisconsin Press, 1989.

Murray, John. "Introduction." In *The Great Bear: Contemporary Writings on the Grizzly,* edited by John Murray, 6–7. Anchorage: Alaska Northwest Books, 1992.

Nash, Gerald. *The American West Transformed: The Impact of the Second World War.* Bloomington: Indiana University Press, 1985.

Nash, Roderick. *The Rights of Nature: A History of Environmental Ethics.* Madison: University of Wisconsin Press, 1989.

———. *Wilderness and the American Mind.* 3d ed. New Haven: Yale University Press, 1982.

Neel, Susan. "A Place of Extremes: Nature, History, and the American West." In *For a New Significance: Re-Envisioning the History of the American West,* edited by Clyde Milner, 105–24. New York: Oxford University Press.

Nelson, Lowery. *The Mormon Village: A Pattern and Technique of Land Settlement.* Salt Lake City: University of Utah Press, 1962.

Nelson, Richard. *Make Prayers to the Raven.* Chicago: University of Chicago Press, 1983.

Netting, Robert. "What Alpine Peasants Have in Common: Observations on Communal Tenure in a Swiss Village." *Human Ecology* 4 (Apr. 1976): 140–41.

Nicolson, Majorie Hope. *Mountain Gloom and Mountain Glory: The Development of the Aesthetics of the Infinite.* Ithaca, N.Y.: Cornell University Press, 1959.

North, Gerald. "The Changing Climate of Texas." In *The Impact of Global Warming on Texas,* edited by Gerald North, Jurgen Schmandt, and Judith Clarkson, 24–49. Austin: The University of Texas Press, 1995.

Norwood, Vera, and Janice Monk, eds. *The Desert Is No Lady: Southwestern Landscapes in Women's Writing and Art.* New Haven: Yale University Press, 1986.

Noss, Reed. "A Regional Landscape Approach to Maintain Diversity." *BioScience* 33 (Dec. 1983): 703.

Nostrand, Richard. *The Hispano Homeland.* Norman: University of Oklahoma Press, 1992.

Novak, Barbara. *Nature and Culture: American Landscape and Painting, 1825–1875.* New York: Oxford University Press, 1979.

Nugent, Walter. "Where Is the American West? Report on a Survey." *Montana, the Magazine of Western History* 42 (summer 1992): 2–23.

Oberholser, Harry. *The Bird Life of Texas.* Edited by Edward Kinkaid Jr. 2 vols. Austin: University of Texas Press, 1974.

Odum, Eugene. *Fundamentals of Ecology.* Philadelphia: W. B. Saunders, 1971.

———. "The Strategy of Ecosystem Development." *Science* 164 (Apr. 1969): 262–70.

Oelschlaeger, Max. *The Idea of Wilderness: From Paleolithic Times to the Present.* New Haven: Yale University Press, 1991.

———, ed. *The Wilderness Condition: Essays on Environmentalism and Civilization.* Washington, D.C.: Island Press, 1992.

Old Lady Horse. "Old Lady Horse (Kiowa) Tells How the Buffalo Disappeared." In *Major Problems in American Indian History,* edited by Albert Hurtado and Peter Iverson, 241–42. Lexington, Mass.: D. C. Heath, 1994.

Oliver, Chad. *Ecology and Cultural Continuity as Contributing Factors in the Social Organization of the Plains Indians.* 69–80. Berkeley and Los Angeles: University of California Press, 1962.

Ord, George. "Biographical Sketch of Alexander Wilson." In *American Ornithology; or, The Natural History of the Birds of the United States,* Alexander Wilson, vol. 9, xxx–xxxiii. 9 vols. Philadelphia, 1808–14.

Osburn, Alan. "Ecological Aspects of Equestrian Adaptations in Aboriginal North America." *American Anthropologist* 85, no. 3 (Sep. 1983): 563–91.

Owen-Smith, N. "Pleistocene Extinctions: The Pivotal Role of Megaherbivores." *Paleobiology* 13 (1987): 351–62.

Paehlke, Robert. *Environmentalism and the Future of Progressive Politics.* New Haven: Yale University Press, 1989.

Parsons, James. "On 'Bioregionalism' and 'Watershed Consciousness.'" *The Professional Geographer* 37 (Feb. 1985): 1–5.

Peña, Devon. "Los Animalitos: Culture, Ecology, and the Politics of Place in the Upper Rio Grande." In *Chicano Culture, Ecology, Politics: Subversive Kin,* edited by Devon Peña, 25–57. Tucson: University of Arizona Press, 1998.

———. "Spanish-Mexican Land Grants in Environmental History." Paper presented at the Western History Association annual meeting. Albuquerque, New Mexico, Oct. 1994. Copy in author's possession.

Peña, Devon, and Ruben Martinez, "The Capitalist Tool, the Lawless, and the Violent: A Critique of Recent Southwestern Environmental History," in Devon Peña, ed., *Chicano Culture, Ecology, Politics: Subversive Kin*, 141–76. Tucson: University of Arizona Press, 1998.

Pennell, Francis W. "Benjamin Smith Barton as Naturalist." *Proceedings of the American Philosophical Society …* 86 (Sep. 1942): 120–21.

Petersen, Shannon. "Bison to Blue Whales: Protecting Endangered Species before the Endangered Species Act of 1973." *Environmental Law and Policy Journal* 22 (spring 1999): 1–26.

Peterson, Charles S. "Albert F. Potter's Wasatch Survey, 1902: A Beginning for Public Management of Natural Resources in Utah." *Utah Historical Quarterly* 39 (summer 1971): 249.

———. "The 'Americanization' of Utah's Agriculture." *Utah Historical Quarterly* 42 (spring 1974): 109–25.

Peterson, Jacqueline. *Sacred Encounters: Father De Smet and the Indians of the Rocky Mountain West.* Norman: University of Oklahoma Press, 1993.

Petulla, Joseph. *American Environmentalism: Issues, Tactics, Priorities.* College Station: Texas A&M University Press, 1980.

Phelan, Richard. *Texas Wild: The Land, Plants, and Animals of the Lone Star State.* New York: Excalibur Books, 1976.

Phillips, George. *Chiefs and Challengers: Indian Resistance and Cooperation in Southern California.* Berkeley and Los Angeles: University of California Press, 1975.

Pinker, Steven. *How the Mind Works.* New York: W. W. Norton, 1997.

Plenty Coups. "Vision in the Crazy Mountains." In *The Wilderness Reader,* edited by Frank
    Bergon, 223–29. New York: Mentor, 1980.

Ponting, Clive. *A Green History of the World: The Environment and the Collapse of Great
    Civilizations.* New York: St. Martin's Press, 1991.

Popper, Deborah Epstein, and Frank Popper. "A Daring Proposal for Dealing with an Inevitable
    Disaster." *Planning* (Dec. 1987): 12–18.

———. "The Fate of the Plains." *High Country News* 20 (1988): 15–19.

Powell, A. Michael, et al., eds. *Third Symposium on Resources of the Chihuahuan Desert Region.*
    Alpine, Tex.: Chihuahuan Desert Research Institute, 1989.

Powell, John Wesley. "Institutions for the Aridlands." *Century Magazine* 40 (May–Oct. 1890): 111–16.

Powell, Peter. *Sweet Medicine.* 2 vols. Norman: University of Oklahoma Press, 1969.

Price, Larry. *Mountains and Man: A Study of Process and Environment.* Berkeley and Los Angeles:
    University of California Press, 1981.

Pyne, Stephen J. *Fire in America: A Cultural History of Wildland and Rural Fire.* Princeton:
    Princeton University Press, 1982.

Quintana, Frances Leon. *Pobladores: Hispanic Americans of the Ute Frontier.* 1974. Privately
    printed reprint, Aztec, N.Mex.

Rakestraw, Lawrence. "Uncle Sam's Forest Reserves." *Pacific Northwest Quarterly* 44 (Oct. 1953):
    145–46.

———. "The West, States' Rights, and Conservation: A Study of Six Public Land Conferences."
    Pacific Northwest Quarterly, 47 (July 1957): 89–99.

Rangel, Emilio, and Eglantina Canales. "Habitat Preservation and Wildlife Management in
    Northern Mexico." In *Third Symposium on Resources of the Chihuahuan Desert Region,*
    edited by Michael A. Powell et al., 19–21. Alpine, Tex.: Chihuahuan Desert Research
    Institute, 1989.

Rankin, Charles, ed. *Legacy: New Perspectives on the Battle of Little Bighorn.* Helena: Montana
    Historical Society Press, 1996.

Rappaport, Roy. "Maladaptation in Social Systems." In *The Evolution of Social Systems,* edited by
    J. Friedman and M. J. Rowlands, 69–71. London: Duckworth, 1977.

———. "Normative Modes of Adaptive Processes: A Response to Anne Whyte." In *Evolution of
    Social Systems,* edited by J. Friedman and M. J. Rowlands, 79–88. London: Duckworth, 1977.

Rathjen, Frederick W. *The Texas Panhandle Frontier.* Austin: University of Texas Press, 1973.

Ray, Arthur. *Indians in the Fur Trade.* Toronto: University of Toronto Press, 1974.

Rehr, Charles. "Buffalo Populations and Other Deterministic Factors in a Model of Adaptive
    Process on the Shortgrass Plains." *Plains Anthropologist* 23, no. 82, pt. 2 (Nov. 1978): 25–27.

Reynolds, Helen. "Some Chapters in the History of the Bitterroot Valley." Master's thesis, State
    University of Montana, Bozeman, 1937.

Richey, Duke. "Valley of Troubles: A History of the Bitterroot Valley since 1930." Master's thesis,
    Environmental Studies, University of Montana, Missoula, 1998.

Rickett, Harold W. *The Central Plains and Mountains.* Vol. 6, *Wild Flowers of the United States.*
    New York: McGraw-Hill, 1966–73.

———. *Wild Flowers of the United States.* 6 vols. New York: McGraw-Hill, 1966–73.

Ricks, Joel E. *Forms and Methods of Early Mormon Settlement in Utah and the Surrounding
    Region, 1847 to 1877.* Logan: Utah State University Press, 1964.

Riebsame, William. "The Dust Bowl: Historical Image, Psychological Anchor, and Ecological
    Taboo." *Great Plains Quarterly* 6 (1986): 127–36.

———. "Sustainability of the Great Plains in an Uncertain Climate." *Great Plains Research* 1
    (1991): 133–51.

————. "Sustainable Development Questioned: The Historical Debate between Adaptationism and Catastrophism in Great Plains Studies." Paper presented at the American Society for Environmental History Conference, Pittsburg, 1993. Copy in author's possession.

————. "The United States Great Plains." In *The Earth as Transformed by Human Action,* edited by B. L. Turner II et al., chap. 34. Cambridge: Cambridge University Press, 1990.

Rister, Carl C. *Border Captives: The Traffic in Prisoners by Southern Plains Indians, 1835–1875.* Norman: University of Oklahoma Press, 1940.

Robbins, Roy. *Our Landed Heritage: The Public Domain, 1776–1970.* Rev. ed. Lincoln: University of Nebraska Press, 1976.

Roberts, B. H. *A Comprehensive History of the Church of Jesus Christ of Latter-Day Saints.* 6 vols. Salt Lake City: Deseret News Press, 1930.

Roberts, N. Keith, and B. Delworth Gardner. "Livestock and the Public Lands." *Utah Historical Quarterly* 32 (summer 1964): 285–300.

Robertson, James, ed. *Louisiana under the Rule of Spain, France, and the United States, 1785–1807.* 2 vols. Cleveland: Arthur H. Clark, 1911.

Rockwell, David. *Giving Voice to Bear: North American Indian Rituals, Myths, and Images of the Bear.* Niwot, Colo.: Robert Rinehart Publishers, 1991.

Rodman, Paul. "Colorado as a Pioneer of Science in the Mining West." *Mississippi Valley Historical Review* 47 (June 1960): 34–50.

Rodriguez, Sylvia. "Land, Water, and Ethnic Identity in Taos." In *Land, Water, and Culture: New Perspectives on Hispanic Land Grants,* edited by Charles Briggs and John Van Ness, 313–403. Albuquerque: University of New Mexico Press, 1987.

————. "The Tourist Gaze, Gentrification, and the Commodification of Subjectivity in Taos." In *Essays on the Changing Images of the Southwest,* edited by Richard Francaviglia and David Narrett, 105–26. College Station: Texas A&M University Press, 1994.

Roe, Frank. *The Buffalo: A Critical Study of the Species in Its Wild State.* Toronto: University of Toronto Press, 1951.

————. *The Indian and the Horse.* Norman: University of Oklahoma Press, 1955.

Roosevelt, Theodore. *Hunting the Grisly.* New York: P. F. Collier and Son, 1893.

Rosenvall, Lynn A. "Defunct Mormon Settlements: 1830–1930." In *The Mormon Role in Settlement of the West,* edited by Richard Jackson, 60. Provo, Utah: Brigham Young University Press, 1978.

Rostlund, Erhard. "The Geographical Range of Historic Bison in the Southeast." *Annals of the Association of American Geographers* 50 (Dec. 1970): 395–407.

Roszak, Theodore, Mary Gomes, and Allen Kanner, eds. *Ecopsychology: Restoring the Earth, Healing the Mind.* San Francisco: Sierra Club Books, 1995.

Rothman, Hal. *Devil's Bargains: Tourism in the Twentieth-Century American West.* Lawrence: Kansas University Press, 1998.

————. "Environmental History and Local History." *History News* 48 (Nov.–Dec. 1993): 8–9.

————. *The Greening of America? Environmentalism in the United States since 1945.* New York: Harcourt Brace, 1997.

————. *On Rims and Ridges: A History of the Los Alamos Area since 1880.* Lincoln: University of Nebraska Press, 1992.

Rudnick, Lois. *Mabel Dodge Luhan: New Woman, New Worlds.* Albuquerque: University of New Mexico Press, 1984.

————. "Re-Naming the Land: Anglo Expatriate Women in the Southwest." In *The Desert Is No Lady: Southwestern Landscapes in Women's Writing and Art,* edited by Vera Norwood and Janice Monk, 10–26. New Haven: Yale University Press, 1986.

Runte, Alfred. *National Parks: The American Experience.* 2d ed. Lincoln: University of Nebraska Press, l987.

Ruskin, John. *Modern Painters.* 5 vols. Vol. 4. Boston: Beacon, 1875.

Sahlins, Marshall. "The Return of the Event, Again." In *Clio in Oceania: Toward a Historical Anthropology,* edited by Aletta Biersack. Washington, D.C.: Smithsonian Institution Press, 1991.

Sahlins, Marshall, and Elman Service, eds. *Evolution and Culture.* Ann Arbor: University of Michigan Press, 1960.

Salthe, Stanley. "*Amphiumatridactylum* Cuvier, Three-toed Congo Eel." In *Catalogue of American Amphibians and Reptiles,* edited by Richard G. Zweifel, 149.1–149.2. New York: Society for the Study of Amphibians and Reptiles, 1971.

Samson, Fred, and Fritz Knopf. "Prairie Conservation in North America." *BioScience* 44 (1994): 418–19.

Samuels, M. L., and J. L. Betancourt. "Modeling the Long-Term Effects of Fuelwood Harvests on Pinyon-Juniper Woodlands." *Environmental Management* 6 (1982): 505–15.

Sauer, Carl O. *Aboriginal Population of Northwestern Mexico.* Berkeley and Los Angeles: University of California Press, 1935.

———. "Grassland Climax, Fire, and Man." *Journal of Range Management* 3 (fall 1950): 16–21.

———. *Seventeenth-Century North America: Spanish and French Accounts.* Berkeley: Turtle Island Foundation, 1980.

Schama, Simon. *Landscape and Memory.* New York: Alfred Knopf, 1995.

Schlesier, Karl, ed. *Plains Indians, A.D. 500–1500: The Archaeological Past of Historic Groups.* Norman: University of Oklahoma Press, 1994.

Schmidt, Robert. "The Mega-Chihuahauan Desert." In *Third Symposium on Resources of the Chihuahuan Desert Region,* edited by A. Michael Powell et al., 105–15. Alpine, Tex.: Chihuahuan Desert Research Institute, 1989.

Schulman, Edmund. *Dendroclimatic Changes in Semiarid America.* Tucson: University of Arizona Press, 1956.

Scully, Vincent. *The Earth, the Temple, and the Gods: Greek Sacred Architecture.* New Haven: Yale University Press, 1962.

Sessions, George. Introduction to pt. 2, "Historical Roots of Deep Ecology." In *Deep Ecology for the 21st Century: Readings on the Philosophy and Practice of the New Environmentalism,* edited by George Sessions, 97–103. Boston: Shambhala Press, 1995.

———, ed. *Deep Ecology for the 21st Century: Readings on the Philosophy and Practice of the New Environmentalism.* Boston: Shambhala Press, 1995.

Seton, Ernest Thompson. *The Biography of a Grizzly.* New York: Grosett and Dunlap, 1927.

———. *Life Histories of Northern Animals.* 2 vols. New York: Charles Scribner's Sons, 1909.

———. *Lives of Game Animals.* 1929. Reprint, Boston: Charles T. Branford, 1953.

Shannon, Fred. "An Appraisal of Walter P. Webb's *The Great Plains: A Study of Institutions and Environment.*" *Critiques of Research in the Social Sciences* 3, Bulletin 46 (1940).

Shelford, Victor E. *The Ecology of North America.* Urbana: University of Illinois Press, 1963.

———. "Preservation of Natural Biotic Communities." *Geology* 14 (1933): 240–45.

Shepard, Jerry. "Singing out of Tune: Historical Perceptions and National Parks on the Great Plains." Ph.D. diss., Texas Tech University, Lubbock, 1995.

Shepard, John, Colleen Boggs, Louis Higgs, and Phil Burgess. *A New Vision of the Heartland: The Great Plains in Transition.* Denver: Center for the New West, 1994.

Shepard, Paul. *Coming Home to the Pleistocene.* Washington: Island Press, 1998.

———. "On the Shift from Hunter-Gathering to Agriculture." In *The Wilderness Condition: Essays on Environment and Civilization,* edited by Max Oelschlaeger, 309–10. Washington, D.C.: Island Press, 1992.

———. *The Others: How Animals Made Us Human.* Washington, D.C.: Island Press/Shearwater, 1996.

———. "A Post-Historic Primitivism." In *The Wilderness Condition: Essays on Environment and Civilization,* edited by Max Oelschlaeger, 40–89. Washington, D.C.: Island Press, 1992.

———. *The Sacred Paw: The Bear in Nature, Myth, and Literature.* Washington, D.C.: Island Press, 1992.

———. *The Tender Carnivore and Sacred Game.* New York: Scribner's, 1973.

Sherow, James. "Workings of the Geodialectic: High Plains Indians and Their Horses in the Arkansas River Valley, 1800–1870." *Environmental History Review* (summer 1992): 61–84.

Shields, Rob. *Places on the Margin: Alternative Geographies of Modernity.* London: Routledge, 1991.

Shimkin, Dimitri Boris. *Wind River Shoshone Ethnography.* Berkeley and Los Angeles: University of California Press, 1947.

Shull, Alisa, and Alan Tipton. "Effective Population Size of Bison on the Wichita Mountains Wildlife Refuge." *Conservation Biology* 1, no. 1 (May 1987): 35–41.

Simmons, Marc. "History of Pueblo-Spanish Relations to 1821." *Indians of the Southwest.* Vol. 9 of *Handbook of North American Indians,* edited by Alfonso Ortiz, table 1, 185. Washington, D.C.: Smithsonian Institution Press, 1979.

Simonian, Lane. *Defending the Land of the Jaguar: A History of Conservation in Mexico.* Austin: The University of Texas Press, 1995.

Simpson, M. B., and D. S. McAllister. "Alexander Wilson's Southern Tour of 1809: The North Carolina Transit and Subscribers to the *American Ornithology.*" *North Carolina Historical Review* 63 (1986): 421–76.

Small, Meredith. *Female Choices: Sexual Behavior of Female Primates.* Ithaca: Cornell University Press, 1993.

Smallwood, William Martin. *Natural History of the American Mind.* New York: Columbia University Press, 1941.

Smith, Eric Alden. "Anthropological Applications of Optimal Foraging Theory: A Critical Review." *Current Anthropology* 24 (Dec. 1983): 628–32.

Smith, Henry Nash. *Virgin Land: The American West in Symbol and Myth.* Cambridge: Harvard University Press, 1950.

Snow, Don. "Squeezing the Daylights out of Zion." *High Country News,* 25 July 1980.

Snyder, Gary. "The Place, the Region, and the Commons." In *The Practice of the Wild: Essays by Gary Snyder,* 25–47. San Francisco: North Point Press, 1990.

Soja, Edward. *Postmodern Geographies: The Reassertion of Space in Critical Social Theory.* London: Verso, 1989.

Spence, Mark. "Crown of the Continent, Backbone of the World: The American Wilderness Ideal and Blackfeet Exclusion from Glacier National Park." *Environmental History* 1 (July 1996): 29–49.

———. *Dispossessing the Wilderness: Indian Removal and the Making of the National Parks.* New York: Oxford University Press, 1999.

Spielman, Katherine. "Late Prehistoric Exchange between the Southwest and Southern Plains." *Plains Anthropologist* 28, no. 102, pt. 1 (Nov. 1983): 257–79.

Spring, David, and Eileen Spring, eds. *Ecology and Religion in History.* New York: Harper and Row, 1974.

Spykerman, Brian. "Shoshoni Conceptualizations of Plant Relationships." Master's thesis, Utah State University, 1977.

Stanford, Dennis, and Jane Day, eds. *Ice-Age Hunters of the Rockies*. Niwot: University of Colorado Press, 1992.

Stegner, Wallace. *Beyond the Hundredth Meridian: John Wesley Powell and the Second Opening of the West*. Boston: Houghton-Mifflin, 1954.

———. "Dead Heart of the West: Reflections on the Great Salt Lake." *Rocky Mountain Magazine* 3 (Nov. 1981): 56–59.

———. "Living Dry." In *The American West as Living Space*. 3–31. Ann Arbor: University of Michigan Press, 1987.

Steiner, Michael. "The Significance of Turner's Sectional Thesis." *Western Historical Quarterly* 10 (Oct. 1979): 437–66.

Steward, Julian. "The Native Population of South America." In *Handbook of South American Indians*, edited by Julian Steward, 655–68. Washington: Bureau of Ethnology, 1949.

Stewart, George. "Utah's Biological Heritage and the Need for its Conservation." *Proceedings*. Utah Academy of Science, Arts and Letters 25 (1947–48): 7–8, 14.

Straus, Lawrence, et al., eds. *Humans at the End of the Ice Age*. New York: Plenum Press, 1996.

Streeter, Thomas W. *Bibliography of Texas, 1795–1845*. 5 vols. 3 pts. Cambridge: Harvard University Press, 1955–60.

Sturtevant, William C., ed., *The Handbook of North American Indians*. 20 vols. Washington, D.C.: Smithsonian Institution Press, 1978–89.

Swagerty, William. "Indian Trade in the Trans-Mississippi West to 1870." Vol. 6 of *Handbook of North American Indians: European-Indian Interaction*, edited by Wilcomb Washburn, 351–74. Washington, D.C.: Smithsonian Institution Press, 1978–89.

Swanton, John R. *Caddoan Indians*. 4 vols. New York: Praeger, 1974.

———. *Source Material on the History and Ethnology of the Caddo Indians*. Smithsonian Institution. Bureau of American Ethnology. Bulletin 132. Washington, D.C.: Government Printing Office, 1942.

Tanner, Adrian. *Bringing Home the Animals: Religious Ideology and Mode of Production of the Mistassini Cree Hunters*. New York: St. Martin's Press, 1979.

Tennant, Alan. *The Snakes of Texas*. Austin: The University of Texas Press, 1984.

Thoen, C. O., and E. M. Himes. "Tuberculosis." In *Infectious Diseases of Wild Mammals*, edited by J. W. Davis et al., 263–74. 2d ed. Ames: Iowa State University Press, 1981.

Thomas, Alfred B., ed. *Forgotten Frontiers: A Study of the Spanish Indian Policy of Don Juan Bautista de Anza, Governor of New Mexico, 1777–1787*. Norman: University of Oklahoma Press, 1932.

Thomas, George. *Development of Institutions under Irrigation with Special Reference to Early Utah Conditions*. New York, 1920.

Thompson, H. Paul. "A Technique Using Anthropological and Biological Data." *Current Anthropology* 7, no. 4 (Oct. 1966): 417–24.

Thornhill, Randy, and Steve Gangestad. "The Evolution of Human Sexuality." *Trends in Ecology and Evolution* 11 (Feb. 1996): 98–107.

Thornhill, Randy, and Nancy Wilmsen Thornhill. "The Evolution of Psychological Pain." In *Sociobiology and the Social Sciences*, edited by Robert Bell and Nancy Bell, 73–103. Lubbock: Texas Tech University Press, 1989.

Thurman, Melburn D. "A New Interpretation of Comanche Social Organization." *Current Anthropology* 23, no. 5 (Oct. 1982): 578–79.

Tobias, Michael. "Dialectical Dreaming: The Western Perception of Mountain People." In *Mountain People*, edited by Michael Tobias, 183–200. Norman: University of Oklahoma Press, 1986.

———, ed. *Mountain People*. Norman: University of Oklahoma Press, 1986.

Tobin, Gregory. "Walter Prescott Webb." In *Historians of the American Frontier: A Bio-Bibliographical Sourcebook,* edited by John Wunder, 713–29. New York: Greenwood Press, 1988.

Toole, K. Ross. *Montana: An Uncommon Land.* Norman: University of Oklahoma Press, 1959.

———. *Twentieth-Century Montana: A State of Extremes.* Norman: University of Oklahoma Press, 1972.

Toynbee, Arnold. "The Religious Background of the Present Environmental Crisis." In *Ecology and Religion,* edited by David Spring and Eileen Spring, 137–50. New York: Harper and Row, 1974

Treshow, Michael, and C. M. Gilmour, eds. *Proceedings.* Conference on the Future of Utah's Environment. Salt Lake City: University of Utah, 1968.

Trigger, Bruce. "Early Native North American Responses to European Contact: Romantic Versus Rationlist Interpretations." *Journal of American History* 77 (Mar. 1991): 1195–215.

Trimble, Stephen. *The Sagebrush Ocean: A Natural History of the Great Basin.* Reno: University of Nevada Press, 1989.

Tuan, Yi-Fu. "New Mexican Gullies: A Critical Review and Some Recent Observations." *Annals of the Association of American Geographers* 57 (1967): 691–703.

———. *Space and Place: The Perspective of Experience.* Minneapolis: University of Minnesota Press, 1977.

———. *Topophilia: A Study of Environmental Perception, Attitudes, and Values.* Englewood Cliffs: Prentice-Hall, 1974.

Turnbull, Colin. "Man Makes the Mountains." In *Mountain People,* edited by Michael Tobias, 69. Norman: University of Oklahoma Press, 1986.

Turner, B. L. et al., eds. *The Earth as Transformed by Human Action.* Cambridge: Cambridge University Press, 1990.

Turner, Frederick. *Spirit of Place: The Making of an American Literary Landscape.* San Francisco: Sierra Club Books, 1989.

Tyler, Royall. "The Japanese Mountains: Crowds, Convenience, and the Sacred." In *Mountain People,* edited by Michael Tobias, 153–55. Norman: University of Oklahoma Press, 1986.

Tyson, Carl Newton. *The Red River in Southwestern History.* Norman: University of Oklahoma Press, 1981.

Tzu, Lao. *Tao Te Ching.* Translated by D. C. Lau. New York: Dutton, 1963.

Ulrich, Robert. "Biophilia, Biophobia, and Natural Landscapes." In *The Biophilia Hypothesis,* edited by Stephen Kellert and E. O. Wilson, 73–137. Washington, D.C.: Island Press, 1993.

Upshur, Thomas T. "Hill and Custis." *The Virginia Magazine of History and Biography* 3 (June 1896): 319–21.

USA Today. 21 and 27 Nov. 1995; 4 Dec. 1997.

Vale, Thomas. "Mountains and Moisture in the West." In *The Mountainous West: Explorations in Historical Geography,* edited by William Wyckoff and Lary Dilsaver, 141–65. Lincoln: University of Nebraska Press, 1995.

Van Ness, John R. "Hispanic Land Grants: Ecology and Subsistence in the Uplands of Northern New Mexico and Southern Colorado." In *Land, Water, and Culture: New Perspectives on Hispanic Land Grants,* edited by Charles Briggs and John Van Ness, 141–214. Albuquerque: University of New Mexico Press, 1987.

Van Slyke, Lyman. *Yangtze: Nature, History, and the River.* Stanford: Stanford Alumni Association, 1988.

Veatch, Arthur C. "The Shreveport Area." In *A Preliminary Report on the Geology of Louisiana,* edited by Gilbert D. Harris and Authur C. Veatch, 149–208. Baton Rouge: Louisiana State University and the State Office of Experiment Stations, 1899.

Vescey, Christopher T., and Robert W. Venables, eds. *American Indian Environments: Ecological Issues in Native American History.* Syracuse: Syracuse University Press, 1980.

Victor, Frances Fuller. *The River of the West: Life and Adventures in the Rocky Mountains and Oregon.* San Francisco: R. J. Trumball, 1870.

Vines, Robert A. *Trees, Shrubs and Woody Vines of the Southwest.* Austin: The University of Texas Press, 1960.

Vogel, Virgil J. *American Indian Medicine.* Norman: University of Oklahoma Press, 1970.

Vogt, Evon, and John Roberts. "A Study of Values." *Scientific American* 195 (July 1956): 25–30.

Wagner, Frederic. "Livestock Grazing and the Livestock Industry." In *Wildlife in America,* edited by Howard Brokaw, 133–35. Washington, D.C.: Council on Environmental Quality, 1978.

Wahlquist, Wayne L. "Population Growth in the Mormon Core Area: 1847–1890." In *The Mormon Role in Settlement of the West,* edited by Richard Jackson, tables 2 and 5. Provo, Utah: Brigham Young University Press, 1978.

Wakefield, John H. "A Study of the Plant Ecology of Salt Lake and Utah Valleys before the Mormon Immigration." Master's thesis, Brigham Young University, Provo, Utah, 1933.

Walker, Don. "The Cattle Industry of Utah, 1850–1900: A Historical Profile." *Utah Historical Quarterly* 32 (summer 1964): 34.

Wallace, Ernest, and E. Adamson Hoebel. *The Comanches: Lords of the South Plains.* Norman: University of Oklahoma Press, 1951.

Wallach, Bret. "The Return of the Prairie." *Landscape* 28 (1985): 1–5.

Wallerstein, Immanuel. *Capitalist Agriculture and the Origins of the European World Economy in the 16th Century.* New York: Academic Press, 1974.

———. *The Modern World System II: Mercantilism and the Consolidation of the European World Economy, 1600–1750.* New York: Academic Press, 1980.

Warren, Louis. *The Hunter's Game.* New Haven: Yale University Press, 1997.

Watson, Alan. *A History of New Bern and Craven County.* New Bern, N.C.: Tryon Palace Comm., 1987.

Weakly, Harry. "A Tree-Ring Record of Precipitation in Western Nebraska." *Journal of Forestry* 41, no. 11 (Nov. 1943): 816–19.

Webb, Walter Prescott. *The Great Plains: A Study in Institutions and Environment.* Boston: Ginn, 1931.

Webb, Walter Prescott, H. Bailey Carroll, and Eldon Stephen Branda, eds. *The Handbook of Texas.* Vol. 2, 449–51. Austin: The University of Texas Press, 1952.

Wedel, Waldo. "Some Aspects of Human Ecology on the Central Plains." *American Anthropologist* 55 (1953): 409–513.

Weist, Katherine. "Plains Indian Women: An Assessment." In *Anthropology on the Great Plains,* edited by Raymond Wood and Margot Liberty, 255–71. Lincoln: University of Nebraska Press, 1980.

West, Elliott. "Called Out People: The Cheyennes and the Southern Plains." *Montana, the Magazine of Western History* 48 (summer 1996): 2–15.

———. *The Contested Plains: Indians, Goldseekers, and the Rush to Colorado.* Lawrence: Kansas University Press, 1998.

Western Literature Association. *Updating the Literary West.* Fort Worth: Texas Christian University Press, 1997.

Westphal, Victor. *Mercedes Reales: Hispanic Land Grants of the Upper Rio Grande Region.* Albuquerque: University of New Mexico Press, 1983.

White, Lynn, Jr. "The Historical Roots of Our Ecological Crisis." *Science* 155 (Mar. 1967): 1203–7.

White, Richard. "American Indians and the Environment." *Environmental Review* 9 (summer 1985): 101–3.

———. "Animals and Enterprise." In *The Oxford History of the American West,* edited by Clyde Milner et al., 247–84. New York: Oxford University Press, 1994.

———. "Native Americans and the Environment." In *Critical Reviews of Recent Writings in the Social Sciences,* edited by William Swagerty, 179–204. Bloomington: Indiana University Press, 1984.

———. *Roots of Dependency.* Lincoln: University of Nebraska Press, 1983.

———. "The Winning of the West: The Expansion of the Western Sioux in the Eighteenth and Nineteenth Centuries." *Journal of American History* 65, no. 2 (Sep. 1978): 319–43.

White, Richard, and William Cronon. "Ecological Change and Indian-White Relations." In *Indian-White Relations,* vol. 4 of *The Handbook of North American Indians,* edited by William C. Sturtevant, 417–29. Washington, D.C.: Smithsonian Institution Press, 1978–89.

Whitman, Walt. *Leaves of Grass.* New York: Bantam Books, 1983.

Whyte, Anne. "Systems as Perceived: A Discussion of 'Maladaption in Social Systems.'" In *Evolution of Social Systems,* edited by J. Friedman and M. J. Rowlands, 73–78. London: Duckworth, 1977.

Widtsoe, John A. "The Relation of Smelter Smoke to Utah Agriculture." *Utah State Agricultural College Experiment Station Bulletin No. 88.* Logan: Utah Department of Agriculture, 1903.

Wilkinson, Charles. *Crossing the Next Meridian: Land, Water, and the Future of the West.* Washington, D.C.: Island Press, 1992.

———. *The Eagle Bird: Mapping a New West.* New York: Pantheon, 1992.

Wilkinson, James. "Reflections on Louisiana." Original in Archivo de Indias, Havana, Cuba. Reproduced in *Louisiana under the Rule of Spain, France, and the United States, 1785–1807.* 2 vols. Vol. 2. Edited by James Robertson, 325–47. Cleveland: Arthur H. Clark, 1911.

Wilkinson, Todd. "Grizzly War." *High Country News* 30 (9 Nov. 1998): 1, 10–14.

Williams, Kenneth. *Systematics and Natural History of the American Milk Snake,* Lampropeltis triangulum. Milwaukee: Milwaukee Public Museum Press, 1978.

Williams, Nancy, and Eugene Hunn, eds. *Resource Managers: North American and Australian Hunter-Gatherers.* 240. Boulder: Westview Press, 1982.

Williams, Ted. "Killer Weeds." *Audubon* 99 (Mar.–Apr. 1997): 22–28.

Wilson, Clyde. "An Inquiry into the Nature of Plains Indian Cultural Development." *American Anthropologist* 65, no. 2 (Apr. 1963): 355–69.

Wilson, Alexander. *American Ornithology; or, The Natural History of the Birds of the United States.* 9 vols. Philadelphia, 1808–14.

Wilson, Edward O. "Biophilia and the Conservation Ethic." In *The Biophilia Hypothesis,* edited by Stephen Kellert and E. O. Wilson, 31–41. Washington, D.C.: Island Press, 1993.

———. *Biophilia: The Human Bond with Other Species.* Cambridge: Harvard University Press, 1984.

———. *Consilience: The Unity of Knowledge.* New York: Alfred Knopf, 1998.

———. "Is Humanity Suicidal?" *In Search of Nature.* 183–99. Washington, D.C.: Island Press, 1996.

———. *On Human Nature.* Cambridge: Harvard University Press, 1978.

———. *Sociobiology: The New Synthesis.* Cambridge: Harvard University Press, 1975.

Wilson, Margo. "Marital Conflict and Homicide in Evolutionary Perspective." In *Sociobiology and the Social Sciences,* edited by Robert Bell and Nancy Bell, 45–62. Lubbock: Texas Tech University Press, 1989.

Wilson, M. L. "The Evolution of Montana Agriculture in Its Early Period." *Mississippi Valley Historical Association Proceedings* 9 (1918): 429–40.

Winterhalder, Bruce. "Concepts in Historical Ecology: The View from Evolutionary Ecology." In *Historical Ecology: Cultural Knowledge and Changing Landscapes,* edited by Carole Crumley, 27–30. Santa Fe: School of American Research Press, 1994.

Wisart, David. *The Fur Trade of the American West, 1807–1840.* Lincoln: University of Nebraska Press, 1979.

———. "Preface to the Paperback Edition." *The Fur Trade of the American West, 1807–1840: A Geographical Synthesis.* iv. Lincoln: University of Nebraska Press, 1996.

Witter, J. F. "Brucellosis." In *Infectious Diseases of Wild Mammals,* edited by J. W. Davis et al., 280–87. 2d ed. Ames: Iowa State University Press, 1981.

Wood, Raymond, and Margot Liberty, eds. *Anthropology on the Great Plains.* Lincoln: University of Nebraska Press, 1980.

Woolley, Ralph. "Our Resources—Water." *Proceedings.* Utah Academy of Sciences, Arts and Letters, 25 (1947–48).

Worster, Donald. "Cowboy Ecology." In *Under Western Skies: Nature and History in the American West.* 34–52. New York: Oxford University Press, 1992.

———. "Doing Environmental History." In *The Ends of the Earth: Perspectives on Modern Environmental History,* edited by Donald Worster, 289–307. New York: Cambridge University Press, 1988.

———. *Dust Bowl: The Southern Plains in the 1930s.* New York: Oxford University Press, 1979.

———. "The Ecology of Order and Chaos." In *The Wealth of Nature: Environmental History and the Ecological Imagination.* 152–69. New York: Oxford University Press, 1993.

———. "History as Natural History." In *The Wealth of Nature: Environmental History and the Ecological Imagination.* 30–44. New York: Oxford University Press, 1993.

———. "John Muir and the Roots of American Environmentalism." In *The Wealth of Nature: Environmental History and the Ecological Imagination.* 184–202. New York: Oxford University Press, 1993.

———. "The Legacy of John Wesley Powell." In *An Unsettled Country: Changing Landscapes of the American West.* 1–30. Albuquerque: University of New Mexico Press, 1994.

———. *Nature's Economy: A History of Ecological Ideas.* New York: Cambridge University Press, 1977.

———. "New West, True West: Interpreting the Region's History." *Western Historical Quarterly* 18 (Apr. 1987): 141–56.

———. "Restoring a Natural Order." In *The Wealth of Nature: Environmental History and the Ecological Imagination.* 170–83. New York: Oxford University Press, 1993.

———. *Rivers of Empire.* New York: Oxford University Press, 1984.

———. "Seeing beyond Culture." *Journal of American History* 76 (Mar. 1990): 1132–36.

———. "The Shaky Ground of Sustainable Development." In *The Wealth of Nature: Environmental History and the Ecological Imagination.* 142–51. New York: Oxford University Press, 1993.

———. *An Unsettled Country: Changing Landscapes of the American West.* Albuquerque: University of New Mexico Press, 1994.

———. "The Warming of the West." In *An Unsettled Country: Changing Landscapes of the American West.* 91–120. Albuquerque: University of New Mexico Press, 1994

———. "The Wilderness Ideal in Canada and the United States." Audiocassette recording. In *Nature and Culture in the Northern West: A Symposium.* Missoula, Mont.: Center for the Rocky Mountain West, 1994.

Wright, Albert Hazen, and Anna Allen Wright. *Handbook of Snakes of the United States and Canada.* 3 vols. Ithaca, N.Y.: Comstock Publishing Association, 1957–62.

Wright, John. *Rocky Mountain Divide: Selling and Saving the West.* Austin: The University of Texas Press, 1993.

———. *Montana Ghost Dance.* Austin: The University of Texas Press, 1998.

Wright, Robert. "Science and Original Sin." *Time* 28 Oct. 1996.

———. *The Moral Animal: The New Science of Evolutionary Psychology.* New York: Pantheon, 1994.

Wrobel, David, and Michael Steiner, eds. *Many Wests: Place, Culture, and Regional Identity*. Lawrence: University Press of Kansas, 1997.

Wunder, John, ed. *Historians of the American Frontier: A Bio-Bibliographical Source Book*. New York: Greenwood Press, 1988.

————. *The Kiowas*. New York: Greenwood Press, 1989.

Wyckoff, William. *Creating Colorado: The Making of a Western American Landscape*. New Haven: Yale University Press, 1999.

Wyckoff, William, and Katherine Hansen. "Settlement, Livestock Grazing and Environmental Change in Southwest Montana, 1860–1990." *Environmental History Review* 15 (winter 1991): 45–72.

Wyckoff, William, and Lary Dilsaver. "Defining the Mountainous West." In *The Mountainous West: Explorations in Historical Geography*. 1–59. Lincoln: University of Nebraska Press, 1995.

————. "Promotional Imagery of Glacier National Park." *The Geographical Review* 87 (Jan. 1997): 1–26.

Young, Stanley P., and Edward A. Goldman. *The Wolves of North America*. 2 vols. Washington, D.C.: The American Wildlife Institute, 1944.

Zimmerman, Michael. "Feminism, Deep Ecology, and Environmental Ethics," *Environmental Ethics* 9 (winter 1987): 21–44.

Zubrow, Ezra. *Prehistoric Carrying Capacity: A Model*. Menlo Park, Calif.: Sunset Books, 1975.

Zweifel, Richard G., ed. *Catalogue of American Amphibians and Reptiles*. New York: Society for the Study of Amphibians and Reptiles, 1971.

Websites

Intertribal Bison Cooperative Website: http://www.intertribalbison.org.crst.htm.

Sierra Club, Ecoregions Website: http://www.sierraclub.org/ecoregions/prairie.html.

INDEX